America's
TEST KITCHEN

Cooking
for Two

2012

THE YEAR'S BEST RECIPES CUT DOWN TO SIZE

BY THE EDITORS OF
AMERICA'S TEST KITCHEN

PHOTOGRAPHY BY
CARL TREMBLAY, KELLER + KELLER, AND DANIEL J. VAN ACKERE

AMERICA'S TEST KITCHEN
17 Station Street, Brookline, MA 02445

AMERICA'S TEST KITCHEN COOKING FOR TWO 2012
The Year's Best Recipes Cut Down to Size

1st Edition

Hardcover: $35 US
ISBN-13: 978-1-936493-07-4   ISBN-10: 1-936493-07-1
ISSN: 2162-6863

Manufactured in the United States of America

10 9 8 7 6 5 4 3 2 1

Distributed by America's Test Kitchen
17 Station Street, Brookline, MA 02445

EDITORIAL DIRECTOR: Jack Bishop
EXECUTIVE EDITORS: Elizabeth Carduff, Lori Galvin
EXECUTIVE FOOD EDITOR: Julia Collin Davison
SENIOR EDITOR: Suzannah McFerran
ASSOCIATE EDITORS: Kate Hartke, Christie Morrison, Adelaide Parker
ASSISTANT EDITOR: Alyssa King
TEST COOKS: Rebecca Morris and Kate Williams
PHOTOSHOOT KITCHEN TEAM:
    ASSOCIATE EDITOR: Chris O'Connor
    ASSISTANT TEST COOKS: Daniel Cellucci, Danielle DeSiato-Hallman, Sara Mayer
DESIGN DIRECTOR: Amy Klee
ART DIRECTOR: Greg Galvan
ASSOCIATE ART DIRECTOR: Matthew Warnick
STAFF PHOTOGRAPHER: Daniel J. van Ackere
ADDITIONAL PHOTOGRAPHY: Keller + Keller and Carl Tremblay
FOOD STYLING: Marie Piraino and Mary Jane Sawyer
PRODUCTION DIRECTOR: Guy Rochford
SENIOR PRODUCTION MANAGER: Jessica Lindheimer Quirk
SENIOR PROJECT MANAGER: Alice Carpenter
PRODUCTION MANAGER: Kate Hux
ASSET AND WORKFLOW MANAGER: Andrew Mannone
PRODUCTION AND IMAGING SPECIALISTS: Judy Blomquist, Heather Dube, Lauren Pettapiece
COPYEDITOR: Barbara Wood
PROOFREADER: Ann-Marie Imbornoni
INDEXER: Elizabeth Parson

PICTURED ON THE FRONT COVER: Glazed Lemon Bundt Cakes (page 277)
PICTURED OPPOSITE TITLE PAGE: Turkey Tamale Pies (page 211)
PICTURED ON BACK OF JACKET: Spring Vegetable Pasta (page 87), Grilled Honey-Glazed Pork Chops with Peach, Red Onion, and Arugula Salad (page 150), Slow-Cooker Turkey Chili (page 227), and Pear Tarte Tatin (page 271)

Contents

THE SMART SHOPPER'S GUIDE

MAKING THE MOST OF THE RECIPES IN THIS BOOK

LET'S FACE IT—WE ALL WASTE FOOD. AND WHEN you're cooking for two, this is an even bigger problem. Sure, there are some stores where you can buy loose leafy greens or a handful of Brussels sprouts, but usually you're stuck with prepackaged produce sold in large quantities. The same is true for canned goods and many other items used in everyday recipes. So what's the solution to this problem? Careful planning and shopping. To that end, we've prepared this guide to key ingredients, both perishable and canned, that are used throughout the book. So if you're making one recipe with half of a red bell pepper or half a can of pinto beans, you can see which other recipes in the book call for them so you don't have to toss the extras.

AVOCADO

	AMOUNT	PAGE
Brown Rice Bowls with Crispy Tofu and Vegetables	½	139
Quinoa and Vegetable Stew	½	123
Smoked Pork Quesadillas	½	200

BEANS, Black

Stuffed Zucchini with Black Beans, Corn, and Chipotle Chiles	¾ cup	130
Turkey Tamale Pies	¾ cup	211

BEANS, Black, or Chickpeas

Crispy Bean Cakes	¾ cup	116

BEANS, Cannellini

French-Style Pork and White Bean Casserole	¾ cup	52
Slow-Cooker Tuscan Chicken Stew with Sausage, White Beans, and Spinach	¾ cup	229
Stuffed Zucchini with Cannellini Beans, Tomato, and Monterey Jack Cheese	¾ cup	128
White Bean Crostini with Lemon and Garlic	¾ cup	54

BEANS, Pinto

Chicken Chimichangas	¾ cup	33
Slow-Cooker Turkey Chili	¾ cup	227

BEANS, Pinto or Refried

	AMOUNT	PAGE
Bean and Cheese Quesadillas	¾ cup pinto beans or 1 cup refried beans	34

BEANS, Refried

Beef Taco Casserole	1 cup	49

CHICKPEAS

Wheat Berry and Arugula Salad	¾ cup	116

BELL PEPPER, Red

Cajun Chicken Chowder with Corn	½	58
Hearty Chicken Chowder	½	58
Italian Bread Salad with Red Bell Pepper and Arugula	½	242
Italian Vegetable Stew	½	120
Quinoa and Vegetable Stew	½	123
Skillet Lasagna with Italian Sausage and Bell Pepper	½	110
Sweet and Tangy Coleslaw with Red Bell Pepper and Jalapeño	½ small	251
Sweet Potato Salad	½	256

BELL PEPPER, Red or Green

Greek-Style Shrimp with Tomatoes and Feta	½	72

BUTTERMILK

Barbecue Grilled Chicken Wings with Tomato-Spinach Salad and Ranch Dressing	¼ cup	160
Creole Grilled Chicken Wings with Tomato-Spinach Salad and Ranch Dressing	¼ cup	160
Crispy Pan-Fried Pork Chops	½ cup	17
Crispy Pan-Fried Pork Chops with Chinese Five-Spice Rub	½ cup	18
Crispy Pan-Fried Pork Chops with Latin Spice Rub	½ cup	18
Easy Fried Chicken	½ cup plus 2 tablespoons	25
Fried Green Tomatoes	⅓ cup	249
Glazed Lemon Bundt Cakes	2 tablespoons	277
Grilled Chicken Wings with Tomato-Spinach Salad and Ranch Dressing	¼ cup	160
Grilled Steak Burgers with Romaine and Blue Cheese Salad	4 teaspoons	143
Tandoori Grilled Chicken Wings with Tomato-Spinach Salad and Ranch Dressing	¼ cup	160
Turkey Tamale Pies	⅓ cup	211

STOCKING THE COOKING-FOR-TWO KITCHEN

IN GENERAL, WHEN YOU'RE COOKING FOR TWO, you really don't need special equipment—the usual battery of pots, pans, knives, and tools will work just fine. (Although if your kitchen isn't stocked with smaller skillets—8- and 10-inch—or a small saucepan, you'll need them for certain recipes in this book.) But for some scaled-down entrées and desserts, we found we needed small baking dishes, pie plates, and more; even a small slow cooker came in handy for our scaled-down slow-cooked recipes (but note that a large slow cooker works fine for the recipes in this book). Fortunately, this equipment is inexpensive and widely available both online and at many retail stores. Plus, when it comes to things like ramekins and small tart pans and pie plates, you'll never need more than two (and sometimes just one will suffice). Here's a list of the cookware we found most useful for the recipes in this book.

SMALL BAKING DISHES

A small baking dish, such as this 8½ by 5½-inch ceramic dish (with straight sides no higher than 2 inches to expose the surface of the food), came in handy when we wanted to scale down our Beef Taco Casserole (page 49). For our rich Chocolate Éclair Cake (page 284), we reached for an even smaller 3-cup baking dish (measuring approximately 7¼ by 5¼ inches). Note that dishes of a comparable size or of a different material can be used in place of these dishes.

GRATIN DISHES

To make two servings of our Baked Tortellini with Radicchio, Peas, and Bacon (page 108) or Ham and Potato Gratins (page 205), we needed a pair of 2-cup gratin dishes (measuring approximately 9 by 6 inches), although dishes of comparable size work, too.

RAMEKINS

Ramekins, in various sizes, are handy for making scaled-down desserts. We found that 6-ounce ramekins were perfect for our petite but rich Hot Fudge Pudding Cakes (page 283), and 12-ounce ramekins were ideal for our Texas-Style Blueberry Cobblers (page 273).

SMALL SLOW COOKER

For our slow-cooker dinners for two, such as Slow-Cooker Gingery Chicken Breasts (page 233) and Slow-Cooker Turkey Chili (page 227), we found a 3- to 3½-quart oval slow cooker easier to maneuver and clean and less space-hogging than the standard 6-quart slow cookers (but the recipes in this book will work equally well in either size).

LOAF PANS

We use both traditional loaf pans (either 8- or 9-inch) and mini loaf pans (which measure approximately 5½ by 3 inches) in the for-two kitchen. We reach for the larger loaf pan for small casseroles, such as our Pasta Roll-Ups with Chicken and Goat Cheese (page 103). The mini loaf pans are ideal for scaled-down quick breads, such as our Zucchini Bread (page 263).

SMALL CAKE PAN

With a 6-inch round cake pan, you can make a perfectly sized cake for two people (see our Cranberry Upside-Down Cake on page 275). For our two-layer Chocolate-Raspberry Torte (page 286), you'll need two 6-inch pans.

SMALL PIE PLATE

For both sweet and savory pies, we rely on 6-inch pie plates. Our individual Turkey Tamale Pies (page 211) call for a pair of these pie plates, but our No-Bake Pumpkin Pie (page 279) requires just one for a perfectly scaled-down dessert.

SMALL TART PANS

When you want to make individual tarts, like our Rustic Walnut Tarts (page 280), two 4-inch tart pans (with removable bottoms) hold just the right amount of crust and filling.

SMALL BUNDT PANS

These 1-cup pans are ideal for making a pair of scaled-down Glazed Lemon Bundt Cakes (page 277).

SMOTHERED PORK CHOPS

EVERYDAY MAIN DISHES

WEEKNIGHT STEAK FAJITAS

STEAK FAJITAS OFTEN STRAY TOO FAR FROM THEIR Southwestern roots, with an overload of toppings to compensate for bland meat and vegetables. We wanted a simple steak fajita recipe that offered tender, beefy steak and vegetables flavored throughout with deep, smoky, spicy notes. And, instead of following the traditional route of grilling our fajitas, we'd bring our recipe indoors and cook them in a skillet, so we could make them any time of year.

Our first task was to choose the right cut of meat. Traditional Mexican fajita recipes typically call for skirt or flank steak, so we tested both. We also decided to consider two other inexpensive cuts: blade steak and flap meat (often used for steak tips). Tasters liked the well-marbled skirt steak and flap meat, but we found the availability of these cuts to be spotty. The flavor of the blade steak was great, but it contained too much internal gristle. Flank steak is more widely available, has a nice beefy flavor, and, when sliced thin against the grain, is very tender. Just 12 ounces of steak provided enough meat for two servings.

NOTES FROM THE TEST KITCHEN

OUR FAVORITE TRADITIONAL SKILLET
We use our skillets all the time, for everything from searing steaks to braising chicken to cooking pasta. While nonstick skillets can be purchased at a reasonable price, traditional skillets cost anywhere from $30 to $150 or more. Preliminary tests of traditional skillets confirmed our suspicion that cheap was not the way to go, but how much do you really need to spend? We tested eight pans from well-known manufacturers. All of the pans tested had flared sides, and most had uncoated stainless steel cooking surfaces, which we prize for promoting a fond (the browned, sticky bits that cling to the interior of the pan when food is sautéed, which help flavor sauces).

We concluded that medium-weight pans (not too heavy and not too light) are ideal—they brown food beautifully and are easy to handle. These pans have enough heft for heat retention and structural integrity, but not so much that they are difficult to manipulate. For its combination of excellent performance, optimum weight and balance, and overall ease of use, the **All-Clad Stainless Steel Fry Pan**, which comes in 8-inch ($90), 10-inch ($105), and 12-inch ($140) sizes, was the hands-down winner.

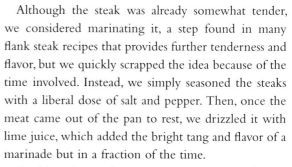

Although the steak was already somewhat tender, we considered marinating it, a step found in many flank steak recipes that provides further tenderness and flavor, but we quickly scrapped the idea because of the time involved. Instead, we simply seasoned the steaks with a liberal dose of salt and pepper. Then, once the meat came out of the pan to rest, we drizzled it with lime juice, which added the bright tang and flavor of a marinade but in a fraction of the time.

Cooking the steak was easy. We pan-seared it to mimic the caramelized exterior and crisp edges of grilled steak. About five minutes per side gave us the right amount of char as well as the preferred level of doneness (we liked medium-rare). Resting the cooked steak for about 10 minutes ensured that its interior stayed juicy.

With our steak perfectly cooked and ready to go, we moved on to the vegetables, sticking with traditional bell pepper and onion. Tasters preferred red bell pepper and red onion—just one of each did the trick. While the steak rested, we sautéed our sliced pepper and onion in the same skillet, taking advantage of the flavorful browned bits left behind from cooking the meat; a little water helped to deglaze the pan. To ensure that our fajitas offered authentic Tex-Mex flavor, we added some chili powder, cumin, and hot sauce to the vegetables, which needed just a few minutes of cooking time.

As for the tortillas, 8- and 10-inch rounds proved to be too big—tasters were biting down on more tortilla than filling; 6-inch tortillas were the perfect size. We warmed our tortillas in the microwave and pulled together our favorite toppings, which we could now use to complement—not cover up—our brightly flavored steak fajitas.

Weeknight Steak Fajitas
SERVES 2

To make these fajitas spicy, add a sliced jalapeño along with the bell pepper. We prefer this steak cooked to medium-rare, but if you prefer it more or less done, see our guidelines on page 154. Although the flavor of the fajitas can stand on its own, accompaniments (chopped avocado, salsa, shredded cheese, lime wedges) may be offered at the table.

12 ounces flank steak, trimmed

Salt and pepper

2 tablespoons vegetable oil

1 tablespoon lime juice

1 red bell pepper, stemmed, seeded, and sliced into ¼-inch-wide strips

1 small red onion, halved and sliced thin

2 tablespoons water

1 teaspoon chili powder

¼ teaspoon ground cumin

¼ teaspoon hot sauce

6 (6-inch) flour tortillas

1. Pat steak dry with paper towels and season with salt and pepper. Heat 1 tablespoon oil in 10-inch skillet over medium-high heat until just smoking. Brown steak well on first side, 3 to 5 minutes.

2. Flip steak and continue to cook until meat registers 120 to 125 degrees (for medium-rare), 3 to 5 minutes longer. Transfer to carving board and drizzle with lime juice. Tent loosely with aluminum foil and let rest for 10 minutes.

3. Add remaining 1 tablespoon oil to now-empty skillet and return to medium-high heat until shimmering. Add bell pepper, onion, water, chili powder, cumin, hot sauce, and ¼ teaspoon salt. Cook, scraping up any browned bits, until onion is softened, about 5 minutes. Transfer to serving platter and tent loosely with foil.

4. Stack tortillas on plate and microwave, covered, until soft and hot, about 1 minute. Slice steak thin against grain, arrange on platter with vegetables, and serve with tortillas.

JUICY PUB-STYLE BURGERS

WHEN YOU'RE MAKING BURGERS FOR TWO, WHY not pull out all the stops? We had in mind a memorably thick, juicy burger full of beefy flavor—the kind served in the best high-end pubs. To that end, we knew we'd skip supermarket ground meat in favor of grinding our own meat. But what we didn't know yet was which cut of beef we would use, how coarsely or finely we would process the meat, and what cooking method would produce a well-seared, thickly crusted burger that was juicy and evenly medium-rare within.

Standing at the butcher case, we were first inclined to have the butcher cut off a portion of the sizable chuck roast. This popular burger cut boasts a robust amount of fat that coats and flavors the meat as it cooks. But it also contains a fair amount of sinew—no problem for a dedicated meat grinder, but more work than our food processor (the test kitchen's go-to alternative to a meat grinder) could handle. Instead, we settled on sirloin steak tips. While not quite as rich as chuck, this cut offers supremely beefy flavor and can easily be ground in a food processor.

Next we moved on to processing the meat. We started by cutting it into 1-inch chunks, freezing it until it was just firm so it wouldn't become overworked in the food processor, and then pulsing it in batches into rough pieces. To ensure a tender burger, we handled the meat gently and simply shaped two loose patties. However, we were disappointed when the patties broke apart when we tried to flip them in the skillet. The problem proved easy to solve by cutting the meat into smaller ½-inch chunks before processing, which helped create a more even grind that stuck together better. We also found that we didn't need to handle the meat so gingerly. Instead of simply mounding two patties together, we first formed the beef into loosely packed meatballs, which we then gently flattened into patties. Both measures gave the burgers just enough structure to hold their shape when flipped.

There was a more pressing issue we needed to address next. More than a few tasters hinted that they missed the richness of well-marbled chuck. Supplementing the steak tips with another, fattier cut of beef—a common restaurant trick—would be one way to boost flavor, but we weren't wild about adding more butchering work to the process. Instead, we experimented with adding straight fat. First we tried olive oil, which was a total flop; it seeped out as soon as the burgers started to cook and did little to flavor the meat. But melted butter, which solidified as it hit the cold meat, created pinhead-size particles of fat strewn throughout the patties, which improved the burgers' flavor and juiciness. Even better, the extra fat boosted the browning on their exterior.

But good browning was about the only thing the exterior had going for it. Between their crisp, craggy shells and deep pink centers, our patties were marred by a thick band of gray meat and no amount of extra fat was going to help. Clearly, we needed to rethink our

JUICY PUB-STYLE BURGERS WITH CRISPY SHALLOTS AND BLUE CHEESE

cooking method. Up to now, we had been following a pretty standard approach for pan-fried burgers: preheating a skillet over high heat until it was good and hot, then cooking the patties to medium-rare for about four minutes per side.

We wondered what would happen if we only used the intense heat of the burner to produce a great crust, then relied on the gentler ambient heat of the oven to prevent the gray band of meat from forming beneath it. We quickly seared the burgers in a skillet and then transferred the whole thing to a 350-degree oven. But the results were only marginally better. The problem was that the portion of the burgers in direct contact with the skillet continued to cook faster than the top half. Lowering the oven temperature to 300 degrees helped, but only a little. That's when we decided to transfer the burgers from the skillet after searing to a cool baking sheet for finishing in the oven. After about five minutes, the burgers emerged with perfect interiors—juicy and rosy throughout.

This being a premium pub-style burger, it needed a few premium (yet simple) toppings. We threw together a quick tangy-sweet sauce to smear on each bun and combined it with aged cheddar and peppercorn-crusted bacon in one variation, and crispy shallots and blue cheese in another.

Admittedly, these burgers require slightly more time and effort than your average supermarket ground beef. But after just one bite, we knew that the fresh, deeply beefy-tasting, incredibly juicy results were well worth the extra trouble.

Juicy Pub-Style Burgers

SERVES 2

Sirloin steak tips are also sold as flap meat. When stirring the butter and pepper into the ground meat and shaping the patties, take care not to overwork the meat, or the burgers will become dense. We prefer these burgers cooked to medium-rare, but if you prefer them more or less done, see our guidelines on page 154. Serve with Pub-Style Burger Sauce (recipe follows).

- 1 pound sirloin steak tips, trimmed and cut into ½-inch pieces
- 2 tablespoons unsalted butter, melted and cooled

Salt and pepper
- 1 teaspoon vegetable oil
- 2 hamburger buns, toasted and buttered

1. Place steak pieces on baking sheet in single layer. Freeze meat until very firm and starting to harden around edges but still pliable, about 25 minutes.

2. Pulse half of meat in food processor until finely ground into 1/16-inch pieces, about 35 pulses, scraping down bowl as needed to ensure that beef is evenly ground. Transfer meat to second baking sheet. Repeat pulsing with remaining half of meat. Spread meat on baking sheet and inspect carefully, removing any long strands of gristle and large chunks of hard meat or fat.

3. Adjust oven rack to middle position and heat oven to 300 degrees. Drizzle melted butter over ground meat and add ½ teaspoon pepper. Gently toss with fork to combine, being careful not to overwork meat. Divide meat into 2 lightly packed balls. Gently flatten into patties ¾ inch thick and about 4½ inches in diameter. Refrigerate patties until ready to cook.

4. Season both sides of patties with salt and pepper. Heat oil in 10-inch skillet over high heat until just smoking. Using spatula, transfer burgers to skillet and cook without moving for 2 minutes. Flip burgers and cook for 2 minutes longer. Transfer patties to clean, dry baking sheet and bake until meat registers 120 to 125 degrees (for medium-rare), 3 to 6 minutes.

5. Transfer burgers to plate and let rest for 5 minutes. Serve on buns, adding toppings and Pub-Style Burger Sauce (if desired).

Pub-Style Burger Sauce

MAKES ABOUT ¼ CUP

- ¼ cup mayonnaise
- 2 teaspoons soy sauce
- 2 teaspoons minced fresh chives
- 1 teaspoon packed brown sugar
- ¾ teaspoon Worcestershire sauce
- 1 small garlic clove, minced
- ¼ teaspoon pepper

Whisk all ingredients together in bowl, cover, and refrigerate until needed.

VARIATIONS

Juicy Pub-Style Burgers with Peppered Bacon and Aged Cheddar

While beef is in freezer, sprinkle ½ teaspoon coarsely ground pepper over 3 slices bacon. Cook bacon in 10-inch skillet over medium heat until crisp, about 10 minutes. Using slotted spoon, transfer bacon to paper towel–lined plate; cut bacon in half crosswise. Pour off all but 1 teaspoon bacon fat from skillet; substitute bacon fat for vegetable oil. Proceed with recipe, topping each burger with ¼ cup shredded aged cheddar cheese before transferring to oven. Top burgers with Pub-Style Burger Sauce (if desired) and bacon just before serving.

Juicy Pub-Style Burgers with Crispy Shallots and Blue Cheese

While beef is in freezer, heat ⅓ cup vegetable oil and 2 thinly sliced shallots in small saucepan over medium-high heat. Cook, stirring frequently, until shallots are golden, 6 to 8 minutes. Using slotted spoon, transfer shallots to paper towel–lined plate and season with salt to taste. Proceed with recipe, topping each burger with ¼ cup crumbled blue cheese before transferring to oven. Top burgers with Pub-Style Burger Sauce (if desired) and crispy shallots just before serving.

NOTES FROM THE TEST KITCHEN

THE BEST KETCHUP

Since the 1980s, most ketchup had been made with high-fructose corn syrup; manufacturers liked this ingredient because it's cheap and easy to mix with other ingredients. But in the past few years, this corn-derived sweetener has been blamed for rising obesity rates and other health problems, so many producers now offer alternatives. From the eight national brands of classic-flavored ketchup we tasted, it was clear that tasters wanted ketchup that was salty, sweet, and tangy and had an assertive tomato flavor. After we tallied up the scores, sure enough, our top three winners were all sweetened with sugar, not corn syrup. In the end, one rose above the rest. **Heinz Organic Tomato Ketchup** came in first, praised by tasters for its "bright and fresh," "well-rounded ketchup-y flavor."

CLASSIC POT ROAST

WITH MELTINGLY TENDER, SLICEABLE MEAT SAUCED with a full-bodied gravy, pot roast is the ultimate in comfort food. But rarely does this homey classic make it onto the table for two. Recipes generally call for a 4- to 5-pound roast, which is way too much for even a pot roast–loving duo. We set out to create a simple recipe for a scaled-down pot roast that would deliver all the hearty flavor and succulent texture of a full-size roast.

While there is no shortage of ways to cook a pot roast, typically a tough cut made tender after hours of cooking in a covered vessel, we wanted to try to stick to the simplest of methods for our roast: Place the meat in a pot with liquid, a few basic seasonings, and vegetables; cover tightly and transfer to a low oven; then walk away until dinnertime. Working from the ground up, we started by considering the cut of meat.

At the supermarket butcher counter, we surveyed our options. Some recipes espoused using a rump or round roast, but these cuts from the back leg of the cow are somewhat lean and lack both flavor and the collagen that is key to turning a tough cut tender. Instead, we decided to try a cut from the shoulder, the chuck-eye roast. This well-marbled roast is full of collagen and is particularly suited to braising, with a long, tapered shape that slices easily. It tends to come in larger sizes, so we had the butcher cut a 1½-pound roast for us.

Most of our roast recipes call for salting the meat before cooking. Salting draws moisture out of the meat, forming a shallow brine that, over time, migrates back into the meat to season it throughout rather than just on the exterior. With roasts, we often advocate letting the salted meat rest for several hours. Since our roast was scaled down, we wondered if we could cut down on the resting time, too. After a number of tests, we determined that although the roast we rested for several hours was indeed quite beefy, the one we rested for just an hour was pretty darn good, too.

After salting and resting the roast, we seared it, a step called for in many recipes, then added a scant ½ cup of water to the saucepan and moved it to a 300-degree oven. Having a tight-fitting lid was essential, and we even sealed the pan with aluminum foil before adding the lid to trap as much liquid as possible. After a few hours, we were greeted by a tender, moist roast and a braising liquid that was nicely thickened (from the collagen in the roast breaking down into gelatin). We could work on the flavor of the gravy later, but for now we wondered if the cooking process could be streamlined even further by cutting out the initial sear.

Browning meat, of course, sets off something called the Maillard reaction, which creates thousands of new compounds that intensify flavor. But in the test kitchen, we had recently tested a handful of low-liquid braises where the meat browned in the oven; because of the minimal amount of liquid much of the meat was exposed during cooking. We decided to do a side-by-side test of two roasts, one seared and one not. When the unseared roast tasted almost as beefy as the seared one, we knew we had found a way to make a simple recipe even simpler.

It was time to think about the gravy. The first thing we did to beef up its flavor was to trade the water for beef broth. Some amount of red wine was also a given. Not only would it add needed depth to the braise, but it also contains glutamates—naturally occurring flavor compounds that enhance savory qualities. We added ¼ cup to keep our liquid levels on the lower side (so as not to dilute our beefy gravy). A spoonful of tomato paste also amped up the savory notes. Garlic and some herbs were obvious additions; we chose bay leaf and thyme, both excellent flavorings in meaty dishes. For aromatics, we liked the trio of shallot, carrot, and celery. To add extra richness, we sautéed them in a little butter before adding our liquid and roast.

By the time we pulled the roast out of the oven, the vegetables had broken down and started to thicken the gravy. We couldn't resist maximizing every bit of their flavor, so we tossed them into the blender with the defatted cooking liquid and a little extra beef broth to keep the consistency saucy. Just before serving, we stirred in a teaspoon of balsamic vinegar and a little more wine for brightness. The resulting gravy was exceptionally rich and full-bodied, perfect for draping over the meat, which was now rested and sliceable.

With a minimum of effort, we had put a classic family favorite back on the table for two—and it was better than ever.

Classic Pot Roast

SERVES 2

This might seem like a lot of meat for two servings, but it will cook down substantially in the oven. Our recommended beef broth is Rachael Ray Stock-in-a-Box Beef Flavored Stock.

1 (1½-pound) boneless beef chuck-eye roast, trimmed
  Salt and pepper
1 tablespoon unsalted butter
1 large shallot, halved and sliced thin
1 small carrot, peeled and cut into ½-inch pieces
1 celery rib, cut into ½-inch pieces
1 small garlic clove, minced
½ cup beef broth, plus extra as needed
¼ cup plus 1 tablespoon dry red wine
1 teaspoon tomato paste
1 bay leaf
1 sprig fresh thyme plus ¼ teaspoon minced
1 teaspoon balsamic vinegar

1. Sprinkle roast with ½ teaspoon salt and place on wire rack set in rimmed baking sheet. Let sit at room temperature for 1 hour.

2. Adjust oven rack to lower-middle position and heat oven to 300 degrees. Melt butter in medium saucepan over medium heat. Add shallot and cook, stirring occasionally, until softened and beginning to brown, 3 to 5 minutes. Add carrot and celery and cook for 5 minutes. Add garlic and cook until fragrant, about 30 seconds. Stir in broth, ¼ cup wine, tomato paste, bay leaf, and thyme sprig and bring to simmer.

3. Pat beef dry with paper towels and season with pepper. Using 3 pieces of kitchen twine, tie meat into loaf shape for even cooking. Nestle meat on top of vegetables. Cover pot tightly with aluminum foil and cover with lid. Transfer pot to oven and cook beef until fully tender and fork slips easily in and out of meat, 3½ to 4 hours, turning meat halfway through cooking.

4. Transfer roast to carving board and tent loosely with foil. Strain liquid through fine-mesh strainer into small measuring cup. Remove bay leaf and thyme sprig, then transfer vegetables to blender.

5. Let liquid settle for 5 minutes, then remove fat from surface using large spoon. Add beef broth if needed to bring liquid amount to ¾ cup. Add liquid to blender with vegetables and blend until smooth, about 1 minute. Transfer sauce to medium saucepan and bring to simmer over medium heat. Off heat, stir remaining 1 tablespoon wine, minced thyme, and vinegar into sauce and season with salt and pepper to taste.

6. Meanwhile, remove twine from roast and slice roast ½ inch thick against grain. Transfer to individual plates, spoon half of sauce over meat, and serve, passing remaining sauce separately.

NOTES FROM THE TEST KITCHEN

THE BEST BLENDERS
A blender has one basic job—to blend food into a uniform consistency, whether it's crushing ice, making smoothies, pureeing soups, or producing lump-free gravies, as in our Classic Pot Roast. Two things are important for success: The blades should be tapered or serrated, and the jar should also be tapered to keep food close to the blade edges. We gathered 10 models of blenders, including basic machines as well as those that boasted fancy new features (such as "dual-wave action" and "reversible motion" blade design), to find out which one performed best. After crushing hundreds of ice cubes and pureeing our way through countless soups and smoothies, we found two winners. The **KitchenAid 5-Speed Blender**, left, impressed us with its brute strength and efficiency—but it cost $150. For a more affordable alternative, we also like the **Kalorik BL Blender**, right, which cost a third of the price at $45. Though noticeably slower than our winner, the Kalorik performed nearly as well and was also the quietest of the bunch, making it our best buy.

MAPLE-GLAZED PORK TENDERLOIN

NEW ENGLANDERS WILL SLATHER MAPLE SYRUP ON just about anything, from pancakes to pineapple. Among the multitude of dishes done right with a dash of maple, classic New England maple-glazed pork tenderloin is one of our favorites. Sweet maple, with its delicate flavor notes of smoke, caramel, and vanilla, makes the ideal accent for pork, which has a faint sweetness all its own. Because one tenderloin serves two perfectly and would cook in minutes, we decided this sweet and savory dish was ideal for our weeknight cooking lineup.

We gathered a number of recipes and commenced testing. Unfortunately, we found that this dish often falls short of its savory-sweet promise. For starters, many of the glazes were too thin to coat the pork properly, some were too sweet, and none had a pronounced maple flavor. Furthermore, many recipes required continually basting the pork in a hot oven, plus they pressed multiple pans into service: a skillet to brown the pork, a saucepan to cook the glaze, and a roasting pan to finish cooking the pork in the oven. Our goal was clear: We needed to create a flavorful glaze that had clinging power so that our pork would really shine—all in one skillet.

We wanted a flavorful crust on our pork, so we began by searing a 12-ounce tenderloin in a nonstick skillet. Instead of immediately transferring the tenderloin to the oven, we set it aside and built the glaze in the same pan. Maple syrup alone was too sweet; whole-grain mustard cut the syrup's sweetness and gave the glaze a tangy, pungent undertone. A little apple cider vinegar heightened this effect and added acidity and depth, and a pinch of cayenne added a little heat. After removing the tenderloin from the pan, we poured off the excess fat and added the glaze ingredients. The flavor was close, but it was a little too one-dimensional. A tablespoon of bourbon brought out the smoky vanilla notes of the maple syrup even further. Now our glaze was perfect. A quick simmer helped concentrate and thicken the glaze, and we were sure this time it would have staying power.

We returned the seared tenderloin to the skillet with the syrup glaze, twirled the pork around in the glaze a couple of times with tongs to coat it, and placed the whole thing in the oven. In the past, when we've glazed

MAPLE-GLAZED PORK TENDERLOIN

a whole pork loin, we relied on a long stay in the oven to thicken the glaze to the right consistency and help it cling. As the loin is rotated in the glaze, layer after layer of the flavorful coating slowly builds up. But our smaller tenderloin needed only about 10 minutes to cook, and we didn't have much glaze to begin with. We definitely didn't have time on our side, and the results were a loose pool of glaze and a bare tenderloin. We were going to have to find a better way to make it stick.

When we were coating the tenderloin with the glaze in the skillet, we noticed that the slick surface of the seared tenderloin was doing nothing to help the syrup adhere. It then occurred to us that glazing a tenderloin wasn't unlike painting a wall. To ensure that the paint adheres properly, you must prepare the surface with a coat of primer. We wondered: Would the secret to great glazed tenderloin be found, likewise, by "priming" its surface with some coating? Flour and cornstarch seemed like good options, so we gave them a go. The cornstarch-encrusted tenderloin did a better job of grabbing the glaze, but it still didn't look as if enough was adhering to the pork. Maybe adding a little sugar would help to create a more ridged texture (like sandpaper). We mixed a teaspoon of sugar into a tablespoon of cornstarch, as well as salt and pepper to season it. We rolled the tenderloin in the mixture and patted it thoroughly to avoid any gummy clumping that could occur if the cornstarch went on unevenly, and then seared it. The sugar melted and caramelized as the meat seared and created a deep brown crust with just the right sandy texture to hold on to a glaze.

Now that we had a surefire way to make the glaze stick to the meat, we placed the seared tenderloin that had been patted with cornstarch back in the pan and coated it with the glaze, then roasted it at 350 degrees. Minutes later, the pork emerged juicy, flavorful, and bathed in a layer of maple glaze. While the pork rested, we combined the glaze with a little extra maple syrup to loosen it, then painted it on the resting pork.

Our maple glaze was simple and required only a few ingredients, so it was easy to come up with two variations. All three are equally satisfying, use only one pan, and hit the table in record time—and you don't have to be a New Englander to appreciate that.

Maple-Glazed Pork Tenderloin
SERVES 2

Don't be tempted to substitute imitation maple syrup—it will be too sweet. Be sure to pat off the cornstarch mixture thoroughly in step 2, as any excess will leave gummy spots on the tenderloin.

- ⅓ cup plus 1 tablespoon maple syrup
- 2 tablespoons whole-grain mustard
- 1 tablespoon bourbon
- 2 teaspoons apple cider vinegar
  Salt and pepper
  Pinch cayenne pepper
- 1 tablespoon cornstarch
- 1 teaspoon sugar
- 1 (12-ounce) pork tenderloin, trimmed
- 2 teaspoons vegetable oil

1. Adjust oven rack to middle position and heat oven to 350 degrees. Stir ⅓ cup maple syrup, mustard, bourbon, vinegar, ¼ teaspoon salt, and cayenne together in small bowl.

2. Combine cornstarch, sugar, ¼ teaspoon salt, and ¼ teaspoon pepper in shallow dish or pie plate. Pat tenderloin dry with paper towels, then roll in cornstarch mixture until evenly coated on all sides; thoroughly pat off excess cornstarch mixture.

3. Heat oil in 10-inch nonstick skillet over medium-high heat until just smoking. Brown tenderloin well on all sides, 6 to 8 minutes; transfer to plate.

4. Pour off excess fat from skillet and return to medium heat. Add syrup mixture, bring to simmer, scraping up any browned bits, and cook until reduced to ⅓ cup, 30 seconds to 1 minute. Return tenderloin to skillet and turn to coat with glaze. Transfer to oven and roast until pork registers 145 degrees, 8 to 12 minutes. Using a potholder (skillet handle will be hot), remove skillet from oven. Transfer tenderloin to carving board, tent with aluminum foil, and let rest for 10 minutes.

5. Being careful of hot skillet handle, transfer glaze left in skillet to small bowl and stir in remaining 1 tablespoon maple syrup. Brush tenderloin with 1 tablespoon glaze, then slice ¼ inch thick. Serve, passing remaining glaze separately.

VARIATIONS

Maple-Glazed Pork Tenderloin with Orange and Chipotle

Substitute 1 teaspoon Dijon mustard for whole-grain mustard and 2 teaspoons finely minced canned chipotle chile in adobo sauce for cayenne. Add 1 tablespoon orange marmalade to bowl along with syrup, mustard, bourbon, vinegar, and salt.

Maple-Glazed Pork Tenderloin with Smoked Paprika and Ginger

Substitute 1 teaspoon Dijon mustard for whole-grain mustard, 1 tablespoon dry sherry for bourbon, and ¾ teaspoon grated fresh ginger and ½ teaspoon smoked paprika for cayenne.

NOTES FROM THE TEST KITCHEN

CREATING TRACTION FOR PORK TENDERLOIN

To create a rough, sandpapery surface so glaze will adhere, roll tenderloin in cornstarch and sugar mixture before browning in pan.

THE BEST MAPLE SYRUP

Sold side by side at the supermarket, genuine maple syrup and so-called pancake syrup (made with high-fructose corn syrup) can range from more than $1 per ounce for the real deal to a mere 14 cents per ounce for an imitation. But price aside, which tastes better? To find out, we pitted four top-selling national brands of maple syrup against five popular pancake syrups. The pancake syrups were universally disliked for their artificial flavor and unnaturally thick texture. Of the maple syrups, those with a good balance of sweetness and maple flavor rose to the top of the pack (tasters downgraded some maple syrups for being too sweet). With its clean, intense maple flavor, moderate sweetness, and just the right consistency, our favorite was **Maple Grove Farms Grade A Dark Amber Syrup**.

CRISPY PAN-FRIED PORK CHOPS

BACK WHEN PORK WAS FAT-STREAKED AND FLAVOR-ful, great pan-fried pork chops came together from nothing more than a coating of seasoned flour and a quick turn in shimmering oil. The finished product—succulent meat encased in a delicate, crisp crust—was utterly simple and on the table in minutes. But now that modern-day pork is bred to be much leaner, a fried pork chop needs more than a scant, spiced-up shell to give it appeal. Most recipes compensate by packing on a more substantial crust—usually a triple layer of flour, eggs, and bread crumbs called a bound breading. Unfortunately, this technique has its own problems, leading to a leathery coating marred by gummy spots, or an overly brittle shell that flakes off with the prick of a fork. Our goal? A bound-breading makeover that would result in a lighter, crispier, more flavorful sheath that stayed where it was put.

To keep this dish fast and easy, we opted to go with ½-inch-thick boneless center-cut loin chops. Shallow-frying these thin, tender chops takes just two to five minutes per side. Plus, four of them fit snugly in a large skillet, perfect for two people.

As for the coating, we needed to examine each ingredient to see what was weighing down the traditional breaded pork chops. First up: the flour. A light dusting is meant to absorb moisture from both the meat and the eggs, creating a tacky base coat that acts as glue for the breading. But the high protein content (10 to 12 percent) in the flour was reacting with the protein in the meat and the egg wash. This contributed to the tough and heavy structure of the breading. In addition, pork exudes far more liquid than chicken, which is frequently prepared in the same manner, and this can create gummy spots in the flour. If our goals were to lighten up the breading and get rid of any gumminess, the flour would have to go.

Fortunately, the only other option we could think of was a good bet: cornstarch. When cornstarch absorbs water, its starch granules swell and release sticky starch that forms an ultra-crisp sheath when exposed to heat and fat. When we swapped the two ingredients, the chops boasted a casing that was indeed lighter and crisper.

CRISPY PAN-FRIED PORK CHOPS

But now we had a new problem—the breading was barely holding on to the meat at all, with shards falling away as soon as we cut into it. After some research, we understood why: When it comes to creating sticky glue, cornstarch and egg wash are not the best pairing. First, cornstarch absorbs liquid less readily than flour. Second, the moisture in raw egg is bound up in its proteins, making it less available to be soaked up—an effect for which not even the juicy pork could compensate. Clearly, a wetter type of wash was in order. We performed several tests using milk, heavy cream, and buttermilk. Tasters liked the subtle tang that buttermilk brought to the breading, so we settled on it, adding a dollop of mustard and a little minced garlic to perk up its flavor even more.

Up to this point, we had been using bread crumbs as the final coat. But with buttermilk as our wash, the crumbs were absorbing too much liquid and weren't staying as crunchy. Fortunately, breading choices abound. We rolled the chops in Ritz crackers (too tender), Melba toast (too bland), cornmeal (too gritty), and Cream of Wheat (too fine)—and crushed cornflakes, which turned out to be the best option. These crisp flakes are a popular way to add craggy texture to oven-fried chicken, so we weren't surprised when they worked here, too. On a whim, we added cornstarch to them before dredging the meat. Once swollen, the starch granules again worked their magic, turning the flakes even crispier in the hot fat.

With all three elements of our breading recalibrated, we prepped one last batch of chops to fry. But just as we were about to put them in the pan, we were called away from the kitchen. When we returned about 10 minutes later, we threw them into a hot skillet as usual. To our surprise, the breading on these chops seemed practically soldered to the meat. Could the stronger grip have something to do with the resting period? To check, we fried up two batches of chops: one immediately after coating, and the other after it had rested for 10 minutes. Sure enough, the coating on the rested chops had a noticeably firmer grasp on the meat. After doing a little research on how cornstarch works, we realized that the brief rest gave the cornstarch layer extra time to absorb moisture to form an even stickier paste. We also discovered a final step we could take to ensure that the crust stayed put: lightly scoring the chops.

Etching a shallow crosshatch pattern onto the meat's surface released moisture and tacky proteins that gave the coating an exceptionally solid footing.

With a crispy, flavorful coating that stayed glued to the meat, our pan-fried pork chops were just about perfect. All we had left was to come up with a couple of spice mixes we could use to season the meat before dredging. A Latin-influenced spice rub with cumin, chili powder, and coriander made our chops pop with every crunchy bite. For an even more international take, we took a cue from Chinese cuisine, which frequently uses Chinese five-spice powder in pork applications. Combined with a little dried ginger, it gave the pork an especially fragrant and warmly spiced flavor. With or without a spice rub, this approach has banished bland pork chops from our weeknight repertoire—for good.

Crispy Pan-Fried Pork Chops
SERVES 2

Don't let the pork chops drain on the paper towels for longer than 30 seconds, or the heat will steam the crust and make it soggy. You can substitute ½ cup store-bought cornflake crumbs for the whole cornflakes. If using crumbs, omit the processing step and mix the crumbs with the cornstarch, salt, and pepper.

- ½ cup cornstarch
- ½ cup buttermilk
- 1 tablespoon Dijon mustard
- 1 garlic clove, minced
- 1½ cups cornflakes
- Salt and pepper
- 4 (3- to 4-ounce) boneless pork chops, ½ to ¾ inch thick
- ⅓ cup vegetable oil
- Lemon wedges

1. Set wire rack in rimmed backing sheet. Place ¼ cup cornstarch in shallow dish or pie plate. In second shallow dish, whisk buttermilk, mustard, and garlic together until combined. Process remaining ¼ cup cornstarch, cornflakes, ¼ teaspoon salt, and ¼ teaspoon pepper in food processor until cornflakes are finely ground, about 10 seconds. Transfer cornflake mixture to third shallow dish.

2. With sharp knife, cut $\frac{1}{16}$-inch-deep slits on both sides of pork chops, spaced ½ inch apart, in crosshatch pattern. Pat pork chops dry with paper towels and season with salt and pepper. Working with 1 pork chop at a time, dredge in cornstarch and shake off excess. Coat in buttermilk mixture, allowing excess to drip off, then dredge in processed cornflakes, gently patting off excess. Transfer coated chops to prepared rack and let sit for 10 minutes.

3. Heat oil in 12-inch nonstick skillet over medium-high heat until shimmering. Carefully place chops in skillet and cook until golden brown and crisp on first side, 2 to 5 minutes. Flip chops and cook until second side is golden brown and crisp and pork registers 145 degrees, 2 to 5 minutes longer. Transfer chops to paper towel–lined plate and let drain for 30 seconds on each side. Serve with lemon wedges.

VARIATIONS

Crispy Pan-Fried Pork Chops with Latin Spice Rub

Omit pepper and combine ¾ teaspoon ground cumin, ¾ teaspoon chili powder, ¼ teaspoon ground coriander, pinch ground cinnamon, and pinch red pepper flakes in small bowl. Coat pork chops with spice rub before breading.

Crispy Pan-Fried Pork Chops with Chinese Five-Spice Rub

Combine 1 teaspoon Chinese five-spice powder, pinch red pepper flakes, and pinch dried ginger in small bowl. Coat pork chops with spice rub before breading.

NOTES FROM THE TEST KITCHEN

CUTTING YOUR CHOPS

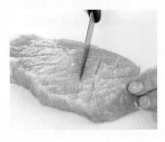

Making shallow cuts in pork chops' surface releases juices and sticky meat proteins that dampen cornstarch and help coating adhere.

SMOTHERED PORK CHOPS

IN CONCEPT, SMOTHERED PORK CHOPS SOUND utterly appealing: Bone-in chops are seared and removed from the skillet, sliced onions are fried in the fat, flour and broth are added, the chops are returned to braise in the flavorful, oniony liquid until tender, and the liquid is reduced to a porky, full-bodied gravy. But the handful of recipes we tried were deeply disappointing. The chops often ended up dry and tough, and the "gravy" was watery and bland. How could such a simple, straightforward recipe—a staple of Southern cooking, at that—fly so far off the rails?

We already had an advantage with our cooking-for-two agenda, since chops are a supermarket mainstay and can be purchased in small quantities. After picking up a variety of cuts, we began cooking to determine which one would give us tender, moist meat. Starting with bone-in chops was a no-brainer; we've learned from experience that the bone helps to keep the meat moist and adds flavor to the sauce. First off, we tried lean yet meaty rib chops and loin chops, which showed up in many recipes we came across. But we were disappointed to find that in test after test, these chops came out dry and tough. Most braised meats are fatty cuts that cook for hours, so we shouldn't have been shocked by the outcome. Next, we tried a batch made with fattier blade chops. Happily, the meat emerged tender and moist—but it did take a full hour and a half. Since we were braising the pork for so long, we thought that the gentle, more even heat of a 300-degree oven made more sense than the stovetop. Now that we had tender, succulent chops, we could work on the onions and sauce.

One onion, sliced thin, seemed like plenty for two chops, yet it brought little flavor to the sauce. We tried caramelizing the onion slices before adding the broth, but this made the sauce too sweet (and took almost an hour). We had better luck cooking the onions in butter over medium heat until they were lightly browned. We further improved the flavor of the sauce by using bold, savory beef broth instead of chicken broth or water and adding dried thyme, a bay leaf, and, at the end, a splash of cider vinegar. For even more pop, we seasoned the chops with a mixture of onion powder, paprika, and cayenne before searing. Now all three components—the pork chops, the sauce, and the onions—were boldly seasoned. But there was still one nagging issue that we needed to resolve.

Although the sauce was nice and thick when the chops went into the oven, it wasn't always that way when the dish came out. During braising, the chops and onions gave up a lot of liquid. The hitch was that it was almost impossible to gauge exactly how much liquid there would be from batch to batch, which meant that sometimes we made perfect gravy but other times it was thin and washed out. For more reliable, consistent results, we waited until the end and thickened a small amount of sauce with a slurry made of cornstarch and a spoonful of beef broth. This worked wonders. We had also tried using flour, but the cornstarch required less cooking, just long enough to thicken the sauce, and didn't contribute any off-flavors. Finally, our sauce was perfectly thick and velvety every time.

We may have added an hour to the usual cooking time for smothered pork chops, but as we ladled the rich gravy over our pair of moist, tender chops, we knew that it was time well spent.

NOTES FROM THE TEST KITCHEN

THE BEST PREMIUM PORK CHOPS
Everything seems to be going upscale nowadays—even pork chops. We wanted to know if pedigreed pork, such as Berkshire (known as Kurobuta in Japan) and Duroc, was worth its premium price tag. We mail-ordered bone-in chops (we stuck to center-cut chops for our tasting) and a roast we cut into chops from five different specialty producers and compared them with supermarket chops. Three mail-order chops were 100 percent Berkshire pork, one was a Berkshire blend, and the last was a Duroc blend. There were startling differences in their color: The pure Berkshire meat was crimson, while the blends were not quite as dark but had more color than the pale supermarket chops. Once pan-seared, the Berkshire meat, from **Snake River Farms**, won us over with its tender texture and intense pork taste. As it turns out, there is a connection between rich flavor and deep color. Color reflects the meat's pH level; the higher the pH, the darker the meat—and the better its flavor and texture. But if you can't justify the splurge—our winning chops run about $10 per pound plus shipping—try to pick out the reddest supermarket chops you can find.

SHOPPING FOR BLADE CHOPS
Supermarkets sometimes mislabel pork chops; this photo shows what you should look for when shopping. Note that the blade chop, which is cut from the shoulder end of the loin, contains a significant amount of fat and connective tissue, which makes it perfect for braising.

Smothered Pork Chops
SERVES 2

Be sure to use blade-cut pork chops, which are cut from the shoulder end of the loin and contain a significant amount of fat and connective tissue. If your chops are thicker than ½ inch, they may take longer to become completely tender.

½ teaspoon onion powder
¼ teaspoon paprika
   Salt and pepper
⅛ teaspoon cayenne pepper
2 (7-ounce) bone-in blade-cut pork chops, ½ inch thick
1 tablespoon vegetable oil
1 tablespoon unsalted butter
1 onion, halved and sliced thin
1 garlic clove, minced
⅛ teaspoon dried thyme
½ cup plus 1 tablespoon beef broth
1 bay leaf
¾ teaspoon cornstarch
½ teaspoon cider vinegar

1. Adjust oven rack to middle position and heat oven to 300 degrees. Combine onion powder, paprika, ¼ teaspoon salt, ¼ teaspoon pepper, and cayenne in small bowl. Pat chops dry with paper towels and rub evenly with spice mixture.

2. Heat oil in 10-inch skillet over medium-high heat until just smoking. Brown chops, 3 to 4 minutes per side; transfer to plate. Melt butter in now-empty skillet over medium heat. Add onion and cook until softened and well browned, 8 to 10 minutes. Add garlic and thyme and cook until fragrant, about 30 seconds. Stir in ½ cup broth and bay leaf, scraping up any browned bits, and bring to boil. Return chops and any accumulated juices to skillet, cover, and transfer to oven. Cook until chops are completely tender and fork slips easily in and out of meat, about 1½ hours.

3. Transfer chops to plate and tent loosely with aluminum foil. Remove bay leaf and strain contents of skillet through fine-mesh strainer into liquid measuring cup; reserve onions. Let liquid settle for 5 minutes, then remove fat from surface using large spoon. Return ⅓ cup defatted pan juices to now-empty skillet and bring to simmer.

4. Whisk remaining 1 tablespoon broth and cornstarch together in bowl until no lumps remain, then whisk mixture into sauce and simmer until thickened, about 30 seconds. Stir in reserved onions and vinegar. Season with salt and pepper to taste and serve.

INDOOR WISCONSIN BRATS AND BEER

GRILLING A PAIR OF FRANKS OR BURGERS IS A SNAP for the cook, but they take up so little space on the grate, it's almost not worth firing up the grill. For an interesting weeknight dinner that brought one of our favorite grilling recipes inside, we turned to a Midwest football season favorite, bratwurst and beer. Typically, a disposable aluminum pan filled with cheap lager and sliced onions is placed on one half of the grill and the sausages on the other half. The sausages are then simmered in the onions and beer to finish cooking. The idea is that the beer and onions flavor the bratwurst, which is then nestled into a bun, smothered with the beer-infused onions, and doused with plenty of mustard. Our goal was to bring this full-flavored, crowd-pleasing meal indoors, but instead of serving a crowd of hungry football fans, it would serve just two.

We started with the star, the meat. Bratwurst is the classic sausage choice in the grilled version. Authentic bratwurst is made from a combination of pork and veal seasoned with a variety of spices, including ginger, nutmeg, and caraway. Our local German butcher supplied the best-quality sausages, but we were also able to find suitable options in our local supermarket's deli department.

In the grilled version, the sausages are first browned on the grill, which deepens their flavor and adds visual appeal. For our indoor adaptation, we moved them to a medium skillet. We found that about five minutes of browning over medium-high heat was enough to intensify the flavor of our pair of sausages and develop a fond in the pan, which we could use to help season the onion. For our skillet version, we simply added the sliced onion—just one—and beer to the skillet with the browned sausages and simmered them together until the sausages were cooked through.

The bratwurst tasted great, but the onion was pale and still called for a flavor boost. For starters, we needed to better utilize the flavorful fond left in the skillet from browning the sausages. For our next test, we sliced the onion thin, then tossed it into the hot skillet after removing the sausages. Letting the onion cook long enough to turn golden brown allowed it to become caramelized and much more flavorful. Then we added the beer bath, scraped up the browned bits, and placed the sausages in the pan. We all agreed that these onions, with their slightly sweet, rich, caramelized flavor, could definitely hold their own next to the brats.

With the onion and brats in good shape, we turned to the beer. We tried dark ales and expensive lagers, but we

---

NOTES FROM THE TEST KITCHEN

THE BEST COARSE-GRAINED MUSTARD
Mustard aficionados argue that the coarse-grained condiment improves any grilled sausage or ham sandwich—unless you pick the wrong jar. The fate of our lunch at stake, we sampled 11 brands. Tasters appreciated the spiciness, tanginess, and pleasant pop of seeds. They disliked mustards with superfluous ingredients such as xantham gum, artificial flavors, and garlic and onion powders. But the more noteworthy factor turned out to be salt. Mustards with a meager quantity ranked low, while the winners contained roughly twice as much of this flavor amplifier. Tying for first place, both the familiar "nasal-clearing" **Grey Poupon Country Dijon**, left, and the newer, "poppier" **Grey Poupon Harvest Coarse Ground**, right, make good pantry staples.

quickly discovered that their big flavors become overly harsh and bitter when reduced—plus we needed less than a cup, so it didn't seem worthwhile to spend the money on a fancier brew. Cheap, mild lagers remained our favorite, as they maintained a mellow, pleasant flavor when simmered for half an hour.

In most outdoor recipes, once the bratwurst and onions have been cooked, the braising liquid is considered spent and it's dumped on the ground. But the caramelized onion and brats had infused the beer with so much flavor that we couldn't bear to see it go to waste. Cooked down, it did a great job of coating our onion and brats, so we decided to amp up its flavor even further. We began by adding mustard to the cooking liquid; this lent brightness and body. A little bit of sugar, pepper, and some caraway seeds added richness and complexity. In the time it took for the sausages to cook through, our liquid had thickened slightly, allowing it to lightly coat the sausages and onion, lending another layer of flavor to the recipe.

With crisp, browned, and flavorful bratwurst and beer and mustard–infused onion slices nestled into a bun—and all done in just 30 minutes—we were sure our indoor recipe could hold its own against the grilled version.

Indoor Wisconsin Brats and Beer

SERVES 2

Liberally pricking the sausages with a fork prior to cooking ensures that they won't burst. We prefer the mellow flavor of Budweiser or Miller Genuine Draft beer in this recipe. Note that bratwurst are often bigger than your average hot dog and therefore require a larger-than-average hot dog roll.

- 1 tablespoon vegetable oil
- 2 (4-ounce) links bratwurst
- 1 onion, halved and sliced thin
- ½ teaspoon packed brown sugar
  Salt and pepper
- ¾ cup beer
- 2 tablespoons whole-grain mustard
- ¼ teaspoon caraway seeds
- 2 teaspoons minced fresh parsley
- 2 large hot dog rolls

1. Heat oil in 10-inch skillet over medium-high heat until shimmering. Brown bratwurst on all sides, about 5 minutes; transfer to plate.

2. Add onion, sugar, and ⅛ teaspoon salt to skillet and cook over medium heat until onion is softened and golden, 8 to 10 minutes. Stir in beer, mustard, caraway seeds, and ¼ teaspoon pepper, scraping up any browned bits, and bring to simmer.

3. Nestle sausages into skillet, reduce heat to medium-low, and cook, turning sausages occasionally, until sausages are no longer pink in center and sauce is slightly thickened, about 12 minutes. Off heat, stir in parsley. Place sausages in rolls, top with onions, and serve.

ORANGE-GLAZED CHICKEN

BRIGHT AND TANGY ORANGE-GLAZED CHICKEN might seem like the ideal easy weeknight dinner for two: Bone-in, skin-on breasts are seared, roasted in the oven, and then painted with an orangey glaze to finish. But though the approach wins points for simplicity, it loses on flavor and texture. As we learned when we road-tested several recipes, the chicken can suffer from painfully sweet glazes, soggy or chewy skin, dry meat, and superficial orange flavor. Our goal was clear: We wanted nicely rendered skin, juicy meat, and balanced, fresh orange flavor. And since we wanted this to be possible for a weeknight, the recipe needed to stay in the realm of uncomplicated.

To begin, we stirred together a basic glaze (a quickly reduced mixture of orange juice and sugar); we would wait until we got our chicken method down before we started to perfect the glaze. We then got to work on technique. Using a 10-inch skillet, we simply seared the breasts skin side down to encourage crisping, then poured the glaze over the chicken and stuck the pan in the oven for 30 minutes. The results were fine but not fantastic: The meat was a tad dry, the skin a tad chewy—far from the moist, juicy meat and nicely rendered skin that we had hoped for. We knew we could do better.

It was clear that simply pan-searing our chicken breasts wasn't going to give us crispy skin. Perusing other chicken recipes that had the same goal of well-rendered skin, we came across an old classic: chicken under a brick. For this technique, a whole chicken is butterflied, so that it lies flat, and then weighted with a brick while it cooks. The weight presses out the fat, and the skin crisps up and becomes nicely browned. Also, the flattened chicken cooks more quickly—a bonus on a weeknight. The test kitchen has sometimes mimicked this technique by weighting chicken with a large, heavy pot. We decided to take a similar approach, but since we were working with a medium skillet and two split chicken breasts cut in half for easier maneuvering, we downgraded the pot to a large saucepan and weighted it with a heavy can of tomatoes. After cooking the chicken under the weighted pan for about 10 minutes, we removed the pan, flipped the chicken, added the glaze, and baked it. The skin had rendered nicely and wasn't chewy in the least.

NOTES FROM THE TEST KITCHEN

WEIGHTING ORANGE-GLAZED CHICKEN

To ensure crisp chicken skin, set weighted saucepan (wrapped in aluminum foil for easy cleanup) on chicken as it browns in pan.

THE BEST MANUAL JUICER

A good juicer should extract maximum juice from a lemon or orange with minimum mess. It shouldn't hurt your hands—or your budget. We bought a bushel of lemons and started squeezing, testing several manual juicers. Our favorite model was the **AMCO Enameled Lemon Squeezer**, $11. Surprisingly easy to use, this press was comfortable and effective, with curved handles and a well-shaped plunger. Squeezing the rounded handles didn't hurt our hands like others of this style, and the seeds were contained. It was also attractive, sporting a bright yellow finish, but hand washing is best if you want to keep the paint from chipping. This model also comes in a smaller green version for limes and a larger orange version for (you guessed it) oranges.

Our recipe was moving right along, but we began to wonder if we couldn't simplify it even further by finishing the chicken right on the stovetop. Once it was flipped, it needed only 10 more minutes of heat, and the skin was incredibly crisp.

Next, we turned to getting decent orange flavor into the meat. We decided that a quick brine might be worthwhile if it increased both flavor and moisture in the chicken. For more orange flavor, we replaced the water in the brine with orange juice, but this produced chicken with absolutely no orange flavor. Stumped, we added orange zest to the brine and tried again, but it didn't help. It finally occurred to us to combine the salt with the zest in the food processor before dissolving it in water. In the past, we've found that processing zest releases its flavorful oils, which the salt then carries into the meat. This time, the chicken drank up the orange flavor.

The glaze was but a minute's work. After brining and cooking our chicken pieces, we set them aside, discarded the fat from the skillet, and poured in orange juice, more zest, cornstarch (to thicken), sugar, and a touch of cayenne for some underlying heat. We returned the chicken, skin side up, to the skillet and let the glaze thicken and the chicken absorb a final bit of flavor. Right before serving the chicken, we gave the pieces a quick turn in the pan—just enough to coat them with the bright, flavorful glaze but not so much that we would compromise the delightfully crisp skin.

Orange-Glazed Chicken

SERVES 2

The fat will render best if you pat the chicken thoroughly dry after removing it from the brine. Brining is crucial to the flavor of this dish; do not omit this step and do not use kosher chicken here. In step 2, weight the saucepan with a 28-ounce can or two 15-ounce cans.

- 4 teaspoons grated orange zest plus ⅓ cup juice
- 1 tablespoon sugar
- ½ teaspoon cornstarch
  Pinch cayenne pepper
- ¼ cup salt
- 2 (12-ounce) bone-in split chicken breasts, trimmed and halved crosswise
- 1 tablespoon vegetable oil

ORANGE-GLAZED CHICKEN

1. Whisk orange juice, ¼ teaspoon orange zest, sugar, cornstarch, and cayenne together in small bowl until no lumps remain; set aside. Process remaining 3¾ teaspoons orange zest and salt together in food processor until finely ground, about 10 seconds. Dissolve orange salt in 1 quart cold water in large container. Submerge chicken in brine, cover, and refrigerate for 30 minutes or up to 1 hour. Remove chicken from brine and pat dry with paper towels.

2. Wrap bottom of large saucepan with aluminum foil, then place 1 large can or 2 smaller cans inside. Heat oil in 10-inch nonstick skillet over medium-high heat until just smoking. Place chicken, skin side down, in skillet and weigh down with prepared saucepan. Cook until well browned and crisp, 10 to 15 minutes. Remove pot and flip chicken skin side up. Reduce heat to medium and cook until chicken registers 160 degrees, 5 to 10 minutes. Transfer chicken to plate and let rest for 5 to 10 minutes.

3. Pour off fat from skillet, add orange juice mixture, and bring to boil over medium heat. Return chicken, skin side up, and any accumulated juices to skillet and simmer until sauce is thick and glossy, 2 to 3 minutes. Turn chicken to coat evenly with glaze. Serve.

EASY FRIED CHICKEN

CRACKLING CRISP, GOLDEN BROWN, AND JUICY— what's not to love about fried chicken? How about having to heat more than a quart of fat on the stovetop? Then there's the mess you have to deal with afterward. And when you're cooking for two, you're frying less chicken, but the amount of oil you need unfortunately doesn't change. We set our sights on a scaled-down fried chicken recipe, one that would deliver the golden brown and crisp coating that we expected—but without the hassle.

Over the years, we've fried a lot of chicken and have discovered a few tricks to help ensure moist meat and an extra-crisp crust. First, we've found that marinating the chicken for at least an hour in a buttermilk brine—buttermilk plus salt—not only seasons but also tenderizes the chicken (buttermilk is a natural tenderizer thanks to its high acidity). Second, we've learned to

add baking powder to the seasoned dredging mixture. As the chicken fries, the baking powder releases carbon dioxide, leavening the crust and increasing its surface area, keeping it light and crisp. Finally, while traditional recipes call for only dry ingredients in their dredging mixture, we've found that adding buttermilk to the dry ingredients before dredging the chicken creates small clumps of batter that become super-crisp as they fry.

We planned to incorporate these tricks into our recipe, but we also thought we'd be better able to replicate deep-fat frying if we first reviewed exactly what it accomplishes. Just like any other high-heat cooking method, deep-fat frying facilitates the Maillard reaction and the creation of hundreds of new flavor compounds that are the hallmark of properly browned food. It also dehydrates, which, along with the flour and chicken skin hardening from a reaction to heat, gives fried chicken its trademark crisp crust. Last, deep-fat frying cooks the food; the trick when frying chicken is finding the right oil temperature to cook the meat through without burning the exterior.

Considering the alternatives to frying, we realized that an oven could obviously reach hot enough temperatures to produce browning and cause dehydration. Maybe it would be possible to get oven-fried chicken closer to the deep-fried original if we simply went with traditional flour-dredged pieces. The idea was a shot in the dark—and it totally missed. After an hour in the oven, our chicken pieces—a pair of bone-in thighs and a bone-in split breast cut in half—were spotty brown, with some regions coated in raw flour and others nearly burnt. Biting into the meat revealed a powdery, brittle crust, not a moist, crisp one. There had to be something else involved with deep-frying that we were missing.

We thought back to a french fry recipe we had developed recently. It turns out that, contrary to popular belief, the higher the temperature of the frying fat, the more it is absorbed by the food being fried. So as a piece of chicken cooks at a relatively hot 300 to 350 degrees, almost all of the moisture in the coating is expelled and replaced with oil. That oil is essential to the flavor and texture of a really good crisp crust—and its absence in the breaded and baked chicken explained the dry, floury results. When the coating's moisture evaporated, there was nothing to replace it. Ultimately, at least some form of frying would be required.

We reviewed our standard fried chicken recipe, which calls for 5 cups of oil, and began testing to get the oil amount as low as we could go. We went all the way down to 1¾ cups—just enough oil that when we nestled the chicken pieces into it they would raise the level to help cook their sides. Then, all we would have to do was flip them over to finish cooking once the first side was golden brown. But we hit a snag.

If we had been using 5 cups, the oil's temperature would have stayed roughly the same after the addition of the chicken. With only 1¾ cups in the pot, however, the temperature dropped dramatically when the chicken was added, to just over 200 degrees from 375. To get the oil back up to the optimal range, we had to crank the flame to high—which fueled a new problem: burnt patches on the parts of the chicken that were in direct contact with the bottom of the pan (and without a full pot of oil to keep the chicken afloat,

this meant a lot of the pieces). To avoid burning, the chicken couldn't stand much more than three or four minutes of frying per side, and that wasn't enough time for it to cook through.

We began to wonder if we had dismissed the oven prematurely. Radiant, circulating heat might be just the ticket to replace the even heating of a deep, hot oil bath and allow our chicken to brown and cook through properly. We decided to try a hybrid method: We would fry the chicken on the stovetop until it formed a light brown crust, then finish it in a hot oven (perched on a wire rack set in a sheet pan to prevent burnt spots and promote air circulation all around the meat) to both cook it through and deepen its color.

Fifteen minutes in the oven was all it took to give our shallow-fried chicken for two a crisp, craggy, golden brown crust. When we tasted it side by side with fried chicken cooked in the usual quart-plus of oil, tasters couldn't tell the two batches apart. But their differences were very apparent when it came time to take care of the cooking fat.

We'd done it—with less than 2 cups of fat, we'd made very crunchy, very crisp, and very tender fried chicken for two. And it was very easy.

NOTES FROM THE TEST KITCHEN

OIL SHORTAGE
Properly frying chicken from start to finish using traditional methods requires lots of messy oil. Our hybrid stove-to-oven method cuts it way back.

| **TRADITIONAL WAY** | **OUR WAY** |
| 5 cups oil | 1¾ cups oil |

DISPOSING OF FRYING OIL
When it's warm, vegetable oil flows easily, and pouring it down the drain may seem like the simplest way to dispose of it. But as it cools, the oil gets thicker, and if it comes in contact with cold water in your plumbing or if the pipes are cold, it may get cold enough to solidify and cause slower draining. To safely and neatly dispose of used oil, wait for it to cool completely, pour it into a lidded container, and put it in the trash.

Easy Fried Chicken
SERVES 2

A Dutch oven with an 11-inch diameter can be used in place of the straight-sided sauté pan. Smaller pieces may cook faster than larger pieces, so remove them from the oven as they reach the correct temperature.

½ cup plus 2 tablespoons buttermilk
    Salt and pepper
½ teaspoon garlic powder
½ teaspoon paprika
    Dash hot sauce
1 (12-ounce) bone-in split chicken breast, trimmed
   and cut in half
2 (6-ounce) bone-in chicken thighs, trimmed
1 cup all-purpose flour
1 teaspoon baking powder
   Pinch cayenne pepper
1¾ cups vegetable oil

1. Whisk ½ cup buttermilk, 1 teaspoon salt, ½ teaspoon pepper, ¼ teaspoon garlic powder, ¼ teaspoon paprika, and hot sauce together in medium bowl. Add chicken and turn to coat. Cover and refrigerate for at least 1 hour or up to 24 hours.

2. Adjust oven rack to middle position and heat oven to 400 degrees. Set wire rack in rimmed baking sheet. Whisk ¼ teaspoon salt, ¾ teaspoon pepper, remaining ¼ teaspoon garlic powder, remaining ¼ teaspoon paprika, flour, baking powder, and cayenne together in large bowl. Add remaining 2 tablespoons buttermilk to flour mixture and mix with fingers until combined and small clumps form. Working with 1 piece of chicken at a time, dredge in flour mixture, pressing mixture so that thick, even coating forms. Place dredged chicken on large plate, skin side up.

3. Heat oil in 11-inch straight-sided sauté pan over medium-high heat to 375 degrees. Carefully place chicken pieces in pan, skin side down, and cook until golden brown, 3 to 5 minutes. Flip chicken and continue to cook until golden brown on second side, 2 to 4 minutes longer. Transfer chicken to prepared rack. Bake until breasts register 160 degrees and thighs register 175 degrees, 15 to 20 minutes. Let chicken rest for 5 to 10 minutes. Serve.

NUT-CRUSTED CHICKEN BREASTS

IN THE COOKING-FOR-TWO KITCHEN, BONELESS, skinless chicken breasts are the ultimate in convenience—after all, they can be prepared in myriad ways and they cook quickly. But occasionally they need to be jazzed up a bit. We decided to take one of our favorite preparations, breaded chicken breasts, to another level by adding chopped nuts to the coating for a more robust flavor element and to boost the crust's crunch factor. But this technique has some issues: The crust can become too dense and leaden, and the rich flavor of the nuts rarely comes through. Plus it's all too easy to dry out a lean boneless breast.

Right away, we found an easy way to ensure juicy, flavorful meat: We salted the breasts (poking them with a fork first helps the salt penetrate) and rested them briefly before dredging and frying. For the crust, we wondered if a simple "breading" of nuts would help, but when we dredged the chicken in flour, dipped it in beaten eggs, and dragged it through almonds that we'd pulverized in the food processor, the crushed pieces barely adhered to the meat. Using bread crumbs in the final dredge, which would absorb liquid from the eggs to help act as glue, was definitely going to be necessary. A mixture of half nuts and half Japanese panko bread crumbs, which are coarser and crunchier than conventional bread crumbs, gave us just the light, crisp texture we wanted. To improve the flavor of the coating, we added Dijon mustard to the egg wash, and lemon zest, fresh thyme, and a dash of cayenne to the nut-crumb mixture.

But the crust still wasn't particularly nutty—and frying the chicken breasts was a hassle. Reviewing our notes on past similar recipes, we noticed a few in which the breaded breasts were baked. No question: "Oven-frying" would be easier. And maybe the circulating oven heat would also toast the nuts and deepen their flavor. We breaded the next batch, arranged the chicken on a wire rack set in a sheet pan, and baked it until it was cooked through. About 20 minutes later, the chicken emerged juicy and shrouded in an even, golden crust but—infuriatingly—no more nutty-tasting than before.

Adding more almonds only robbed the crust of the panko's crispness. Pretoasting them helped, but not enough to warrant the extra step. What we really needed was a way to add more nuttiness without adding more nuts. Then it hit us. We've achieved exactly this result in other recipes by calling on a powerhouse ingredient: browned butter. Gently heating butter until its milk solids take on a rich, deeply bronzed color brings out its inherent nuttiness. We gave it a shot, swirling a tab of butter in a skillet for about five minutes and then cooking the panko, ground nuts, and a minced shallot in the browned butter until fragrant and russet-colored. Tasters reached for second helpings of this latest batch. The tried-and-true combination of chopped nuts, lemon zest, and thyme didn't fail us, and our new brown butter technique took our chicken to greater heights.

For a variation that had a stronger citrus note, we switched out the lemon zest for orange and complemented our new flavoring with oregano in place of the thyme. The technique worked equally well with pecans, pistachios, and hazelnuts, making this an easy weeknight dish we could turn to again and again.

NUT-CRUSTED CHICKEN BREASTS WITH LEMON AND THYME

Nut-Crusted Chicken Breasts with Lemon and Thyme

SERVES 2

This recipe also works well with pecans, pistachios, and hazelnuts.

- 2 (6- to 8-ounce) boneless, skinless chicken breasts, trimmed
- Salt and pepper
- ½ cup whole almonds, chopped coarse
- 2 tablespoons unsalted butter, cut into 2 pieces
- 1 small shallot, minced
- ½ cup panko bread crumbs
- 1 teaspoon finely grated lemon zest, plus lemon wedges for serving
- ½ teaspoon minced fresh thyme
- Pinch cayenne pepper
- 2 large eggs
- 1½ teaspoons Dijon mustard
- ½ cup all-purpose flour

1. Adjust oven rack to lower-middle position and heat oven to 350 degrees. Set wire rack in rimmed baking sheet. Using fork, poke thicker half of each breast 5 to 6 times. Place on prepared rack and sprinkle each breast evenly with ⅛ teaspoon salt. Refrigerate, uncovered, while preparing coating.

2. Pulse nuts in food processor until they resemble coarse meal, about 20 pulses. Melt butter in 10-inch skillet over medium heat. Cook, swirling pan constantly, until butter turns golden brown and has nutty aroma, about 3 minutes. Add shallot and ⅛ teaspoon salt and cook, stirring constantly, until just beginning to brown, about 2 minutes. Reduce heat to medium-low, add ground nuts and panko, and cook, stirring often, until golden brown, 10 to 12 minutes. Transfer nut mixture to shallow dish or pie plate and stir in lemon zest, thyme, and cayenne.

3. Lightly whisk eggs, mustard, and ⅛ teaspoon pepper together in second shallow dish. Place flour in third shallow dish. Pat chicken dry with paper towels. Working with 1 breast at a time, dredge in flour, shaking off excess, then coat with egg mixture, allowing excess to drip off. Coat all sides of breast with nut mixture, pressing gently so that crumbs adhere. Return nut-breaded breasts to wire rack.

4. Bake until thickest part of chicken registers 160 degrees, 20 to 25 minutes. Let chicken rest for 5 to 10 minutes. Serve with lemon wedges.

VARIATION

Nut-Crusted Chicken Breasts with Orange and Oregano

Substitute ½ teaspoon orange zest for lemon zest, orange wedges for lemon wedges, and ½ teaspoon oregano for thyme.

CHICKEN POT PIE WITH SAVORY CRUMBLE TOPPING

HOMEY AND SATISFYING, CHICKEN POT PIE IS THE epitome of comfort food. But this family favorite usually serves six to eight people. What if you're not cooking for a crowd? We wanted a streamlined chicken pot pie that served two perfectly. The typical recipe is a huge investment of time and energy—you have to cook and break down a chicken, make a sauce, parcook vegetables, and prepare, chill, and roll out a pie crust—so we hoped to find some shortcuts that would bring chicken pot pie back to the dinner table for two—and do it in record time.

The first step was to figure out just how much chicken we needed and how to cook it. We settled on an 8-ounce boneless, skinless chicken breast, so that there would be room for vegetables, sauce, and pastry. Using a boneless breast, instead of a bone-in piece, ensured that the chicken cooked fairly quickly. When we sautéed the skinless breast in a little oil, it inevitably developed a crusty, browned exterior that tasters found unappealing in pot pie. We turned to poaching the chicken instead.

It took just one test to tell us we were on the right path. Poaching worked just as well and just as fast as sautéing, and it kept the chicken moist throughout. Since we wouldn't have the browned bits, or fond, left behind in the pan from sautéing the chicken to contribute rich flavor, we substituted chicken broth for water as the poaching liquid. Already, our downsized chicken breast worked better than a whole bird in two ways. First, the meat cooked in a fraction of the time. Second, the smaller amount of chicken required less broth to cook in, and the resulting liquid provided a concentrated base for a velvety, relatively full-bodied sauce that didn't need reducing. Plus, with the skin and bones already removed, the meat was easy to handle and shredded nicely into bite-size morsels.

Now, what should we do about the vegetables? Our tasters clamored for the traditional combination of onions, carrot, celery, and peas, which sounded just right to us, too. A whole onion, however, overpowered the rest of the vegetables, so we swapped it out for a shallot. Cooking the chicken together with the vegetables, while undeniably efficient, resulted in meat and sauce that tasted like vegetable soup base, and vegetables that turned mushy and tasted bland. Cooking the two elements separately—the chicken in broth, the vegetables in a little oil—was the only way to tease out and maintain their distinct flavors and textures in the finished dish. The whole process turned out to be less fussy than we thought; during the five minutes or so that it took to sauté the vegetables, we could shred the chicken.

As for the sauce, stirred together from a butter-and-flour roux, the poaching liquid, and milk, it tasted clean and nicely chicken-y. But without the benefit of a fond from dark, caramelized bits of roasted chicken or the deeply concentrated jus of a pot-roasted bird as a flavor base, it lacked a certain savory depth. What we needed were some powerhouse ingredients to give it a boost—and fortunately we had some test kitchen precedent to fall back on.

Whenever we need to make a full-flavored stew or soup in an hour or less, we turn to foods that are rich in glutamates—these foods help us develop maximum flavor in a short amount of time. Many of these are pantry items that we tend to keep on hand—tomato paste, red wine, soy sauce, and anchovies—as well as mushrooms and Parmesan cheese. Red wine, of course, was out of the question, and the idea of salty little fish in our scaled-down pot pie did not appeal. However, sautéed mushrooms were a no-brainer. Together with a small spoonful each of soy sauce and tomato paste (both cooked in the pan until browned and caramelized), they served as a base for our sauce and enhanced its savory character. And because the amounts of soy sauce and tomato paste were so tiny, no one even guessed they were in the mix. We then brightened the filling with a squirt of fresh lemon juice and some minced parsley and added the frozen peas right before transferring everything to a small baking dish.

NOTES FROM THE TEST KITCHEN

MAKING THE CRUMBLE TOPPING
Prebaking the crumbles before sprinkling them over the pie ensures that they stay crisp in the oven.

Crumble topping mixture into irregularly shaped pieces onto parchment paper–lined rimmed baking sheet and bake in 450-degree oven until they start to brown, 6 to 8 minutes.

BUILDING DEEP FLAVOR IN HALF THE TIME
Most chicken pot pies require hours to build a full-flavored sauce. We cut time but not flavor by building a sauce that takes advantage of the browning process and three glutamate-rich ingredients.

MUSHROOMS
Sautéed cremini mushrooms begin to build flavor.

TOMATO PASTE
Tomato paste added to the pan caramelizes to create more flavor.

SOY SAUCE
The sugars in soy sauce also brown, further boosting flavor.

CHICKEN POT PIE WITH SAVORY CRUMBLE TOPPING

It was time to put a lid on it—but exactly what sort of crust was not yet clear. Though we would miss cracking a fork through a rich, buttery seal of golden pie crust, we could think of two reasons traditional pie pastry wouldn't work here: First and foremost, we were aiming for a streamlined, speedy pot pie. Second, baking the pie long enough for the crust to finish would almost certainly wreak havoc on our carefully calibrated filling, drying out the chicken and turning the vegetables to mush. Of the simpler from-scratch options, cream biscuits came to mind. We needed just a few biscuits, and these quick-cooking Yankee-style pastries came together in a jiffy; but most tasters felt that despite their nicely browned, craggy peaks, the soft, tender undersides offered too little textural contrast with the creamy filling. A chicken pie—even a speedy one—needs a crisp, buttery top.

Then a fellow test cook mentioned a more rugged-textured topping she had stumbled across at a local restaurant: a vegetable stew with a garlic-cheddar "crumble" crust. Not quite biscuit, not quite pie crust, this savory topping turned out to be a snap to prepare—just rub butter into flour, salt, and leavening; toss in some grated cheese (we used glutamate-rich Parmesan) and pepper; bind the lot together with a bit of cream; and crumble it over the filling. It also offered a lightly crunchy exterior and tender interior, plus an appealingly rough-hewn appearance. It wouldn't be traditional, but since expediency was our primary goal, it was worth a shot.

Since the chicken filling was already fully cooked, we decided to prebake the crumble before scattering it over the casserole, so that a brief stint in the oven would be all the pie needed. Prebaking would also ensure that the crumble didn't lose any of its wonderful crispness. Fortunately, crumbling the mixture onto a sheet pan and baking it while we made the filling fit smoothly into our method. At that point, the topped casserole needed a mere 15 minutes to brown and start bubbling up the sides.

Our streamlined chicken pot pie with crispy crumble topping didn't take nearly as long as the traditional full-size pot pie, but it was every bit as satisfying.

Chicken Pot Pie with Savory Crumble Topping
SERVES 2

This recipe relies on two unusual ingredients: soy sauce and tomato paste. Do not omit them. They don't convey their distinctive tastes but greatly deepen the savory flavor of the filling. When making the topping, do not substitute milk or half-and-half for the heavy cream. You will need an 8½ by 5½-inch baking dish for this recipe (see page 3).

CRUMBLE TOPPING
- ⅔ cup all-purpose flour
- ½ teaspoon baking powder
-   Salt and pepper
-   Pinch cayenne pepper
- 2 tablespoons unsalted butter, cut into ½-inch pieces and chilled
- ¼ cup grated Parmesan cheese
- ¼ cup plus 1 tablespoon heavy cream

FILLING
- 1 (8-ounce) boneless, skinless chicken breast, trimmed
- 1¼ cups low-sodium chicken broth
- 1½ tablespoons vegetable oil
- 4 ounces cremini mushrooms, trimmed and sliced thin
- 1 shallot, minced
- 1 small carrot, peeled and cut into ¼-inch pieces
- 1 small celery rib, cut into ¼-inch pieces
-   Salt and pepper
- ½ teaspoon soy sauce
- ½ teaspoon tomato paste
- 2 tablespoons unsalted butter
- 3 tablespoons all-purpose flour
- ½ cup whole milk
- 1 teaspoon lemon juice
- 1 tablespoon minced fresh parsley
- ¼ cup frozen baby peas

1. FOR THE TOPPING: Adjust oven rack to upper-middle position and heat oven to 450 degrees. Line rimmed baking sheet with parchment paper. Combine flour, baking powder, ⅛ teaspoon salt, ⅛ teaspoon pepper, and cayenne in bowl. Sprinkle butter pieces over top of flour mixture. Using fingers, rub butter into flour mixture until it resembles coarse cornmeal. Stir in Parmesan. Stir in cream until just combined. Crumble dough onto

prepared pan into irregularly shaped pieces ranging from ½ to ¾ inch each. Bake until fragrant and starting to brown around edges, 6 to 8 minutes; set aside.

2. FOR THE FILLING: Meanwhile, line rimmed baking sheet with aluminum foil. Bring chicken and broth to simmer in medium saucepan. Reduce heat to medium-low, cover, and cook until chicken registers 160 degrees, 8 to 10 minutes. Transfer chicken to medium bowl. Let cool slightly, then using two forks, shred chicken into bite-size pieces. Pour broth through fine-mesh strainer into liquid measuring cup, reserving 1 cup.

3. Heat oil in now-empty saucepan over medium heat until shimmering. Add mushrooms, shallot, carrot, celery, ¼ teaspoon salt, and ¼ teaspoon pepper; cover and cook, stirring occasionally, until mushrooms have released their juices and vegetables are just tender, about 5 minutes.

4. Uncover and stir in soy sauce and tomato paste. Increase heat to medium-high and cook, stirring frequently, until liquid has evaporated and mushrooms are well browned, 5 to 7 minutes; transfer vegetables to bowl with chicken.

5. Melt butter in now-empty saucepan over medium heat. Stir in flour and cook for 30 seconds. Slowly whisk in reserved chicken broth and milk. Bring to simmer, scraping up any browned bits, and cook until sauce fully thickens, about 1 minute. Off heat, stir in lemon juice and 2 teaspoons parsley, then stir in chicken mixture and peas. Season with salt and pepper to taste.

6. Pour chicken mixture into 8½ by 5½-inch baking dish. Scatter crumble topping evenly over filling. Bake pot pie on prepared baking sheet until filling is bubbling and topping is well browned, 12 to 15 minutes. Sprinkle with remaining 1 teaspoon parsley and serve.

CHICKEN CHIMICHANGAS

THE CHIMICHANGA IS A STAPLE IN MEXICAN-American restaurants from coast to coast—and for good reason. It's basically a burrito taken up a notch. It has the same hearty meal's worth of tender meat, rice, cheese, beans, heat, and spice rolled into a flour tortilla. What gives it the edge is deep-frying: The shell becomes exquisitely crisp and flaky, and the cheese oozes into

gooey nirvana. Add the parade of toppings—guacamole, salsa, sour cream, enchilada sauce—and it's no wonder people are passionate about chimichangas. But if you're hoping to enjoy this dish for dinner tonight, you might be disappointed, since each of the components—seasoned meat, rice, and beans—must be prepped and cooked before being rolled up and fried. We hoped that making just a pair of chimis—as opposed to a big batch—might make prep go more quickly so we could enjoy these crispy, crunchy, spicy burritos any night of the week.

First things first: Chimichangas can be made with beef or chicken. We opted for chicken, hoping it would cut down on prep work and cooking time. We tested a number of classic recipes and spent a long day boiling rice in one pot, sautéing a bone-in, skin-on chicken breast in a pan, and soaking and boiling dried beans in another pot. All of that work, and we weren't even close to being done. We still had to pile the filling into each tortilla and roll it into a cylinder, tucking in the edges as we went. After several hours of preparation, we dropped these oversize burritos into our fourth pot of the day, this one filled with hot oil. A few minutes later, we fished them out. Their exterior was crisp, even buttery, but the folded edges had unsealed in the oil, letting the filling escape and burn. There was no doubt in our minds that in order for this recipe to make it into our weeknight repertoire, we would need to repair and streamline it.

First, the easy decisions: We would use canned beans instead of dried, specifically pinto beans, which had trumped red kidney and black beans in early tests for their creaminess and versatility. Next, we would start with a boneless, skinless chicken breast so that we could avoid the steps of skinning and boning the chicken. We moved on to the procedure.

Dismayed by the sink full of dirty dishes, we tried cooking everything in a single pot. We sautéed an onion and garlic in a little oil; stirred in chili powder and cumin; and tossed in the whole raw chicken breast (we would chop the meat after it was cooked), raw rice, and the canned, drained beans. To poach the chicken and cook the rice, we poured in flavorful chicken broth, covered the pot, and waited. Our one-pot plan had mixed results. On the plus side, the chicken was nicely cooked. On the minus side, the rice was crunchy, and overall the dish was lackluster. We knew our more convenient changes were to blame. The quicker-cooking boneless, skinless chicken and canned beans sure cut back on our time, but in the process we had sacrificed flavor and texture. We headed back to the drawing board.

The chicken cooked faster than the rice, and since we couldn't slow down the bird's cooking speed, we would help the rice get a move on. We tried using instant rice, but it was chalky and sticky. We cycled back to ordinary long-grain rice. To give it a head start, we microwaved it with some chicken broth until the broth was absorbed. We added this partially cooked rice to the pot with the other ingredients, and in just 15 minutes, the rice was tender.

To give the filling depth and flavor, we added extra spices to the rice and broth as they parcooked in the microwave, hoping that the rice would drink up the flavors. But this didn't work so well, because we hadn't bloomed the dried spices in advance to release their flavor compounds. Since that would be yet another step, we looked for an alternative. Happily, minced canned chipotle chiles yielded a smoky, well-seasoned broth that flavored the rice nicely.

We combined our now tasty and easy filling with shredded cheddar cheese and cilantro, rolled up the chimichangas, and dropped these 1-pound burritos into 2 quarts of hot oil. It was a nightmare. Not only was the potential for pain scary, but once again the filling leaked out and burned. We were then hit with an idea: What if we tried shallow-frying? We had just successfully used this method for our Easy Fried Chicken (page 25) and couldn't think of one good reason not to try it here. Switching from deep- to shallow-frying, with just 3 cups of oil, let us ease the unwieldy chimichangas into the pan without any oil splashing.

To address the problems we were having with the filling leaking out, we tried securing the ends with toothpicks. No luck—the picks burned and broke into shards, and the filling leaked out in every direction. What we needed was some kind of glue. Taking a cue from the papier-mâché classes of kindergartens past, we mixed up a homemade food "glue" of equal parts flour and water, brushing the paste on the edges of the tortilla before rolling and frying each chimichanga. This time, the chimichangas stayed in one piece. Unfortunately, the tightly tucked edges had created folds of extra tortilla at the end that came out of the oil doughy, not crisp. So we decided to practice a little tortilla origami. We tried and rejected several shapes and folding strategies before hitting on the idea of folding each tortilla as though we were wrapping a present and, as before, sealing the edges with the flour-water paste. In the oil, these thinner edges became decidedly crunchy—a perfect match for the rest of the big, golden, crisp tortilla and its spicy, delicious, and easy-to-make filling.

NOTES FROM THE TEST KITCHEN

ASSEMBLING CHICKEN CHIMICHANGAS

1. Place filling in middle of warm tortilla. Brush tortilla's circumference with flour-and-water paste.

2. Fold 2 opposite sides toward center and press to seal. Then brush open flaps with remaining paste. Fold flaps in and again press firmly to seal chimichanga shut.

Chicken Chimichangas

SERVES 2

Serve with sour cream, salsa, or guacamole if desired. See page 34 for a recipe to use up the leftover pinto beans.

- 1   cup low-sodium chicken broth
- 1¼ teaspoons minced canned chipotle chile in adobo sauce
- ¼   cup long-grain white rice
      Salt and pepper
- 1   (6-ounce) boneless, skinless chicken breast, trimmed
- 1   tablespoon plus 3 cups vegetable oil
- 1   small onion, chopped fine

1 garlic clove, minced

¼ teaspoon chili powder

¼ teaspoon ground cumin

¾ cup canned pinto beans, rinsed

2 ounces sharp cheddar cheese, shredded (½ cup)

2 tablespoons minced fresh cilantro

1 tablespoon all-purpose flour

1 tablespoon water

2 (10-inch) flour tortillas

1. Set wire rack in rimmed baking sheet. Whisk broth and chipotle together in small liquid measuring cup. Combine ½ cup chipotle broth, rice, and ⅛ teaspoon salt in bowl. Cover and microwave until liquid is completely absorbed, 3 to 5 minutes. Pat chicken dry with paper towels and season with salt and pepper.

2. Heat 1 tablespoon oil in small saucepan over medium-high heat until shimmering. Add onion and cook until softened, about 5 minutes. Stir in garlic, chili powder, and cumin and cook until fragrant, about 30 seconds. Add remaining ½ cup chipotle broth, par-cooked rice, and beans and bring to boil.

3. Reduce heat to medium-low and nestle chicken into pot. Cover and cook until rice is tender and chicken registers 160 degrees, about 15 minutes, flipping chicken halfway through cooking. Transfer chicken to carving board and let rest for 5 to 10 minutes, then cut into ½-inch pieces. Transfer rice and bean mixture to medium bowl and stir in chicken, cheese, and cilantro.

4. Whisk flour and water together in small bowl. Stack tortillas on plate and microwave, covered, until pliable, about 30 seconds. Working with 1 tortilla at a time, place half of chicken mixture in center of warm tortilla. Brush edges of tortilla with half of flour paste. Wrap top and bottom of tortilla tightly over filling. Brush ends of tortilla with remaining paste and fold into center, pressing firmly to seal.

5. Heat remaining 3 cups oil in Dutch oven over medium-high heat to 325 degrees. Place chimichangas, seam side down, in oil. Fry, adjusting burner as necessary to maintain oil temperature between 300 and 325 degrees, until chimichangas are deep golden brown, about 2 minutes per side. Transfer chimichangas to prepared rack to drain briefly. Serve.

USE IT UP: REFRIED BEANS OR PINTO BEANS

Bean and Cheese Quesadillas

SERVES 2

If you're using pinto beans, mix them with 2 tablespoons vegetable oil before mashing them. These quesadillas are mildly spicy; if you'd like more heat, increase the hot sauce to 1 teaspoon.

1 cup canned refried beans or ¾ cup rinsed canned pinto beans, mashed

1 tablespoon minced fresh parsley, cilantro, or scallions

½ teaspoon hot sauce

Salt and pepper

2 (10-inch) flour tortillas

2 ounces Monterey Jack cheese, shredded (½ cup)

1½ teaspoons vegetable oil

1. Combine beans, parsley, and hot sauce in bowl. Season with salt and pepper to taste. Working with 1 tortilla at a time, spread half of filling over 1 side of tortilla, leaving ½-inch border. Sprinkle ¼ cup cheese over filling. Fold tortilla over filling, pressing firmly to seal.

2. Heat oil in 12-inch nonstick skillet over medium-high heat until shimmering. Cook quesadillas until golden brown and crisp on both sides, about 4 minutes. Transfer to cutting board and cut into wedges. Serve.

BRAISED CHICKEN THIGHS

IF YOU'RE LOOKING FOR A SIMPLE YET HEARTY supper, look no further than braised chicken. Tender, moist pieces of chicken dressed with a boldly flavored sauce and served with mashed potatoes or polenta make for one comforting plate. Chicken thighs, with their rich, dark meat, would make the perfect starting point on our path toward an utterly satisfying braised supper; they're easy to purchase in smaller amounts, and they are less prone to drying out than chicken breasts. But the long cooking time would present two big challenges—it could lead to soggy skin and boring, washed-out flavors. We'd have to figure out a way around both potential pitfalls.

We started by determining the minimum amount of cooking time necessary to render our chicken thighs fork-tender. This was, after all, a dish we wanted to be able to make any night of the week, so the fuss factor came second only to the flavor. We cooked batches of bone-in, skin-on thighs in a 400-degree oven, a 325-degree oven, and a 200-degree oven. The 400-degree oven was out of the question: While the meat was cooked through in just 30 minutes, it didn't allow enough time for connective tissue to break down, and the meat was tough and rubbery. Braised in a 200-degree oven, the chicken was wonderfully moist and tender—but only after three hours. The best compromise between time and temperature was the 325-degree oven. At this heat level, the chicken needed to stay in the oven for about an hour and 15 minutes for meat that was tender and juicy. With some groundwork laid, we began assembling our dish.

First, we thoroughly browned the thighs in a large saucepan—a Dutch oven, the traditional choice for a braise, was overkill for our smaller amount of meat, and the pot surface burned where it was exposed. Then we transferred the chicken to a plate and built our braising liquid in the empty pan. We added a sliced onion and some garlic for a robust backdrop, followed by a little flour for thickening power, and a mixture of chicken broth and white wine for both savory and acidic notes. We then returned the chicken to the pot, tossed on the cover, and popped it into the oven. About 75 minutes later, we lifted the lid and took a bite. We had two liquid-related problems on our hands: The skin was soggy and waterlogged, and the braising liquid itself, while slightly thickened by the flour, still lacked body and complexity.

We quickly realized that the problem was the saucepan lid, which was trapping moisture inside the pot. The simple solution, we reasoned, was to remove the lid. As long as all but the top of the meat stayed submerged in the simmering liquid, we figured, it should cook properly and allow the skin to stay crisp. We figured wrong: The skin still came out flabby. Maybe our problem was more fundamental. Could it be that we were using

the wrong cooking vessel entirely? The high sides of a saucepan are designed for trapping heat and steam, but we needed something that allowed steam to escape.

A skillet is an odd choice for a dish that's traditionally cooked covered, but we decided to give it a go anyway. Finally, our chicken was crisp-skinned on top, meltingly tender and juicy within, and deeply infused with the flavors of the wine and aromatics. Even better, now that we were cooking with the lid off, the sauce was slowly reducing and concentrating during its stay in the oven.

Despite its great flavor, the sauce was still missing something. Placing a strip of lemon zest and a full sprig of fresh thyme in the skillet before braising added some depth as well as a lemony identity, but it was the hit of lemon juice and pat of butter stirred in at the end that really brightened things up. Now our emboldened sauce was rife with citrusy notes that played nicely off the rich flavor of the chicken thighs.

Braised Chicken Thighs with Lemon
SERVES 2

Serve with boiled potatoes, mashed potatoes, egg noodles, or polenta.

4	(6-ounce) bone-in chicken thighs, trimmed
	Salt and pepper
1	teaspoon olive oil
1	small onion, halved and sliced thin
2	garlic cloves, sliced thin
1	teaspoon all-purpose flour
1	cup low-sodium chicken broth
½	cup dry white wine
1	sprig fresh thyme
1	bay leaf
1	(2-inch) strip lemon zest plus 1½ teaspoons juice
1	tablespoon unsalted butter

1. Adjust oven rack to lower-middle position and heat oven to 325 degrees. Pat chicken dry with paper towels and season with salt and pepper. Heat oil in 10-inch skillet over medium-high heat until just smoking. Brown chicken well on both sides, 8 to 10 minutes; transfer to plate.

2. Pour off all but 1 tablespoon fat from skillet and return to medium heat. Stir in onion and cook until softened, about 5 minutes. Stir in garlic and cook until fragrant, about 30 seconds.

3. Stir in flour and cook for 1 minute. Stir in broth, wine, thyme, bay leaf, and lemon zest, scraping up any browned bits, and bring to simmer. Nestle chicken, along with any accumulated juices, into sauce skin side up (skin should be above surface of liquid). Transfer skillet to oven and bake, uncovered, until meat is very tender but not falling off bone, about 1¼ hours. (Check chicken after 15 minutes; broth should be barely bubbling. If bubbling vigorously, reduce oven temperature to 300 degrees.) Using a potholder (skillet handle will be hot), remove skillet from oven. Transfer chicken to serving platter, tent loosely with aluminum foil, and let rest while finishing sauce.

4. Being careful of hot skillet handle, remove thyme, bay leaf, and lemon zest from sauce. Bring sauce to simmer over medium-high heat and cook until sauce is reduced to ¾ cup, 3 to 5 minutes. Off heat, whisk in lemon juice and butter and season with salt and pepper to taste. Pour sauce over chicken and serve.

CRISPY SALMON CAKES

WHEN DONE WELL, SALMON CAKES ARE TENDER AND moist on the inside, crisp and golden brown on the outside. Unfortunately, most of the ones we've tried stray far from this ideal. Their interior is mushy and their flavor overly fishy. And then there's the fussy breading, which can lead to clumpy, greasy results. Given that salmon fillets are a staple at the fish counter, we set out to perfect this seaside favorite and bring it to the table for two.

We decided early on that these cakes would need to be made with raw salmon—the cakes we had tested with precooked salmon lacked moisture and had a "fishier" taste to them. But making raw salmon cakes was no joy either. Even though we were working with just 10 ounces of salmon, which seemed appropriate for two diners, hand-chopping slippery raw fish into

¼-inch pieces was sticky and tedious. And then having to put the cakes through the standard breading process of flour, beaten eggs, and then fresh bread crumbs before pan-frying them was just plain messy. Cutting the salmon into larger chunks wasn't an option—with bigger salmon bits, the cakes fell apart, even with strong binders like bread crumbs and mayonnaise. That said, colleagues deemed the cakes made from raw salmon "pretty darn good." They were tender and moist inside and boasted a pleasantly rich, almost creamy flavor. They just needed a bit of flavor enhancement and, for the sake of weeknight cooking, an easier method.

To this end, we took out our food processor. We cut the fillet into 2-inch pieces, chucked them in, and let the processor whirl. This resulted in big chunks of salmon bound by finely ground fish paste; when we tried pulsing them for longer to get smaller pieces, formed the mixture into rounds, and fried them, the finished cakes had a ground-meat consistency that was dense rather than delicate.

But that ground-meat analogy gave us an idea. When we made our Juicy Pub-Style Burgers (page 9), we ground the meat ourselves using an easy three-step process: We cut the meat into ½-inch pieces, froze them briefly to firm them up, and then ground them into smaller chunks in the food processor. The method ensures small, discrete pieces rather than mush. But before we added a half-hour of freezer time to our procedure, we tried cutting the salmon into smaller pieces and grinding them in smaller batches. We cut the salmon into 1-inch chunks and pulsed them for just two pulses. This approach—pulsing, rather than letting the processor run continuously—allowed for more even chopping. Some of the pieces were still a bit bigger than the ideal ¼-inch morsels and some were smaller, but taken as a whole, they produced a cake very similar to those we had made with hand-minced fish.

Having succeeded in making the chopping easier, we now could address an issue that had been annoying us from the start: The raw cakes were so wet that dipping them in egg made them slippery and awkward to handle. Adding more bread crumbs made the patties drier and firmer, but now the delicate sweetness of the fish was masked. We had a radical thought: Was the full-on

CRISPY SALMON CAKES

breading process really necessary? What if we ditched the egg and flour and simply coated the salmon cakes in bread crumbs before frying? This made the patties easier to handle, and the bread crumbs clung surprisingly well to the fish on their own, but the results weren't stellar. Without a little bit of flour to act as a buffer from the moisture in the cakes, the fresh bread crumbs came out too pale and soft. But when we traded the fresh crumbs for ultra-crisp Japanese panko, the salmon cakes emerged from the pan crisp and golden brown. For convenience, we decided to use panko for the binder as well.

Curious why the traditional breading procedure proved unnecessary in this case—which, fortunately, both cut down on mess and resulted in a simpler process—we consulted a few of our food science books. A typical breading process works because the egg contains sticky soluble proteins called ovalbumins that (along with the flour) help hold the mixture together. But it turns out that salmon also contains tacky soluble proteins, called myosins, that migrate to the surface with the moisture in the fish and help the bread crumbs stick. Salmon has more of these water-soluble proteins than many other kinds of fish, making it the perfect candidate for a nontraditional breading and our just-panko coating.

When it came to cooking the cakes, we decided that not only would pan-frying be the quickest method, it would also keep the fishiness in check. After pondering the merits of oven-frying our cakes, we found that the unsaturated fat in the salmon oxidizes both when it is exposed to air and when it is cooked, so the longer the cooking time, the stronger the "fishy" flavor would be.

Now that we had settled on a technique, it was time to jazz up the cakes' somewhat plain taste in a way that would enhance the fish flavor rather than disguise it. We added some finely chopped shallot for depth and some parsley for freshness. Lemon juice brightened the flavor and cut the richness of the salmon, and a half-teaspoon of mustard and a pinch of cayenne added punch. For a variation honoring a classic brunch mainstay, we substituted minced smoked salmon for 2 ounces of the fresh salmon, dill for the parsley, and added chopped capers for brininess.

Served with a quick and easy tartar sauce, these moist yet crisp salmon cakes managed to be both elegant fare and comfort food.

Crispy Salmon Cakes with Sweet and Tangy Tartar Sauce

SERVES 2

If buying a skin-on salmon fillet, purchase 11 ounces of fish. This will yield 10 ounces of fish after skinning. When processing the salmon it is OK to have some pieces that are larger than ¼ inch. It is important to avoid overprocessing the fish.

TARTAR SAUCE

- ⅓ cup mayonnaise
- 1 tablespoon sweet pickle relish
- 1½ teaspoons capers, rinsed and minced
- 1 teaspoon white wine vinegar
- ¼ teaspoon Worcestershire sauce
- ¼ teaspoon pepper
- Salt

SALMON CAKES

- 2 tablespoons plus ½ cup panko bread crumbs
- 1 tablespoon minced fresh parsley
- 1 tablespoon mayonnaise
- 2 teaspoons lemon juice
- 1 small shallot, minced
- ½ teaspoon Dijon mustard
- Salt and pepper
- Pinch cayenne pepper
- 10 ounces skinless salmon, cut into 1-inch pieces
- ⅓ cup vegetable oil

1. FOR THE TARTAR SAUCE: Whisk all ingredients together; season with salt and pepper to taste.

2. FOR THE SALMON CAKES: Combine 2 tablespoons panko, parsley, mayonnaise, lemon juice, shallot, mustard, ½ teaspoon salt, ¼ teaspoon pepper, and cayenne in bowl. Pulse salmon in food processor until coarsely chopped into ¼-inch pieces, about 2 pulses. Transfer salmon to bowl with panko mixture and gently mix until uniformly combined.

3. Place remaining ½ cup panko in shallow dish or pie plate. Using ⅓-cup measure, scoop level amount of salmon mixture and transfer to plate; repeat to make 4 cakes. Carefully coat each cake with bread crumbs, gently patting into disk measuring 2¾ inches in diameter and 1 inch thick. Return coated cakes to plate.

4. Heat oil in 10-inch skillet over medium-high heat until shimmering. Place salmon cakes in skillet and cook without moving until golden brown, about 2 minutes. Carefully flip cakes and cook until second side is golden brown, 2 to 3 minutes. Transfer cakes to paper towel–lined plate to drain for 1 minute. Serve with tartar sauce.

VARIATION

Crispy Salmon Cakes with Smoked Salmon, Capers, and Dill

Substitute 1 tablespoon chopped fresh dill for parsley. Reduce amount of fresh salmon to 8 ounces and salt to ⅛ teaspoon. Add 2 ounces finely chopped smoked salmon and 1½ teaspoons rinsed and minced capers to bowl with salmon mixture.

NOTES FROM THE TEST KITCHEN

SECRETS TO CRISPY SALMON CAKES

1. Hand-chop fish into 1-inch pieces before adding them to food processor. (If they are too big, fish will be mix of large chunks and finely ground paste.)

2. Carefully pulse chopped fish into ¼-inch bits, about 2 pulses. Then mix with bread crumb binder and flavorings.

3. Gently coat shaped cakes with coarse panko bread crumbs. Salmon's high concentration of tacky water-soluble proteins glues crumbs to patties without need for egg or flour.

GLAZED SALMON FILLETS

THERE ARE FEW BETTER WAYS TO HIGHLIGHT THE rich, silky flesh of salmon than by offsetting it with a sweet-tart glaze. Most recipes call for using the broiler to get the right texture in the salmon and instill it with the glaze's flavor. Unfortunately, using such extreme heat makes it hard to pinpoint the proper doneness of the fish, resulting in salmon with a leathery, overcooked exterior and burnt glaze. We wanted to find a better way to put two buttery, moist, flavorful salmon fillets on the table for dinner tonight.

To start, we looked to a common restaurant technique. Slow-cooked salmon is a popular restaurant dish these days, one that trades the intense heat of the broiler for the low, slow heat of the oven, which renders the fish terrifically moist and tender. The likely trade-off would be a well-lacquered exterior, but we thought it was worth a shot. We set the oven to 300 degrees, placed the rack in the middle position, and gently cooked the fish plain (we would address the glaze later). After 10 minutes, the salmon was cooked perfectly.

Now that our salmon was succulent and pink throughout, we had only one problem: Tasters missed the slightly crusty, flavorful browned exterior of the broiled fish. Cranking the heat back up was out of the question. Instead, we briefly seared each side of the fish in a hot skillet before transferring it to the low oven. But while the crust was nicely browned, one bite revealed that we had virtually negated the benefits of our slow-cooking technique. The outer layer of the fish was tough and dry—reminiscent of what happens with broiling.

What we needed to do was more rapidly caramelize the fillets before their exteriors had a chance to turn tough and leathery—and that's when we remembered a favorite test kitchen technique: To expedite browning on everything from pork tenderloin to tuna, we lightly sprinkle the flesh with sugar. Here, we tried brown sugar (for its subtle molasses flavor), and it took only a minute for a delicate, flavorful crust to form. We then seared the skin side of the fish for another minute to promote even cooking and transferred the skillet to the oven. Seven minutes later, we had just what we wanted: a golden brown exterior and a pink, wonderfully moist interior.

That just left us with the glaze. We combined more brown sugar with vinegar, then added mirin, soy sauce, and mustard to create a teriyaki-inspired varnish that would serve as a perfect foil to the rich, fatty salmon. We brought the mixture to a boil in a saucepan; reduced it for five minutes, until it was thick enough to coat the back of a spoon; then brushed it over the seared salmon fillets. But even before we got the fish into the oven, much of the glaze slid off and pooled in the bottom of the pan. We had to find a way to get it to stay in place.

An obvious remedy was to further thicken the glaze, so we tried adding a small amount of cornstarch to the mixture. The result? Better, but too much of the sauce still dribbled down the sides of the fish. Adding more cornstarch was not an option; any more than ½ teaspoon rendered the mixture gummy and gloppy. We were running out of ideas when an altogether different approach occurred to us: What if instead of trying to create a tackier glaze, we worked on getting the salmon itself to have more "stickability"? The success we had with our Maple-Glazed Pork Tenderloin (page 12) gave us hope that rubbing cornstarch on the surface of the fish would add texture, essentially creating tiny nooks and crannies to trap the glaze.

Fingers crossed, we combined ⅛ teaspoon of cornstarch with the brown sugar we were already rubbing on the fish, plus ⅛ teaspoon of salt for seasoning, and then seared the fillets. As we had hoped, the surface was now quite coarse, mottled all over with tiny peaks and valleys. We proceeded with the recipe, spooning the glossy glaze over the salmon and then transferring it to the low oven. This time the mixture stuck, resulting in a glistening, well-lacquered exterior.

With our glaze holding fast to the fillets, we whipped up two more variations: a fruity pomegranate version spiked with balsamic vinegar, and an Asian barbecue mixture drawing sweetness from hoisin sauce and tartness from rice vinegar.

With a foolproof recipe for buttery, tender salmon in our arsenal, the only issue we had left to contend with was which flavorful glaze to pick.

Glazed Salmon Fillets

SERVES 2

Prepare the glaze before you cook the salmon. If your nonstick skillet isn't ovensafe, sear the salmon as directed in step 2, then transfer it to a rimmed baking sheet, glaze it, and bake it as directed in step 3.

- ½ teaspoon packed brown sugar
- ⅛ teaspoon cornstarch
-   Salt and pepper
- 2 (6- to 8-ounce) center-cut skin-on salmon fillets
- 1 teaspoon vegetable oil
- 1 recipe glaze (recipes follow)

1. Adjust oven rack to middle position and heat oven to 300 degrees. Combine sugar, cornstarch, ⅛ teaspoon salt, and ⅛ teaspoon pepper in small bowl. Pat salmon dry with paper towels and sprinkle sugar mixture evenly over flesh side of salmon, rubbing to distribute evenly.

2. Heat oil in 10-inch ovensafe nonstick skillet over medium-high heat until just smoking. Place salmon, flesh side down, in skillet and cook until well browned, about 1 minute. Using tongs, carefully flip salmon and cook, skin side down, for 1 minute.

3. Off heat, spoon glaze evenly over salmon fillets. Transfer skillet to oven and roast until center is still translucent when checked with tip of paring knife and registers 125 degrees (for medium-rare), 7 to 10 minutes. Serve.

Soy-Mustard Glaze

MAKES ABOUT ¼ CUP

Mirin, a sweet Japanese rice wine, can be found in Asian markets and the international section of most supermarkets.

- 5 teaspoons packed brown sugar
- 1 tablespoon soy sauce
- 1 tablespoon mirin
- 1½ teaspoons sherry vinegar
- 1½ teaspoons whole-grain mustard
- 1½ teaspoons water
- ½ teaspoon cornstarch
-   Pinch red pepper flakes

Whisk all ingredients together in small saucepan. Bring to simmer over medium-high heat and cook until thickened, about 1 minute. Off heat, cover to keep warm.

Pomegranate-Balsamic Glaze

MAKES ABOUT ¼ CUP

- 2 tablespoons pomegranate juice
- 5 teaspoons packed brown sugar
- 1 tablespoon balsamic vinegar
- 1½ teaspoons whole-grain mustard
- ½ teaspoon cornstarch
- Pinch cayenne pepper

Whisk all ingredients together in small saucepan. Bring to simmer over medium-high heat and cook until thickened, about 1 minute. Off heat, cover to keep warm.

Asian Barbecue Glaze

MAKES ABOUT 3 TABLESPOONS

Asian chili-garlic sauce can be found in Asian markets and the international section of most supermarkets.

- 1 tablespoon ketchup
- 1 tablespoon hoisin sauce
- 1 tablespoon rice vinegar
- 1 tablespoon packed brown sugar
- 1½ teaspoons soy sauce
- 1½ teaspoons toasted sesame oil
- 1 teaspoon Asian chili-garlic sauce
- ½ teaspoon grated fresh ginger

Whisk all ingredients together in small saucepan. Bring to simmer over medium-high heat and cook until thickened, about 1 minute. Off heat, cover to keep warm.

BAKED SOLE FILLETS

WE LOVE THE SUBTLE FLAVOR AND FINE TEXTURE of sole, but it can be nearly impossible to translate this fish into a simple, foolproof weeknight meal. For starters, every cooking method has its drawbacks. Both sautéing and pan-frying yield nice golden color, but a hot skillet can overcook the thin fillets in a flash. Plus, sole is a fairly wide fillet, meaning a pair of them often fit a little too snugly in the skillet for our comfort. Poaching is gentler, but it also leaves the fish a bit bland without a flavorful poaching liquid and separate sauce for serving.

Baking seemed like the best option—it would be forgiving and convenient, with the ambient heat of the oven cooking the fish through at a gentle, even rate. But we wanted to gussy up the dish somehow with a minimal amount of effort—and we didn't want to just fall back on a pan sauce. It was time to think of some new ways to approach baked sole.

Simply laying the fillets flat on a baking sheet seemed promising, until they broke into pieces when we transferred them to dinner plates—not what we had in mind for an elegant dinner for two. Rolling them into compact bundles eased the transport from baking dish to plate, and looked impressive, but the trade-off was a thicker piece of fish that cooked unevenly.

But the technique itself—baking rolled fillets—showed promise and won presentation points with tasters, so we experimented with oven temperatures (from 300 all the way up to 450 degrees) to even out the cooking. After 30 minutes at 325 degrees, the fillets were nicely done from edge to center. Covering the baking dish with foil offered the delicate fish further protection from the drying heat of the oven.

With the cooking method settled, we set out to ramp up the still-flat flavor. Salt, pepper, and lemon zest for brightness were shoe-ins. Fresh herbs would also be a must, so we tried a few different ones to see what combination would work best. A little minced parsley with some chives worked OK, but while the chives were definitely a keeper for the hint of onion flavor they gave the fish, the parsley didn't do much in terms of flavor. With such a simple meal, every ingredient needs to contribute, so we looked to another herb for help. A small amount of minced tarragon went a long way in providing a fresh, aniselike flavor and worked well with the chives' mild, grassy notes.

After seasoning the fillets and sprinkling on the herb and lemon zest mixture, we drizzled them with melted butter, rolled them, drizzled on more butter, and put them in the oven. The butter contributed richness and ensured that the exterior didn't dry out, but the overall flavor was still somewhat mild. Once we worked a clove of minced garlic into the butter and brushed a spoonful of Dijon mustard over each fillet, the flavor popped.

All we had left to address was the baked fillets' one-note texture and fairly dull appearance. A topping of panko (Japanese-style bread crumbs) toasted in butter

BAKED SOLE FILLETS WITH HERBS AND BREAD CRUMBS

along with garlic offered both crunch and a golden crown, but adding a measure of herbs to the crumbs once they were cooled made it even better. As for when to add the crumbs to the fish, they absorbed moisture and lost their lovely crispness when added at the outset, but they lacked cohesion with the fish when sprinkled on after cooking. We compromised with a hybrid technique, removing the foil with five to 10 minutes remaining, basting the fillets with the pan juices, topping them with most of the toasted crumbs, and then returning them to the oven uncovered. Just before serving, we sprinkled on the remaining spoonful of crumbs. This way, most of the crumbs fused to the fish, and the final showering offered delicate crispness.

Fuss-free and foolproof, these crumb-topped, herb-filled fillets were exactly what we had hoped to create: fish suitable for a weeknight dinner, yet impressive and elegant enough to serve on a special occasion.

Baked Sole Fillets with Herbs and Bread Crumbs

SERVES 2

Try to purchase fillets of similar size. If using smaller fillets (about 3 ounces each), serve 2 fillets per person and reduce the baking time in step 3 to 20 minutes. We strongly advise against using frozen fish in this recipe. Freezing can undermine the texture of the fish, making it hard to roll. Fresh basil or dill can be used in place of the tarragon.

- 2 tablespoons minced fresh chives
- 1 teaspoon minced fresh tarragon
- ¼ teaspoon finely grated lemon zest, plus lemon wedges for serving
- 2 tablespoons unsalted butter
- 1 garlic clove, minced
- 2 (6-ounce) skinless sole or flounder fillets
  Salt and pepper
- 1 teaspoon Dijon mustard
- ⅓ cup panko bread crumbs

1. Adjust oven rack to middle position and heat oven to 325 degrees. Combine chives and tarragon in small bowl. Measure out 1 teaspoon herb mixture and set aside. Stir lemon zest into remaining herbs.

2. Melt 1 tablespoon butter in 8-inch skillet over medium heat. Add ½ teaspoon garlic and cook, stirring often, until fragrant, about 1 minute. Set skillet aside.

3. Pat fillets dry with paper towels and season both sides with salt and pepper. Turn fillets skinned side up with tail end pointing away from you. Spread ½ teaspoon mustard on each fillet, sprinkle each evenly with about 1 tablespoon herb–lemon zest mixture, and drizzle each with 1 teaspoon garlic butter. Tightly roll fillets from thick end to form cylinders. Set fillets, seam side down, in 8-inch square baking dish. Drizzle remaining 1 teaspoon garlic butter over fillets, cover baking dish with aluminum foil, and bake for 25 minutes.

4. Meanwhile, wipe out skillet and melt remaining 1 tablespoon butter over medium heat. Add panko and cook, stirring often, until crumbs are deep golden brown, 5 to 8 minutes. Reduce heat to low, add remaining garlic, and cook, stirring constantly, until garlic is fragrant and evenly distributed throughout crumbs, about 1 minute. Transfer to small bowl and season with salt and pepper to taste. Let cool, then stir in reserved 1 teaspoon herb mixture.

5. Remove baking dish from oven. Baste fillets with melted garlic butter from baking dish and sprinkle with all but 1 tablespoon bread crumb mixture. Continue to bake, uncovered, until fish flakes apart when gently prodded with paring knife and registers 140 degrees, 6 to 10 minutes longer. Using thin metal spatula, transfer fillets to individual plates, sprinkle with remaining 1 tablespoon bread crumb mixture, and serve with lemon wedges.

NOTES FROM THE TEST KITCHEN

THE BEST MULTI-EVENT KITCHEN TIMER
Even when you're cooking for two, if you're preparing a main dish for dinner, you most likely also have a side or two cooking away on the stovetop or in the oven. That's when a good multi-event timer, which enables you to monitor the progress of several recipes at once, comes in handy. We recently tested seven models in search of one that is strong, easy to read, and straightforward to set. To test durability, we knocked each one off the counter several times and manhandled it with sticky, dough-covered hands. Under this treatment, one timer quit and two others cracked. Our favorite brand is the **American Innovative Chef's Quad Timer**, $29.99, which proved to be durable, sturdy, and easy to read.

SPICE-RUBBED PORK TENDERLOIN WITH FENNEL, TOMATOES, AND ARTICHOKES

CHAPTER 2

ONE-DISH SUPPERS

PAN-SEARED STEAKS WITH CRISPY POTATOES

FOR MOST PEOPLE, A FINE STEAK DINNER MEANS A trip to a fancy steakhouse, since turning out perfectly cooked steak at home can be a gamble. We set out to develop a foolproof technique for chophouse-caliber pan-seared steaks. And on the side we wanted none other than crispy potato wedges. To keep things simple, we decided to rely on just one skillet to get our meat and potatoes on the table with little fuss—and cleanup.

We started with the steak. For a perfectly seared steak, we knew from experience that a heavy skillet is key for even heat distribution, as is the right level of heat. To achieve the best crust, we had to make sure of two

NOTES FROM THE TEST KITCHEN

THE BEST INEXPENSIVE NONSTICK SKILLET

We've always recommended buying inexpensive nonstick skillets, because with regular use the nonstick coating inevitably scratches, chips off, or becomes ineffective. Why spend big bucks on a pan that will last only a year or two? To find the best nonstick pan on the market, we tested seven contenders under $50 against our longtime favorite, the All-Clad Stainless 12-inch Nonstick Frying Pan, $129.99, and the Best Buy from our previous testing, the Calphalon Simply Calphalon Nonstick Omelette Pan, $55. We tested the nonstick effectiveness of each pan by frying eggs and stir-frying beef and vegetables. To see which pans cooked food evenly and had good size and heft but were comfortable to maneuver, we made crêpes in each. We also ran them through a number of durability tests. We'd like to say our new favorite pan, the **T-Fal Professional Total Non-Stick Fry Pan**, aced every test, but a loose handle that resulted from the durability testing was a sign that it's not high-end cookware. Still, at $34 for the 12.5-inch pan ($29.95 for the 10.25-inch pan, and $25 for the 8-inch pan), it's a bargain, and it was the only pan in the lineup to give us the best of both worlds: an exceptionally slick, durable nonstick coating and top performance in cooking. As for the All-Clad, it is a solidly built pan and a terrific piece of cookware, but its coating became slightly worn by the end of our tests (meanwhile, the T-Fal remained perfectly slick). Because the All-Clad boasts a lifetime warranty, we still recommend it, but we'll be buying the T-Fal from now on for our own kitchens.

things: that the oil in the skillet was just smoking before we added the steaks and that the skillet was not over-crowded. If the oil wasn't hot enough, or if the steaks were jammed too tightly together, the meat ended up stewing rather than searing. Since we'd be cooking only enough steak for two, we wouldn't need a large skillet, which would leave some surface area uncovered, leading to scorched oil; our steaks fit perfectly in a medium-size 10-inch pan. And because moving the steaks releases their liquid, once they were in the pan, we let them be. We'd sear the steaks on the first side, flip them, and then let them cook through over lower heat.

Cooking method established, we turned to the steaks themselves. Since we needed only enough meat for two, we'd need to choose our steaks carefully. We bypassed the gargantuan porterhouse and T-bone steaks in favor of more reasonable cuts, ultimately testing filet mignon, flank steak, and strip steak. The filet mignon was tender but lacking in beefy flavor, and the flank steak didn't quite have the hearty, steakhouse feel. But a 12-ounce strip steak, cut in half to make two individual steaks, offered plenty of beefy flavor and also felt substantial on the plate. Since these steaks tend to be thicker (around 1½ inches), we were able to get a really good crust on the exterior without overcooking the interior. Getting a deep brown crust on the first side took about five minutes. Once that crust had developed, we flipped the steaks, reduced the heat, and continued cooking until they were medium-rare, which took another five minutes. We undercooked the steaks a bit to allow for carryover cooking (while the steaks rest, the meat continues to cook).

Next we tackled the potatoes. We wanted a potato that we could cut into wedges and that would hold up to high-heat crisping, so we knew we didn't want to use fluffy, high-starch russets that would stick and fall apart in the pan. Instead, we tried both Yukon Golds and red potatoes. The waxy Yukons never quite gave us the desired fluffy-on-the-inside, crisp-on-the-outside texture, but the red potatoes worked very well. As a bonus, red potatoes turned out to be a great timesaver: Their tender skin didn't even require peeling.

As far as our cooking method was concerned, we knew deep-frying was out—it was too messy and would require another pot. Sautéing the potatoes in the same skillet we had used to sear our steaks meant that the potatoes would get a flavor boost from the steak's fat. However, dumping a handful of raw potato wedges into a hot skillet with a modicum of fat left behind from cooking the steak left us chewing on charred fries with raw centers. Adding extra oil helped us achieve more evenly golden potatoes, but it did little to solve the undercooked middles. We wondered if parcooking the potatoes in the microwave before adding them to the skillet would help. This meant we could jump-start the potatoes while the steaks seared, and then sauté them (in only the residual fat from searing the steaks) just long enough to finish cooking their interiors and crisp up their exteriors. This worked like a charm, giving us golden, crunchy potatoes with a light and fluffy interior.

While purists won't want to adorn their steak with anything other than a sprinkling of salt and pepper, our tasters felt that an herb sauce would brighten the meal and elevate it to the next level. Inspired by an Argentine complement to steak, chimichurri sauce, we gathered parsley, garlic, olive oil, and red wine vinegar for a quick, fresh sauce that we could throw together in the food processor.

Finally, we had created a restaurant-caliber home-cooked steak dinner for two. It was quick to prepare and easy to cook, and it definitely went beyond the standard meat-and-potatoes supper.

Pan-Seared Steaks with Crispy Potatoes and Parsley Sauce

SERVES 2

We prefer to use medium to large potatoes, measuring 2 to 4 inches in diameter, for this recipe. We prefer this steak cooked to medium-rare, but if you prefer it more or less done, see our guidelines on page 154.

PARSLEY SAUCE

- ½ cup fresh parsley leaves
- ¼ cup extra-virgin olive oil
- 1 shallot, minced
- 2 tablespoons red wine vinegar
- 1 tablespoon water
- 2 garlic cloves, minced
- ½ teaspoon salt
- ⅛ teaspoon red pepper flakes

STEAK AND POTATOES

- 12 ounces medium to large red potatoes, cut into 1-inch wedges
- 2 tablespoons vegetable oil
   Salt and pepper
- 1 (12-ounce) boneless strip steak, 1½ inches thick, trimmed and cut in half crosswise

1. FOR THE PARSLEY SAUCE: Process all ingredients together in food processor until well combined, about 20 seconds, scraping down bowl as necessary. Transfer to small bowl, cover, and set aside.

2. FOR THE STEAK AND POTATOES: Toss potatoes with 1 tablespoon oil in bowl and season with salt and pepper. Microwave, covered, until potatoes begin to soften, about 5 minutes, stirring halfway through cooking. Drain potatoes well.

3. Meanwhile, pat steaks dry with paper towels and season with salt and pepper. Heat remaining 1 tablespoon oil in 10-inch nonstick skillet over medium-high heat until just smoking. Cook steaks until well browned on first side, 3 to 5 minutes.

4. Flip steaks, reduce heat to medium, and continue to cook until steaks register 125 degrees (for medium-rare), 5 to 7 minutes longer. Transfer steaks to platter, tent loosely with aluminum foil, and let rest for 10 minutes.

5. Return skillet with remaining fat to medium heat until shimmering. Add potatoes and cook until golden brown and tender, about 10 minutes. Transfer potatoes to platter, drizzle sauce over steak and potatoes, and serve.

BEEF TACO CASSEROLE

WHILE THEY MAY NOT BE AUTHENTICALLY MEXICAN, ground beef tacos have earned a special place at the American dinner table. As a quick, kid-friendly meal, the ground beef taco has a simplicity and comfort-food appeal that are undeniable. But when you're cooking for two, taco night might seem a little humdrum. For a dish that would bring beef tacos to another level, we decided to take them apart and put them back together in a simple casserole, perfectly portioned for two, with a spicy, flavorful, beefy filling, a crunchy taco-shell layer, and cheesy garnishes built right in.

We started with the beef filling, testing ground beef that ranged from 80 to 93 percent lean with a handful of basic taco spices. We quickly learned that there is such a thing as too much fat. Pools of orange oil seeped out of the beef mixture made with ground chuck (aka 80 percent lean beef). Even the 85 percent lean option, our favorite for ground beef chili, cooked up slick and oily. At the other end of the spectrum, the filling made with 93 percent lean beef (extra-lean) was dry and sandy. Ultimately, we went with 90 percent lean beef, which was full-flavored without being greasy; a half-pound gave us the perfect amount for a two-person casserole.

We didn't want to use a dusty taco seasoning packet; we wanted to season our ground beef with fresh flavor. To that end, we sautéed a small minced onion and a couple of cloves of garlic for both moisture and flavor.

NOTES FROM THE TEST KITCHEN

THE BEST TORTILLA CHIPS

Hit the snack aisle at the supermarket and you'll think tortilla chips have surpassed potato chips as America's favorite snack food. There are dozens of flavors and shapes to choose from. So how do you pick the best of the bunch? Despite their being made from just a handful of ingredients—corn flour or stone-ground corn, oil, and salt—we found great variation in flavor among the different samples that we tried. As a general rule, we favored thin, delicate chips made from finely ground cornmeal. As opposed to the thicker tortilla chips, these chips were described as "thin and crispy" and were perceived as being fresher. In terms of salt, the chips with a higher salt content generally fared better than those with less salt— no surprise there. So which were our favorites? Our favorite widely available tortilla chips were **Tostitos 100% White Corn Restaurant Style Tortilla Chips**, which tasters liked for their "delicately crisp" texture. **Santitas Authentic Mexican Style White Corn Tortilla Chips** also finished on top, praised for their "mild and salty" flavor and "sturdy" texture; their "great crunch" topped the crispness charts.

For spices, we turned to chili powder. A single teaspoon didn't pack enough heat, so we quickly doubled up for the right kick. Small amounts of both ground cumin and ground coriander added savory, complex flavor. To deepen their flavor, we cooked, or bloomed, the spices with the onion and garlic in oil before adding the beef.

Now our filling needed a sauce to bind it together. First, we tried a small can of tomato sauce, which provided a good consistency but little flavor. Canned diced tomatoes gave us a consistency closer to what we were after, but the flavor was still lacking. Swapping out the diced tomatoes for canned Ro-Tel tomatoes (which incorporate green chiles) worked much better. The green chiles in the Ro-Tel can provided a jolt without any extra work on our part, and the tomatoes' chunky texture gave the filling some variety. A little cider vinegar and brown sugar provided a sweet and sour tang.

Happy with the beef, we moved on to the other layers. Beans seemed an obvious candidate. After trying both canned whole and refried beans in our working recipe, we settled on the refried because they provided a distinct, creamy layer. To bump up the flavor of the canned beans, we combined them with some of our Ro-Tel tomatoes and cilantro, giving our beans complexity without adding items to our shopping list. With these changes made, our beans were close to perfect, but they needed a little more heat. A teaspoon of hot sauce did the trick. We spread this mixture on the bottom of our mini casserole dish, then added the beef mixture on top.

While taco toppings vary a bit from table to table, shredded cheese is always a requirement. We tried both cheddar and Monterey Jack, and although neither was bad, tasters found the cheddar a little greasy and the Monterey Jack too mild. We found our answer in Colby Jack, a blend of Colby and Monterey Jack cheeses. The cheddar-esque flavor of the Colby, combined with the creaminess of the Monterey Jack, was ideal, especially when sprinkled between the layers of our casserole.

Finally, it was time to find the best way to incorporate the taco-shell element. We crumbled a few crisp shells on top of the casserole and added another smattering of cheese. While this gave us a crunchy, flavorful topping, we were a bit irked by the nearly full package of taco shells left behind. We wondered if tortilla chips would serve as a more sensible stand-in for the taco shells. Luckily, these stayed just as crisp as the taco shells after a quick stay in the oven. Just 15 minutes was enough to melt the cheese, meld the flavors, and brown the topping of our petite casserole.

For a fresh finish, we sprinkled the top layer with a little more cilantro before serving. Our taco casserole now packed all the texture and flavor expected from taco night into an unexpected, but every bit as satisfying, dinner for two.

Beef Taco Casserole

SERVES 2

If you can't find Ro-Tel tomatoes, substitute ¾ cup canned diced tomatoes and one 4-ounce can chopped green chiles, reserving 3 tablespoons of the tomato juice and 1 tablespoon of the chile juice. You will need an 8½ by 5½-inch baking dish for this recipe (see page 3). See page 34 for a recipe to use up the leftover refried beans.

   1 cup canned refried beans
   1 (10-ounce) can Ro-Tel tomatoes, drained with
      ¼ cup juice reserved
2½ tablespoons minced fresh cilantro
   1 teaspoon hot sauce
   3 ounces Colby Jack cheese, shredded (¾ cup)
   2 teaspoons vegetable oil
   1 small onion, chopped fine
      Salt and pepper
   2 garlic cloves, minced
   2 teaspoons chili powder
   ¼ teaspoon ground cumin
   ¼ teaspoon ground coriander
   8 ounces 90 percent lean ground beef
   ½ teaspoon cider vinegar
   ¼ teaspoon packed brown sugar
1½ ounces tortilla chips or taco shells, broken into
      1-inch pieces (1⅓ cups)

1. Adjust oven rack to upper-middle position and heat oven to 475 degrees. Mix refried beans, one-half of drained tomatoes, 1½ tablespoons cilantro, and hot sauce together in bowl, then smooth mixture into 8½ by 5½-inch baking dish. Sprinkle ¼ cup cheese over beans.

2. Heat oil in 10-inch skillet over medium heat until shimmering. Add onion and ¼ teaspoon salt and cook

until onion is softened, about 5 minutes. Stir in garlic, chili powder, cumin, and coriander and cook until fragrant, about 30 seconds.

3. Stir in beef and cook, breaking up meat with wooden spoon, until no longer pink, 3 to 5 minutes. Stir in remaining tomatoes, reserved tomato juice, vinegar, and sugar. Bring to simmer and cook until mixture is thickened and nearly dry, about 8 minutes. Season with salt and pepper to taste.

4. Spread beef mixture in baking dish and sprinkle with ¼ cup cheese. Scatter tortilla chips over top, then sprinkle with remaining ¼ cup cheese.

5. Bake until filling is bubbling and top is spotty brown, 8 to 10 minutes. Let casserole cool for 10 minutes, then sprinkle with remaining 1 tablespoon cilantro. Serve.

PORK TENDERLOIN WITH VEGETABLES

WHEN DONE RIGHT, NOTHING CAN MATCH THE fine-grained, buttery-smooth texture of pork tenderloin. And because of its size—the tenderloin is relatively long and thin—it cooks quickly, not to mention that a single tenderloin is the perfect amount for two hungry diners. But generally speaking, since most of the flavor in a cut of meat comes from the fat that surrounds and marbles the muscles, lean cuts like pork tenderloin have a tendency to be bland. As such, they benefit from bold seasoning, often in the form of a dry rub, marinade, or sauce. We decided we would first need to determine how to flavor our pork, and then we could focus on selecting a complementary side dish—one that would also cook quickly—allowing us to deliver a well-rounded dinner for two in under an hour.

When cooking pork tenderloin, we typically start by searing it on the stovetop to brown the exterior and add flavor. But we wondered if a dry rub might allow us to skip the step of browning, adding both flavor and color to our tenderloin without the extra work. Seasoning with salt and pepper would provide a solid base, but we wanted a distinct flavor profile to guide the rest of the dish. Herbes de Provence, a dried herb blend that usually includes thyme, fennel seeds, savory, rosemary, marjoram, and lavender, would give our pork

NOTES FROM THE TEST KITCHEN

ENHANCED OR UNENHANCED PORK?

Because modern pork is remarkably lean and therefore somewhat bland and prone to dryness if overcooked, a product called "enhanced" pork has overtaken the market. In fact, it can be hard to find unenhanced pork. Enhanced pork has been injected with a solution of water, salt, sodium phosphate, sodium lactate, potassium lactate, sodium diacetate, and varying flavor agents to bolster flavor and juiciness; these enhancing ingredients add 7 to 15 percent extra weight. After several taste tests, we have concluded that although enhanced pork is indeed juicier and more tender than unenhanced pork, the latter has more pure pork flavor. Some tasters also picked up artificial, salty flavors in enhanced pork. It can also leach juice that, once reduced, will result in overly salty sauces. We prefer natural pork, but the choice is up to you.

PREPARING FENNEL

1. Cut off stems and feathery fronds. (Fronds can be minced and used as garnish, if desired.)

2. Trim very thin slice from base and remove any tough or blemished outer layers from bulb.

3. Cut bulb in half through base. Use small, sharp knife to remove pyramid-shaped core.

4. Slice each fennel half into ½-inch-thick strips.

a definitive identity without requiring a number of different herbs and spices. After a very potent first test, we learned that a little of this blend goes a long way; a mere teaspoon was sufficient to flavor and coat our 12-ounce tenderloin without overwhelming the pork.

Because pork tenderloin is thin and lean, a relatively brief stay in a hot oven works best to avoid overcooking. The high temperature aids in browning the outside of the meat, while the short cooking time ensures a tender, moist interior. We found that roasting the tenderloin at 450 degrees for about 30 minutes was all we needed to bring the interior of the pork to a rosy 145 degrees. To optimize browning on the exterior of the pork, we turned the tenderloin over halfway through the cooking time.

Finding a vegetable accompaniment for such a quick-cooking meat was tricky; after just 30 minutes of roasting time, most root vegetables are still raw, and more delicate vegetables, such as green beans or asparagus, are overcooked. Thinking again about our Provençal-inspired rub, we wondered if fennel might work—its sweet, delicate flavor would be the perfect complement to our pork tenderloin. We began with two fennel bulbs and cut them into ½-inch-thick slices. After tossing them with olive oil, we placed them in the baking dish with the pork. After 30 minutes of roasting, the pork was done, but the fennel was still crunchy. We transferred the pork to a carving board and returned the fennel to the oven, but in the 10 to 15 minutes the pork rested, the fennel still didn't finish cooking.

The fennel needed a jump start—and perhaps some company in the baking dish. While tasters liked the mild flavor of the fennel, they also thought this dish could handle some bolder, brighter additions. We decided to reduce the amount of fennel we were using to one bulb and supplement it with some frozen artichoke hearts, halved niçoise olives, and half a pint of cherry tomatoes. After parcooking the fennel in the microwave, we tossed it with the artichoke hearts, olives, and a little olive oil. We spread the mixture in the baking dish and placed the tenderloin on top. This time, the vegetables were almost perfectly cooked when the pork was done. We removed the pork, stirred in our cherry tomatoes and a sprinkle of lemon zest, and returned the vegetables to the oven to finish cooking. When we retrieved the vegetables 10 minutes later, the fennel was tender, the tomatoes had softened and begun to release their juice, and the bright aroma of lemon filled the kitchen.

In about 45 minutes, we were transported to Provence with an inspired weeknight dinner that was low on fuss and high on flavor.

Spice-Rubbed Pork Tenderloin with Fennel, Tomatoes, and Artichokes

SERVES 2

Herbes de Provence, a blend of dried herbs such as thyme, fennel seeds, savory, rosemary, marjoram, and lavender, is available in the spice aisle of supermarkets. To thaw frozen artichokes quickly, microwave them, covered, for 3 to 5 minutes, drain well in a colander, and thoroughly pat dry with paper towels.

- 1 (12-ounce) pork tenderloin, trimmed
- 1 teaspoon dried herbes de Provence
- Salt and pepper
- 1 fennel bulb, stalks discarded, bulb halved, cored, and sliced ½ inch thick
- 5 ounces frozen artichoke hearts, thawed and patted dry
- ¼ cup pitted niçoise or kalamata olives, halved
- 1 tablespoon extra-virgin olive oil
- 6 ounces cherry tomatoes, halved
- 1 teaspoon grated lemon zest
- 1 tablespoon minced fresh parsley

1. Adjust oven rack to lower-middle position and heat oven to 450 degrees. Pat pork dry with paper towels, then season with herbes de Provence, salt, and pepper.

2. Combine fennel and 1 tablespoon water in bowl, cover, and microwave until fennel is softened, 2 to 3 minutes. Drain fennel well, then toss with artichokes, olives, and oil and season with salt and pepper.

3. Arrange vegetables in 8-inch square baking dish. Lay pork on top of vegetables and roast until center of meat registers 145 degrees, 25 to 30 minutes, flipping pork halfway through roasting.

4. Transfer pork to carving board, tent loosely with aluminum foil, and let rest for 10 minutes. Meanwhile, stir cherry tomatoes and lemon zest into vegetables and continue to roast until fennel is tender and tomatoes have softened, about 10 minutes longer.

5. Stir parsley into vegetables and season with salt and pepper to taste. Slice pork ¼ inch thick and serve with vegetables.

FRENCH-STYLE PORK AND WHITE BEAN CASSEROLE

A TRADITIONAL FRENCH BEAN AND MEAT STEW, cassoulet is a rich, comforting dish. Typically composed of garlicky white beans (starting with dried beans means an overnight soak), pork sausage (made by hand), and duck leg confit (cooked and preserved in fat) and topped with buttery bread crumbs, cassoulet can take up to three days to make, and the ingredients can be both hard to find and difficult to prepare. While deeply flavorful and incredibly satisfying, this stew is somewhat impractical even when cooking for a crowd, so making just two servings seemed downright silly. Could we find a way to create a much simpler, but just as decadent, two-person casserole inspired by the flavors of this iconic French dish? That was our goal.

To start, we looked at our cooking method. We knew that to get the most out of what we hoped would be a streamlined list of ingredients, we'd need to build a flavorful base and braise our meat until it was perfectly tender. Furthermore, since our casserole was destined to be so small, we knew we'd need to choose our cooking vessel carefully. A Dutch oven, the usual choice for cassoulet, was much too large for the small amount of ingredients we'd be cooking. Instead, we tested a working recipe in small and medium saucepans, as well as in 8- and 10-inch skillets. The saucepans' high sides didn't allow for enough evaporation, and the 10-inch skillet led to an overreduced sauce because of the wide surface area. The 8-inch skillet, on the other hand, held all of our ingredients perfectly and gave us just the right ratio of saucy filling to crisp topping. We decided that using the one pan for the whole procedure—browning the meat, building the sauce, and then covering the skillet to cook the meat and beans over low heat on the stove—made the most sense and kept things easy (and dirty pots to a minimum).

Cassoulet typically includes a triumvirate of sausage, duck confit, and pork. Since buying and cooking small amounts of all three seemed absurd for our scaled-down casserole, we set out to trim the ingredient list, starting with the duck confit. After all, the premade stuff is hard to find, and it takes an eternity to make at home. Instead, our white bean casserole would use a simpler combination of pork and sausage. After ruling out hard-to-find French sausages, we found that both kielbasa and andouille sausages gave us the smokiness we desired. Kielbasa was a bit easier to find, so it got our vote. We then looked over the pork options in the meat case and finally settled on boneless country-style pork ribs. Unlike spareribs and baby back ribs, country-style ribs are cut more toward the shoulder (where the pork butt comes from), so they have more fat and flavor. And unlike pork shoulder (another classic candidate), country-style ribs are available in small amounts, making it easy to buy just what we needed for our two-person casserole.

To get the most flavor out of the ribs, we cut them into 1-inch pieces and browned them in our skillet; once they were golden, we added a small chopped onion and a clove of garlic to sauté with the pork. From the spice cabinet, we pulled out thyme and a bay leaf, flavors that we thought would enhance but not overpower our beans, ribs, and kielbasa. A small dollop of tomato paste brought out the sausage's sweet notes and added another layer of savory complexity. Now we were ready for the beans.

While cassoulet is traditionally prepared with kidney-shaped French white beans that are difficult to find stateside, we thought that cannellini beans would work just fine. Since we were aiming for a quick casserole, we reached for canned beans—there would be enough flavorful ingredients in this dish that we suspected no one would miss the flavor of dried beans. Half a can of beans was just the right amount for our casserole; they had a solid presence, but they didn't crowd the pan or overwhelm the meat.

Turning to our sauce, we added ½ cup of chicken broth and ¼ cup of vermouth to the skillet for a bright base. We then added the beans and some canned diced tomatoes, turned the heat to low, covered the skillet, and let it all simmer gently for close to an hour. Unfortunately, by the time the pork was tender, our beans had cooked to mush. We decided to stagger the cooking time and add the beans during the last 20 minutes of cooking. Since the kielbasa needed only to heat through, we saved it for the end.

Finally, for the bread topping, we knew we wanted to take a fuss-free approach, but it still had to convey the rustic feel of cassoulet. Bread crumbs got lost in the filling, so we opted for croutons. A single dinner roll, cut into ¾-inch pieces and tossed with olive oil, gave us just the right amount to scatter over the top

of our small casserole. A quick 15-minute stint in the oven was just enough to crisp the topping and heat the kielbasa through.

At this point, eager tasters were ready to dig in—but they had to wait. Through a little trial and error, we found that our casserole was best after a 15-minute rest: The bread cubes absorbed some of the cooking liquid, and the pork and beans cooled to a manageable temperature. Our casserole now had that rustic French feel and flavor, but it was streamlined and updated enough for a couple of modern diners.

French-Style Pork and White Bean Casserole
SERVES 2

Canned navy or great Northern beans can be substituted for the cannellini beans. You will need an 8-inch skillet with a tight-fitting lid for this recipe. Be sure to let the casserole rest for 15 minutes before serving to allow it to set. See page 54 for a recipe to use up the leftover cannellini beans and a recipe to use up the leftover diced tomatoes.

8 ounces boneless country-style pork ribs, trimmed and cut into 1-inch pieces
  Salt and pepper
2 tablespoons olive oil
1 small onion, chopped fine
1½ teaspoons tomato paste
1½ teaspoons minced fresh thyme or ½ teaspoon dried
1 garlic clove, minced
1 bay leaf
½ cup low-sodium chicken broth
½ cup canned diced tomatoes, drained
¼ cup dry vermouth or dry white wine
¾ cup canned cannellini beans, rinsed
4 ounces kielbasa, halved lengthwise and sliced ¼ inch thick
1 rustic dinner roll, cut into ¾-inch pieces

1. Pat pork dry with paper towels and season lightly with salt and pepper. Heat 1 tablespoon oil in 8-inch skillet over medium-high heat until just smoking. Lightly brown pork on all sides, about 5 minutes.

2. Reduce heat to medium, stir in onion and ¼ teaspoon salt, and cook, stirring occasionally, until onion is

FRENCH-STYLE PORK AND WHITE BEAN CASSEROLE

softened, about 5 minutes. Stir in tomato paste, thyme, garlic, and bay leaf and cook until fragrant, about 30 seconds. Stir in broth, tomatoes, and vermouth, scraping up any browned bits, and bring to simmer. Cover, reduce heat to medium-low, and simmer for 30 minutes.

3. Adjust oven rack to middle position and heat oven to 450 degrees. Stir beans into skillet and continue to simmer, covered, until pork is tender, 20 to 25 minutes longer. Off heat, stir in kielbasa and remove bay leaf.

4. Toss bread with remaining 1 tablespoon oil and season with salt and pepper to taste. Sprinkle bread on top of pork and bean mixture, transfer skillet to oven, and bake, uncovered, until bread is toasted and golden, about 15 minutes. Let rest for 15 minutes before serving.

USE IT UP: CANNELLINI BEANS

White Bean Crostini with Lemon and Garlic
SERVES 2

You will need one 5- to 6-inch-long ciabatta-style roll for this recipe; it should yield 6 to 8 slices. Using both mashed and whole beans is key to the texture of this appetizer.

- 1 ciabatta roll (5 to 6 inches long), cut into ½-inch-thick slices
- 3 tablespoons extra-virgin olive oil
  Salt and pepper
- ¾ cup canned cannellini beans, rinsed
- 1 tablespoon lemon juice
- 1 small garlic clove, minced
- 1½ teaspoons minced fresh parsley, basil, or mint

1. Adjust oven rack to middle position and heat oven to 400 degrees. Arrange bread slices in single layer on baking sheet and bake until bread is dry and crisp, about 10 minutes, flipping slices halfway through baking. Brush with 1 tablespoon oil and season with salt and pepper to taste.

2. Using fork, coarsely mash half of beans with 1 tablespoon oil, lemon juice, garlic, and parsley. Stir in remaining beans and season with salt and pepper to taste. Spread bean mixture evenly over toasts, then drizzle with remaining 1 tablespoon oil. Serve.

USE IT UP: CANNED DICED TOMATOES

Quick Tomato Salsa
SERVES 2

Be sure to drain the salsa right before serving, or else it will become watery.

- ½ cup canned diced tomatoes, drained
- 1 small shallot, chopped
- 1 tablespoon fresh cilantro or parsley leaves
- 1 teaspoon lime juice
  Pinch cayenne pepper
  Salt and pepper

Pulse tomatoes, shallot, cilantro, lime juice, and cayenne in food processor until roughly chopped, about 8 pulses. Transfer to fine-mesh strainer set over bowl and drain for about 1 minute. Season with salt and pepper to taste and serve.

CRUNCHY PORK CHOPS WITH ACORN SQUASH

THE BEST BAKED BREADED PORK CHOPS DELIVER an incredibly satisfying experience: tender, moist pork surrounded by a crunchy coating that crackles apart with each bite. But all too often, these chops fall short of that ideal. Opt for the convenience of a packaged product from the supermarket for your breading and the result is a thin, sandy crust. Making your own breading with fresh crumbs can be problematic as well—often you end up with a soggy, patchy crust that won't stick to the meat. Our goal was to cook a juicy, flavorful chop with a crisp, substantial crust that would stay on the meat from fork to mouth. In addition, we wanted a well-paired side dish that would cook alongside the chops for an easy one-dish supper.

Our first task was choosing the pork chops. For ease of preparation we decided on boneless chops, which gave us two options: sirloin and center-cut chops. We settled on center-cut, which are widely available and cook more evenly. Chops that were between ¾ and 1 inch thick provided the best ratio of pork to coating.

For our initial tests, we decided to use the test kitchen's standard bound breading method (dusting with flour, dipping in beaten egg, and rolling in toasted bread crumbs) while we determined the best cooking technique. Simply breading the chops, tossing them on a sheet pan, and baking made the bottoms soggy. Placing the chops on a wire rack set on the baking sheet definitely helped, as did increasing the oven temperature from 350 to 425 degrees. The coating was now crisp all over.

Up until now, we had been making our own bread crumbs in the food processor and toasting them on a baking sheet in the oven until dry and brown. These crumbs produced a good crust, but we wondered if there was an even easier option. Potato chips and crackers are common shortcut breadings; they are already crunchy and are easy to crush by hand or with a mallet. We tested all the usual suspects but found them to be soggy, bland, greasy, or insubstantial.

Then we thought of panko, Japanese-style bread crumbs. The chops made with panko straight from the bag were ultra-crisp, but we wanted to add more flavor to them. Toasting the panko would definitely improve color and flavor, but was there a faster way to do it that didn't involve dirtying another pan? A colleague of ours suggested using the microwave. While untraditional, we gave it a shot, tossing the panko with some olive oil, salt, and pepper. After just a few minutes in the microwave, the panko was dark golden brown. A little Parmesan cheese added to the bread crumbs after they had cooled contributed a welcome boost of flavor.

We now needed something more substantial than our plain egg wash to get these thick, coarse crumbs to adhere to the chops. Dijon mustard is a typical partner for pork chops, so we thought it could work as a flavorful substitute for the egg wash. Although the Dijon gave the chops good flavor, a straight swap was too intense. Keeping the beaten egg and adding a tablespoon and a half of Dijon thickened the mixture nicely and contributed just enough mustard flavor to our breading. A little thyme was a welcome herbal addition. Our coating was now crisp and tasted great—and best of all, it stayed on the chops.

With the available space on the sheet pan next to the chops, we had plenty of room for our side. Winter squash came to mind; its creamy texture and sweetness would pair nicely with the pork's crisp coating.

We chose earthy, sweet acorn squash; just half of a squash provided two ample servings. We experimented with cooking the halved squash whole and then cutting it into 1-inch pieces, but in the end we found it best to cut the squash into two wedges of the same size. This shape was attractive as well as easy to portion.

Since the squash would take longer to cook than the pork, we followed the procedure we had used in our Spice-Rubbed Pork Tenderloin with Fennel, Tomatoes, and Artichokes (page 51) and gave it a head start in the microwave, cooking the wedges until they just began to soften. Now when the pork was finished cooking, the squash was tender and starting to brown and had a sweeter, more pronounced flavor. To accentuate this sweetness, we brushed the flesh with melted butter, brown sugar, and a pinch of cayenne before roasting. This mixture caramelized and browned in the oven, giving the squash a burnished, glazed appearance. Paired with our crisp breaded pork chops, the glazed squash made the perfect costar in this satisfying yet simple dinner for two.

Crunchy Parmesan-Crusted Pork Chops with Glazed Acorn Squash

SERVES 2

Be sure to leave the bread crumbs uncovered when microwaving them in step 2 or they will not brown. See page 56 for a recipe to use up the leftover acorn squash.

½ cup panko bread crumbs

1½ teaspoons olive oil

Salt and pepper

¼ cup grated Parmesan cheese

2 tablespoons all-purpose flour

1 large egg

1½ tablespoons Dijon mustard

¼ teaspoon minced fresh thyme or pinch dried

2 (6- to 8-ounce) boneless pork chops, ¾ to 1 inch thick, trimmed

½ acorn squash (12 ounces), seeded and cut into 2 wedges

3 tablespoons unsalted butter, melted

1½ tablespoons packed dark brown sugar

Pinch cayenne pepper

Lemon wedges

1. Adjust oven rack to middle position and heat oven to 425 degrees. Line rimmed baking sheet with aluminum foil. Spray wire rack with vegetable oil spray and set rack in prepared sheet.

2. Toss panko with oil in shallow dish or pie plate and season with salt and pepper. Microwave crumbs, uncovered, stirring often, until deep golden brown, about 2 minutes. Let crumbs cool, then stir in Parmesan. Place flour in second shallow dish. In third shallow dish, whisk egg, mustard, and thyme together until combined.

3. Cut 2 slits about 2 inches apart through fat around outside of each pork chop. Pat chops dry with paper towels and season with salt and pepper. Working with 1 chop at a time, dredge in flour, shaking off excess, then coat with egg mixture, allowing excess to drip off. Coat chops with toasted crumbs, pressing gently so that crumbs adhere. Lay breaded pork chops on 1 side of prepared wire rack.

4. Meanwhile, place squash, cut side up, on plate, brush with 1 tablespoon melted butter, and season with salt and pepper. Microwave squash until it begins to soften but still holds its shape, 8 to 10 minutes.

5. Arrange squash, cut side up, on prepared rack opposite pork. Stir remaining 2 tablespoons melted butter, sugar, and cayenne together, then brush over squash.

6. Bake pork chops and squash until meat registers 145 degrees and squash is lightly browned and tender, 18 to 25 minutes. Let pork chops and squash rest on rack for 5 minutes. Serve with lemon wedges.

NOTES FROM THE TEST KITCHEN

CUTTING ACORN SQUASH SAFELY

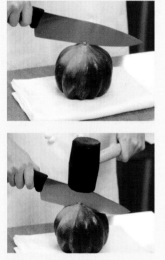

1. Hard winter squash can be difficult (and dangerous) to prep. To cut squash open safely, place squash on damp kitchen towel (which will hold squash in place) and position knife on top.

2. Strike back of knife with rubber mallet to drive knife into squash. Continue to hit knife with mallet until knife cuts through squash. Once squash is halved, you can easily remove seeds and continue to cut up squash as desired.

PREVENTING CURLED PORK CHOPS

To prevent chops from curling, cut 2 slits about 2 inches apart through fat around outside of each raw chop. This method works whether you're using boneless or bone-in pork chops.

USE IT UP: ACORN OR BUTTERNUT SQUASH

Easy Squash Soup
SERVES 2

Serve this simple, creamy soup with crusty bread.

- ½ acorn squash or butternut squash (12 ounces), seeded and cut into 2 wedges
- 1 small fennel bulb, stalks discarded, bulb halved and cored (see page 50)
- 1 shallot, peeled and halved
- 2 tablespoons olive oil
- Salt and pepper
- 1½ cups low-sodium chicken broth, plus extra as needed
- 2 tablespoons heavy cream
- Pinch ground ginger
- Pinch cayenne pepper

1. Adjust oven rack to middle position and heat oven to 400 degrees. Line baking sheet with aluminum foil. Toss squash, fennel, shallot, and oil together in bowl and season with salt and pepper. Place vegetables, cut side down, on prepared pan. Roast until skewer inserted into vegetables meets no resistance, 25 to 30 minutes. Let vegetables cool slightly, then remove skin from squash. Transfer vegetables to blender.

2. Add broth to blender and process until smooth, 1 to 2 minutes, adding up to 1 additional cup broth as needed to adjust consistency. Strain soup though fine-mesh strainer into small saucepan. Stir in cream, ginger, and cayenne. Bring soup to brief simmer and season with salt and pepper to taste. Serve.

HEARTY CHICKEN CHOWDER

THOUGH MOST PEOPLE THINK OF SEAFOOD WHEN it comes to chowder, in the landlocked center of the country, chicken chowders are the status quo. These creamy soups include the quintessential chowder ingredients—pork (salt pork or bacon), potatoes, and milk or cream—but they trade the clams and fish for more accessible chicken. We thought this type of rustic, hearty chowder would make a great supper for a household of two, so we set out to create our own scaled-down version. It had to be rich and creamy, with tender bites of chicken and potato throughout, and, most important, we didn't want to deal with a big pot of leftovers.

The best chicken chowder recipes rely on a time-honored technique that builds layers of flavor: First, either salt pork or bacon is rendered, then aromatics are cooked in this flavorful fat. Next, chicken broth is added along with chicken, potatoes, and additional vegetables. Once everything is tender and the chicken is cooked through, dairy—usually milk or cream—is stirred in to add richness. We decided to first create a flavorful base, then test the chicken, potatoes, and finally the dairy and any extra vegetables, determining additional seasonings along the way.

Generally, pork provides the flavor foundation for chowder, so this is where we began our testing. Pork is most often found in chowders in one of its cured forms: bacon or salt pork. Though salt pork is the more traditional choice, we needed a small amount, so we turned to more readily accessible bacon—one slice did the trick. We used the rendered bacon fat to sauté a large shallot, a clove of garlic, and a bit of thyme and then turned to our liquid base. For thickening power, we added a spoonful of flour and let it cook in the fat for a minute to rid it of its raw flavor. Two cups of chicken broth provided the liquid element.

Now that we had a flavorful base to work with, we had to make a decision about our chicken. We knew that the easiest method would be to poach the chicken right in the broth; this step would cook the chicken gently while adding flavor to the store-bought broth. A single boneless, skinless chicken breast cooked quickly and was easy to shred into bite-size pieces after poaching. With our foundation in place, we could now concentrate on the potatoes.

The ideal chowder potato absorbs the flavor of the broth and provides satisfying, creamy bites in the final soup. But which type of potato would give us this result? Russet potatoes went from tender to crumbly and mushy in a matter of minutes. Red potatoes were plagued with the opposite problems; they stayed too firm and absorbed little of the broth's flavor. In the end, Yukon Gold potatoes were the perfect spud: They provided a small amount of starch for thickening our chowder and absorbed rich flavors from the broth without turning to mush. A single potato was just the right amount for our two-person chowder.

Finally, it was time to consider the vegetables, dairy, and finishing touches. Carrots are another staple in many chicken chowder recipes—we found that one small carrot, sliced thin, was well received by tasters. Half of a red bell pepper, with its sweetness and light crunch, won tasters over, too, with its freshness and color.

For the dairy element, which gives chowder its ultra-creamy texture, tasters preferred the richness of cream to both half-and-half and milk. Added at the end of cooking along with the shredded chicken (which just needed to warm through), a quarter-cup of cream filled out the soup and balanced its flavors. While this chowder now had great texture and balance, tasters were still asking for something more.

Up to this point, we had been leaving the crisped bacon in the pot and building the soup right on top of it. Guessing that crispy bacon might provide a welcome contrast to the soft textures of our chowder, we removed half of the cooked bacon and sprinkled it on as a garnish at the end. Now our chicken chowder provided all of the flavors and heartiness expected from a traditional chowder—plus a little extra kick with our crunchy bacon topping.

NOTES FROM THE TEST KITCHEN

SHREDDING CHICKEN OR PORK

Hold 1 fork in each hand, with tines facing down. Insert tines into meat and gently pull forks away from each other, breaking meat into bite-size pieces or large chunks.

Hearty Chicken Chowder

SERVES 2

The chicken breast will not be fully submerged during poaching; be sure to flip it halfway through poaching to ensure even cooking.

   1   **slice bacon, chopped fine**
   1   **large shallot, minced**
   1   **garlic clove, minced**
   ¼   **teaspoon minced fresh thyme or pinch dried**
   1   **tablespoon all-purpose flour**
   2   **cups low-sodium chicken broth**
   1   **Yukon Gold potato, peeled and cut into ½-inch pieces**
   1   **small carrot, peeled and sliced ¼ inch thick**
   1   **(8-ounce) boneless, skinless chicken breast, trimmed**
   ½   **red bell pepper, stemmed, seeded, and cut into ½-inch pieces**
   ¼   **cup heavy cream**
   1½ **teaspoons minced fresh parsley**
       Salt and pepper

1. Cook bacon in medium saucepan over medium heat until crisp, 5 to 7 minutes. Using slotted spoon, transfer half of bacon to paper towel–lined plate.

2. Add shallot to bacon and fat left in saucepan and cook until softened, 3 to 5 minutes. Stir in garlic and thyme and cook until fragrant, about 30 seconds. Stir in flour and cook for 1 minute.

3. Gradually whisk in broth, scraping up any browned bits. Stir in potato and carrot. Nestle chicken into sauce and bring to simmer. Simmer gently, uncovered, until chicken registers 160 degrees, 10 to 15 minutes, flipping chicken halfway through cooking. Transfer chicken to plate, let cool slightly, then shred into bite-size pieces.

4. Meanwhile, return chowder to medium heat and stir in bell pepper. Continue to simmer until vegetables are tender, 10 to 15 minutes longer. Off heat, stir in shredded chicken and cream and let sit until heated through, about 2 minutes. Stir in parsley and season with salt and pepper to taste. Sprinkle with reserved bacon and serve.

VARIATION

Cajun Chicken Chowder with Corn
Add 1 small, finely chopped celery rib to pot with shallot. Add ½ teaspoon Cajun seasoning to pot with garlic and thyme. Omit carrot. Add ¼ cup frozen corn along with bell pepper.

QUICK CHICKEN FRICASSEE

MADE THE CLASSIC FRENCH WAY BY POACHING chicken pieces, mushrooms, and pearl onions in stock and saucing them with a cream-enriched reduction of the cooking liquid, chicken fricassee captures both richness and clean chicken flavor all on one plate. But there are two reasons the dish has fallen out of favor in recent years: It can be a bit heavy and one-note for the modern palate, and many traditional versions are quite fussy and time-consuming, especially when cooking for two. Still, we were intrigued by the luxe texture and straightforward chicken flavor of this dish, and we had ideas for a few refinements—namely, a streamlined technique that would make the dish quick and practical for two, and a brighter, more complex sauce.

First up: The thick bone-in chicken parts in the traditional French recipe would have to go, as they required nearly 30 minutes of poaching. Instead, we decided to try boneless, skinless breasts, which cook quickly and require little preparation. A pair of chicken breasts not only fit nicely in our 10-inch skillet, but they were mostly cooked through after the initial sear.

Unfortunately, now that we were going without skin and bones in our chicken, we had lost substantial flavor. Browning the meat in a combination of butter and oil added back some richness, but still, we'd need to find a shortcut to help develop serious meaty flavor in our sauce.

In the past we've built up savory flavor by thoroughly browning vegetables until they develop their own fond. We took the same tack here but made two key changes to the traditional fricassee components: First, we swapped the pearl onions for a regular chopped onion, which would provide more surface area for browning and caramelization. Second, because mushrooms are an excellent source of glutamates—compounds that significantly boost meaty flavor in food—we upped their amount as high as we could go in our 10-inch pan (we ended up at a half-pound).

Sure enough, sautéing these ingredients for about 10 minutes with white wine coated the pan with a layer of dark browned bits. Just before deglazing with chicken broth, we stirred in a little garlic and a spoonful of flour to help gently thicken the sauce. Finally, we slid the chicken back into the skillet to finish cooking. Within 10 minutes, the breast meat was cooked through and the poaching liquid had reduced to a rich, savory gravy.

QUICK CHICKEN FRICASSEE

The final step was to finish the sauce with dairy. Tasters found that the traditional choice of heavy cream muted the flavors, and the next logical option, half-and-half, left the sauce thin. Sour cream was much better, adding body and a pleasant tang. But this sauce was finicky; if the heat was a tad too high, the sour cream separated, giving the sauce an unpleasant broken texture. To create a more foolproof sauce with a satiny-smooth consistency, we tried a technique found in many fricassee recipes: whisking an egg yolk into the sauce. Yolks contain the emulsifier lecithin, and we were guessing it would have the same impact on our gravy as it does in mayonnaise—keeping fat (in this case from the sour cream) suspended in water. We whisked a yolk into the sour cream before incorporating the mixture into the thickened broth and were pleased to find that it not only kept the sour cream in check but also turned the sauce incredibly silky. All that was left was to add a bit of lemon juice for acidity, ground nutmeg for earthiness, and a smattering of minced tarragon for brightness.

Although our timesaving approach was not a traditional "fricassee," it still captured the chicken flavor with a smooth, creamy sauce and, best of all, made an excellent weeknight option for two.

Quick Chicken Fricassee

SERVES 2

You will need a 10-inch skillet with a tight-fitting lid for this recipe. Serve with crusty bread.

2	**(6-ounce) boneless, skinless chicken breasts, trimmed**
	Salt and pepper
1	**tablespoon unsalted butter**
1	**teaspoon olive oil**
8	**ounces cremini mushrooms, trimmed and sliced ¼ inch thick**
1	**small onion, chopped fine**
2	**tablespoons dry white wine**
1½	**teaspoons all-purpose flour**
1	**small garlic clove, minced**
¾	**cup low-sodium chicken broth**
2½	**tablespoons sour cream**
1	**large egg yolk**
1	**teaspoon lemon juice**
1	**teaspoon minced fresh tarragon or parsley**
⅛	**teaspoon ground nutmeg**

1. Pat chicken dry with paper towels and season with salt and pepper. Melt butter and oil in 10-inch skillet over medium-high heat. Brown chicken on both sides, about 8 minutes; transfer to plate.

2. Add mushrooms, onion, and wine to now-empty skillet and cook, stirring occasionally, until liquid has evaporated and mushrooms are browned, 8 to 10 minutes. Add flour and garlic and cook for 1 minute. Gradually whisk in broth and bring mixture to simmer, scraping up any browned bits and smoothing out any lumps. Return chicken and any accumulated juices to skillet. Reduce heat to medium-low, cover, and simmer until chicken registers 160 degrees, 5 to 10 minutes.

3. Transfer chicken to platter and tent loosely with aluminum foil. Whisk sour cream and egg yolk together in bowl. Whisking constantly, slowly stir ¼ cup sauce into sour cream mixture to temper. Slowly whisk sour cream mixture back into sauce until smooth. Stir in lemon juice, tarragon, and nutmeg and season with salt and pepper to taste. Pour sauce over chicken and serve.

CHICKEN BONNE FEMME

A CREOLE CLASSIC, CHICKEN BONNE FEMME COMbines browned chicken with bacon and potatoes in a flavorful sauce. Its name, which means "good woman," harks back to an earlier time and refers to this dish being made by a housewife rather than by a trained chef. But ironically, classic recipes seem better suited to commercial kitchens than the home kitchen—by the time we had completed a sample recipe, we had dirtied a pile of pots and pans, having fried chicken and potatoes (separately), made the sauce, and combined the various elements. We sought to scale back and speed up this Louisiana specialty, making it perfect for the for-two home kitchen while keeping all of its rich flavor intact.

First, we tackled the procedure. We wanted to turn this dish into an easy, one-pan supper, so we immediately ruled out frying the chicken and potatoes separately. Our thoughts turned to braising, which would allow us to brown the chicken and potatoes sequentially, finish cooking them in a bit of liquid, and then make the sauce from that flavorful liquid. But since we were cooking for two, we'd need to choose our braising vessel carefully. A heavy Dutch oven would be far too large for our smaller amount of food, but a 10-inch skillet would be too small. We settled somewhere in the middle with a 12-inch skillet.

The decision to braise rather than fry the chicken pointed us toward chicken thighs, which stand up well to low, slow cooking, but we'd have to figure out what to do about the skin. Though the skin lends flavor to the meat and protects the thighs from drying out during browning, it would lose its crispness after simmering in the braising liquid. As a compromise, we browned the thighs with the skin on, then removed the skin before braising. The bits left behind in the pan from browning, also known as fond, along with the fat rendered from the skin, gave us the deep flavor we wanted without any unwanted flabby, leathery skin in the finished dish.

Bacon is a key flavor in bonne femme, but the amount called for in many traditional recipes is overkill, even when scaled down for our two-person version. We made numerous batches of bonne femme, reducing the quantity of bacon slice by slice, until we reached a reasonable two slices, which provided plenty of smoky-sweet richness and flavorful rendered fat in which to brown the chicken.

Next, we tackled the potato element. Only a few classic recipes specified a particular type, so we decided to test a wide range of choices, from high-starch russets, to medium-starch Yukon Golds, to low-starch red potatoes. The russets fell apart in the pan, and the Yukons never became soft and creamy. On the other hand, unpeeled red potatoes turned tender and creamy while still remaining intact over the long braise.

Our potatoes picked, we turned to the cooking technique. We knew that we wanted the potatoes to be definitively browned so that they'd hold their own

alongside the rich, dark meat of the chicken thighs. Since we'd already built up layers of flavorful fat from rendering the bacon and browning the chicken, we decided to use this flavor-packed liquid to amp up our potatoes. Cooking the small potatoes whole worked fine, but when we tried cutting them in half to maximize their surface area, we truly struck gold—these potatoes had a deeply browned crust and a gloriously creamy interior.

Last up was the sauce. The rather greasy, flour-thickened sauce of the classic dish would have to go; we pictured a lighter version that would be easy to build from the pan drippings left after browning the chicken and potatoes. We added some dry white wine to counter the rich bacon, then poured in a bit of chicken broth to balance the wine. In addition to a small chopped onion and a couple of cloves of garlic, we stirred in fresh thyme, hot sauce, and parsley to bolster our bonne femme's Creole credentials.

Modernized but true to its Louisiana origins, this Chicken Bonne Femme was just right for a two-person home kitchen.

Chicken Bonne Femme

SERVES 2

To ensure even cooking and browning, use red potatoes no larger than 1½ inches around. You will need a 12-inch skillet with a tight-fitting lid for this recipe.

4	(6-ounce) bone-in chicken thighs, trimmed
	Salt and pepper
2	slices bacon, chopped fine
12	ounces small red potatoes, halved
1	small onion, chopped fine
2	garlic cloves, minced
1	teaspoon minced fresh thyme or ¼ teaspoon dried
⅓	cup dry white wine
¼	cup low-sodium chicken broth
½	teaspoon hot sauce
1	tablespoon minced fresh parsley

1. Pat chicken dry with paper towels and season with salt and pepper. Cook bacon in 12-inch skillet over medium heat until crisp, about 8 minutes. Using slotted spoon, transfer bacon to paper towel–lined plate. Heat fat left in skillet over medium-high heat until

PARMESAN AND BASIL–STUFFED CHICKEN BREASTS WITH ROASTED CARROTS

just smoking. Brown chicken well on both sides, 10 to 15 minutes; transfer to plate. Let cool slightly, then remove skin.

2. Pour off all but 1 tablespoon fat from skillet and return to medium heat. Arrange potatoes, cut side down, in skillet and cook, without stirring, until bottoms are golden brown, about 5 minutes. Stir in onion and cook until softened, about 5 minutes. Add garlic and thyme and cook until fragrant, about 30 seconds. Stir in half of bacon, wine, broth, and hot sauce and bring to simmer.

3. Nestle chicken into skillet and add any accumulated juices. Cover, reduce heat to low, and simmer until potatoes are tender and meat registers 175 degrees, about 25 minutes. Sprinkle with remaining bacon and parsley. Season with salt and pepper to taste and serve.

STUFFED CHICKEN BREASTS WITH ROASTED CARROTS

STUFFED CHICKEN BREASTS MAKE FOR A MORE elegant, dressed-up take on simple baked chicken, but many recipes boast a mile-long ingredient list and can be a challenge to assemble. We set out to make a no-fuss cheese filling—we thought a creamy filling would complement the tender, juicy meat nicely—and an easy method for stuffing the chicken, no finicky butterflying or pounding required. Finally, we had one last request: We wanted to find a simple side dish to roast alongside our chicken to make a complete meal.

First we needed to figure out how to fill the chicken breasts. Although chicken breasts are commonly boned before being stuffed, research yielded a fair number of bone-in recipes. It seemed worth a try, since using bone-in chicken had great potential for moist, flavorful meat, and we love the crisp, roasted skin of bone-in chicken. Since we were after the easiest method possible, we decided to first try stuffing a working mixture of cream cheese, salt, and pepper under the skin. Working carefully, we loosened the skin and fit a couple of spoonfuls of the cheese mixture underneath, then transferred the chicken to a baking sheet and roasted it. The skin held the filling in place, and when the chicken emerged from the oven it was moist

and tender, with a creamy, tangy, saucelike filling that basted the breasts as they cooked. Our results were nearly flawless, but one problem remained—the skin was flabby and inedible.

We wondered if increasing the oven temperature would help to crisp the skin. We had been baking the chicken breasts at 375 degrees, so next we tried cooking the chicken at 400 degrees, 425 degrees, and 450 degrees. The skin on the chicken cooked at 450 degrees was golden brown and crisp and the meat was perfectly cooked. To further encourage browning, we tested brushing both oil and melted butter on the skin. Both worked well, but butter was the clear winner for flavor.

With our method in place, we could focus on perfecting the flavor of the stuffing. Tasters liked the creaminess and tang of the cream cheese, but its flavor was too mild for our tastes. So we tried adding a few more ingredients, including herbs, spices, cheeses, and olives. We quickly discovered that melting cheeses such as cheddar tended to ooze out from under the skin, even when combined with the cream cheese. Parmesan and goat cheese, however, were winners, in terms of both flavor and binding ability. As for other ingredients, tasters favored a handful of bold additions—olive oil and a generous quantity of basil complemented our Parmesan, and chopped kalamata olives and heady oregano paired well with the goat cheese.

Finally, we moved on to our side dish. We considered a number of vegetables but ultimately settled on roasted carrots, as their earthy sweetness would be an excellent counterpoint to the potent flavors of the filling. For an elegant presentation, we cut our carrots on the bias into ½-inch-thick ovals, then tossed them with a little brown sugar and melted butter and spread them on the sheet pan opposite the chicken.

Unfortunately, since we were roasting a small amount of carrots, they spread out into too thin a layer, and their exposed edges burned in the high heat of the oven before the chicken could finish cooking. A colleague had a suggestion to remedy this problem. To cook the carrots more gently without adding an extra step, he suggested mounding the slices in a small pile so that they could steam in their own juices. While it sounded promising, this method gave us chewy carrots that were not even close to caramelized on the edges. We'd need to get more creative. Since we knew we wanted the carrots to both steam and brown, we thought that perhaps we could combine the mounding and spreading steps. We made a small pile of carrots next to the chicken. Halfway through roasting, we spread the carrots into an even layer. When the chicken was finished 15 minutes later, the carrots emerged tender on the inside and nicely browned on the outside. Now perfectly cooked, these simple roasted carrots were the perfect match for our golden, juicy stuffed chicken breasts.

Parmesan and Basil–Stuffed Chicken Breasts with Roasted Carrots

SERVES 2

It is important to buy chicken breasts with the skin still attached and intact, otherwise the stuffing will leak out. Be sure to spread the carrots in an even layer halfway through baking to ensure that they cook through and brown properly.

- 1 ounce Parmesan cheese, grated (½ cup)
- 1 ounce cream cheese, softened
- 2 tablespoons chopped fresh basil
- 1 tablespoon extra-virgin olive oil
- 1 small garlic clove, minced
  Salt and pepper
- 2 (12-ounce) bone-in split chicken breasts, trimmed
- 1 tablespoon unsalted butter, melted
- 6 small carrots, peeled and sliced ½ inch thick on bias
- 1½ teaspoons packed dark brown sugar

1. Adjust oven rack to middle position and heat oven to 450 degrees. Line rimmed baking sheet with aluminum foil. Mix Parmesan, cream cheese, basil, oil, garlic, pinch salt, and pinch pepper together in small bowl.

2. Pat chicken dry with paper towels, season with salt and pepper, then gently loosen center portion of skin covering each breast. Using spoon, place one-half of cheese mixture under skin, in center of each breast. Gently press on skin to spread out cheese mixture.

3. Arrange chicken, skin side up, on 1 side of baking sheet. Brush chicken with one-half of melted butter. Toss carrots with remaining melted butter and sugar and season with salt and pepper. Mound carrots in pile on baking sheet, opposite chicken.

4. Bake until chicken registers 160 degrees and carrots are browned and tender, 30 to 35 minutes, rotating pan and spreading out carrots into even layer halfway through baking. Let chicken and carrots rest on baking sheet for 5 minutes. Serve.

VARIATION

Goat Cheese and Olive–Stuffed Chicken Breasts with Roasted Carrots

Omit Parmesan, basil, and olive oil. Add 1½ ounces softened goat cheese, 2 tablespoons finely chopped pitted kalamata olives, and 1 teaspoon minced fresh oregano to cream cheese mixture.

CHICKEN WITH ARTICHOKES AND OLIVES

CHICKEN WITH ARTICHOKES AND OLIVES, SIMMERED in a sauce of tomatoes, white wine, garlic, and herbs, is a classic Mediterranean dish, but not one that necessarily lends itself well to a two-person meal. The flavorful sauce requires far too much time on the stove, and the starring vegetables, fresh artichokes, are tricky and time-consuming to prepare. Still, given the exciting flavors of the dish, we were compelled to design a version that not only would taste of the Mediterranean but would also come together easily, without a pile of leftovers.

Traditionally this dish involves braising bone-in chicken pieces (usually a whole bird, broken down) for a long time—not an option on a Tuesday night. Since we were cooking only enough chicken for two, we needed just a couple of pieces that were about the same size. Roasting bone-in, skin-on chicken breasts seemed like a good plan, if we could find a way to easily incorporate the sauce into the same dish. We decided first on a basic method: We'd brown our chicken in a pan until the skin rendered and crisped, then use the residual fat to sauté our aromatics. We'd add our artichokes and tomatoes, and then build a simple wine-and-broth-based sauce, return the chicken to the pan (partially submerged in the sauce but with the crispy skin high and dry), and cook it all off in a hot oven.

The first step, searing the chicken, was simple. The next, choosing our vegetables, was not. We knew we wanted artichokes and tomatoes to make up the rest of the dish, but both come in a variety of preparations from fresh to canned. Fresh artichokes were out of the question because of the work involved. Canned artichokes tasted tinny, and the jarred variety were briny and soft, and they turned to mush when they hit the pan. Frozen artichokes, on the other hand, had a firm, appealing texture, even though they needed a bit of help in the flavor department. For the tomatoes, we wanted to stick with the most readily available options. After a few tests, we nixed canned diced tomatoes and chopped beefsteak tomatoes in favor of cherry tomatoes, which added fresh flavor and held their shape throughout cooking.

For our aromatic components, we chose one small onion, a couple of cloves of garlic, and a bit of tomato paste (for even deeper tomato flavor). Fresh herbs were a must, and tasters preferred thyme and parsley to oregano and basil (the other likely candidates). We added the thyme along with the garlic and saved the parsley for a fresh finish. For our olive component, kalamatas were an easy choice for their mild, fruity flavor and availability in most supermarkets. We cut these in half so they'd retain a presence among all of the other elements.

After about half an hour in the oven, our dish emerged looking promising. The chicken skin was nice and crisp, and the vegetables were cooked through and saucy. However, the flavors were still letting us down, and the artichokes were the worst offenders.

We knew that one way to boost flavor in a bland, watery vegetable like frozen artichokes is through browning. We didn't want to tack any more time onto this supposedly quick recipe, so we altered the procedure to take advantage of the time we had. Instead of adding the artichokes to the pan with the chicken broth and wine, we sautéed them with the onion until golden brown. Then we simply added the tomatoes, chicken broth, and wine to the skillet later on, before roasting the chicken. The sautéed artichokes were noticeably improved, with a deeper flavor and sturdier texture.

The flavors were now good but very strong, and the combination of wine, olives, and garlic had left us craving something sweet. We considered adding a pinch of sugar to the sauce to balance things out, then reconsidered and tried orange juice, hoping to boost the acidity along with the sweetness. We simply substituted 2 tablespoons of orange juice for half of the wine, then simmered them together in the pan. With our sauce balanced, our Mediterranean chicken finally offered the best of both worlds—tender vegetables and moist chicken with crisp skin, plus a boldly flavored, vibrant sauce.

NOTES FROM THE TEST KITCHEN

CHOOSING THE RIGHT SIZE SKILLET

When cooking for four or more, a large 12-inch skillet usually does the job, but using the same pan to cook for two can result in disaster. Certain dishes, like our Pan-Seared Steaks with Crispy Potatoes and Parsley Sauce (page 47) and Quick Chicken Fricassee (page 60), would scorch in a 12-inch skillet because there would be too much hot surface area (and heat) for too little food. Instead, we reach for a 10-inch skillet for these dishes. (Whereas other dishes, like Chicken Bonne Femme, page 61, and Indonesian-Style Fried Rice, page 74, are the exception, as the large surface area is necessary to accommodate the mélange of ingredients.) With a mix of skillet sizes on hand, you'll be able to make anything from Indoor Wisconsin Brats and Beer (page 21) to Glazed Salmon Fillets (page 40). (See pages 6 and 46 for information on our top-rated traditional and nonstick skillets.)

Mediterranean Chicken with Artichokes and Olives

SERVES 2

To thaw frozen artichokes quickly, microwave them, covered, for 3 to 5 minutes, drain well in a colander, and thoroughly pat dry with paper towels.

2	(12-ounce) bone-in split chicken breasts, trimmed
	Salt and pepper
1	tablespoon olive oil
1	small onion, chopped fine
5	ounces frozen artichoke hearts, thawed and patted dry
6	ounces cherry tomatoes, halved
2	garlic cloves, minced
¾	teaspoon tomato paste
½	teaspoon minced fresh thyme or ⅛ teaspoon dried
¼	cup low-sodium chicken broth
2	tablespoons dry white wine
2	tablespoons orange juice
¼	cup pitted kalamata olives, halved
1½	teaspoons minced fresh parsley

1. Adjust oven rack to middle position and heat oven to 450 degrees. Pat chicken dry with paper towels and season with salt and pepper. Heat oil in 10-inch skillet over medium-high heat until smoking. Cook chicken, skin side down, until well browned, about 5 minutes; transfer to plate.

2. Pour off all but 1 tablespoon fat from skillet and return to medium heat until shimmering. Add onion and cook, stirring often, until softened and browned, 5 to 8 minutes. Add artichokes and cook until beginning to brown, about 2 minutes. Add tomatoes and cook until beginning to soften, about 2 minutes. Stir in garlic, tomato paste, and thyme and cook until fragrant, about 30 seconds. Add broth, wine, and orange juice and bring to simmer, scraping up any browned bits. Add olives and season with salt and pepper to taste.

3. Nestle chicken into sauce, skin side up, and bake until it registers 160 degrees, about 30 minutes. Let chicken rest for 5 to 10 minutes. Sprinkle with parsley and serve.

LEMON-HERB COD WITH CRISPY POTATOES

COD AND POTATOES IS A CLASSIC PAIRING, BUT most folks think of fish and chips when they think of this duo. We wanted a more elegant preparation for fish and potatoes that didn't require heating up a vat of oil. In the test kitchen, cooking fish fillets and potatoes on a sheet pan is standard practice, so we set out to join cod and spuds into one simple supper, all cooked on a sheet pan. The biggest challenge would be to nail down the cooking time—since fish cooks quickly but potatoes take a good chunk of time, cooking them together could result in rubbery fish and rock-hard potatoes. And while the clean flavor and lean nature of cod are much of its appeal, it runs the risk of tasting plain. Our goals were clear: to find a way to boost the flavor of mild cod, and also to cook the fish and potatoes together, so that they were ready at the same time and perfectly done.

Putting aside flavor for the moment, we focused on finding a cooking method that would deliver perfectly cooked potatoes and fish. We already knew that just throwing them in the oven together wouldn't work. And since chunks of potato would need a significant amount of time in the oven to become tender and spotty brown before we could add the fish, we figured that slicing the potatoes thin would speed up the process. Additionally, slicing the potatoes would allow us to take advantage of the surface area of the baking sheet, exposing more of the potatoes' flesh to the dry heat of the oven and the hot pan. We hoped this would result in some browning and crisping.

After a few tests, we settled on two potatoes, cut into ¼-inch-thick slices. These slices were thin enough to cook quickly but thick enough to cut by hand without the aid of special equipment (pulling out a mandoline to slice two potatoes wasn't worth the hassle). Instead of spreading the potato slices across the oiled baking sheet in a single layer, we shingled them into two piles that would serve as beds for each piece of cod. When the potatoes were tender and starting to brown (which took about 30 minutes in a 425-degree oven), we placed the fish on top and put the sheet pan back in the oven. Cod is a relatively wet fish, so it stands up well to high heat; 15 minutes later it was perfectly cooked and moist.

Unfortunately, our large baking sheet didn't fare so well. The excess oil burned in spots where it wasn't covered by food and lent an unpleasant flavor to the meal.

We knew we'd need a smaller pan. An 8-inch square baking dish was too small (especially when we tried to maneuver a spatula under the cooked fish and potatoes to neatly remove them), so we opted for a roomier 13 by 9-inch glass baking dish.

Up to this point, the russet had been our potato of choice, but we were curious to see if other varieties might be better. We tried red potatoes and Yukon Golds, but tasters found both a bit waxy. The traditional russet, with its tender bite and earthy flavor, was the unanimous favorite. The russet also formed tighter, more cohesive layers owing to its higher starch content. This allowed us to slide a spatula under the potato slices and fish and serve the whole thing intact for an attractive presentation.

Now that our fish and potatoes were cooked to perfection, it was time to focus on infusing them with flavor. We kept the potatoes simple: a little olive oil, garlic, salt, and pepper did the trick. The lean fish, however, could benefit from a more substantial preparation. We decided that a compound butter would add plenty of flavor and richness. We stirred minced thyme and lemon juice into softened butter and rubbed it on the fish before baking. This kept the fish moist and added flavor, but the thyme didn't spend long enough in the oven to mellow; tasters thought it overwhelmed the mild cod. Nevertheless, they liked the flavor combination, so we just needed an alternate method of incorporating it.

NOTES FROM THE TEST KITCHEN

MAKING LEMON-HERB COD WITH CRISPY POTATOES

1. Shingle potato slices into two piles of 3 tight rows, measuring about 4 by 6 inches. Then gently push rows together so that potatoes are tidy and cohesive.

2. After parcooking potatoes, carefully place 1 cod fillet, skinned side down, on top of each set of potatoes. Top fish with butter pieces, thyme sprigs, and lemon slices and return to oven to finish cooking.

Backing up, we considered the layered arrangement of the fish and potatoes. What if we layered the components of the herb butter—butter, thyme, and lemon—on top of the fish? After placing the cod on the potatoes, we scattered pieces of butter on top, then topped each fillet with a sprig of thyme, followed by a few slices of lemon. This technique was a success: The butter and lemon basted the fish as it baked, and the thyme gently flavored the fish. This method not only worked better than the compound butter, but it was much easier; no chopping herbs or waiting for the butter to soften. Best of all, the attractive, layered appearance of our fillets and potato slices made for an elegant update of a timeless classic.

Lemon-Herb Cod with Crispy Garlic Potatoes
SERVES 2

Halibut or haddock can be substituted for the cod. You will need about 18 potato slices.

- 2 tablespoons olive oil
- 2 (8-ounce) russet potatoes, sliced ¼ inch thick
- 2 garlic cloves, minced
  Salt and pepper
- 2 (6-ounce) skinless cod fillets, 1 to 1½ inches thick
- 1 tablespoon unsalted butter, cut into ¼-inch pieces
- 2 sprigs fresh thyme
- ½ lemon, sliced thin

1. Adjust oven rack to lower-middle position and heat oven to 425 degrees. Brush 13 by 9-inch baking dish with 1 tablespoon oil.

2. In bowl, toss potatoes with remaining 1 tablespoon oil and garlic and season with salt and pepper. Shingle potatoes into baking dish in 2 rectangular piles measuring 4 by 6 inches. Roast potatoes until spotty brown and just tender, 30 to 35 minutes, rotating dish halfway through roasting.

3. Pat cod dry with paper towels and season with salt and pepper. Carefully place 1 fillet, skinned side down, on top of each potato pile. Top cod with butter pieces, thyme sprigs, and lemon slices. Roast fish and potatoes until fish flakes apart when gently prodded with paring knife and registers 140 degrees, about 15 minutes.

4. Slide spatula underneath potatoes and fish, gently transfer to individual plates, and serve.

BAKED SNAPPER WITH ROASTED RATATOUILLE

BAKED SNAPPER WITH ROASTED RATATOUILLE

HAVING SUCCESSFULLY CREATED AN ELEGANT roasted fish dinner (see our Lemon-Herb Cod with Crispy Garlic Potatoes, page 67), we were on the lookout for another simple yet sophisticated seafood dish. But this time, we were after something instilled with the bright and sunny flavors of Mediterranean cuisine. Ratatouille, a Provençal dish that combines tomatoes, eggplant, squash, garlic, and herbs, seemed perfect. As with our cod and potatoes, we knew both main dish and side would need to be carefully coordinated to deliver perfectly cooked, moist fish and tender, flavorful vegetables that were done at exactly the same time.

To start, we considered the type of fish. We thought red snapper, which has a firm texture and clean, mild flavor, would pair well with ratatouille; using skin-on fillets ensured that the fish held together during baking. Though red snapper is generally available year-round, we found a few alternatives that would work just as well, including Arctic char, catfish, grouper, and tilefish. For the time being, we rubbed our fillets with a bit of olive oil and seasoned them with salt and pepper. Since we planned to roast our fish atop the vegetables in the oven, we moved on to the side dish and cooking method next.

In most ratatouille recipes each vegetable is cooked separately before being combined with olive oil, garlic, and herbs; this both maximizes the vegetables' flavor and texture and rids them of excess liquid that would make for a waterlogged ratatouille. But cooking the eggplant, zucchini, and tomatoes separately before mixing them together and cooking them further in the oven was more work than we had in mind. Looking for a simpler method, we decided to cut out the stovetop time and just toss the vegetables together in a small baking dish and roast them in the oven at a high temperature. We hoped this would concentrate their flavors and evaporate those exuded juices that turn many versions of ratatouille soupy and one-dimensional. Once they started to cook down, we could place our snapper fillets on top and let both elements finish together.

To nail down the right temperature, we started at 425 degrees. At this level of heat, most of the liquid from the vegetables had cooked off, and the vegetables retained their distinct flavors and some texture, but they were unevenly cooked and even a little burnt around the edges. The texture of the fish also suffered at such a high temperature, with spots that were slightly overdone. Reducing the temperature little by little, we ultimately found that 375 degrees worked best. Now the vegetables were perfectly cooked—and not waterlogged in the least—and the fish was moist and succulent. Adding the fish only after the vegetables had begun to soften ensured that both were ready at the same time.

With our basic method established, we reconsidered the amounts and preparation of the individual vegetables. A large eggplant gave us an unbalanced, eggplant-heavy ratatouille, so we decided to use a small one. A single medium zucchini provided the right amount of squash. Cutting both the zucchini and eggplant into ½-inch cubes gave us substantial chunks of vegetable that didn't cook down too much in the finished dish. Though many recipes call for salting the eggplant and zucchini prior to cooking to drain off their excess moisture, the long stay in the oven made this step (thankfully) unnecessary.

Canned diced tomatoes ensured that we could make our snapper and ratatouille supper year-round. At first, we thought we'd need to thoroughly drain the tomatoes to prevent the ratatouille from becoming soggy, but when we did this, the ratatouille was too dry and the vegetables once again burned around the edges. Instead, we stirred in the whole can, juice and all, to moisten the vegetables and prevent those pesky burnt spots. Thinly sliced shallots, minced garlic, thyme, and

NOTES FROM THE TEST KITCHEN

THE BEST RASP GRATER
Rasp-style graters have long been a test kitchen favorite for their ability to finely grate ingredients like citrus zest, chocolate, Parmesan cheese, and ginger. In search of the absolute best grater, we headed into the test kitchen to put the four major brands through their paces, focusing on ease of use and efficiency. The winner? The **Microplane Classic 40020 Zester/Grater**, $14.95, breezed through all four tasks, producing piles of zest, cheese, chocolate, and ginger with minimal effort. With its razor-sharp teeth, comfortable handle, and a design that's maneuverable over round or irregular shapes, it's our hands-down favorite.

basil offered the right amount of aromatic and herbal background. A sprinkle of vinegar at the end added a much-needed acidic punch.

Though both the ratatouille and fish were now perfectly cooked, the ratatouille was much more boldly flavored than the mild snapper, so we decided to create a simple marinade for the fish to infuse it with more flavor. Letting the fillets rest in a mixture of olive oil, garlic, basil, and lemon zest gave them more presence in our dish, and as a bonus, we didn't need to add any time to our recipe—we simply marinated the fish while the ratatouille got its head start in the oven.

We now had a cohesive and rustic fish dish with all of the big, bright flavors of the Mediterranean—and we didn't even have to leave our own kitchen.

Baked Snapper with Roasted Ratatouille

SERVES 2

You can substitute Arctic char, catfish, cod, grouper, or tilefish fillets for the snapper. Be sure to remove the fish from the marinade after 30 minutes. Small eggplants can be hard to find; if you need to purchase a larger size, see the eggplant "Use It Up" at right.

  1 (14.5-ounce) can diced tomatoes
  1 zucchini or summer squash (8 ounces), cut into
     ½-inch pieces
  1 small eggplant (6 ounces), cut into ½-inch pieces
  2 shallots, halved and sliced ¼ inch thick
  ¼ cup extra-virgin olive oil
  4 garlic cloves, minced
  ½ teaspoon minced fresh thyme or
     ⅛ teaspoon dried
     Salt and pepper
  1 tablespoon chopped fresh basil
  1 teaspoon grated lemon zest, plus lemon wedges
     for serving
  2 (6-ounce) snapper fillets, 1 to 1¼ inches thick
  1½ teaspoons red wine vinegar

1. Adjust oven rack to middle position and heat oven to 375 degrees. Combine tomatoes, zucchini, eggplant, shallots, 1 tablespoon oil, one-half of garlic, and thyme in bowl and season with salt and pepper.

2. Spread vegetable mixture in 8-inch square baking dish. Roast until vegetables are browned and softened,

50 to 60 minutes, stirring halfway through cooking.

3. Meanwhile, whisk remaining 3 tablespoons oil, remaining garlic, 2 teaspoons basil, and lemon zest together in bowl. Pat fish dry with paper towels and season with salt and pepper. Add fillets to bowl and turn to coat. Cover and refrigerate for 30 minutes.

4. Remove fillets from marinade and gently nestle into roasted vegetables. Bake until fish flakes apart when gently prodded with paring knife and registers 140 degrees, about 10 minutes. Sprinkle with remaining 1 teaspoon basil and vinegar. Serve with lemon wedges.

USE IT UP: EGGPLANT

Roasted Eggplant Dip
SERVES 2

Tahini is a sesame paste that is widely available in the international foods aisle of many supermarkets. Be sure to stir the tahini thoroughly before measuring.

8–10 ounces eggplant, halved lengthwise and scored
      in 1-inch-deep crosshatch
   2 tablespoons extra-virgin olive oil
      Salt and pepper
   2 teaspoons tahini
   2 teaspoons lemon juice
   ¼ teaspoon minced garlic
   ⅛ teaspoon ground cumin
   1 tablespoon Greek-style yogurt or sour cream

1. Adjust oven rack to middle position and heat oven to 375 degrees. Line 8-inch square baking dish with aluminum foil. Brush eggplant with 1½ tablespoons oil and season with salt and pepper. Lay eggplant, cut side down, on prepared dish and roast until very soft and skin is shriveled, about 1 hour. Let cool slightly, about 5 minutes. Scoop eggplant pulp into fine-mesh strainer set over bowl and let drain for 5 minutes.

2. Pulse drained eggplant pulp, tahini, lemon juice, garlic, cumin, ⅛ teaspoon salt, and pinch pepper in food processor until coarsely pureed, about 5 pulses. Transfer eggplant mixture to bowl and stir in yogurt and remaining 1½ teaspoons oil until combined. Cover and refrigerate until chilled, about 30 minutes. Season with salt and pepper to taste. Serve.

GREEK-STYLE SHRIMP WITH TOMATOES AND FETA

FROZEN SHRIMP ARE THE PERFECT INGREDIENT IN the for-two kitchen—you can stash a bag in the freezer and use just as much as you need, so there's no waste. Looking for a more exciting way to add shrimp to our one-dish repertoire than falling back on the usual stir-fry, we hit on shrimp *saganaki*, a classic Greek specialty of tender shrimp baked in a tomato sauce under crumbles of feta cheese. We thought this brightly flavored dish would be a great way to bring the sweet, briny flavors of shrimp to the weeknight table for two, so we set out to create our own scaled-down version.

Admittedly, not everyone was sold on a dish that included both seafood and cheese. In the bad versions we came across, tough, rubbery shrimp were hidden under store-bought tomato sauce and a desiccated layer of salty cheese. Since shrimp are incredibly easy to overcook, our main challenge would be to get them just right—that is, tender, juicy, and just cooked through, not tough and rubbery. But before we fired up the oven, we had to choose the right size shrimp.

A few quick tests determined that jumbo or extra-large shrimp (16 to 20 to a pound or 21 to 25 to a pound, respectively) were best; they were appropriate for two main-dish portions, and their large size meant that peeling and deveining was a relatively quick process. Twelve ounces—6 ounces per person—made for two satisfying servings.

Choosing a cooking method, however, wasn't quite so easy. The traditional approach—layering the tomato sauce and shrimp in a baking dish, sprinkling feta over the top, and slipping the dish into a hot oven—produced an unexpected problem: The shrimp around the perimeter cooked more quickly and were noticeably tougher than the ones in the center. We tried a lower oven temperature, which gave us more evenly cooked shrimp, but they were unfortunately still not tender.

At this point, we decided that it didn't make sense to use the oven for what really could be a quick and easy skillet dish. So we threw tradition overboard and went stovetop. Taking the simplest approach first, we seared the shrimp quickly in a very hot 10-inch skillet, then added the sauce and feta. This tack was simple for sure, but the flavors didn't meld; our dish was just seared shrimp topped with tomato sauce and cheese. Next, reasoning that simmering the shrimp and tomatoes together would allow for an even exchange of flavors, we added the shrimp raw to the tomato sauce and briefly simmered them over high heat until they were cooked through. Tasters were pleased with the richer, more unified flavor of this batch.

Unfortunately, though, the shrimp were still a little tough. What if we turned down the heat? This method might also give the flavors in the dish more time to blend. Sure enough, as we gradually decreased the heat, the dish became better and better. Cooked gently at the barest simmer, the shrimp were at their most tender and succulent, and the dish had a fuller flavor, too.

While the shrimp now were cooked just right—perfectly tender but not underdone—they still tasted a little dull. As with our Baked Snapper with Roasted Ratatouille (page 70), we found that a quick marinade did a lot to boost the flavor of the shellfish. We combined olive oil, minced garlic, grated lemon zest, salt, and pepper, tossed in the shrimp, and let them sit for a few minutes. Though the shrimp had more flavor, they were not distinctively Greek-tasting. Some of the recipes we turned up in our initial research suggested ouzo. Though it required a trip to a liquor store, the ouzo—a lightly sweet, anise-based Greek liqueur—was an undeniable improvement: Adding just a touch to the marinade brought a welcome complexity of flavor and aroma.

Now it was time for the tomato sauce. We wanted a sauce with some sweetness to balance the feta's sharpness, as well as some earthiness to complement the brininess of the cheese and shrimp. After experimenting with various forms of tomato—fresh, canned whole, and canned diced—we settled on one can of diced tomatoes, which was not only the most convenient but also the most intensely flavored option. As for flavorings, minced garlic and shallot sautéed in olive oil were naturals for this Mediterranean sauce, as were diced bell pepper for sweetness, red pepper flakes for enlivening heat, and dry white wine for acidity. To finish with a Greek flourish, we added another dash of the ouzo we now had on the shelf.

We still had the feta to consider. We began by using a modest ¼ cup of crumbled feta and gradually ratcheted it all the way up to a generous ¾ cup, so that some would melt into the sauce and the rest would remain as a flavorful presence on top. For final touches, we drizzled a spoonful of extra-virgin olive oil over the top, then sprinkled on a little dill—its unique grassy, tangy notes had the big benefit of tasting distinctly Greek. Served with rice or crusty bread, this simple dish was an exciting new way to bring shrimp to the table for two.

NOTES FROM THE TEST KITCHEN

OUZO SUBSTITUTES

Ouzo, the popular anise-flavored spirit of Greece, lends our Greek-Style Shrimp with Tomatoes and Feta a nuanced flavor that we like. But since ouzo is not in everyone's liquor cabinet, here are two alternatives.

PERNOD	**VODKA AND ANISE SEEDS**
Though slightly sweeter than ouzo, this French anise-flavored liqueur is the next best thing.	One tablespoon of vodka plus ⅛ teaspoon of anise seeds makes a fine substitute for 1 tablespoon of ouzo.

THE BEST FETA CHEESE

In Greece, salty, crumbly curds of feta are still made by methods dating back to the Trojan War, and in 2005 the European Union ruled that only cheese produced in that country from at least 70 percent sheep's milk can rightfully bear the name. Here in the United States, domestic and imported imitators abound, and we wanted to see how they compared to the real deal. We tasted five brands—two Greek fetas, one French version, and two American cheeses—both plain and in our Greek-Style Shrimp with Tomatoes and Feta. Tasters lamented the lack of "funky," "grassy" tang in the domestic cheeses (all of which were made with 100 percent cow's milk), preferring the "barnyard" taste of the sheep's and goat's milk imports. In the end, **Mt. Vikos Traditional Feta**, a true feta from Greece, won out.

Greek-Style Shrimp with Tomatoes and Feta
SERVES 2

This dish is fairly spicy; to make it milder, reduce the amount of red pepper flakes. If you can't find ouzo, see "Ouzo Substitutes" at left. You can use jumbo-size shrimp (16 to 20 per pound) if you prefer, but you will need to increase the cooking time to 7 to 11 minutes. Serve with crusty bread or Simple White Rice (page 73).

- 12 ounces extra-large shrimp (21 to 25 per pound), peeled and deveined
- 2 tablespoons extra-virgin olive oil
- 1½ tablespoons ouzo
- 3 garlic cloves, minced
- ½ teaspoon grated lemon zest
- Salt and pepper
- 2 shallots, minced
- ½ red or green bell pepper, stemmed, seeded, and cut into ¼-inch pieces
- ¼ teaspoon red pepper flakes
- 1 (14.5-ounce) can diced tomatoes, drained with ¼ cup juice reserved
- 2 tablespoons dry white wine
- 3 ounces feta cheese, crumbled (¾ cup)
- 1 tablespoon minced fresh dill

1. Toss shrimp, 1½ teaspoons oil, 1½ teaspoons ouzo, one-third of garlic, and lemon zest together in bowl until combined and season with salt and pepper.

2. Heat 1 tablespoon oil in 10-inch skillet over medium heat until shimmering. Add shallots, bell pepper, and ⅛ teaspoon salt and stir to combine. Cover and cook, stirring occasionally, until vegetables release their moisture, 3 to 5 minutes. Uncover and continue to cook, stirring occasionally, until moisture evaporates and vegetables have softened, 3 to 5 minutes longer. Add remaining garlic and pepper flakes and cook until fragrant, about 30 seconds. Add remaining 1 tablespoon ouzo, tomatoes and reserved juice, and wine. Continue to simmer, stirring occasionally, until flavors have melded and sauce is slightly thickened, about 5 minutes longer. Season with salt and pepper to taste.

3. Reduce heat to medium-low and add shrimp along with any accumulated juices to pan; stir to coat. Cover and simmer, stirring occasionally, until shrimp are opaque throughout, 6 to 9 minutes. Off heat, sprinkle evenly with feta. Drizzle remaining 1½ teaspoons oil evenly over top and sprinkle with dill. Serve.

Simple White Rice

SERVES 2

You will need a small saucepan with a tight-fitting lid to make this recipe.

    1   teaspoon vegetable oil
    ¾   cup long-grain white or jasmine rice, rinsed
    1¼ cups water
    ¼   teaspoon salt

1. Heat oil in small saucepan over medium heat until shimmering. Stir in rice and cook until edges of grains begin to turn translucent, about 2 minutes. Stir in water and salt and bring to boil. Reduce heat to low, cover, and simmer until all liquid is absorbed, 18 to 22 minutes.

2. Off heat, uncover saucepan and place clean kitchen towel, folded in half, over saucepan, then replace lid. Let rice sit for 10 minutes, then fluff with fork. Serve.

INDONESIAN-STYLE FRIED RICE

LEFTOVER WHITE RICE IS A FREQUENT REALITY IN any household. Worst-case scenario, it sits neglected in the back of the fridge until being tossed out a week later. A better option, and one known by many a frugal chef, is to repurpose the leftovers into fried rice. The recipe is a snap: Take cold cooked rice, stir-fry it with whatever meat, vegetables, and aromatics are on hand, and toss it with a sauce that lightly coats the mixture and rehydrates the grains. When done well, the result is a satisfying one-dish meal.

And yet after years of eating hodgepodge versions, in which the rice is cooked together with scraps of meat and random vegetables, we wanted something a bit more inspired. Indonesia's spin on the approach, *nasi goreng*, provides an answer. In this Southeast Asian rendition, the grains themselves are more thoroughly seasoned with a pungent chili paste called *sambal*, along with fermented shrimp paste and a syrupy-sweet soy sauce known as *kecap manis*. Then, instead of being loaded up with miscellaneous meats and vegetables, the rice is garnished with egg and crisp fresh vegetables, for a final product with seriously complex flavor and texture. Would we be able to find the best way to replicate this dish for the two-person American kitchen?

A quick survey of Indonesian fried rice recipes revealed the source of this dish's heady flavor: chili paste. This coarse mixture is nothing more than a puree of shallots, garlic, and fresh Thai chiles. In most recipes, sautéing the chili paste in oil is the first step in the process. This way, the paste develops complexity and heat before the other ingredients hit the pan.

The chili paste, we discovered, wasn't hard to reproduce. We easily found the ingredients at the supermarket, and the paste was a snap to make, requiring just a few quick pulses in the food processor. As for duplicating the flavors of the hard-to-find shrimp paste, glutamate-rich anchovies packed a rich, salty punch but were a little too fishy. Pungent fish sauce made a better substitute but didn't single-handedly capture the paste's brininess. For that, we ended up going directly to the source, sautéing 6 ounces of chopped shrimp with the chili paste.

Bottled versions of kecap manis consist of soy sauce and palm sugar, which has a rich, almost caramelized flavor. To replicate this condiment, we tried simply adding dark brown sugar to soy sauce. But brown sugar's subtle caramel notes alone weren't enough to capture kecap manis's complex flavor and viscosity. We had much better luck in our next test, when we added a spoonful of molasses to the mix. Molasses not only added another layer of earthy sweetness, but it also gave our sauce the thickness it needed to coat the rice.

In a series of quick motions, we sautéed the chili paste, added the shrimp, then stirred in the sweet soy mixture and fish sauce and, finally, 3 cups of cold leftover rice. Each bite of this fried rice revealed that famously addictive balance of sweetness, heat, and pungency. A scattering of sliced scallion and a squirt of lime juice gave the rice a fresh finish.

All that remained was adding the traditional trimmings: a fried egg or omelet and fresh-cut cucumbers and tomatoes. The latter two were no problem, but we had to determine the best way to prepare the egg. Everyone agreed that avoiding the last-minute work of egg frying would be a plus. With that in mind, we whipped up a quick omelet, which we rolled into a tight log, sliced into spirals, and set aside until we were ready to garnish.

With its sweet-salty flavors, spicy kick, and contrasting textures, this take on fried rice had officially eclipsed the more familiar humdrum versions. And best of all, we had found a cure for the curse of leftover rice.

Indonesian-Style Fried Rice

SERVES 2

If Thai chiles are unavailable, you can substitute two serranos or two medium jalapeños. You can reduce the spiciness of this dish by removing the ribs and seeds from the chiles. If you don't have cooked white rice, follow the recipe for Simple White Rice on page 73, spread the rice on a rimmed baking sheet, and let it cool in the refrigerator for 30 minutes before using. If desired, serve with sliced cucumbers and tomato wedges.

- 2 shallots, peeled
- 2 green or red Thai chiles, stemmed
- 2 garlic cloves, peeled
- 1 tablespoon packed dark brown sugar
- 1 tablespoon molasses
- 1 tablespoon soy sauce
- 1 tablespoon fish sauce
- Salt
- 2 large eggs
- 2 tablespoons vegetable oil
- 6 ounces extra-large shrimp (21 to 25 per pound), peeled, deveined, tails removed, and cut into thirds
- 3 cups cooked white rice, chilled
- 1 scallion, sliced thin
- Lime wedges

1. Pulse shallots, chiles, and garlic in food processor until coarse paste forms, about 20 pulses, scraping down sides of bowl as necessary. Transfer mixture to small bowl and set aside. In second small bowl, stir together sugar, molasses, soy sauce, fish sauce, and ¼ teaspoon salt. Whisk eggs and pinch salt together in medium bowl.

2. Heat 1½ teaspoons oil in 12-inch nonstick skillet over medium heat until shimmering. Add eggs and gently tilt skillet to evenly coat bottom. Cover and cook until bottom of omelet is spotty golden brown and top is just set, about 1½ minutes. Slide omelet onto cutting board and gently roll up into tight log. Using sharp knife, cut log crosswise into 1-inch segments, leaving segments rolled.

3. Heat remaining 1½ tablespoons oil in now-empty skillet over medium heat until shimmering. Add chile mixture and cook until mixture turns golden, 3 to 5 minutes. Increase heat to medium-high, add shrimp, and cook, stirring constantly, until exterior of shrimp is just opaque, about 2 minutes.

4. Push shrimp to sides of skillet to clear center; stir molasses mixture to recombine and pour into center of skillet. When molasses mixture bubbles, add rice and cook, stirring and folding constantly, until shrimp is cooked, rice is heated through, and mixture is evenly coated, about 3 minutes. Off heat, stir in scallion and transfer fried rice to individual plates. Garnish with egg segments and lime wedges. Serve immediately.

NOTES FROM THE TEST KITCHEN

RE-CREATING THE FLAVORS OF INDONESIA

For our scaled-down Indonesian-Style Fried Rice, we didn't want to hunt down esoteric ingredients. The various components that give this dish complex flavors and textures can be found at your local supermarket.

Soy sauce sweetened with dark brown sugar and molasses approximates the flavors of the Indonesian condiment kecap manis.

We create an Indonesian chili paste by coarsely pureeing fresh Thai chiles, shallot, and garlic and sautéing them in oil to develop their flavors.

The combination of fish sauce and fresh shrimp captures the rich, briny essence of hard-to-find Asian shrimp paste.

A thin Asian-style omelet that gets rolled into a log and sliced into spirals brings tender texture to the dish.

INDONESIAN-STYLE FRIED RICE

MA PAO TOFU

MA PAO DOUFU, OR MA PAO TOFU AS IT'S KNOWN in the United States, combines garlic, Asian bean paste, and spicy Sichuan peppercorns with ground pork and tofu to create a dish that's rich, spicy, saucy, and highly addictive. This quick-cooking dish is a staple on Chinese restaurant menus and a favorite of many of our test cooks, so gathering opinions about the dish was easy. We were unprepared, though, for the passion it inspired. Ma pao tofu is not a dish to be taken lightly; we would have our work cut out for us if we were going to capture the perfect combination of soft, creamy tofu, flavorful pork, and spicy chili oil, all the while scaling it down to make just two servings.

Any tofu dish worth its weight should begin with the right amount of the right kind of tofu. Since we didn't want an odd piece of leftover tofu in the fridge, we opted for one 14-ounce block for this dish; this amount seemed right given that it's really the tofu, not the pork, that is the star of the dish. Many stir-fries use firm or extra-firm tofu—they hold up to constant stirring and high heat better than their soft or silken counterparts. But given the soft, silky texture of the tofu in traditional ma pao tofu, we knew that firm, extra-firm, and even medium weren't the way to go. At the other end of the spectrum, we dismissed silken tofu, as we wanted the tofu to remain in distinct chunks instead of disappearing into tiny curds.

That left us with soft tofu. We gave it a test run in a basic working recipe. We sautéed a bit of ginger and garlic, added a basic sauce of chicken broth, water, soy sauce, rice wine, and sugar, letting it simmer and concentrate in flavor, then added the tofu toward the end, cooking it just long enough to heat through. Tasters agreed that the texture of this tofu was still too firm. After a little more research, we noticed that some traditional recipes referred to ma pao tofu as a braised tofu dish. Would a traditional braising technique over low, slow heat give the soft tofu the proper texture, softening it just as it softens a tough cut of meat? We gave it a shot, adding the soft tofu with the sauce, reducing the heat, and then simmering the tofu for 10 minutes. We noticed a difference in texture but wondered if we

could push this approach even further. An additional 10 minutes of simmering gave our tofu just the right silky, soft texture, just like the restaurant versions.

Now we were ready to build a flavor base. Pork is a traditional ingredient in ma pao tofu, so we started by browning and cooking through a small amount of ground pork (just 4 ounces), then setting it aside and stirring it into the sauce and tofu at the end to heat it through. But tasters felt the browned pork overwhelmed the delicate tofu. For our next test, we added the pork to the aromatics and cooked it over medium heat for a couple of minutes, just long enough to cook it completely (without browning). Then we set it aside and stirred it in at the end as we had before. This was an improvement, but the pork was a little chewy. Would the pork, like the tofu, benefit from an extended simmer in the sauce? In our next test, we cooked the pork for just a minute, to break it up, then stirred in the sauce, added the tofu, and left the dish to simmer for 20 minutes. This gave us meltingly tender pork, but it needed a little flavor boost. For our final pork test, we let the pork marinate in a bit of soy sauce while we prepped the remaining ingredients. This step did the trick, giving us tender, flavorful pork that subtly permeated the entire dish.

Finding the best way to prepare the tofu and pork had been challenging, but determining the exact blend of flavors that give this dish its distinctive taste would prove even more difficult. While most recipes use the heat (and vibrant red color) of readily available chili oil as an integral ingredient, they also rely on more esoteric ingredients like broad bean or chili bean paste to give the sauce meaty depth. As much as we loved the flavor of the bean paste, we felt that a substitute was necessary to keep this two-person recipe within the realm of weeknight cooking. The bean paste added some heat, which could easily be replaced by adding more chili oil, but the rich, salty flavor it possessed would be harder to replicate. Increasing the soy sauce helped some, but we needed another source to add complexity. Rooting around in our pantry for a solution, we spied fish sauce. Granted, it's a Southeast Asian, not a Chinese, condiment, but just a small amount gives such dishes as pad thai and Vietnamese pho an essential salty complexity. Likewise, a small amount of fish sauce gave this dish the depth it was missing. A full teaspoon of ground Sichuan peppercorns gave it the anise flavor and tongue-numbing sensation for which the dish is famous. To thicken the sauce at the end of cooking, we added a tablespoon of cornstarch, mixed with water, before stirring in a generous 5 teaspoons of chili oil as a finishing touch.

Every bit as flavorful as the real deal but streamlined for two, our ma pao tofu was an exotic new option, perfect for livening up any old Monday night.

Ma Pao Tofu

SERVES 2

Soft tofu is important to the texture of this dish; do not substitute silken, medium, or firm tofu. Sichuan peppercorns impart intense flavor and heat to this dish, and we strongly encourage you to seek them out—neither black nor white peppercorns can be substituted. This dish is fairly spicy; to make it milder, reduce the amount of chili oil. Serve with Simple White Rice (page 73).

SAUCE

- 1 cup low-sodium chicken broth
- ¼ cup water
- 1 tablespoon soy sauce
- 1 tablespoon fish sauce
- 2 teaspoons Chinese rice wine or dry sherry
- 1 teaspoon sugar

STIR-FRY

- 14 ounces soft tofu, cut into ½-inch dice
- 4 ounces ground pork
- 1 teaspoon soy sauce
- 2 garlic cloves, minced
- 2 teaspoons grated fresh ginger
- 2 teaspoons vegetable oil
- 1 teaspoon Sichuan peppercorns, ground or crushed fine
- 2 scallions, whites minced, greens sliced thin on bias
- 1 tablespoon cornstarch
- 1½ tablespoons water
- 5 teaspoons chili oil, plus extra for serving

1. FOR THE SAUCE: Whisk all ingredients together in bowl.

2. FOR THE STIR-FRY: Spread tofu out on several layers of paper towels and let drain for 20 minutes. Meanwhile toss pork with soy sauce in bowl, cover, and refrigerate for at least 10 minutes or up to 1 hour. In separate bowl, combine garlic, ginger, 1 teaspoon vegetable oil, and peppercorns.

3. Heat remaining 1 teaspoon vegetable oil in 10-inch nonstick skillet over medium heat until shimmering. Add scallion whites and cook until softened, about 1 minute. Add garlic mixture and cook, mashing mixture into pan, until fragrant, about 30 seconds.

4. Add pork and cook, breaking up meat with wooden spoon, until no longer pink, about 1 minute. Whisk sauce to recombine, then add to skillet. Gently stir in tofu, cover, and simmer over low heat until tofu and pork are very tender and flavor of sauce has deepened, about 20 minutes.

5. In small bowl, whisk cornstarch and water together. Gently stir cornstarch mixture into skillet, being careful not to break up tofu. Bring to simmer and cook, stirring often, until sauce has thickened, 2 to 3 minutes. Stir in chili oil, transfer to platter, and sprinkle with scallion greens. Serve with additional chili oil.

NOTES FROM THE TEST KITCHEN

ALL ABOUT SICHUAN PEPPERCORNS

From 1968 until 2005, Sichuan peppercorns, which are berries from a spiny shrub indigenous to the Sichuan province of China, were banned from the United States (they were thought to be potential carriers of a tree disease that could harm citrus crops). But with their return a few years ago, they are appearing more and more frequently in authentic Sichuan recipes in the States. The peppercorns have purplish-red husks and shiny black seeds. It is preferable to buy Sichuan peppercorns with the shiny black seeds removed, as it's the reddish-brown husks that are used for their aromatic, gently floral fragrance and their telltale numbing effect on the tongue.

MEATY SKILLET LASAGNA

CHAPTER 3

PASTA FOR DINNER

LINGUINE WITH QUICK TOMATO SAUCE

SURE, IT'S EASY ENOUGH TO POP OPEN A JAR OF sauce for a weeknight spaghetti dinner, especially if you're preparing just two servings. But the truth is, preparing a simple, from-scratch tomato sauce doesn't take that much longer, and it doesn't require an extensive ingredient list. We set out to create a flavorful pasta sauce with a nicely thickened texture; it had to coat each strand of pasta perfectly, and it had to offer bold, bright, fresh tomato flavor in every bite.

To get our bearings, we started by digging up a number of recipes and giving them a try. There was considerable agreement among the staff as to what worked and what didn't. Most recipes used a pretty standard list of ingredients: tomatoes, basil, olive oil, and garlic. But a number of recipes broke from the norm. Butter was used in a few sauces to add some richness, but we nixed it because we found that it dulled the bright, slightly acidic flavor of the tomatoes. Tomato paste, which we frequently use in the test kitchen to add depth and savory flavor to long-simmered sauces, braises, and stews, also showed up in a handful of recipes. However, nobody was enthusiastic about the rather one-dimensional flavor it produced in our test recipes.

In general, we liked the brighter, fresher tomato flavor of sauces that had cooked for a short period of time—10 to 15 minutes seemed to work best. Canned tomatoes provided more consistent results, and we didn't have to wait until the height of summer to make our sauce. Also, we preferred sauces that tasted predominantly of tomatoes, with the garlic and basil relegated to accent notes. The better recipes also had a nice balance of sweetness and acidity that gave the sauce some depth; these sauces included just a little bit of sugar, which kept the acidity of the tomatoes in check without making the sauce too sweet.

Now that we had a general sense of what we liked—fresh tomato flavor accented by basil and garlic, with a hint of sweetness to balance the tomatoes—we set out to nail down the specifics. For the tomatoes, we tested crushed, diced, and whole and simmered each in a saucepan with a couple of cloves of garlic. The crushed tomatoes gave us an overly thick sauce reminiscent of the jarred stuff, and diced tomatoes produced a sauce that was too chunky. The whole tomatoes resulted in a sauce that was much closer to what we had in mind. Pulsing them in the food processor instead of chopping them by hand took just a second and promised a mostly smooth sauce with a few smaller bites of tomato.

Unfortunately, the short cooking time that ensured a sauce with fresher flavor meant that the extra liquid from the tomatoes didn't have time to reduce, yielding a slightly thin and watery sauce. We tried cooking the tomatoes just a little longer to cook off the extra liquid, but, as we expected, this dulled their flavor. Draining the can of tomatoes before tossing them in the food processor solved the problem. Now our sauce was nicely thickened after its brief simmer, plus its flavor was deep and robust.

With the consistency just right, we looked to figure out the additional flavorings. We determined that ¼ teaspoon of sugar, stirred in after the sauce had finished simmering and become more concentrated in flavor, provided just the right level of sweetness. When it came to the garlic, tasters were pleased with the aromatic background provided by two cloves. For the basil, we tested a variety of amounts and ultimately settled on just 2 tablespoons, which gave the sauce the right level of freshness and a bit of color.

With the supporting players figured out, our quick tomato sauce was perfect, and it offered just the right consistency and flavor. It was such a success that we

were inspired to develop a variation: a bold, assertive sauce that traded the whole tomatoes from our master recipe for the fire-roasted variety. Now we had two speedy tomato sauces that we could make any night of the week—and both of them were worlds better than anything we'd ever had from a jar.

Linguine with Quick Tomato Sauce
SERVES 2

Since the acidity of canned whole tomatoes varies from brand to brand, you'll need to adjust the amount of sugar to suit your taste. For a spicy sauce, add ½ teaspoon red pepper flakes to the oil with the garlic. See page 82 for a tip on how to measure out long strands of pasta without using a scale.

- 1 **(28-ounce) can whole peeled tomatoes, drained**
- 5 **teaspoons extra-virgin olive oil**
- 2 **garlic cloves, minced**
- 2 **tablespoons chopped fresh basil**
  Sugar
  Salt
- 6 **ounces linguine**

1. Pulse drained tomatoes in food processor until coarsely chopped and no large pieces remain, 6 to 8 pulses. Cook oil and garlic together in medium saucepan over medium heat, stirring often, until fragrant but not browned, about 2 minutes. Stir in processed tomatoes. Bring to simmer and cook until slightly thickened, 10 to 15 minutes.

2. Stir in basil and ¼ teaspoon sugar. Season with salt and additional sugar to taste.

3. Meanwhile, bring 4 quarts water to boil in large pot. Add pasta and 1 tablespoon salt and cook, stirring often, until al dente. Reserve ½ cup cooking water, then drain pasta and return it to pot. Add sauce to pasta and toss to combine. Season with salt and pepper to taste and add reserved cooking water as needed to adjust consistency. Serve.

VARIATION

Linguine with Quick Fire-Roasted Tomato Sauce
Substitute 1 (28-ounce) can drained whole fire-roasted tomatoes for whole tomatoes. Add ¼ teaspoon smoked paprika to oil with garlic.

LINGUINE WITH FENNEL, GARLIC, AND LEMON

ITALIANS HAVE A DEFINITE APPRECIATION FOR sweet, anise-scented fennel, which they incorporate into everything from salads to pastas to soups and braises. One popular dish involves braising the vegetable in an aromatic broth and then tossing everything with pasta and a smattering of grated Parmesan. Braising gives the bulb an entirely new dimension and renders it tender, sweet, and utterly addictive. We thought this dish would make for a simple yet tasty pasta dinner for two.

We began by researching the best way to braise the fennel. Some recipes called for browning thick slices of fennel in a skillet before submerging them in liquid and letting them bubble away for an hour or more. In others, the fennel was first braised before being moved to a pan to develop a caramelized exterior. Still other recipes skipped the browning altogether; the braising liquid was reduced to a rich glaze that coated the tender pieces of fennel as they cooked. Of the recipes we tried, we favored those in which the fennel was braised first, then allowed to brown; in these, the fennel was able to retain its flavorful, lightly browned exterior, leading to a more intense, sweet, aniselike flavor in the finished dish.

With our method determined, we moved on to figuring out the best liquid for braising. The recipes we'd seen used mostly water, chicken broth, and wine, either alone or in combination. We tried the chicken broth first, but when combined with the fennel, it led to a dish that was overly sweet. Using only wine made the dish too acidic. In the end, tasters favored a combination of wine and water.

When it came to the cooking vessel, we found that a medium skillet was just the right size to hold our single bulb of fennel, which we'd sliced thin for an elegant look, along with the braising liquid. In a larger pan, our thin slices of fennel burned unless we added more liquid (which resulted in too much sauce later on), and in a smaller pan, our fennel was crowded and steamed (and braising in two batches seemed too finicky for this humble dish). Covering the skillet ensured that the fennel released its moisture, which added flavor to the braising liquid. After about 5 minutes, we uncovered the pan and let the excess moisture cook off. The fennel had taken on a nice golden hue and was incredibly tender.

HOW TO COOK PASTA

If you ask 10 cooks how they cook pasta, you're likely to get 10 different answers. In an effort to standardize pasta cookery, we've come up with these guidelines that will guarantee perfect pasta every time.

USE 4 QUARTS OF WATER IN A LARGE POT: This may sound like a lot of water for just two servings, but it will ensure that the pasta cooks evenly and doesn't clump.

SKIP THE OIL AND USE PLENTY OF SALT: Many people dump oil into boiling pasta water, thinking it will keep the pasta from sticking together, but this is a myth. Adding oil does not prevent sticking; frequent stirring does. Skip the oil but make sure to add salt—roughly 1 tablespoon for 4 quarts of water—or the pasta will taste bland.

TASTE PASTA OFTEN FOR DONENESS: Reading the instructions on the box is a good place to start, but for al dente pasta, you may need to shave a few minutes off the recommended time. When you are a minute or two shy of the recommended cooking time, begin tasting for doneness.

SAVE SOME COOKING WATER: Wait! Before you drain that pasta, measure about ½ cup of the cooking water from the pasta pot with a liquid measuring cup. Then drain the pasta and immediately toss it with the sauce. (Don't let the pasta sit in the colander too long; it will get very dry very quickly.) When you toss your sauce with the pasta, add some (or all) of the reserved pasta cooking water to thin the sauce as needed.

MEASURING PASTA SHAPES

The best method for measuring pasta is to weigh it using a scale. However, if you do not own a scale, we have provided the equivalent cup measurements for various shapes. Use dry measuring cups for the most accurate measurements, and pack them full.

PASTA TYPE	4 OUNCES	6 OUNCES
Farfalle	1⅔ cups	2½ cups
Rigatoni, Rotini	1½ cups	2⅓ cups
Penne, Ziti	1¼ cups	2 cups
Campanelle	1¼ cups	2 cups
Orecchiette	1 cup	1¾ cups

When 6 ounces of uncooked linguine, spaghetti, fettuccine, or vermicelli are bunched together into a tight circle, the diameter measures about 1⅛ inches.

1⅛"

Now we had perfectly cooked fennel, but it was lacking in richness. Adding extra-virgin olive oil seemed like our best bet, but adding it at the end of cooking left us with greasy fennel and an overly assertive olive flavor. What if we incorporated the oil into the braising step? Two tablespoons proved to be just the right amount; to keep the braising liquid in check, we cut down on the water and wine accordingly.

At this point, our pasta dish needed some help in the flavor department. A couple of cloves of garlic added aromatic backbone, and fennel seeds echoed the sweet notes of our braised fennel. Grated lemon zest added a light, citrusy flavor that paired well with the fennel's sweetness, and lemon juice contributed brightness. Tasters liked the flavor of the dish now but felt that the acidic notes were overwhelming. Loath to do away with the lemon juice, we simply replaced the wine in the braising liquid with more water. All we had left to do was cook our pasta and toss everything together.

Topped with grated Parmesan, our flavorful fennel and pasta dish was the perfect homage to simple, yet sophisticated, Italian cuisine.

Linguine with Fennel, Garlic, and Lemon

SERVES 2

Be sure to mince the garlic well so that its flavor is evenly distributed throughout the dish. See the box at left for a tip on how to measure out long strands of pasta without using a scale.

- 1 fennel bulb, 2 tablespoons fronds chopped, stalks discarded, bulb halved, cored, and sliced thin (see page 50)
- 2 tablespoons extra-virgin olive oil
- 2 tablespoons water
  Salt and pepper
- 2 garlic cloves, minced
- ½ teaspoon fennel seeds
- ¼ teaspoon grated lemon zest plus 1½ teaspoons juice
- 6 ounces linguine
- 2 tablespoons grated Parmesan cheese, plus extra for serving

1. Bring sliced fennel, oil, water, and ¼ teaspoon salt to boil in 10-inch skillet over medium-high heat. Reduce heat to medium-low, cover, and simmer until fennel is tender, 5 to 8 minutes.

LINGUINE WITH FENNEL, GARLIC, AND LEMON

2. Uncover and cook until liquid evaporates, about 2 minutes. Stir in garlic, fennel seeds, and ¼ teaspoon pepper and cook until fragrant, about 30 seconds. Off heat, stir in fennel fronds and lemon zest and juice. Cover and keep warm.

3. Meanwhile, bring 4 quarts water to boil in large pot. Add pasta and 1 tablespoon salt and cook, stirring often, until al dente. Reserve ½ cup cooking water, then drain pasta and return it to pot. Add fennel mixture and Parmesan to pasta and toss to combine. Season with salt and pepper to taste and add reserved cooking water as needed to adjust consistency. Serve with extra Parmesan.

QUICK MUSHROOM RAGU

WE LOVE TRADITIONAL LONG-SIMMERED RAGU (see Classic Pork Ragu on page 105), but when we want a dish that offers just as much depth of flavor and meaty richness in a fraction of the time, we turn to mushroom ragu. Based on a Tuscan dish known as *spaghetti alla boscaiola*, or "woodsman's pasta," this ragu combines the naturally hearty texture of fresh mushrooms with the concentrated meaty flavor of dried ones and is ready and on the table in 30 minutes.

Our working recipe started with pancetta, which is used to give mushroom ragu some meaty flavor and richness. Chopped bits of the salt-cured pork are first rendered, then the fat is used to sauté the remaining ingredients. Pancetta's meaty flavor, though subtle, adds backbone to the sauce while still relinquishing the leading role to the mushrooms.

Since fresh mushrooms give the sauce bulk, we decided to go with one of the meatiest kinds: the portobello. We started with a single mushroom and removed its gills—the dark, feathery grooves on the cap's underside—prior to cooking to keep the sauce from turning muddy-looking. We then chopped the portobello into bite-size pieces that would blend into the sauce yet maintain a noticeable presence.

With the meaty texture from the fresh mushrooms in check, we turned to the dried mushrooms to instill our sauce with ultra-concentrated flavor. Smoky porcini are among the most savory of the dehydrated varieties, and they seemed the natural choice in this Tuscan-inspired dish. We began by soaking ¼ ounce in hot water for 5 minutes, then minced the damp, shriveled pieces and added them to our skillet along with the rendered pancetta, a little olive oil, the chopped portobello, and sliced garlic. After about five minutes, the fresh mushrooms had started to brown. Next, we added chopped fresh tomatoes, and after about 20 minutes of simmering, the sauce had thickened nicely. When we tasted it, however, we were disappointed to find that it had nothing close to the earthy richness we wanted.

We thought adding another portobello cap might help add deeper flavor, but it barely made an impact, and it gave us too much sauce for two servings. A far more potent solution was to double the amount of dried porcini. This so greatly deepened the flavor that we decided to keep going. We strained the soaking liquid left over from rehydrating the mushrooms, which we knew would have picked up a lot of porcini flavor, and added it to the sauce. Replacing the water in the recipe with chicken broth fortified the ragu even more. The mushroom flavor was finally bold and hearty; now we could return to the tomatoes.

We switched to canned tomatoes, which are more reliable than fresh most of the year, and tried several types. Crushed tomatoes proved too thick, and diced tomatoes didn't break down enough. Tasters preferred the softer yet hearty texture of whole tomatoes that we had crushed by hand, which gave us a sauce with chunks of tomato; a single 14.5-ounce can yielded just the right amount for two servings. Two teaspoons of tomato paste rounded out the flavor of the sauce. Minced rosemary added some woodsy notes that fit in with the flavor profile of the dish.

Even without an abundance of meat and hours of simmering, our mushroom ragu was worthy of the name—and every bit as hearty and satisfying.

NOTES FROM THE TEST KITCHEN

REMOVING PORTOBELLO GILLS

The black gills on the underside of a portobello mushroom cap can make a sauce, soup, or stew taste muddy and appear unappetizingly dark. To avoid this, simply scrape the gills off using a spoon before cooking.

Quick Mushroom Ragu

SERVES 2

Use a spoon to scrape the dark brown gills from the portobello, or the ragu's flavors may be dulled and the sauce can turn unappetizingly dark. See page 82 for a tip on how to measure out long strands of pasta without using a scale.

- ½ cup low-sodium chicken broth
- ½ ounce dried porcini mushrooms, rinsed
- 2 tablespoons extra-virgin olive oil
- 2 ounces pancetta, cut into ½-inch pieces
- 1 large portobello mushroom cap, gills removed, cut into ½-inch pieces
- 2 garlic cloves, sliced thin
- 2 teaspoons tomato paste
- 1 teaspoon minced fresh rosemary
- 1 (14.5-ounce) can whole peeled tomatoes, drained, roughly crushed by hand
- Salt and pepper
- 6 ounces spaghetti
- Grated Pecorino Romano cheese

1. Microwave broth and porcini together in covered bowl until steaming, about 1 minute. Let sit until softened, about 5 minutes. Drain mushrooms through fine-mesh strainer lined with coffee filter, reserve broth, and finely chop mushrooms.

2. Heat 1 tablespoon oil in 10-inch skillet over medium heat until shimmering. Add pancetta and cook until rendered and crisp, 3 to 5 minutes. Add chopped porcini, remaining 1 tablespoon oil, portobello, garlic, tomato paste, and rosemary and cook, stirring occasionally, until all liquid has evaporated and tomato paste starts to brown, 5 to 7 minutes. Stir in reserved broth and tomatoes, increase heat to high, and bring to simmer. Reduce heat to medium-low and simmer, stirring occasionally, until thickened, 15 to 20 minutes. Season with salt and pepper to taste.

3. Meanwhile, bring 4 quarts water to boil in large pot. Add pasta and 1 tablespoon salt and cook, stirring often, until al dente. Reserve ½ cup cooking water, then drain pasta and return it to pot. Add sauce to pasta and toss to combine. Season with salt and pepper to taste and add reserved cooking water as needed to adjust consistency. Serve with Pecorino.

SPRING VEGETABLE PASTA

PASTA PRIMAVERA, THE ITALIAN RESTAURANT staple, might be named for spring, but the usual dish often goes astray with a heavy, dull cream sauce, thus tasting nothing like spring. The vegetables often require painstaking preparation and individual blanching, and the cream-, butter-, and cheese-enriched sauce too easily turns overly rich and heavy. We wanted a true spring vegetable pasta, with a few thoughtfully chosen vegetables and a light but full-bodied sauce that clung well to the noodles and brought the dish together. And since we were making just two servings, the preparation had to be streamlined.

We began by selecting a flavorful combination of spring vegetables. We landed on a pair of classics—asparagus and green peas—plus garlic and leeks for their aromatic depth and sweetness, and mint, a natural match for peas. We also decided at the outset to do away with the tedious blanching step. We found that by sautéing the vegetables in stages in a large saucepan, we were able to ensure that each one maintained its crisp-tender texture while taking on a touch of flavorful browning. First in went the leeks, followed by the chopped asparagus, the minced garlic, and finally the frozen baby peas, which needed only a minute over the heat to lend sweetness to the mix.

But as we'd learned from countless recipes we tested, simply tossing sautéed vegetables with the pasta didn't add up to a dish that was any greater than the sum of its parts. What we needed was a way to tie the dish together and give it depth of flavor—a job that's usually reserved for the sauce. We started with vegetable broth as the base of the sauce. To give it depth, we simmered the broth with the pile of scraps we'd peeled and trimmed away from the vegetables (the green parts of the leeks and the woody ends of the asparagus), along with some extra garlic and peas. But once we'd strained the broth and added the cream and butter—necessary to give the sauce body—any flavor advantage we had gained was lost. Cutting back on the dairy didn't help; the resulting sauce was so thin that it just slid off the pasta. It was clear that the vegetables alone weren't enough to give the dish flavor.

We needed to find some way to infuse flavor into the pasta, rather than merely coating it with a

SPRING VEGETABLE PASTA

vegetable sauce. That's when a colleague reminded us that Italian cookery has a tradition of parboiling pasta in water and then letting it finish cooking for a minute or two in whatever sauce is being served. The technique has a twofold benefit: As the pasta cooks, it absorbs some of the sauce and takes on its flavors. In exchange, the noodles release some of their starches into the sauce, which helps build body. We prepared another batch, this time boiling the pasta (spaghetti, for now) for a couple of minutes in the water, draining it, and then allowing it to finish cooking in our enhanced vegetable broth. Tasters agreed that while this was a step in the right direction, the results were still too subtle. Instead of merely finishing the pasta in the flavorful broth, what if we used it to cook the pasta from the outset?

The concept is well established in Italian cooking—it's a classic risotto technique, in which the rice and broth work together to produce a glossy, full-bodied "sauce" that thoroughly flavors and coats each grain. When we tried the approach with pasta, the results weren't quite perfect, but they were promising: The noodles, which we had boiled in a modest 3 cups of liquid (2 cups of broth, 1 cup of water) until they were al dente and the saucepan was almost dry, emerged more flavorful and lightly coated with the silky, starchy pot liquor. In fact, the sauce was thick enough that we didn't even need to add any cream or butter to give it body.

Now that we were on a roll, we wondered if we could stretch the risotto technique even farther. Traditionally, the raw rice grains "toast" for a few minutes in some hot fat before the liquid is added, taking on a nutty richness. Adapting this technique for the pasta recipe seemed like a natural move, except for the problem of the long spaghetti strands, which we'd need to break up first. It seemed easier to just change the shape of the noodle. After testing half a dozen shorter shapes, we opted for bell-shaped campanelle: They held on to the sauce nicely, without clinging to one another or compressing into a mass.

Now that we had the right pasta shape, we went back to the cooking technique. After sautéing the vegetables, we wiped out the pot, added a splash of extra-virgin olive oil, and toasted the pasta until it started to color. Taking another hint from the classic risotto method,

we poured in some dry white wine (its crisp acidity would brighten the sauce), stirring the mixture until most of the liquid had cooked off, then added the hot broth and cranked up the heat to a boil. Ten minutes later, the results were remarkably improved: tender pasta pieces coated with a light but lustrous and creamy sauce that more than hinted at the sweet, grassy flavors of the vegetables.

Once the sautéed vegetables were incorporated, all the dish needed was a little flavor tweaking here and there. Along with the minced garlic, we added a pinch of red pepper flakes and, just before serving, some chopped mint and a handful of grated Parmesan. Finally, we brightened the whole dish with a bit of lemon zest and juice.

At last, our spring vegetable pasta truly tasted like spring.

Spring Vegetable Pasta

SERVES 2

Other pasta shapes can be substituted for the campanelle; however, their cup measurements may vary (see page 82). The test kitchen's preferred brand of vegetable broth is Swanson Vegetarian Vegetable Broth.

2 leeks, white and light green parts halved lengthwise, sliced ½ inch thick, and washed thoroughly (3 cups); 1½ cups roughly chopped dark green parts, washed thoroughly

8 ounces asparagus, tough ends snapped off, chopped coarse, and reserved; spears cut on bias into ½-inch lengths

1 cup frozen baby peas, thawed

2 garlic cloves, minced

2 cups vegetable broth

1 cup water

2 tablespoons extra-virgin olive oil
   Salt and pepper
   Pinch red pepper flakes

6 ounces (2 cups) campanelle

½ cup dry white wine

¼ cup grated Parmesan cheese, plus extra for serving

1 tablespoon minced fresh mint

¼ teaspoon grated lemon zest plus 2 teaspoons juice

1. Place dark green leek trimmings, asparagus trimmings, ½ cup peas, one-half of garlic, vegetable broth, and water in medium saucepan. Bring to simmer over high heat, then lower heat to medium-low and gently simmer for 10 minutes.

2. Strain broth through fine-mesh strainer into measuring cup, pressing on solids to extract as much liquid as possible (you should have 2½ cups broth; if necessary, add water as needed to measure 2½ cups). Discard solids and return broth to saucepan. Cover and keep warm over low heat.

3. Heat 1 tablespoon oil in large saucepan over medium heat until shimmering. Add sliced leeks and pinch salt and cook, covered, stirring occasionally, until leeks begin to brown, 5 to 7 minutes. Add asparagus pieces and cook until crisp-tender, 4 to 6 minutes. Add remaining garlic and pepper flakes; cook until fragrant, about 30 seconds. Add remaining ½ cup peas and continue to cook for 1 minute. Transfer vegetables to plate and set aside. Wipe out saucepan.

4. Heat remaining 1 tablespoon oil in now-empty saucepan over medium heat until shimmering. Add pasta and cook, stirring frequently, until just beginning to brown, 4 to 6 minutes. Add wine and cook, stirring constantly, until fully absorbed, about 2 minutes.

5. Add hot broth, increase heat to medium-high, and bring to boil. Cook, stirring frequently, until most of liquid is absorbed and pasta is al dente, 8 to 10 minutes.

6. Off heat, stir in vegetables, Parmesan, 1 teaspoon mint, and lemon zest and juice. Season with salt and pepper to taste and sprinkle with remaining 2 teaspoons mint. Serve with extra Parmesan.

PASTA WITH SUN-DRIED TOMATO PESTO

TRADITIONAL PESTO IS A BRIGHT GREEN SAUCE that gets its distinctive color and flavor from a considerable amount of fresh basil. Nowadays, however, many pestos trade the basil for any number of starring ingredients, like fresh greens (think spinach and arugula) or more potent, shelf-stable flavorings (like roasted red peppers or sun-dried tomatoes). We liked the idea of using a pantry-friendly ingredient as the defining flavor in a pesto that could be made any time of year, even in the dead of winter. With their sweet and sunny flavor profile, sun-dried tomatoes seemed like just the right pick for our anytime pesto.

First, we took a closer look at the main ingredient. Sun-dried tomatoes are available dried (like raisins) or packed in oil with flavorings. Many of the dried tomatoes, which must be hydrated in hot water before being used, tasted too salty, bitter, strong, or musty, and their texture was either mushy or tough. Tasters much preferred the pleasantly chewy consistency of the oil-packed sun-dried tomatoes but disliked the flavor of the oil and spices they were packed in.

The flavor issue was easy enough to address: Before we tossed the tomatoes into the food processor to combine them with the other ingredients, we drained and rinsed them to rid them of their universally unpleasant marinades. In addition to excising undesired flavors, this

THE BEST SUN-DRIED TOMATOES

Here in the test kitchen, we prefer oil-packed sun-dried tomatoes to their leatherlike counterparts. After conducting a taste test, we can say with certainty that not all oil-packed sun-dried tomatoes taste the same, at least straight from the jar. Our favorite brand is **Trader Joe's Sun-Dried Tomatoes**, which are packed in olive oil, garlic, herbs, spices, and sulfur dioxide (to retain color). These sun-dried tomatoes offer just the right balance of flavors and sweetness.

TOASTING GARLIC

To temper harsh flavor of raw garlic, toast unpeeled cloves in small skillet over medium heat until color of cloves deepens slightly, about 7 minutes. Let garlic cool, then peel and chop cloves.

THE BEST ROTARY GRATER

Rather than risk scraping our knuckles on a box or rasp-style grater, we prefer to shred cheese tableside with a rotary grater. To find a rotary grater that worked quickly with the least amount of pressure possible, we asked testers with various hand sizes to try four models, handing them everything from hard Parmesan to semisoft cheddar, soft mozzarella, and even a chunk of chocolate. The biggest factor in performance turned out to be the size of the barrel: Models with smaller barrels came in with slow grating times, while models with wider barrels zipped through grating tasks. The other major considerations—handle comfort and cleanup—were all about simplicity. Graters that disassembled quickly and contained fewer pieces made cleanup a breeze. The **Zyliss All Cheese Grater**, $19.95, won out for its simple design, with an extra-wide barrel and comfortable handle. For an added bonus, it's also dishwasher-safe.

step also helped the tomatoes break down more easily in the food processor, rather than getting clogged around the blade. Next we considered the other ingredients, starting with the garlic.

Though pestos tend to be quite garlicky in flavor given their uncooked nature, we wanted our pesto to taste first and foremost of sun-dried tomatoes. The garlic would have to take a backseat. But what would be the best way to tame its flavor? We considered several approaches—roasting, sautéing, and infusing olive oil with garlic flavor—but ultimately none of them made sense given the small amount of garlic we were working with (just one clove). We finally hit on simply toasting the clove in a small skillet, which took just a few minutes. This tamed the garlic's harsh notes and loosened the skin from the clove for easy peeling.

Next, we moved on to the nuts. Pine nuts, the traditional choice for basil pesto, were up first. They yielded the smoothest, creamiest pesto, but their flavor was too mild to stand up to the intense flavor of the sun-dried

tomatoes. We gave almonds a go next, but they gave the pesto a coarse, granular texture. Our tasters preferred walnuts, which gave our pesto some texture (but not too much) and a noticeably nutty flavor. To bring out their full flavor, we toasted them, too.

For the extra-virgin olive oil, it was important to use high-quality oil for the best flavor. Grated cheese added sharpness and saltiness; tasters preferred the flavor of traditional Parmesan. A teaspoon of lemon juice contributed some necessary freshness. A small amount of sugar prevented our pesto from tasting overly acidic.

After processing the garlic, tomatoes, cheese, walnuts, and sugar, we slowly added the olive oil, lemon juice, and water—this ensured that our pesto was nicely emulsified and pleasantly smooth. For the pasta shape, tasters preferred farfalle, which offered nooks and crannies that the pesto could cling to.

With a minimum of effort, we had created a bold, bright, summery pesto—but we could make it anytime, not just when it was hot and sunny outside.

Pasta with Sun-Dried Tomato Pesto

SERVES 2

We prefer to buy sun-dried tomatoes that are packed in oil, rather than those that are packaged just dried. Not only do they have more flavor, but their texture is softer and they are more easily incorporated into the pesto. Other pasta shapes can be substituted for the farfalle; however, their cup measurements may vary (see page 82).

- 1 garlic clove, unpeeled
- ⅓ cup oil-packed sun-dried tomatoes, rinsed, patted dry, and chopped coarse
- ¼ cup grated Parmesan cheese, plus extra for serving
- 2 tablespoons walnuts, toasted
- ¼ teaspoon sugar
   Salt and pepper
- ¼ cup water
- 3 tablespoons extra-virgin olive oil
- 1 teaspoon lemon juice
- 6 ounces (2½ cups) farfalle

1. Toast garlic in 8-inch skillet over medium heat, shaking pan occasionally, until fragrant and color of clove deepens slightly, about 7 minutes. Let garlic cool slightly, then peel and chop.

2. Process garlic, tomatoes, Parmesan, walnuts, sugar, and ⅛ teaspoon salt in food processor until smooth, about 30 seconds, scraping down sides of bowl as needed. With processor running, slowly drizzle in water, oil, and lemon juice until incorporated, about 30 seconds.

3. Meanwhile, bring 4 quarts water to boil in large pot. Add pasta and 1 tablespoon salt and cook, stirring often, until al dente. Reserve ½ cup cooking water, then drain pasta and return it to pot. Add pesto to pasta and toss to combine. Season with salt and pepper to taste and add reserved cooking water as needed to adjust consistency. Serve with extra Parmesan.

LINGUINE WITH FRESH CLAM SAUCE

TOO OFTEN PASTA WITH CLAM SAUCE IS A SOGGY mess of canned clams tossed with overcooked pasta. We knew we could do better, especially if we used fresh clams.

First, we needed to identify the best clams for the job. In Italy, tiny clams are often used for this dish, but these are hard to find stateside. Instead of mail-ordering our mollusks, we looked for another variety and hit upon littlenecks, which are slightly larger than the traditional clams used in Italy. We steamed them, which took mere minutes, and were thrilled by their sweet, briny flavor. Clearly we were on the right track.

To find out if any other clams would work, we also tried larger cherrystones and giant quahogs, which we had to chop into pieces after steaming. The cherrystones worked just as well as the littlenecks, but the quahogs were a flop. No matter how long or briefly we cooked them, they were tough, and they lacked the distinctive, fresh brininess of the other clams. Littlenecks and cherrystones were the clear winners for our clam sauce; 2 pounds provided just enough clam meat for two servings of pasta.

At this point, we had been steaming the clams in a large saucepan. We decided that using the same pan to build the sauce would keep our procedure streamlined and dirty dishes to a minimum. To give our sauce a savory backbone, we started by sautéing a few aromatics—a shallot and a single clove of garlic were sufficient. A small amount of red pepper flakes added some heat. For earthy complexity, we stirred in a bay leaf.

NOTES FROM THE TEST KITCHEN

BUYING AND STORING CLAMS
When shopping, look for tightly closed clams (some shells may gape slightly but should close when they are tapped) and avoid any that are cracked, broken, or sitting in a puddle of water. They should smell clean, not sour or sulfurous, and the shells should appear moist. Clams should be scrubbed before cooking to get rid of the grit and sand. The best way to store clams is in the refrigerator in a colander of ice set over a bowl; discard any water that accumulates so that the shellfish are never submerged.

LINGUINE WITH FRESH CLAM SAUCE

Now it was time to add the clams and steaming liquid, which would form the base of the sauce. Up to this point, we'd been using water to steam the clams, but there had to be a more flavorful alternative. Clam juice seemed as if it would be overkill; indeed, when we tried it, it gave us an overly salty, briny sauce, especially once the clams had opened and released their juices. White wine worked much better, providing the perfect slightly acidic background. A small amount of butter added richness without weighing down the dish.

To add even more flavor, we stirred in fresh parsley and some dried oregano for depth. But tasters demanded another element, something fresh-tasting and acidic to keep our clam sauce from becoming one-dimensional and overly rich. A single chopped tomato did the trick, brightening the flavor as well as the look of the dish.

We were so satisfied with our efforts that we decided to create a Spanish-inspired variation, combining the clams with spicy chorizo, which added an intense flavor punch and welcome heat. Peppery arugula, stirred in at the end of cooking, added freshness and bright color to the dish.

Linguine with Fresh Clam Sauce

SERVES 2

When shopping for clams, choose the smallest ones you can find. Be sure to scrub the clams thoroughly to get rid of grit and sand before cooking. Note that the clams can be very briny, so be sure to taste the final dish before seasoning with additional salt. See page 82 for a tip on how to measure out long strands of pasta without using a scale.

- 1 tablespoon extra-virgin olive oil
- 1 shallot, minced
- 1 garlic clove, minced
- ⅛ teaspoon red pepper flakes
- 2 pounds littleneck or cherrystone clams, scrubbed
- ¼ cup dry white wine
- 1 bay leaf
- 1 tomato, cored and chopped fine
- 3 tablespoons unsalted butter, cut into ¼-inch pieces
- 2 tablespoons fresh parsley leaves
- ¼ teaspoon dried oregano
   Salt and pepper
- 6 ounces linguine

1. Heat oil in large saucepan over medium-high heat until shimmering. Add shallot and cook until softened, 2 to 3 minutes. Stir in garlic and pepper flakes and cook until fragrant, about 30 seconds. Stir in clams, wine, and bay leaf. Cover and simmer, shaking pan occasionally, until clams begin to open, about 6 minutes.

2. Uncover and continue to simmer until all clams have opened and sauce is slightly reduced, about 2 minutes. Discard any clams that refuse to open and remove bay leaf. (If clams release sand into sauce, remove clams and strain sauce; return sauce and clams to clean pot and continue.) Gently stir in tomato, butter, parsley, and oregano. Continue to cook until butter has melted and tomatoes are heated through, about 1 minute longer. Off heat, season with pepper to taste.

3. Meanwhile, bring 4 quarts water to boil in large pot. Add pasta and 1 tablespoon salt and cook, stirring often, until al dente. Reserve ½ cup cooking water, then drain pasta and return it to pot. Add clam mixture to pasta and toss to combine. Season with salt and pepper to taste and add reserved cooking water as needed to adjust consistency. Serve.

VARIATION

Spanish-Style Linguine with Clams and Chorizo
This pasta is based on the Spanish tradition of combining clams and pork sausage.

Add 2 ounces chorizo sausage, halved lengthwise and cut into ¼-inch half-moons, to oil; cook until lightly browned, then add shallot. Omit parsley and oregano. Before serving, stir in 2 cups coarsely chopped arugula until wilted.

PAD THAI

PAD THAI FOR SMALLER HOUSEHOLDS ALMOST always involves a phone call and a deliveryman. After all, the authentic versions have a mile-long ingredient list that includes at least a few hard-to-find ingredients. But with its mix of flavors and textures, balancing sweet, sour, and spicy with tender noodles, briny shrimp, crisp bean sprouts, and fried egg, we didn't see any reason this exotic, satisfying dish should be written off the menu when cooking for two. We wanted to develop a recipe that was full of authentic flavor but streamlined enough that it would be easy enough to prepare in the for-two home kitchen.

Since pad thai is a noodle dish, we decided to start there. Flat rice noodles, often called rice sticks, the type of noodles used in pad thai, are often only partially cooked, particularly when used in stir-fries. We found three different methods of preparing them: soaking them in room-temperature water, soaking them in hot tap water, and boiling them. We began with boiling, but the drained noodles glued themselves together while waiting in the colander. When we managed to stir-fry them, they wound up soggy and overdone. Noodles soaked in room-temperature water remained fairly stiff, and required a longer cooking time that made the pad thai drier and stickier. Soaking the noodles in hot tap water for about 20 minutes was a little better, but the resulting noodles were still a bit stiff. We finally tried soaking the noodles in water that had been brought to a boil and then removed from the heat. Bingo! Drained, they were loose and separate, and they cooked through easily with stir-frying for a tender yet resilient texture.

Sweet, salty, sour, and spicy are the flavor characteristics of pad thai and none should dominate; they should coexist in harmony. Although the cooking time is short, the ingredient list isn't. Fish sauce supplies a salty-sweet pungency, sugar gives sweetness, the heat comes from ground chiles, vinegar provides acidity, and tamarind rounds out the dish with its fruity, earthy, sweet-tart molasses-tinged flavor. Garlic and sometimes shallots contribute their heady, robust flavors.

With these ingredients in hand, we set off to find out which ones were key to success and how much of each to use to achieve balanced flavor. While we usually rely on 6 ounces of pasta to serve two, the richness of pad thai prompted us to go easy on the noodles; we settled on 4 ounces instead. Two tablespoons of fish sauce and sugar were ideal. One-eighth of a teaspoon of cayenne (many recipes call for Thai chiles, but for the sake of simplicity, we opted not to use them) brought a low, even heat—not a searing burn—and 2 teaspoons of rice vinegar (preferred in pad thai for its mild acidity and relatively complex fermented-grain flavor) greatly vivified the flavors.

Tasters liked the flavor of one garlic clove, and just one small shallot produced a round, full sweetness and depth of flavor. To coax the right character out of

these two aromatics, we cooked them until they were lightly browned; they now tasted mellow, sweet, and mildly toasty.

Tamarind was the most enigmatic ingredient on our list. Tamarind is a fruit that grows as a round brown pod about five inches long and is often sold as a paste (in a hard, flat brick) or as a sticky concentrate. It is central to the unique flavor of pad thai, but we wondered if it was, in fact, essential. Could we replicate the flavor of this specialty ingredient with pantry staples? Since tamarind contributes tartness, as well as a sweetness similar to molasses, we tried substituting

NOTES FROM THE TEST KITCHEN

DEVEINING SHRIMP

1. Hold shelled shrimp between your thumb and forefinger and cut down length of its back, about ⅛ to ¼ inch deep, with sharp paring knife.

2. If shrimp has vein, it will be exposed and can be pulled out easily. Once you have freed vein with tip of knife, just touch knife to paper towel and vein will slip off knife and stick to towel.

ALL ABOUT RICE NOODLES

In Southeast Asia and southern regions of China, rice noodles are used in an array of dishes, including soups, stir-fries, and salads. These delicate noodles are made from rice flour and water, and they come in several different widths from extra-small to extra-large; for our Pad Thai, we prefer a medium-width noodle, similar to linguine in size (about ¼ inch wide). Unlike other pasta, rice noodles should not be boiled; we've learned that they have a tendency to overcook very quickly, resulting in a mushy, sticky mess. Instead, it is best to bring a pot of water to a boil, then remove the pot from the heat and steep the noodles gently in the hot water.

equal parts lime juice and water and increasing the sugar slightly. This mixture came close to replacing the tamarind's acidity, but the complex sweetness was missing. What if we switched from granulated sugar to molasses-flavored brown sugar? Light brown sugar was promising, but not quite rich enough. Dark brown sugar gave us just the flavor we were seeking; increasing the amount by half a tablespoon provided even fuller, richer flavor.

The other ingredients in pad thai are sautéed shrimp, scrambled eggs, chopped peanuts, bean sprouts, and scallions. For more textural intrigue and to achieve authentic pad thai flavor, dried shrimp and Thai salted preserved radish are often used, as well. For our pad thai for two, however, we felt that the sautéed shrimp and fish sauce contributed all the salty "shrimpness" we needed—dried shrimp seemed unnecessary. Ditto for the preserved radish, a specialty product that adds piquant, savory crunch. Since we already had the crunch of bean sprouts and peanuts, we figured we had the texture angle covered.

All that was left to finish the pad thai was a trio of garnishes. After mixing some scallion greens into the noodles, we reserved the rest to sprinkle on top with more chopped peanuts and some fresh cilantro. Easy to prep and even faster to cook, our streamlined pad thai for two was an exotic break from the ordinary.

Pad Thai

SERVES 2

We prefer the rich molasses flavor of dark brown sugar in this recipe, but you can substitute light brown sugar in a pinch. Because this dish cooks very quickly, it is important to have everything prepared and within easy reach at the stovetop when you begin cooking.

SAUCE

- 3 tablespoons lime juice
- 3 tablespoons water
- 2½ tablespoons dark brown sugar
- 2 tablespoons fish sauce
- 1½ tablespoons vegetable oil
- 2 teaspoons rice vinegar
- ⅛ teaspoon cayenne pepper

NOODLES, SHRIMP, AND GARNISH

- 4 ounces (¼-inch-wide) dried flat rice noodles
- 2 tablespoons vegetable oil
- 6 ounces medium shrimp (41 to 50 per pound), peeled and deveined
  Salt
- 1 small shallot, minced
- 1 garlic clove, minced
- 1 large egg, lightly beaten
- 2 ounces (1 cup) bean sprouts
- 2 tablespoons chopped unsalted roasted peanuts, plus extra for garnish
- 2 scallions, green parts only, sliced thin
- 2 tablespoons fresh cilantro leaves

1. FOR THE SAUCE: Whisk all ingredients together in bowl and set aside.

2. FOR THE NOODLES, SHRIMP, AND GARNISH: Bring 4 quarts water to boil in large pot. Remove boiling water from heat, add rice noodles, and let stand, stirring occasionally, until noodles are just tender, about 10 minutes. Drain noodles and set aside.

3. Heat 1 tablespoon oil in 10-inch nonstick skillet over medium-high heat until just smoking. Add shrimp and pinch salt and cook, stirring occasionally, until shrimp are opaque and browned around edges, 2 to 3 minutes; transfer shrimp to plate.

4. Add remaining 1 tablespoon oil, shallot, garlic, and pinch salt to now-empty skillet, return to medium heat, and cook, stirring constantly, until light golden brown, about 1½ minutes. Stir in egg and cook, stirring constantly, until scrambled and barely moist, about 20 seconds.

5. Add drained rice noodles and toss to combine. Add sauce, increase heat to medium-high, and cook, tossing constantly, until noodles are evenly coated, about 1 minute.

6. Add cooked shrimp, bean sprouts, peanuts, and one-half of scallions and continue to cook, tossing constantly, until noodles are tender, about 2 minutes. (If not yet tender, add 2 tablespoons water to skillet and continue to cook until tender.) Transfer noodles to serving platter, sprinkle with remaining scallions, cilantro, and extra peanuts, and serve.

SHRIMP FRA DIAVOLO

ITS NAME MEANS "BROTHER DEVIL" IN ITALIAN, SO it should come as no surprise that shrimp fra diavolo is intensely spicy, thanks to a generous helping of red pepper flakes. But there's more to it than that. The complexly flavored sauce also gets its bold, brash attitude from a combination of wine, garlic, and tomatoes. Tender, briny shrimp contribute a sweetness that balances the heat and spice, and al dente pasta provides the perfect neutral carrier for all of the flavors. Even though shrimp fra diavolo is usually relegated to restaurant fare,

NOTES FROM THE TEST KITCHEN

HOW TO FLAMBÉ SHRIMP

1. Remove skillet from heat and, using long kitchen match, carefully ignite cognac.

2. Once cognac is ignited, shake skillet back and forth until flames go out completely.

THE BEST SPAGHETTI

Spaghetti makes a versatile partner for just about any type of sauce. Plus, it promises a cheap dinner—or, at least, it used to. When we recently checked out brands at the supermarket, we saw a few boxes priced around a dollar, while others cost four times that. We recently sampled eight brands of spaghetti to find out if we had to spend more money for great pasta. After cooking and tasting six Italian imports and two domestic brands dressed simply with olive oil and tossed with a tomato sauce, we found our winner. Our favorite spaghetti—and also one of the two cheapest brands we tasted (less than $2 a pound)—was an Italian import. Tasters preferred **De Cecco Spaghetti (No. 12)** for its "clean wheat flavor" and "firm" strands with "good chew."

it's not terribly complicated to make and takes less than 30 minutes to prepare from start to finish. Given its quick-cooking nature and lively flavor profile, we thought this bold dish would make the perfect addition to our pasta-for-two roster.

We began by testing a number of recipes but were disappointed when they all came up short, lacking depth and unity of flavor. The shrimp contributed little to the overall flavor of the sauce, serving merely as a bulky, lifeless garnish. The same held true for the garlic, the flavor of which was often unpleasantly sharp, even acrid. In our ideal fra diavolo, not only would the shrimp themselves be firm, sweet, and well seasoned, but they would commit their flavor to the sauce as well.

After just a few tests, it was clear that the way the shrimp were cooked had a tremendous effect not just on their texture and flavor but also on the overall flavor of the sauce. In most fra diavolo recipes we encountered, plain raw shrimp were added to the almost-finished sauce; basically, the shrimp braised in the sauce. While these shrimp remained tender, tasters agreed that their flavor was barely developed. We tried seasoning the shrimp with olive oil, salt, and red pepper flakes, searing them quickly in a very hot pan, then adding them to the sauce just before serving. Every taster noted that the shrimp themselves—and therefore the sauce—had a stronger, more unified flavor. The sear also improved the flavor of the red pepper flakes, as they now contributed an earthy, toasty note to the sauce in addition to pure heat.

Though the searing helped, we wanted to coax still more flavor from the shrimp. Several of the fra diavolo recipes we consulted included cognac. We added cognac to the pan with the seared shrimp and flambéed it for a minute until the flame died down. The combined forces of cognac and flame made a big difference in the flavor. Not only did many tasters detect the spirit's own complexity, but also they felt that the shrimp boasted more flavor. This sauce had substantial backbone, something that had been missing from the earlier recipes we tried.

In addition to serious heat from the red pepper flakes, shrimp fra diavolo typically includes a hefty dose of garlic. We wanted enough garlic to make the devil proud, and our tasters agreed. We made our sauce time and again, going up one clove at a time. In the end, we preferred a sauce that packed in a whopping six cloves

SHRIMP FRA DIAVOLO

of garlic. To ensure that our big dose of garlic didn't add bitterness to the sauce, we sautéed it slowly over low heat until it became golden, sticky, mellow, and nutty. Now there was no trace of bitterness, and the sauce acquired a sweeter, deeper dimension. We reserved a tablespoon of raw garlic to add to the sauce at the end of cooking, along with a bit of olive oil. Tasters appreciated the bright, fruity flavor of these raw ingredients, which complemented the rich, potent notes of the sauce.

Finally, we focused on the last two major components of fra diavolo: tomatoes and wine. We tested canned diced tomatoes (drained of excess liquid), canned crushed tomatoes, canned whole tomatoes (which we chopped by hand), and fresh tomatoes. The winner was drained canned diced tomatoes; tasters preferred their solid texture to the saucier consistency of crushed tomatoes, and fresh tomatoes were too inconsistent to consider. Tasters also preferred white wine over red wine and white vermouth, and we found that adding a little bit of sugar helped prevent the sauce from tasting too acidic due to the tomatoes and wine.

At last, our shrimp fra diavolo was perfect—and we didn't have to make a deal with the devil to get there.

Shrimp Fra Diavolo
SERVES 2

This pasta has some devilish heat to it; for more heat, add more red pepper flakes. Before flambéing, be sure to roll up long shirtsleeves, tie back long hair, and turn off the exhaust fan and any lit burners; see page 95 for more information on flambéing. See page 82 for a tip on how to measure out long strands of pasta without using a scale.

    8   ounces large shrimp (26 to 30 per pound),
        peeled and deveined
    ½   teaspoon red pepper flakes
        Salt and pepper
    3   tablespoons extra-virgin olive oil
    2   tablespoons cognac or brandy
    6   garlic cloves, minced
    1   (14.5-ounce) can diced tomatoes, drained
    ½   cup dry white wine
    ¼   teaspoon sugar
    2   tablespoons minced fresh parsley
    6   ounces linguine or spaghetti

1. Toss shrimp with ¼ teaspoon pepper flakes and ¼ teaspoon salt. Heat 1 tablespoon oil in 10-inch skillet over medium-high heat until just smoking. Add shrimp to skillet in single layer and cook, without stirring, until bottoms of shrimp turn spotty brown, about 30 seconds.

2. Remove skillet from heat and stir shrimp. Off heat, sprinkle cognac evenly over shrimp and let warm through, about 5 seconds. Wave lit match over skillet until cognac ignites, then shake skillet to distribute flames. When flames subside, transfer shrimp to bowl and set aside. Let skillet cool for about 2 minutes.

3. Add 1 tablespoon oil and one-half of garlic to cooled skillet and cook over low heat, stirring often, until garlic foams and is sticky and straw-colored, about 5 minutes.

4. Stir in remaining ¼ teaspoon pepper flakes, tomatoes, wine, sugar, and ¼ teaspoon salt. Bring to simmer and cook until thickened, 3 to 5 minutes. Stir in remaining garlic, parsley, and reserved shrimp with any accumulated juices and continue to simmer until shrimp are heated through, about 1 minute longer.

5. Meanwhile, bring 4 quarts water to boil in large pot. Add pasta and 1 tablespoon salt and cook, stirring often, until al dente. Reserve ½ cup cooking water, then drain pasta and return it to pot. Add shrimp sauce and remaining 1 tablespoon oil to pasta and toss to combine. Season with salt and pepper to taste and add reserved cooking water as needed to adjust consistency. Serve.

PENNE WITH CHICKEN AND VEGETABLES

FOR A QUICK WEEKNIGHT MEAL, NOTHING BEATS pasta for ease of preparation. Add some chicken, vegetables, and a flavorful sauce and you've got an instant hit on your hands. Penne with chicken and mushrooms is one classic option, and when done right, the result is a lightly sauced, perfectly cooked, flavorful penne supper. Unfortunately, this simple combination often produces disappointing results—dry chicken, bland pasta, and slimy mushrooms blanketed by a flavorless cream sauce. We wanted to develop a foolproof method for preparing penne with chicken and mushrooms, and, to keep things streamlined, we wanted to see if we could use just one skillet to do it.

We started by figuring out the best cooking method for the chicken. Right off the bat, we decided that an 8-ounce boneless, skinless chicken breast was the best choice for this dish; it's both easy to prepare and ideal for quick weeknight meals. We considered various cooking methods, including poaching and sautéing. Given that we planned on building our sauce in the same pan, we went with sautéing—it left some browned bits, also known as fond, behind on the bottom of the pan, which

would contribute deep, savory flavor to our sauce later on. After slicing the chicken thinly, we added it to the pan and cooked it over high heat for just a few minutes. When the chicken was just cooked through, we set it aside until the sauce and pasta were ready (then we would stir it back in to warm it).

For the sauce, we started with a simple base of chicken broth and water. After a number of tests, we learned that 2½ cups of liquid was the right amount to cook 2 cups of penne. Cooking the pasta right in the sauce was beneficial to both: The starches released by the pasta worked to thicken the sauce, while the starchy surface of the pasta absorbed maximum flavor from the sauce. We found that a vigorous simmer was necessary to properly cook the pasta and reduce the liquid to the ideal saucy consistency. A little white wine, added to the skillet before stirring in the broth and water, provided a balanced acidic note. We also tested adding cream, but tasters favored a lighter, cleaner sauce. Next, we focused on the mushrooms.

All too often, mushrooms are piled up and cooked with insufficient heat, causing them to steam, rather than brown. Determined to avoid this pitfall, we cranked the heat to medium-high and kept the mushroom amount small enough (4 ounces for two servings) to allow them to spread out and make use of the skillet's surface area. They had softened sufficiently after about five minutes, but we continued to cook them until they had browned. In addition to giving the mushrooms flavor and texture, the fond, once deglazed with white wine, lent flavor to the whole dish.

With the chicken, mushrooms, and pasta perfectly cooked, we considered a few last tweaks to the sauce. A generous amount of garlic and a touch of red pepper flakes rounded out the flavors, and a handful of rich, pungent Gorgonzola added sharp flavor that contrasted nicely with the hearty mushrooms and gave our sauce a slightly creamy texture. Satisfied with our one-dish approach to this classic, we moved on to develop some interesting and flavorful variations.

For a brightly flavored dinner that whisked us away to the Mediterranean, we included sweet cherry tomatoes and briny kalamatas. We quartered the cherry tomatoes to help them release their juice and flavor the sauce. A second take on our penne with chicken dish combined

---

NOTES FROM THE TEST KITCHEN

SLICING CHICKEN BREASTS THINLY

1. To slice chicken breasts thinly, cut them across grain into ¼-inch-wide strips that are 1½ to 2 inches long. Cut center pieces in half so that they are same length as end pieces.

2. For tenderloins, cut them on diagonal to produce pieces of meat that are roughly same size.

THE BEST WINE OPENER

Lever-style corkscrews are designed to use leverage rather than muscle power to pull the cork, but many such models are unwieldy and bulky. We wanted a wine opener that could cleanly and effortlessly remove any type of cork, took minimal cajoling (the fewer steps, the better), and fit neatly in a drawer. So we gathered 17 models ranging in price from $8 to $100—besides lever-style openers, we also included waiter's corkscrews (in which the lever rests on one side of the lip of the bottle), twisting pull models, and winged designs—and opened cases of wine until we narrowed our choices to seven. After wine-opening novices and experts alike test-drove our finalists on both natural and synthetic corks, the sleek, economical, lever-style **Oggi Nautilus Corkscrew**, $24.99, was dubbed the premier pick.

peppery arugula, crunchy toasted pine nuts, and a healthy dose of lemon juice for a fresh, light pasta supper.

Our reinvented penne, chicken, and vegetable dinners were so flavorful and so easy, the only problem we had left was figuring out which one to make first.

Penne with Chicken, Mushrooms, and Gorgonzola

SERVES 2

Other pasta shapes can be substituted for the penne; however, their cup measurements may vary (see page 82). Make sure the pasta cooks at a rapid simmer or the pasta will overcook before the sauce is reduced.

- 1 (8-ounce) boneless, skinless chicken breast, trimmed and sliced thin
  Salt and pepper
- 2 tablespoons olive oil
- 4 ounces white mushrooms, trimmed and quartered
- 3 garlic cloves, minced
- 1 teaspoon minced fresh oregano or ¼ teaspoon dried
  Pinch red pepper flakes
- ½ cup dry white wine
- 1½ cups low-sodium chicken broth
- 1 cup water
- 6 ounces (2 cups) penne
- 1 ounce Gorgonzola cheese, crumbled (¼ cup), plus extra for serving
- 1 tablespoon unsalted butter
- 1 tablespoon minced fresh parsley

1. Pat chicken dry with paper towels and season with salt and pepper. Heat 1 tablespoon oil in 10-inch non-stick skillet over medium-high heat until just smoking. Add chicken, break up any clumps, and cook, without stirring, until beginning to brown, about 1 minute. Stir chicken and continue to cook until just cooked through, 1 to 2 minutes longer. Transfer chicken to bowl, cover, and set aside.

2. Add remaining 1 tablespoon oil and mushrooms to now-empty skillet and cook over medium heat, stirring occasionally, until mushrooms have released their moisture and are golden brown, 7 to 10 minutes. Stir in garlic, oregano, and pepper flakes and cook until

fragrant, about 30 seconds. Stir in wine, scraping up any browned bits, and cook until nearly evaporated, about 2 minutes.

3. Stir in broth, water, pasta, and ¼ teaspoon salt and bring to rapid simmer. Cover and simmer vigorously, stirring often, until pasta is tender and sauce is thickened, 12 to 15 minutes.

4. Reduce heat to low and stir in cooked chicken with any accumulated juices, Gorgonzola, and butter. Cook, tossing gently, until pasta is well coated with sauce, 1 to 2 minutes. Season with salt and pepper to taste and sprinkle with parsley. Serve with extra Gorgonzola.

VARIATIONS

Penne with Chicken, Cherry Tomatoes, and Olives
Substitute 1 small finely chopped onion for mushrooms and cook until softened, 5 to 7 minutes. Add 6 ounces quartered cherry tomatoes and ¼ cup coarsely chopped pitted kalamata olives to pasta along with cooked chicken. Substitute 1 ounce (½ cup) grated Parmesan cheese for Gorgonzola.

Penne with Chicken, Arugula, Pine Nuts, and Lemon
Substitute 1 small finely chopped onion for mushrooms and cook until softened, 5 to 7 minutes. Add 3 ounces (3 cups) baby arugula to pasta along with cooked chicken. Substitute 1 ounce (½ cup) grated Parmesan cheese for Gorgonzola. Stir 2 tablespoons toasted pine nuts, ¼ teaspoon grated lemon zest, and 1½ teaspoons lemon juice into pasta along with parsley.

CHICKEN RIGGIES

HAVING SUCCESSFULLY DEVELOPED A RECIPE FOR chicken with pasta in a light, bright sauce, we looked to create another, but this time we wanted it to have a bold, potent flavor profile. That's when we came across Chicken Riggies. This dish hails from Utica, New York, where it is widely celebrated (including at an annual festival called "RiggieFest"). Uticans brim with home-town pride for this Italian-American specialty: rigatoni with tender chicken and vegetables in a spicy, creamy tomato sauce. We thought this dish was just what we were after, and we looked to scale it down for two but keep its big, bold flavors completely intact.

We gathered a number of recipes for riggies and headed into the test kitchen. The better recipes offered a cascade of bold flavors—garlic, onions, spicy pickled peppers, and Pecorino Romano cheese—enriched with cream and paired with bites of tender, juicy chicken breasts and al dente pasta. The disappointing recipes suffered from rubbery or dried-out chicken and desiccated vegetables in an overreduced and underwhelming cream sauce.

Looking at our test recipes again, we noticed that every one was essentially the same: Brown the chicken, then add the vegetables and sauce ingredients, and simmer the sauce for up to an hour—with the chicken and vegetables sitting in it. This explained why the chicken was often rubbery and the vegetables mushy. The remedy for both problems was less cooking time. Eight minutes proved perfect for tenderizing the mushrooms and bell pepper without obliterating their texture. To spare them from stewing in the sauce, we removed them from the pan after cooking and added them back in at the very end. A similar treatment for the chicken—brown it and remove it from the pan—improved its texture as well.

It was time to move on to the basics of the sauce. Since there are no tomato chunks in riggies, we skipped canned diced tomatoes and cycled through tomato puree, tomato paste, plain canned sauce, jarred marinara sauce, and crushed tomatoes. Tasters preferred the last for their bright flavor and rustic texture, but crushed tomatoes are usually available only in 28-ounce cans, and one can resulted in too much sauce for two. Instead, we used a small can of whole tomatoes, which we pulsed in the food processor; now our sauce had just the right texture and consistency.

Many recipes include white wine or sherry, and some recommend chicken broth, but tasters voted them off the ingredient list because they muted the other flavors too much. For the aromatics, one small onion contributed sweetness, and two cloves of garlic and some dried oregano, plus a hefty dose of grated Pecorino Romano cheese, gave the sauce authentic Italian flavor. Some versions of riggies included olives, which tasters liked, so we included ⅓ cup of halved kalamatas.

Hot pickled cherry peppers are essential in riggies for both heat and vinegary tang. A single tablespoon of chopped peppers lent just enough punch for two servings, and we reinforced their telltale flavor by introducing a mere tablespoon of the pepper brine. A relatively conservative ⅓ cup of heavy cream balanced the high-impact ingredients without turning the dish into a full-fledged cream sauce.

But given such a flavorful sauce, the chicken was fading into the background. Spying the jar of cherry peppers on the counter, we got the idea of making a marinade with some of the brine to infuse the chicken with more flavor. We added salt and a little olive oil to a single tablespoon of brine, tossed in the chicken, and waited. A modest 30 minutes in the briny, salty vinaigrette hugely improved the chicken's flavor. The chicken was so flavorful, in fact, that we questioned the extra step of browning it. In the end, we found that poaching the marinated chicken in the sauce at the end of cooking kept it extra-tender and tasting great.

Chicken Riggies

SERVES 2

If you find only sweet cherry peppers, add ¼ to ½ teaspoon red pepper flakes with the garlic in step 2. Other pasta shapes can be substituted for the rigatoni; however, their cup measurements may vary (see page 82). You can substitute Parmesan cheese for the Pecorino Romano cheese.

- 1 (8-ounce) boneless, skinless chicken breast, cut into 1-inch pieces
- 1 tablespoon jarred sliced hot cherry peppers, chopped fine, plus 2 tablespoons cherry pepper brine
- 2 tablespoons olive oil
  Salt and pepper
- 1 (14.5-ounce) can whole peeled tomatoes
- 4 ounces white mushrooms, trimmed and quartered
- 1 red bell pepper, stemmed, seeded, and cut into 1-inch pieces
- 1 small onion, cut into 1-inch pieces
- 2 garlic cloves, minced
- ¾ teaspoon dried oregano

CHICKEN RIGGIES

1/3 cup heavy cream

1/3 cup pitted kalamata olives, halved lengthwise

4 ounces (1½ cups) rigatoni

1 ounce Pecorino Romano cheese, grated (½ cup)

1. Combine chicken, 1 tablespoon cherry pepper brine, 2 teaspoons oil, and ¼ teaspoon salt in zipper-lock bag and refrigerate for 30 minutes or up to 1 hour. Pulse tomatoes in food processor until coarsely chopped and no large pieces remain, about 6 pulses.

2. Heat 2 teaspoons oil in 10-inch skillet over medium-high heat until shimmering. Stir in mushrooms, bell pepper, and ⅛ teaspoon salt and cook until browned, 8 to 10 minutes. Transfer vegetables to bowl; set aside. Add remaining 2 teaspoons oil and onion to now-empty skillet and cook over medium heat until softened, about 5 minutes. Stir in cherry peppers, garlic, and oregano and cook until fragrant, about 30 seconds.

3. Add processed tomatoes, cream, and ⅛ teaspoon pepper and bring to boil. Reduce heat to medium and simmer, stirring occasionally, until sauce is very thick, 10 to 15 minutes. Stir in chicken and reserved vegetables, cover, and simmer until chicken is cooked through, 5 to 7 minutes. Off heat, add remaining 1 tablespoon cherry pepper brine and olives. Cover to keep warm.

4. Meanwhile, bring 4 quarts water to boil in large pot. Add pasta and 1 tablespoon salt and cook, stirring often, until al dente. Reserve ½ cup cooking water, then drain pasta and return it to pot. Add sauce and Pecorino to pasta and toss to combine. Season with salt and pepper to taste and add reserved cooking water as needed to adjust consistency. Serve.

NOTES FROM THE TEST KITCHEN

THE SECRET TO CHICKEN RIGGIES
Jarred cherry peppers give the sauce in Chicken Riggies its tangy flavor. For more spicy tang, we marinate the chicken in olive oil and cherry pepper brine.

PASTA ROLL-UPS WITH CHICKEN

ONE OF THE HEADACHES OF MAKING MANICOTTI IS needing to boil, cool, and then stuff the pasta tubes. At some point during the process, some tubes inevitably stick together or tear, forcing you to start the time-consuming process over again with more pasta (or cook—and waste—more than you need). Scale it down for two, and you still have the same tedious task to deal with. Wanting to create an easier approach to stuffed pasta for two, we started by thinking outside the tube. We would use softened no-boil noodles to roll, rather than stuff, our filling. Then, since we were already turning manicotti on its head, we decided to swap the traditional red sauce for a rich (but not heavy) white sauce and the simple cheese filling for a more substantial chicken filling.

We started with the filling. Quick-cooking and mild enough to pair with a variety of ingredients, boneless, skinless chicken breast was our best bet. Since we would be making a rich sauce and stuffing the roll-ups with cheese, the richness of dark thigh meat would be overkill. We knew that a single 8-ounce breast would provide enough meat for two servings, but how should we cook it? For optimal moistness and flavor, poaching the chicken seemed the way to go. We went a step further in building flavor by poaching the chicken in low-sodium chicken broth. In addition to being fast and easy (the chicken was done in about 12 minutes), this method gave us flavorful, tender chicken, which we could assemble into portions as we pleased. Another bonus of this method was that the leftover poaching broth, infused with flavor by the chicken, gave us the perfect base for our sauce.

But before we could jump ahead to the sauce, we had to finish the filling. For the cheese, we knew we wanted something more intensely flavored than ricotta to pair with the chicken, so we tested a few possibilities. Gorgonzola was too overpowering, and fontina was too dull and grainy. Goat cheese, however, was perfect. It was more flavorful than ricotta but still creamy, and we found that its flavor was nicely brightened by the addition of lemon zest and juice. Some briny olives sharpened the goat cheese and lent some bite. We tried black and green olives and quickly discovered that the black olives turned the filling an unappealing purple hue. Luckily, tasters were in favor of the cleaner flavor of the green olives anyway. Some chopped fresh basil added distinctive Mediterranean flair and finished the filling perfectly.

Next we addressed the sauce. With the reserved poaching broth ready to go, we had the base of a classic French sauce called velouté, which is basically roux-thickened broth. Deciding to start bare-bones and build the flavor of the sauce as needed, we made a roux by cooking equal parts butter and flour. We then whisked in the reserved broth and some heavy cream and simmered until thickened. The sauce was rich and appropriately clingy, but—no surprise—it tasted a little dull. White wine cut the richness and started building depth. For more complexity, we added minced shallot and garlic (sautéing them in the butter before adding the flour). After stirring some of the sauce into our filling to both moisten and bind it, we turned to assembling our casserole.

We briefly soaked no-boil noodles in boiling water to make them pliable before shaping. Then we mounded the chicken filling on one end of the pasta and rolled the pasta around it (like a sushi roll). This method kept the chicken in uniform pieces and helped the filling stay moist. We covered the pasta with the remaining sauce and baked it until the noodles were fully softened and the filling was hot throughout. Though the overall flavor was spot-on, the filling was separated and loose and lacked cohesion. To help bind our filling together, we tried adding some mozzarella, which proved key to marrying the ingredients.

Baking the casserole took some finesse, as the bright and subtle flavors of the filling were easily killed with extended stints in the oven. After some experimentation, the key proved to be using a low-heat/high-heat method. We baked the casserole, covered, at 350 degrees until it just started to bubble around the edges. We then removed the cover and quickly broiled the casserole to brown the top. This last technique was the final touch needed to perfect our fresh take on stuffed pasta.

Our pasta roll-ups were a new take on traditional manicotti, but they were every bit as flavorful and satisfying as the original.

Pasta Roll-Ups with Chicken and Goat Cheese
SERVES 2

We prefer Barilla no-boil lasagna noodles for their delicate texture that resembles fresh pasta. It's important not to overbake this dish; be sure to remove the casserole from the oven once the sauce begins to bubble around the edges.

CHICKEN AND SAUCE

 1 (8-ounce) boneless, skinless chicken breast, trimmed
1¾ cups low-sodium chicken broth
 2 tablespoons unsalted butter
 2 shallots, minced
 1 garlic clove, minced
2½ tablespoons all-purpose flour
 2 tablespoons dry white wine
 ½ cup heavy cream
    Salt and pepper

FILLING AND NOODLES

 4 ounces goat cheese, crumbled (1 cup)
 2 ounces whole-milk mozzarella cheese, shredded (½ cup)
 ¼ teaspoon grated lemon zest plus 1 teaspoon juice
    Salt and pepper
 3 tablespoons chopped fresh basil
 2 tablespoons chopped pitted green olives
 6 no-boil lasagna noodles
 ¼ cup grated Parmesan cheese

1. FOR THE CHICKEN AND SAUCE: Adjust oven rack to middle position and heat oven to 350 degrees. Combine chicken and broth in medium saucepan, cover, and simmer over medium heat until chicken registers 160 degrees, 12 to 18 minutes, flipping chicken halfway through cooking.

2. Transfer chicken to plate and pour liquid into measuring cup. Let chicken cool slightly, then, using two forks, shred meat into bite-size pieces.

3. Wipe saucepan dry, add butter, and melt over medium heat. Add shallots and cook until softened, 2 to 3 minutes. Stir in garlic and cook until fragrant, about 30 seconds. Stir in flour and cook for 1 minute. Slowly whisk in wine and simmer until nearly evaporated, about 30 seconds.

4. Gradually whisk in reserved broth and cream and simmer, whisking often, until sauce is thickened and measures about 1⅔ cups, 2 to 4 minutes. Off heat, season with salt and pepper to taste, then cover to keep warm.

5. FOR THE FILLING AND NOODLES: In large bowl, combine goat cheese, mozzarella, lemon zest and juice, ⅛ teaspoon salt, and ¼ teaspoon pepper until uniform. Gradually stir ½ cup sauce into cheese mixture, then fold in shredded chicken, 2 tablespoons basil, and olives; set aside.

6. Fill large bowl halfway with boiling water. Slip noodles into water, one at a time, and let soak until pliable, about 5 minutes, separating noodles with tip of knife to prevent sticking. Remove noodles from water and place in single layer on clean kitchen towels.

7. Spread ½ cup sauce on bottom of 9 by 5-inch loaf pan. Mound ¼ cup chicken-cheese mixture evenly on bottom of each noodle and compact into tidy log. Roll noodle up around filling and lay seam side down in baking dish. Spoon remaining sauce evenly over filled noodles, covering pasta completely.

8. Cover pan tightly with aluminum foil and bake until edges are just bubbling, about 30 minutes, rotating pan halfway through baking. Remove pan from oven. Adjust oven rack 6 inches from broiler element and

heat broiler. Remove foil from baking dish, sprinkle pasta with Parmesan, and broil until top is spotty brown, 3 to 5 minutes. Let casserole cool for 10 minutes, then sprinkle with remaining 1 tablespoon basil. Serve.

VARIATION

Pasta Roll-Ups with Chicken, Sun-Dried Tomatoes, and Pine Nuts

Substitute 2 tablespoons oil-packed sun-dried tomatoes, rinsed, patted dry, and chopped fine, for olives. Add 2 tablespoons toasted pine nuts to filling along with chicken.

CLASSIC PORK RAGU

THOUGH MOST FOLKS THINK A HEARTY, STICK-TO-your-ribs meat sauce involves numerous ingredients and hours spent getting them ready for simmering, there's a simpler, more rustic alternative favored by many Italian cooks that starts with just canned tomatoes and a stray piece of meat. The meat (often a pork chop or two) is browned, the fat drained, and the sauce built in the empty pan with the tomatoes and just a handful of aromatics and seasonings. Then the browned meat is added back to the sauce to simmer away until it's fall-off-the-bone tender. Finally, the meat is shredded and stirred into the sauce, which is then served over pasta with a good sprinkling of grated cheese. Though the method is simple, the resulting sauce is anything but, full of deep, rich, hearty flavor. We liked the idea of scaling this recipe down for two; it would still deliver big, meaty flavor, but without a ton of work.

The meat is the heart of this recipe, so that's where we began our testing. We tried pork chops from the blade, loin, and sirloin, but even the fattiest chops were dry and tough after braising. We wanted the meat to almost melt when added back to the tomato sauce. We needed a piece of meat with more marbling so that it would not dry out during braising.

We thought about a cut from the shoulder—either picnic or Boston butt—because this part of the pig has more fat than the loin, where most chops come from. The problem with these shoulder roasts was their

---

NOTES FROM THE TEST KITCHEN

MAKING PASTA ROLL-UPS

1. Using spoon, mound ¼ cup chicken-cheese mixture on bottom of each noodle, then compact filling into tidy log.

2. Roll noodle up and around filling, then lay roll-up, seam side down, in single row, in loaf pan.

size; the smallest at the market was 4 pounds—far too much meat for two servings. We considered having the butcher cut a specific amount of meat from one of these large roasts, but this was supposed to be an easy, rustic sauce, and special-ordering was not in the game plan.

Spareribs are fattier than roasts from the shoulder, so we gave them a try. The braised meat from spareribs was better than the Boston butt—it was unctuous and rich. But again, we found that spareribs are sold in an entire rack that weighs 3 or more pounds—which meant we'd have a pile of spareribs left over. Was there a more economical way to scale down this peasant sauce?

Another cruise through the meat aisle at our local grocery store yielded a small packet of country-style ribs. Taken from the backbone, at the juncture of the shoulder and loin, country-style ribs are very flavorful and resilient because of the relatively high amount of fat and connective tissue between the bones. A long, slow simmer at a moderate temperature breaks down the connective tissue, turning it into rich gelatin, which in turn keeps the meat moist. These ribs proved perfect for the dish, and their flavor, in fact, improved the longer they simmered. Since much of the weight of the ribs is due to bone, we found that a 12-ounce portion was perfect, resulting in just enough sauce for two dishes of pasta.

Simmered with a can of drained, processed whole tomatoes (which worked well in our quick tomato sauce, page 81) and flavored with shallot, garlic, rosemary, and red wine, the meaty ribs delivered rich, deep, savory flavor. This long-simmered meat sauce can't be rushed—the cooking time is about 90 minutes, even for our small batch—but it is well worth the (mostly hands-off) wait.

Classic Pork Ragu

SERVES 2

Pork spareribs can be substituted for the country-style ribs. To prevent the sauce from becoming greasy, trim all external fat from the ribs before browning. Other pasta shapes can be substituted for the ziti; however, their cup measurements may vary (see page 82).

1 (28-ounce) can whole peeled tomatoes, drained with ¼ cup juice reserved
12 ounces bone-in country-style pork ribs, trimmed
    Salt and pepper
2 teaspoons olive oil
1 large shallot, minced
2 garlic cloves, minced
1½ teaspoons minced fresh rosemary
½ cup dry red wine
6 ounces (2 cups) ziti
    Grated Pecorino Romano cheese

1. Pulse tomatoes in food processor until coarsely chopped and no large pieces remain, 6 to 8 pulses. Pat ribs dry with paper towels and season with salt and pepper.

2. Heat oil in 10-inch skillet over medium-high heat until just smoking. Brown ribs well on all sides, 8 to 10 minutes; transfer to plate.

3. Add shallot and ¼ teaspoon salt to now-empty skillet and cook over medium heat until softened, 2 to 3 minutes. Stir in garlic and rosemary and cook until fragrant, about 30 seconds. Stir in wine, scraping up any browned bits, and simmer until reduced by half, about 2 minutes.

4. Stir in tomatoes and reserved tomato juice. Nestle browned ribs into sauce, along with any accumulated juices, and bring to gentle simmer. Reduce heat to low, cover, and gently simmer, turning ribs occasionally, until meat is very tender and falling off bones, about 1½ hours.

5. Transfer ribs to plate and let cool slightly. Using 2 forks, shred pork into bite-size pieces, discarding fat and bones. Return shredded meat to sauce, bring to simmer, and cook until heated through and slightly thickened, 2 to 3 minutes. Season with salt and pepper to taste.

6. Meanwhile, bring 4 quarts water to boil in large pot. Add pasta and 1 tablespoon salt and cook, stirring often, until al dente. Reserve ½ cup cooking water, then drain pasta and return it to pot. Add sauce to pasta and toss to combine. Season with salt and pepper to taste and add reserved cooking water as needed to adjust consistency. Serve with Pecorino.

BAKED TORTELLINI

IN THE WORLD OF BAKED PASTA, BAKED TORTELLINI provides an updated spin on the classic casserole. When done right, the result is a sophisticated pasta dish that utilizes flavors and ingredients that are more upscale than those you'd find in most casseroles. We thought this refined, bistro-style fare would make the perfect dressed-up addition to our collection of pasta dishes for two, and we knew the key was matching the delicate flavor of the tortellini with an equally refined sauce and well-chosen add-ins.

NOTES FROM THE TEST KITCHEN

THE BEST PANKO

Light and flaky, panko bread crumbs, which originated in Japan, add big crunch and a neutral flavor to recipes. Once the domain of specialty shops and Asian markets, panko bread crumbs are now available in most supermarkets. We tested four supermarket brands, as a coating for baked chicken and pan-fried pork cutlets, to find the best one. While we couldn't distinguish differences in taste among brands, our test kitchen tasting did reveal differences in texture. Our favorite is **Ian's Panko Bread Crumbs**, which provided a much more substantial crunch than the other brands.

THE BEST TORTELLINI

Though handmade tortellini is delicious, it's quite an undertaking when you're cooking for two. Fortunately, we found a good runner-up in store-bought tortellini, which offers both good flavor and tender texture in a fraction of the time. To find the best one, we recently sampled seven supermarket brands of cheese tortellini, including two refrigerated, two dried, and three frozen. Our winner, surprisingly, was a dried brand, **Barilla Tortellini Three Cheese**. It was praised for a filling that tasters called "creamy," "pungent," and "tangy," thanks to its bold mixture of ricotta, Emmentaler, and Grana Padano cheeses. Another factor in Barilla's win was the texture of the pasta: The delicate wrapper of these petite tortellini was strong enough to contain the filling during boiling, but not overly gummy or prone to blowouts like other brands.

We started with dried tortellini, which the test kitchen prefers over both the frozen and fresh varieties. In taste tests, we've found the dried tortellini offer a flavorful filling and a tender, supple texture. Unlike the unfilled pastas that are used in other pasta casseroles, tortellini don't continue cooking in the oven, so we found that they needed to be fully cooked on top of the stove.

Moving on to the sauce, we wanted something with an indulgent edge but that wasn't too heavy. We started with a combination of chicken broth and heavy cream, which produced a respectable flavor that was neither too rich nor too lean. Thickening the sauce with a little flour was necessary to give it the ability to coat the tortellini and vegetables. Shallots, garlic, fresh thyme, and Parmesan lent robust flavor, but we were still not satisfied. Starting the sauce off by sautéing a little bacon gave it some necessary oomph, but it wasn't until we added white wine that we knew we were getting somewhere. The wine added a mildly acidic note that helped to cut through the bacon and cream without obscuring their flavors, and it gave this sauce a necessary hint of elegance.

With the tortellini and sauce figured out, we still needed to round out the casserole with some vegetables. We wanted to add some interesting flavors yet keep the prep work and cooking to a minimum. Slightly bitter radicchio came to mind. It took only moments to chop half a head of radicchio into bite-size pieces, and it required no precooking—we simply stirred it into the tortellini and sauce before moving the casserole to the oven. There, it would braise in the sauce, and the combination of cream and chicken broth would mellow its bitterness. To offset the radicchio in terms of both flavor and color, we turned to an even more low-maintenance vegetable: peas. We tossed the peas, still frozen, into the pan with the radicchio (we have found that frozen peas are a more reliable choice than fresh in terms of consistent quality).

To bake our tortellini, we divided them between two small gratin dishes, which made for an attractive presentation. But after sampling our mini baked casseroles, we felt they were missing some textural contrast and decided that a crunchy bread crumb topping would be the perfect solution. Instead of dragging out the

BAKED TORTELLINI WITH RADICCHIO, PEAS, AND BACON

food processor just to pulverize a single slice of bread, we substituted panko, the flaky Japanese bread crumbs that are a mainstay in the test kitchen pantry. Tossed with olive oil and sprinkled over the pasta, the panko developed a golden brown color and satisfying crunch that contrasted with the soft texture and richness of the tortellini.

Even though it offered all the homey satisfaction of a baked pasta dish, our baked tortellini was elegant enough to turn any night into a special occasion.

Baked Tortellini with Radicchio, Peas, and Bacon

SERVES 2

You can substitute fresh tortellini if desired. You will need two shallow 2-cup gratin dishes (measuring approximately 9 by 6 inches; see page 3), or you can substitute one 8-inch square baking dish.

¾ cup panko bread crumbs

4 teaspoons olive oil

Salt and pepper

8 ounces dried cheese tortellini

2 slices bacon, chopped fine

2 shallots, minced

3 garlic cloves, minced

1 teaspoon minced fresh thyme

2 tablespoons all-purpose flour

¼ cup white wine

1½ cups low-sodium chicken broth

½ cup heavy cream

1 ounce Parmesan cheese, grated (½ cup)

½ small head radicchio (3 ounces), cored and chopped into ½-inch pieces

½ cup frozen peas

1. Stir panko, 1 tablespoon oil, and pinch salt together in bowl; set aside. Adjust oven rack to middle position and heat oven to 400 degrees.

2. Bring 4 quarts water to boil in large pot. Add tortellini and 1 tablespoon salt and cook, stirring often, until tender. Drain tortellini and return them to pot. Toss tortellini with remaining 1 teaspoon oil and set aside.

3. Meanwhile, cook bacon in 10-inch nonstick skillet over medium heat until crisp, 5 to 7 minutes. Add shallots and cook, stirring occasionally, until softened, 2 to 3 minutes. Add garlic and thyme and cook until fragrant, about 30 seconds. Add flour and cook, stirring constantly, until golden, about 1 minute. Whisk in wine and cook until almost evaporated, about 1 minute. Slowly whisk in broth and cream, bring to simmer, and cook, whisking often, until slightly thickened, 1 to 2 minutes. Off heat, stir in Parmesan and season with salt and pepper to taste.

4. Add sauce, radicchio, and peas to tortellini and toss gently to combine. Divide pasta mixture evenly between two shallow 2-cup gratin dishes (measuring approximately 9 by 6 inches) and sprinkle with panko topping. Bake until topping is browned and crisp, about 15 minutes. Serve.

USE IT UP: RADICCHIO

Radicchio-Apple Slaw

SERVES 2

You can substitute 1 minced small shallot for the scallion. To prep the apples, cut the cored apples into ¼-inch-thick planks, then stack the planks and cut them into thin matchsticks.

½ small head radicchio (3 ounces), halved, cored, and sliced thin

1 Granny Smith apple, cored and cut into 2-inch-long matchsticks

1 scallion, sliced thin

1 tablespoon olive oil

1 tablespoon cider vinegar

1 teaspoon Dijon mustard

Salt and pepper

Sugar

Combine radicchio, apple, and scallion in medium bowl. Whisk oil, vinegar, mustard, pinch salt, pinch pepper, and pinch sugar together in small bowl. Pour over radicchio mixture and toss to coat. Cover and refrigerate for at least 30 minutes or up to 24 hours. Season with salt, pepper, and sugar to taste. Serve.

SKILLET LASAGNA

WITH ITS LAYERS OF GOOEY CHEESE, TENDER PASTA, and flavorful, tomatoey meat sauce, lasagna is a crowd-pleaser that never goes out of style—but the operative word here is *crowd-pleaser*. Most recipes serve six to 10, which means a lot of leftovers for a household of two. Yet we don't think lasagna should be out of the question when you're cooking for two, so we sought a way to scale this dish down but still keep all its comfort-food appeal intact. To up the ante, we decided to do away with the baking dish altogether and see if we could use just one skillet to prepare our scaled-down lasagna.

To keep our lasagna on the stovetop, our plan was simple: We would first brown the meat, then build a flavorful sauce in which to cook our lasagna noodles. Finally, we would add a blend of cheeses (ricotta, Parmesan, and mozzarella are traditional for lasagna) and consider other flavors along the way. We reached for our skillet—a 10-inch pan seemed the right size to hold both sauce and noodles—and headed into the test kitchen.

Most lasagna sauces simmer for hours, giving the ingredients and flavors a chance to blend, but since speed is a key to weeknight dinner success, we decided to keep things simple. We started with just an onion and a clove of garlic for our aromatics; these gave the sauce its depth. Adding meat was a given so that our lasagna would be hearty and satisfying. Half a pound of ground beef worked well; for the best flavor and richness, we selected 85 percent lean ground beef. For a flavor variation, tasters liked a combination of Italian sausage and sweet red pepper.

We next turned to the type of tomatoes we would use in the sauce. We started our tests with tomato puree, but this made a sauce that was too heavy; the pasta sat on top of the sauce and cooked unevenly. Adding a little water created a better medium in which to cook the pasta, but the resulting lasagna was bland. Abandoning tomato puree, we turned to whole peeled tomatoes pulsed briefly in a food processor. This gave the sauce a slightly chunky and substantial texture—and there was just enough liquid to cook the pasta. So that the lasagna noodles would fit in the pan and cook evenly, we had to break them into smaller pieces of about 2 inches in length. Since we wouldn't be able to slice and serve our casserole, this also ensured that it would be easy to serve and eat.

To replicate the cheesiness of traditional lasagna, we stirred in ricotta, shredded mozzarella, and grated Parmesan, but this didn't quite give us the results we were looking for. Once it was mixed in, the sweet creaminess of the ricotta was lost, and the sauce turned into a grainy, pink mess. We had success when we stirred in the mozzarella and Parmesan first, then placed dollops of ricotta on top of the lasagna and covered the pan, allowing the mozzarella to melt and the ricotta to heat through but still remain a distinct element. The ricotta also created an attractive pattern over the top of the dish. A sprinkling of freshly chopped basil further enhanced the look and flavor of our easy, streamlined skillet lasagna for two.

Meaty Skillet Lasagna
SERVES 2

Do not substitute no-boil lasagna noodles for the traditional, curly-edged lasagna noodles here because the no-boil noodles will fall apart. We recommend using either whole-milk or part-skim ricotta here, but do not use nonfat ricotta, which has a very dry texture and bland flavor.

- 1 (28-ounce) can whole peeled tomatoes
- 2 teaspoons olive oil
- 1 small onion, chopped fine
-    Salt and pepper
- 1 garlic clove, minced
-    Pinch red pepper flakes
- 8 ounces 85 percent lean ground beef
- 5 curly-edged lasagna noodles (4¼ ounces), broken into 2-inch lengths
- ¼ cup shredded mozzarella cheese
- 2 tablespoons grated Parmesan cheese
- ⅓ cup ricotta cheese
- 2 tablespoons chopped fresh basil

1. Pulse tomatoes in food processor until coarsely ground and no large pieces remain, 6 to 8 pulses.

2. Heat oil in 10-inch nonstick skillet over medium heat until shimmering. Add onion and ¼ teaspoon salt and cook until softened, about 5 minutes. Stir in garlic and pepper flakes and cook until fragrant, about 30 seconds. Add ground meat and cook, breaking up meat with wooden spoon, until lightly browned and no longer pink, 3 to 5 minutes.

BREAKING LASAGNA NOODLES

To make sure that the lasagna noodles cook through evenly in the skillet and are easier to eat, we break them into 2-inch pieces using our hands. Be sure to use traditional, not no-boil, lasagna noodles here.

3. Scatter pasta over meat, then pour processed tomatoes over pasta. Cover, increase heat to medium-high, and cook, stirring often and adjusting heat to maintain vigorous simmer, until pasta is tender, about 20 minutes.

4. Off heat, stir in one-half of mozzarella and one-half of Parmesan. Season with salt and pepper to taste. Dollop heaping tablespoons of ricotta over noodles, then sprinkle with remaining mozzarella and Parmesan. Cover and let stand off heat until cheese melts, 2 to 4 minutes. Sprinkle with basil and serve.

VARIATION

Skillet Lasagna with Italian Sausage and Bell Pepper

Substitute 8 ounces Italian sausage, casings removed, for ground beef. Add ½ red bell pepper, stemmed, seeded, and chopped coarse, to skillet with onion.

GREEK LASAGNA (PASTITSIO)

WITH OUR ITALIAN-STYLE LASAGNA PERFECTLY scaled down for two, we decided to tackle what's known as "Greek lasagna" next. Pastitsio is a rich casserole composed of pasta, a tomatoey meat sauce (spiced with a little cinnamon), plenty of cheese, and a creamy white sauce, all layered and baked. Sounds great—except that most recipes for pastitsio make enough to feed a small army. We wanted a pastitsio that served just two but preserved all the rich, creamy goodness and flavor of the full-size version.

We dug out a number of Greek cookbooks and tested recipes for pastitsio. To our dismay, we found them bland and heavy rather than rich and satisfying.

The creamy white sauce, or béchamel, was uninspired, the meat sauce greasy and timid, and the pasta bloated and mushy. Certainly we could improve matters.

Béchamel, a dairy-based white sauce thickened with a butter and flour roux, is the defining element of pastitsio. It's often used both to sauce the pasta and as a top layer, with eggs added to give it a firm, light, custardy texture. Since béchamel is usually mildly seasoned, it stood to reason that it was responsible for the blandness we encountered in our test recipes.

To create a lighter, more flavorful béchamel, we started by reconsidering the dairy element. Ultimately, we banished the heavy cream called for in many recipes, because it led to an overly rich sauce; whole milk produced a sauce that was plenty rich. To boost the flavor, we increased the amount of savory, sharp Pecorino Romano cheese, which is the most common substitute for the traditional but hard-to-find Greek *kefalotyri* cheese. Finally, we took a tip from one Greek cookbook we had consulted and added some thick Greek yogurt; just a couple of tablespoons added a welcome tang and extra complexity to the béchamel.

For the custardy béchamel topping, different recipes introduced eggs in various numbers and configurations. We tried making the béchamel using one or two whole eggs, combinations of whole eggs with an extra yolk or two, and yolks alone. The simplest approach of whisking a single whole egg into the béchamel prevailed, providing a casserole cap that was both smooth and firm enough to slice neatly.

Though lamb is traditional in the meat sauce, it can taste gamy and lead to a greasy dish, so we opted for ground beef. The leanest choice in most supermarkets, 93 percent, kept the grease factor well in check; just 6 ounces provided enough heartiness and flavor. Tomatoes are the second sauce ingredient, and plain tomato sauce, with some added tomato paste for punch, won out over canned diced, crushed, and pureed tomatoes. Onions, garlic, oregano, and cinnamon are the requisite flavorings. We employed all four but found that a whole onion was too much and swapped it for a shallot. Adding a few tablespoons of red wine bolstered the acidity enough to balance the richness of the meat sauce and béchamel.

Next, we considered the pasta. Traditional recipes call for long, slender tubes similar to bucatini or perciatelli, but tasters found these hard to eat, favoring short, small shapes instead. Elbow macaroni in particular were easy on the fork and compacted into a tidy layer. Boiling the macaroni to parcook it, then letting it finish in the oven, helped avoid mushy pasta. Since the pasta adds more substance than flavor, we cut the quantity to just 2 ounces, which helped give both the custardy béchamel layer and the meat sauce a stronger presence.

Finally, we assembled our pastitsio in a small baking dish and topped it off with more Pecorino Romano to give the creamy topping a flavor boost. We baked it just long enough to take on an appealing golden crown. After a single bite, it was clear we had restored classic pastitsio to its rich, creamy, satisfying state, and it fed only two—not a whole Greek army.

Pastitsio

SERVES 2

You will need a 3-cup baking dish measuring 7¼ by 5¼ inches for this recipe (see page 3). Be sure to use whole Greek yogurt in this recipe; do not substitute 2 percent or 0 percent Greek yogurt here.

PASTA AND MEAT SAUCE
- 2 ounces (½ cup) elbow macaroni
  Salt and pepper
- 2 teaspoons olive oil
- 1 shallot, minced
- 1 tablespoon tomato paste
- 2 garlic cloves, minced
- ¼ teaspoon dried oregano
- ¼ teaspoon ground cinnamon
- 6 ounces 93 percent lean ground beef
- ¼ cup red wine
- ⅓ cup tomato sauce

BÉCHAMEL SAUCE
- 2 tablespoons unsalted butter
- 2½ tablespoons all-purpose flour
- 1½ cups whole milk
- 1 ounce Pecorino Romano cheese, grated (½ cup)
  Salt and pepper
- 1 large egg
- 2 tablespoons plain Greek yogurt

1. FOR THE PASTA AND MEAT SAUCE: Adjust oven rack to middle position and heat oven to 425 degrees. Bring 4 quarts water to boil in large pot. Add pasta and 1 tablespoon salt and cook until nearly al dente, 3 to 4 minutes. Drain in colander and rinse with cold water until cool. Drain again and transfer to bowl.

2. Meanwhile, heat oil in 10-inch skillet over medium heat until shimmering. Add shallot and cook until softened, 2 to 3 minutes. Stir in tomato paste, garlic, oregano, and cinnamon and cook until paste begins to darken, about 1 minute. Add ground meat and ⅛ teaspoon salt and cook, breaking up meat with wooden spoon, until lightly browned and no longer pink, 3 to 5 minutes.

3. Stir in wine and cook until almost evaporated, about 1 minute. Add tomato sauce and simmer until slightly thickened, 2 to 3 minutes. Season with salt and pepper and transfer to bowl; set aside. Wipe skillet clean.

4. FOR THE BÉCHAMEL SAUCE: Melt butter in now-empty skillet over medium heat. Add flour and cook, stirring constantly, until golden and fragrant, about 1 minute. Slowly whisk in milk and bring to boil. Reduce heat to medium-low and simmer until thickened and reduced to 1 cup, 5 to 7 minutes. Off heat, whisk in ¼ cup Pecorino until smooth. Season with salt and pepper to taste.

5. Stir ⅓ cup béchamel sauce into pasta until combined. Transfer pasta to 7¼ by 5¼-inch baking dish. Beat egg in now-empty pasta bowl until smooth. Whisk 2 tablespoons béchamel into egg to temper, then whisk tempered egg mixture back into remaining béchamel. Stir in yogurt.

6. Spread meat sauce over pasta, then evenly pour béchamel-egg mixture over top. Sprinkle with remaining ¼ cup Pecorino and bake until edges begin to puff and turn golden, 15 to 20 minutes. Let cool for 10 minutes. Serve.

NOTES FROM THE TEST KITCHEN

THE BEST ELBOW MACARONI
With so many brands of elbow macaroni on the market, which one should you buy? Are they all the same? To find out, we rounded up eight contenders and tasted them simply dressed with vegetable oil and in a macaroni and cheese recipe. What we found is that an Italian brand (which makes pasta for the American market domestically) won our tasting by a large margin. Our tasters praised **Barilla Elbows** for their "wheaty," "buttery" flavor and "firm texture," and they especially liked that these elbows have small ridges and a slight twist that "holds sauce well."

BROWN RICE BOWLS WITH CRISPY TOFU AND VEGETABLES

CHAPTER 4

VEGETARIAN SUPPERS

WHEAT BERRY AND ARUGULA SALAD

WHEN YOU'RE COOKING VEGETARIAN FOR TWO, salads are probably on the menu quite often—they're easy to put together and bring a distinctive freshness to the dinner hour. But in all honesty, the most common iteration, a pile of greens rounded out with a few vegetables and some cheese, leaves us hungry and craving a midnight snack. For a satisfying yet exciting dinner salad that was still fairly effortless, we looked to incorporate a whole grain, plus a few other well-chosen, complementary ingredients, all of which would be tossed with a brightly flavored dressing. We knew we had several issues to tackle, so we started with the most important: choosing the right grain.

We began by testing quinoa, amaranth, and millet, but we found that their fine grains got lost among the leafy greens. Then a fellow test cook suggested wheat berries—whole, unprocessed wheat kernels. Their nutty flavor and chewy texture won tasters over, and their larger shape enabled them to hold their own among the salad greens.

Now we needed to settle on the best way to cook our wheat berries. In many recipes the kernels are simply cooked like pasta, simmered in water, so we decided to follow suit. After an hour of simmering, the grains had a nice, chewy texture, but we were disappointed to find that their flavor had been somewhat diluted. Taking another cue from pasta-cooking techniques, we decided to add salt to the cooking water. Working with our standard ratio of 1 tablespoon of salt to 4 quarts of water, we cooked up another batch of wheat berries. This time we had an unexpected result: After an hour

of cooking, the wheat berries were still incredibly hard. It turns out that the salinity of the water was preventing the wheat from absorbing it. We decided to test separate batches, each with a different amount of salt, and go down on the amount of water proportionately while we were at it (4 quarts seemed like a waste for our small amount of wheat berries). After numerous tests, we ultimately scaled the salt down to ¼ teaspoon and the water to 2 quarts; this salinity allowed the wheat berries to achieve the proper tenderness and lent the best flavor boost. After draining the grains and letting them cool, we were ready to move on to the rest of the salad.

With simplicity in mind for this supper for two, we considered the additional components of our salad. Starting with the greens, we nixed romaine from the get-go since we knew we would need a lettuce with a stronger presence. Baby spinach wouldn't work either—its flavor was too delicate in this application. Arugula ended up being the answer, lending a peppery flavor that complemented our slightly nutty grain. For piquant flavor and a touch of color, we added some chopped roasted red peppers as well.

For the dressing, we wanted a simple vinaigrette with bright, bold flavors. Orange juice provided sweetness and acidity; to concentrate its flavor, we reduced it on the stovetop, then let it cool briefly before stirring in the other ingredients. Lime juice added fresh, tart notes, and minced cilantro reinforced the clean flavors of our salad. A spoonful of honey tempered the acidity of the orange juice and lime juice; a bit of cumin and cayenne provided the perfect amount of spice.

Tasters were pleased with the lively flavors in our salad but commented that the dish needed more substance, so we added canned beans. We vetoed both cannellini beans and black beans; the cannellini were too delicately flavored to stand up to the hearty wheat berries, and the black beans were too overpowering. Chickpeas worked much better—they retained a noticeable presence in the salad, and their nutty and buttery flavor complemented the bright citrus dressing.

Though our revamped dinner salad was pretty good at this point, we thought a bit of cheese might put it over the top. We considered a few varieties, but in the end, crumbled feta won out. It created a cool, creamy counterpoint to our boldly flavored dressing and the hearty, nutty wheat berries.

NOTES FROM THE TEST KITCHEN

ALL ABOUT WHEAT BERRIES
Wheat berries are whole, unprocessed kernels of wheat. Since none of the grain has been removed, wheat berries are a great source of fiber, protein, iron, and other minerals. Compared to more refined forms of wheat (cracked wheat, bulgur, and flour), wheat berries require a long cooking time. We find it easiest to cook them like pasta, simply simmering them in a lot of water until tender with some chew.

WHEAT BERRY AND ARUGULA SALAD

Wheat Berry and Arugula Salad

SERVES 2

The wheat berries will still retain a chewy texture once fully cooked.

SALAD

- ½ cup wheat berries
- Salt and pepper
- ¾ cup canned chickpeas, rinsed
- ¼ cup jarred roasted red peppers, rinsed, patted dry, and chopped fine
- 1 ounce feta cheese, crumbled (¼ cup)
- 3 ounces (3 cups) baby arugula

DRESSING

- ½ cup orange juice
- 2 tablespoons minced fresh cilantro
- 1 tablespoon lime juice
- 1 tablespoon extra-virgin olive oil
- 1 teaspoon honey
- 1 garlic clove, minced
- ¼ teaspoon ground cumin
- ⅛ teaspoon salt
- Pinch cayenne pepper

1. FOR THE SALAD: Bring 2 quarts water to boil in large pot. Stir in wheat berries and ¼ teaspoon salt, partially cover, and cook, stirring often, until wheat berries are tender but still slightly chewy, about 1 hour. Drain wheat berries, spread them out on rimmed baking sheet, and let cool to room temperature, about 30 minutes.

2. FOR THE DRESSING: Meanwhile, bring orange juice to simmer in small saucepan over medium-high heat. Reduce heat to medium and simmer until juice is syrupy and has reduced to ¼ cup, 8 to 10 minutes. Transfer reduced juice to medium bowl and refrigerate until cool, about 10 minutes. Whisk in cilantro, lime juice, oil, honey, garlic, cumin, salt, and cayenne.

3. Combine cooled wheat berries, chickpeas, peppers, and feta in large bowl. Drizzle one-half of dressing over wheat berry mixture and toss gently to coat. Season with salt and pepper to taste.

4. In separate bowl, toss arugula with remaining dressing. Divide arugula between 2 plates and top with wheat berry mixture. Serve.

USE IT UP: CHICKPEAS OR BLACK BEANS

Crispy Bean Cakes

MAKES 2 CAKES

Add hot sauce to taste, if desired.

- ¾ cup canned chickpeas or black beans, rinsed
- 2 teaspoons plus 3 tablespoons vegetable oil
- 2 scallions, sliced thin
- 1 garlic clove, minced
- ¼ teaspoon ground cumin
- Salt and pepper
- 1 egg, lightly beaten
- 2 tablespoons plus ⅓ cup panko bread crumbs

1. Mash ½ cup beans, 2 teaspoons oil, scallions, garlic, cumin, ⅛ teaspoon salt, and ⅛ teaspoon pepper together in medium bowl until mostly smooth. Gently stir in remaining ¼ cup beans, one-half of beaten egg, and 2 tablespoons panko. Divide bean mixture in half, gently patting each into disk measuring 3 inches in diameter and about 1 inch high.

2. Place remaining egg in shallow dish and remaining ⅓ cup panko in second shallow dish. Coat bean cakes with egg, allowing excess to drip off, then dredge in panko, pressing gently so that crumbs adhere.

3. Heat remaining 3 tablespoons oil in 8-inch skillet over medium-high heat until shimmering. Add cakes and cook until golden brown, about 2 minutes per side. Transfer cakes to paper towel–lined plate. Serve.

THIN-CRUST PIZZA

AS MUCH AS WE LIKE THE CONVENIENCE OF DIALING up a pizza, nothing beats fresh, homemade pizza hot from the oven—that is, if you know what you're doing. We wanted a really great, parlor-quality pizza. It had to offer a crisp and slightly chewy crust, a bright tomato sauce, and plenty of creamy cheese on top—and it had to be scaled down for two. We knew it might take a bit of work, but we were up for the challenge.

Most of the effort and testing went into perfecting the pizza dough, which, after all, really makes or breaks a homemade pizza recipe. Pizza dough is made from just flour, water, salt, and yeast, so each element has to count. We first took a look at the flour. For a slightly chewy and spottily charred pie, we found that high-protein bread flour was our best choice. The higher protein in the bread flour encourages gluten development and browning, as well as firmer, stronger dough; this extra elasticity came in handy when it was time to stretch and shape it.

Our dough was promising great things so far, but we knew that pizza perfection was a long way away. First off, instead of being thin and just a little floppy, the crust was bready and overinflated, with a texture more like that of focaccia than pizza. Plus, the dough lacked any kind of flavor, save for the strong yeastiness. Simply reducing the yeast would help to reduce the puffy crust, but it would also wipe out what little flavor the dough had. Could we keep the same amount of yeast and somehow fix the puffy crust problem? We needed to think outside the box.

We knew that when the ingredients for pizza dough are first mixed, tiny "seed" bubbles form. These then expand at two different points in the procedure: once when the dough is "proofed" (when the dough is first given time to rise) and again during the first few minutes of baking. Logically, the larger the bubbles in the dough prior to baking, the more open and puffy the final crust will be. We realized that dough proofed at room temperature has much larger air bubbles than dough that is chilled, so instead of letting our dough proof on the counter, we decided to try sticking it in the refrigerator to proof. The next day, we pulled it out, divided and shaped it into rounds, and let it warm to room temperature while the baking stone was preheating. Bingo! This gave us just the thin crust we wanted, plus we got a few added bonuses out of the deal. The dough proved much easier to work with because the colder temperature slowed down the gluten development, making the dough looser and more pliable. Chilling also had the added benefit of creating more flavorful dough. Why? Because at lower temperatures, yeast produces not only less carbon dioxide (aka air bubbles) but also more of the side products—sugar, alcohol, and acids—that contribute to flavor.

Then we wondered, If 24 hours of cold fermentation had such a dramatic effect, what would happen if we left the dough in the fridge even longer? Three days later, we had an even more flavorful crust on our hands,

but any longer and the yeast would start producing too much carbon dioxide, rendering the dough too puffy. While this method wasn't exactly quick, the dough was a snap to pull together. Plus, the long rest wasn't altogether inconvenient; with a little planning, it was a great way to get pizza night started in advance.

We had our perfect foundation; all we had left to do was tweak the toppings. The no-cook sauce we had been using as a placeholder—half a cup of canned whole tomatoes, garlic, olive oil, and spices combined in the food processor—needed just a quick jolt of flavor, so we added a splash of red wine vinegar to enhance the tomatoes' bright acidity. As for the cheese, we supplemented the creamy, stretchy mozzarella with a fistful of sharp, salty, finely grated Parmesan. With a little time and advance planning, we'd turned out the perfect parlor-style, thin-crust pie right from our own oven.

Thin-Crust Pizza

SERVES 2

If you don't have a baking stone, bake the pizza on an overturned and preheated rimmed baking sheet. It is important to use ice water to prevent overheating the dough while in the food processor.

DOUGH

1½ cups (8¼ ounces) bread flour
1 teaspoon sugar
¼ teaspoon instant or rapid-rise yeast
⅔ cup ice water
1½ teaspoons vegetable oil
¾ teaspoon salt

SAUCE

½ cup canned whole peeled tomatoes, drained
1 teaspoon extra-virgin olive oil
1 small garlic clove, minced
¼ teaspoon red wine vinegar
¼ teaspoon dried oregano
⅛ teaspoon salt
⅛ teaspoon pepper

PIZZA

¼ cup grated Parmesan cheese
4 ounces whole-milk mozzarella cheese, shredded (1 cup)

1. FOR THE DOUGH: Process flour, sugar, and yeast together in food processor until combined, about 2 seconds. With processor running, slowly add water and process until dough is just combined and no dry flour remains, about 10 seconds. Let dough sit for 10 minutes.

2. Add oil and salt to dough and process until dough forms satiny, sticky ball that clears sides of bowl, about 30 seconds. Transfer dough to lightly oiled counter and knead briefly until smooth, about 1 minute. Shape dough into ball, place in large, lightly oiled bowl, and cover tightly with greased plastic wrap. Refrigerate for at least 24 hours or up to 3 days.

3. FOR THE SAUCE: Process all ingredients together in food processor until smooth, about 15 seconds, scraping down bowl as needed. Transfer to small bowl and refrigerate until ready to use.

4. TO BAKE THE PIZZA: Position oven rack 4½ inches from top of oven, set pizza stone on rack, and heat oven to 500 degrees. Let stone heat for 1 hour. Place dough on lightly oiled baking sheet, cover loosely with lightly greased plastic, and let sit at room temperature for 1 hour.

5. Coat dough generously with flour and place on well-floured counter. Using fingertips, gently flatten into 8-inch disk, leaving 1 inch of outer edge slightly thicker than center. Using hands, gently stretch disk into 12-inch round, working along edges and giving disk quarter turns as you stretch.

6. Transfer dough to well-floured peel and stretch into 13-inch round. Spread tomato sauce over dough, leaving ¼-inch border around edge. Sprinkle Parmesan evenly over sauce, followed by mozzarella.

7. Carefully slide pizza onto stone and bake until crust is well browned and cheese is bubbly and beginning to brown, 10 to 12 minutes, rotating pizza halfway through baking. Transfer pizza to wire rack and let cool for 5 minutes. Slice and serve.

ITALIAN VEGETABLE STEW

ITALY'S ANSWER TO RATATOUILLE, *GIAMBOTTA* turns a bounty of summer vegetables into a comforting, filling mélange of fresh flavors and satisfying textures— in theory. In practice, most recipes result in characterless bowls of stewed vegetables. Add off-season vegetables to the mix, and you get a veggie stew with all the freshness and flavor of canned soup. We set out to banish the bland and create two fresh and satisfying bowls of this rustic Italian-inspired stew, any time of year.

We got to work researching different recipes. True to the simple roots of this dish, most recipes called for layering the vegetables in a large pot, covering them with broth and/or water, sprinkling seasonings over the top, and letting everything stew until tender. But even when we generously garnished our bowls with chopped fresh basil and grated Italian cheese, the stew that resulted tasted bland and had zero texture. Given the number of high-moisture vegetables in the pot—zucchini, tomatoes, bell peppers, and eggplant are the traditional mix—it came as little surprise that the resulting stew was watery and insipid. In some recipes the remedy for this deluge of flavorlessness was salting the vegetables before they were added to the pot. While these versions were slightly better, they took twice as long to prepare and sometimes turned out too salty. If we wanted to turn out a rich-tasting bowl of Italian vegetable stew that still had some bite to it, it was clear that we would have to find a way to rid our vegetables of excess moisture so that we could keep all their bright, fresh flavor in the pot.

We began by selecting the tomatoes, as they would provide the underlying flavor profile of our stew. Because one of our goals was to prepare this stew year-round, we needed to consider the canned options. Packed at the height of ripeness, canned tomatoes offer consistently good tomato flavor. We tested tomato puree, crushed tomatoes, diced tomatoes, and whole tomatoes. Tomato puree and crushed tomatoes produced soupy stews, but both diced and whole tomatoes delivered decent results after half an hour of gentle simmering. In the end, tasters preferred the taste and texture of whole tomatoes chopped into smaller pieces.

Yet even with the addition of the chopped tomatoes, tasters felt the stew lacked real tomato punch. We found that three simple steps amplified the tomato flavor significantly. First, we sautéed the chopped tomatoes to bring out their flavor and achieve some caramelization. Second, we added a teaspoon of tomato paste to the sautéed tomatoes for more concentrated flavor. Third, we reserved the juice the tomatoes had been packed in and added it to the pot later on with our vegetable broth and water. We partially covered our saucepan (a Dutch oven proved too large for our smaller amount of ingredients) so that the broth and tomato juice would achieve a thickened consistency. At last, we had the deep tomato flavor we were looking for. Pleased with our base, we concentrated on the eggplant and zucchini.

We figured that first we'd nail down the cooking times. By adding the eggplant and zucchini (cut into substantial 1-inch chunks) when we added the broth and tomato juice and removing a sample of each at intervals, we were able to pinpoint the range in which they were done. Between 35 and 40 minutes, tasters found the zucchini to be tender yet slightly firm and the eggplant tender and creamy. Unfortunately, an old problem had reared its ugly head again. Although our vegetables were properly cooked, they tasted washed out and dull, and our stew had become slightly brothy and watery.

We knew that the best way to reduce extra liquid in the pan and develop rich flavor in our vegetables was to use dry heat. We decided to treat the eggplant and zucchini as we would meat—we browned each vegetable in olive oil at the start of cooking. Not only did this technique boost the flavor of both veggies and drive off excess moisture, but it also provided some browned bits on the bottom of the pan (also called fond), which lent serious richness to the stew. To compensate for the browning, we cut a few minutes from the simmering time. Now we could focus on the stew's remaining elements.

Since the tomatoes, eggplant, and zucchini had required such careful handling, we expected the same of the red bell pepper. To our surprise and delight, tasters were pleased when we simply sautéed it (with a shallot) to form the aromatic base. Added this early, it softened and melded with the flavors of the stew. Next, we examined options for the stew's starchy component. While a handful of recipes called for pasta, the majority relied on potatoes for starchiness. Tasters quickly approved of this path, pleased with the character and heartiness provided by some spuds. We needed only one potato and quickly ruled out using a russet, which absorbed the stew's richness but crumbled into a mess. Tasters preferred the more buttery Yukon Gold, because it sopped up the stew's deep flavor while also maintaining its shape.

Finally, we added fresh oregano and garlic to the mix and finished our bowls with grated Pecorino Romano and a drizzle of extra-virgin olive oil. Whether prepared in the dead of winter or at the height of summer, this satisfying stew for two provides full, rich flavor and big bites of tender vegetables.

Italian Vegetable Stew

SERVES 2

Do not peel the eggplant as the skin helps hold it together during cooking. Small eggplants can be hard to find; if you need to purchase a larger size, see page 70 for a recipe to use up the leftover eggplant.

- 3 tablespoons extra-virgin olive oil, plus extra for serving
- 1 small eggplant (6 ounces), cut into 1-inch pieces
- 1 small zucchini (6 ounces), halved lengthwise, seeded, and cut into 1-inch pieces
- 1 (14.5-ounce) can whole peeled tomatoes, drained with juice reserved and chopped coarse
- 1 large shallot, minced
- ½ red bell pepper, stemmed, seeded, and cut into ½-inch pieces
- 1 teaspoon tomato paste
   Salt and pepper
- 3 garlic cloves, minced
- ¼ teaspoon minced fresh oregano or pinch dried
- 1½ cups vegetable broth
- ½ cup water
- 1 Yukon Gold potato, peeled and cut into ½-inch pieces
- 2 tablespoons chopped fresh basil
- ¼ cup grated Pecorino Romano cheese

1. Heat 1 tablespoon oil in medium saucepan over medium-high heat until shimmering. Brown eggplant lightly on all sides, 5 to 7 minutes; transfer to medium bowl. Repeat with 1 tablespoon oil and zucchini; transfer to bowl with eggplant.

2. Heat remaining 1 tablespoon oil in now-empty saucepan over medium heat. Add tomatoes, shallot, bell pepper, tomato paste, ¼ teaspoon salt, and ¼ teaspoon pepper and cook until dry and beginning to brown, 11 to 13 minutes.

3. Stir in garlic and oregano and cook until fragrant, about 30 seconds. Stir in broth and water, scraping up any browned bits. Stir in reserved tomato juice and potato and bring to boil.

4. Gently stir in browned eggplant and zucchini, cover pot partially (leaving about 1 inch of pot open), and simmer gently until vegetables are tender and stew has thickened, 25 to 35 minutes. Off heat, stir in basil and season with salt and pepper to taste. Divide stew between 2 bowls, drizzle with extra oil, and sprinkle with Pecorino. Serve.

NOTES FROM THE TEST KITCHEN

THE BEST LIQUID MEASURING CUP

The liquid measuring cup is a basic kitchen tool, where accuracy matters more than looks and form should follow function. But when we perused stores recently, we found cup after wacky cup, with silly shapes and candy colors, made of materials that were flimsy, with markings that ran from minimal (no quarter-cups or thirds) to ridiculously excessive (pints, tablespoons, and cubic centimeters). Unsure whether any of these innovative shapes or features might prove useful, we gathered 15 glass, silicone, and plastic 2-cup liquid measures and tested them for accuracy, durability, resistance to heat, and user-friendliness. Some cups were downgraded because they gave us inaccurate measurements; others resulted in inaccurate measurements simply because they were too difficult to read, with small type and busy designs. In the end, we liked the **Good Cook by Bradshaw International 2-Cup Measuring Cup**, $3.99. While we'd prefer a more substantial glass cup, this lightweight, crisply marked plastic model was accurate and easy to read and provided all the measurements we need.

QUINOA AND VEGETABLE STEW

FINDING A STEW THAT'S HEARTY, SATISFYING, AND meat-free isn't always easy. Enter naturally high-protein quinoa. In countries such as Peru, along the Andean highlands, quinoa plays a starring role in many dishes, among them a quinoa stew. It traditionally includes a good mix of vegetables, with potatoes and corn at the forefront, and while some recipes might also call for meat, many rely solely on the quinoa for protein. The meatless version struck us as an exciting, unexpected new dish to add to our roster of vegetarian suppers for two.

In our research, we learned that although recipes might have varied ingredient lists, they all followed the same basic cooking method. First, a mix of cumin, coriander, and annatto powder was cooked in oil until fragrant. Next, onion, garlic, green pepper, and tomato were added and sautéed to form the background notes. Broth, water, or a combination of the two was then stirred into the pot, as were the native potatoes and giant kernels of Andean corn. When these were almost tender, quinoa was added and allowed to simmer until cooked through. Garnished with diced avocado, cilantro, and salty *queso fresco,* the authentic stews were hearty, delicious, and filling. This method seemed like the right place to start, but we needed to find a way to work around the obscure ingredients, such as annatto powder and Peruvian varieties of potatoes and corn.

After cooking a few of the recipes that included annatto powder, we were able to identify its flavor and understand its overall contribution to the stew. Ground from the red pulp found inside achiote seeds (which are from the annatto tree), annatto powder is used extensively in South American and Caribbean cooking. We found its flavor to be slightly sweet and earthy, with just a hint of peppery bitterness. Although its flavor can be somewhat subtle, the color it lends to foods is anything but. Just a teaspoon was enough to turn a pot of our stew a rich shade of crimson. After examining our notes, we quickly realized that annatto powder has a flavor profile and color similar to those of sweet paprika. To test whether we could substitute readily available paprika for hard-to-find annatto, we bloomed a few tablespoons of each in vegetable oil. Tasting them side by side, we had a difficult time telling the difference. Once they were mixed into the stew, any slight discrepancies disappeared completely. To round out the spice profile, we added cumin and coriander until the flavor was balanced and rich. To prevent the spices from burning (which happened in many of the recipes we tested), we added them to the pot after we had sautéed our aromatics.

For our aromatics, we first tried onion, green bell pepper, tomato, and garlic. This combination was perfectly fine, but tasters complained about the flavor of the pepper (or lack thereof); it turned army green and bland by the time the stew was done. Red bell pepper, on the other hand, remained sweet and fire-engine red. Tasters all agreed that the bell pepper provided enough brightness and acidity for us to do away with the tomato, which simplified our ingredient list a little more. After adding some vegetable broth to the softened aromatics, we had to make a decision about the other vegetables that would give our stew its authentic South American feel.

Without access to native Peruvian potatoes or Andean corn at our local supermarkets, we had to find acceptable substitutes. After getting our hands on some Peruvian potatoes and comparing them with our domestic varieties, we found the texture of red potatoes to be the closest option. A single spud proved to be adequate for our stew. As for the corn, nothing came close to the dense, chewy, and nutty Andean corn, but tasters almost unanimously preferred the sweeter stew made with our own locally grown corn anyway (frozen corn worked well as a substitute). Happy with the hearty mix of vegetables, next we focused on the quinoa.

Having cooked quinoa before, we knew it could go from crunchy to mushy almost instantly. Wary of overcooking the quinoa, we added it after the potato had softened. After about 10 minutes, we were rewarded with firm yet cushy bites of quinoa. Although the quinoa still had some texture to it, we now found that the broth lacked body. One colleague suggested stretching the cooking time of the quinoa as far as we could—just a few extra minutes would help it release additional starch into the stew without causing the quinoa to soften too much. After a few more minutes of gentle simmering, the quinoa offered a slight chew

NOTES FROM THE TEST KITCHEN

PITTING AND DICING AVOCADOS

1. After slicing avocado in half around pit, lodge edge of knife blade into pit and twist to remove. Use large wooden spoon to pry pit safely off knife.

2. Using dish towel to hold avocado steady, make ½-inch crosshatch incisions in flesh of each avocado half with knife, cutting down to but not through skin.

3. Separate diced flesh from skin with soupspoon inserted between skin and flesh, gently scooping out avocado cubes.

QUINOA AND VEGETABLE STEW

and had also given up sufficient starch so that the broth now had substantial body.

All that was needed now were a few thoughtfully chosen garnishes. We liked the traditional combination of salty queso fresco (feta cheese makes a good substitute), creamy avocado, and citrusy cilantro. Our quinoa stew was now the best of both worlds: a humble ode to its authentic roots, and a streamlined yet flavorful offering for the modern-day table for two.

Quinoa and Vegetable Stew

SERVES 2

This stew tends to thicken as it sits; add additional warm vegetable broth as needed before serving to loosen. Be sure to rinse the quinoa to remove its bitter coating (known as saponin). We prefer to use a medium red potato, measuring 2 to 3 inches in diameter, in this recipe.

- 1 tablespoon vegetable oil
- 1 small onion, cut into ½-inch pieces
- ½ red bell pepper, stemmed, seeded, and cut into ½-inch pieces
- 2 garlic cloves, minced
- 1 teaspoon paprika
- ¾ teaspoon ground coriander
- ½ teaspoon ground cumin
- 2 cups vegetable broth
- ½ cup water
- 1 red potato, cut into ½-inch pieces
- ⅓ cup quinoa, rinsed
- ⅓ cup fresh or frozen corn
  Salt and pepper
- 2 ounces queso fresco or feta cheese, crumbled (½ cup)
- ½ avocado, pitted and cut into ½-inch pieces
- 3 tablespoons minced fresh cilantro
  Lime wedges

1. Heat oil in medium saucepan over medium heat until shimmering. Add onion and bell pepper and cook until softened, 5 to 7 minutes. Stir in garlic, paprika, coriander, and cumin and cook until fragrant, about 30 seconds. Stir in broth, water, and potato and bring to boil. Reduce to gentle simmer and cook for 10 minutes.

2. Stir in quinoa and continue to simmer for 8 minutes. Stir in corn and simmer until potato and quinoa are just tender, 6 to 8 minutes. Season with salt and pepper to taste and divide stew between 2 bowls. Sprinkle with queso fresco, avocado, and cilantro. Serve with lime wedges.

MUSHROOM AND FARRO RAGOUT

TYPICALLY, A RAGOUT IS MADE WITH MEAT OR poultry; mushroom ragout, however, is a rich, well-seasoned stew made with a variety of meaty mushrooms. This luxurious, hearty dish takes on intense, deep flavor when made with an assortment of exotic wild mushrooms, but we wanted to keep our grocery shopping to a minimum (no mail-ordering) and looked to develop a recipe that was every bit as rich and robust, but that relied on the mushroom selection at the supermarket to get there. To add even more substance to this stew, we decided to add a grain to the mix.

We wanted our ragout to include mushrooms that offered variety in flavor, texture, and appearance, and we focused our efforts on the varieties commonly found at the supermarket: cremini, portobello, white, and shiitake mushrooms. We quickly whittled down the list to just three varieties. Since cremini are baby portobellos, we decided to cut them from the competition. We opted for portobellos—they are meaty in texture and can be cut into thick, hearty slices. We also chose to include white mushrooms. While their flavor pales in comparison to portobellos, sautéing does give them more bite. Finally, shiitakes offered a savory richness to the mix.

With our list of fresh mushrooms pared down and providing interest in terms of both texture and flavor, we looked to add more intensity with some dried mushrooms. Here in the test kitchen, we often turn to dried porcini mushrooms to instill long-simmered soups and stews with deep, savory flavor. Indeed, tasters appreciated the richness provided by a small amount of dried porcini. A quarter of an ounce proved just the right amount—any less than that and the flavor impact was minimal; any more, and the dried porcini were overpowering.

With our mushrooms selected, we turned our attention to choosing the right grain that would turn our mushroom stew into a satisfying supper. We considered quinoa, but it was too small and disappeared in our ragout next to the bigger bites of mushroom. We knew that wheat berries would take a while to cook (about an hour), and we suspected the mushrooms would already require ample time on their own to soften, so we looked for something that would be ready in less time. We hit upon farro next, which is a whole-grain form of wheat that has a slightly sweet, nutty flavor and chewy texture. Tasters found the farro flavorful enough to have its own identity in the ragout while still letting the mushrooms take center stage.

Next, we turned our attention to the aromatics. Carrot and celery looked out of place in the stew, and their flavors and textures took away from the mushrooms and farro rather than enhancing them. We then performed a number of tests focusing on alliums. We tried leeks, shallots, onion, and garlic. The leeks were too delicate in flavor and texture; shallots turned out to be too subtle as well. An onion, however, stood up nicely to the assortment of assertive mushroom flavors. Garlic added a pungent note and depth.

While we usually use olive oil or vegetable oil to sauté aromatics for stews, butter is the traditional fat used in ragout. We tried both and found that tasters preferred butter for the richness it provided; it also helped thicken the liquid in the stew. For the liquid, we relied on vegetable broth; its sweetness balanced the earthiness of the mushrooms.

To cut through the richness, most mushroom stews also contain wine. We found that white wine didn't have enough heft to brighten the flavors. Red wine was too strong and sharp. Next we tried dry sherry. Fortified wines like dry sherry and Madeira are often found in mushroom ragouts, and testing showed us why. They are stronger in flavor than white wine but not as overpowering as red wine.

Many mushroom ragout recipes include tomatoes for brightness. We tried both canned whole tomatoes, which we chopped, and tomato paste. The tomato paste dulled both the flavor and the color of our stew, so we stuck with canned whole tomatoes that we coarsely chopped, which added some color and freshness.

With our main ingredients in hand, we set out to figure out the cooking method. After sautéing our onion, we added the mushrooms and cooked them until they were well browned; this gave us a stew with deep flavor. Though it took a little extra time, it was well worth it—allowing a layer of browned bits, or fond, to form on the bottom of the pan fortified the flavor of the vegetable broth once it was added to simmer. Next, we added the garlic and some thyme, which we preferred over other herbs for the way it enhanced the earthiness of the mushrooms, followed by the tomatoes and farro.

After about 30 minutes, our farro was perfectly tender yet chewy, and the mushrooms had a meaty texture and more concentrated flavor than when they started. After this amount of time, though, our ragout was a bit thin and lacking in richness. We decided to stir in another pat of butter. This move put our ragout over the top—the butter enriched the flavor of our ragout, thickened its texture, and gave the liquid a bit of a glossy shine. For a finishing touch, we stirred in a spoonful of balsamic vinegar; its sharpness balanced the deep tones of the mushrooms.

Mushroom and Farro Ragout
SERVES 2

Farro is a grain that can be found alongside other grains or near the pasta in specialty or gourmet markets. You can substitute Madeira wine for the dry sherry if necessary.

- 2 tablespoons unsalted butter
- 1 small onion, chopped fine
- ¼ ounce dried porcini mushrooms, rinsed and minced
  Salt and pepper
- 2 portobello mushroom caps, gills removed, halved, and sliced ½ inch thick
- 5 ounces white mushrooms, trimmed and halved if small or quartered if large
- 2 ounces shiitake mushrooms, stemmed and sliced ¼ inch thick
- 2 garlic cloves, minced
- 1 teaspoon minced fresh thyme
- 2 tablespoons dry sherry

3 cups vegetable broth

½ cup canned whole peeled tomatoes, drained with juice reserved and chopped coarse

½ cup farro

1 tablespoon minced fresh parsley

¾ teaspoon balsamic vinegar

1. Melt 1 tablespoon butter in medium saucepan over medium heat. Add onion, porcini, and ⅛ teaspoon salt and cook until softened and lightly browned, 8 to 10 minutes.

2. Stir in portobellos, white mushrooms, and shiitake mushrooms, cover, and cook, stirring occasionally, until mushrooms have released their moisture, 8 to 10 minutes. Uncover and continue to cook until dark fond forms on bottom of saucepan, 10 to 15 minutes longer.

3. Stir in garlic and thyme and cook until fragrant, about 30 seconds. Stir in sherry, scraping up any browned bits, and cook until almost completely evaporated, about 1 minute.

4. Stir in broth, tomatoes, reserved juice, and farro and bring to boil. Reduce to gentle simmer, cover pot partially (leaving about 1 inch of pot open), and cook until ragout is thickened and farro is tender, 30 to 35 minutes.

5. Off heat, stir in remaining 1 tablespoon butter, parsley, and vinegar. Season with salt and pepper to taste and serve.

BUTTERNUT SQUASH RISOTTO

BUTTERNUT SQUASH RISOTTO IS A BISTRO FAVORITE for good reason. With its creamy, al dente rice surrounding bites of tender, slightly sweet, buttery squash, this classic is incredibly satisfying, rich in both flavor and texture. But try to bring this seemingly simple dish home for two, and you'll most likely be disappointed—potential pitfalls include sticky, gummy, bland rice and mushy, overcooked squash. We sought a recipe for butternut squash risotto for two that offered creamy rice fully infused with deep butternut squash flavor and flecked with both hints of broken-down squash as well as more substantial, but still tender, bites of squash.

We began by figuring out the best way to prepare and cook the butternut squash. In order to maintain the textural integrity of the squash pieces, we found that dicing and then cooking the squash worked better than roasting squash halves and then removing the flesh, which caused the squash to fall apart. For the cooking method, we tried roasting the squash pieces, but most tasters found the concentrated sweetness that resulted from the dry, intense heat too distracting. The other obvious method, sautéing the squash pieces in a skillet, did not produce the color and flavor development we had hoped for. The solution was as easy as letting the squash cook for a few minutes without stirring or turning it, allowing one side to caramelize slightly; once the squash was golden brown, we gently stirred it and let it cook a few more minutes until it was tender. This produced the color and flavor we were after without the overt sweetness that resulted from the oven-roasting approach.

Next, we moved on to figuring out the best way to incorporate our cooked squash into the rice (later on, we could focus on finessing our risotto). After a few tests, it was clear that the cooked squash could not be added to the rice all at once. Added early on, the squash dissolved and lost its personality; added later in cooking, it never became sufficiently integrated. Our first approach was to mash half of the cooked squash pieces and then sauté them with the toasted rice, folding in the intact pieces at the end. Although the rice now had a ton of squash flavor, it also took on an unappealing gummy texture. The solution was simple. We added half of the cooked squash pieces with the toasted rice—without mashing them—and then gently folded in the remaining half at the end. Now we had a perfect marriage of flavors and textures.

All the butternut squash needed now was a rich, creamy rice base upon which it could be layered. In keeping with risotto-making tradition, we began by sautéing the aromatics in some melted butter before adding short-grain Arborio rice, the usual choice for risotto. While this is normally done in a saucepan, we knew we could probably get away with using the same 10-inch nonstick skillet we had used to cook the squash (giving us one less pot to wash).

After the rice had toasted with a mix of garlic and onion, we added ¼ cup of white wine for extra acidity and brightness. Because of the strong flavors in the risotto, the wine flavor was faint at best. Increasing the wine to ½ cup gave the rice the acidity and complexity needed to balance the sweetness of the squash. Once the rice grains had fully absorbed the wine, we stirred in half of the cooked squash.

Traditional risotto recipes are time-consuming since small amounts of broth or water are added to the pan, which must be stirred constantly for over half an hour. The test kitchen had previously discovered a more streamlined, quicker method, which calls for preheating the broth (we liked vegetable broth combined with water to mitigate its sweetness) in a separate saucepan and then adding the bulk of it (we used 2 cups) to the rice once the wine has been absorbed. This speeds up the cooking and means less stirring at the outset. The remaining liquid is then added in smaller ½-cup increments, and the rice is stirred more frequently to prevent the bottom of the skillet from drying out.

Once the rice was al dente, we stirred in another pat of butter for richness, minced sage for woodsy flavor, and grated Parmesan for a salty, nutty tang. Our risotto was now incredibly creamy and rich, and the squash was perfectly tender, but it could still use a bump up in nutty, buttery squash flavor.

A glance around the test kitchen led us to the leftover squash seeds and fibers on a cutting board. Could we use these somehow to further elevate the squash flavor in our risotto? In our next test, we sautéed the seeds and fibers separately to deepen their flavor (similar to the way we sauté, or bloom, spices to bring out their flavor), then added them to the saucepan with the broth (we would strain the broth later). We proceeded with our recipe as we'd been doing and doled out two picture-perfect dishes of squash risotto. Surprisingly, this one simple step had yielded a complex and easy-to-detect boost in squash flavor without adding more sweetness.

With such an easy and foolproof recipe for creamy, flavorful risotto at our fingertips, we knew we'd never have to hit up a bistro to enjoy this satisfying dish again.

Butternut Squash Risotto
SERVES 2

Infusing the vegetable broth and water with the squash's seeds and fibers helps to reinforce the earthy squash flavor. See page 56 for a recipe to use up the leftover butternut squash.

- 1 tablespoon olive oil
- 1 pound butternut squash, peeled, seeded, and cut into ½-inch pieces (1¾ cups), seeds and fibers reserved
  Salt and pepper
- 2½ cups water
- 2 cups vegetable broth
- 2 tablespoons unsalted butter
- 1 small onion, chopped fine
- 1 garlic clove, minced
- ¾ cup Arborio rice
- ½ cup dry white wine
- 1 ounce Parmesan cheese, grated (½ cup)
- 1 teaspoon minced fresh sage

1. Heat oil in 10-inch nonstick skillet over medium-high heat until shimmering. Add squash in even layer and cook without stirring until golden brown, about 5 minutes; stir in ⅛ teaspoon salt and ⅛ teaspoon pepper. Continue to cook, stirring occasionally, until squash is tender and browned, 5 to 7 minutes longer; transfer squash to bowl and set aside.

2. Add reserved squash fibers and seeds to now-empty skillet and cook over medium heat, stirring frequently to break up fibers, until lightly browned, about 4 minutes. Transfer to medium saucepan and add water and broth; cover saucepan and bring mixture to simmer over high heat, then reduce heat to medium-low to maintain bare simmer for 5 minutes. Strain hot broth through fine-mesh strainer into medium bowl, pressing on solids to extract as much liquid as possible. Return strained broth to saucepan and discard solids in strainer. Cover saucepan and set over low heat to keep broth hot.

3. Meanwhile, melt 1 tablespoon butter in now-empty skillet over medium heat. Stir in onion, ¼ teaspoon salt, and ¼ teaspoon pepper and cook until softened, about 5 minutes. Stir in garlic and cook until fragrant, about 30 seconds. Add rice to skillet and cook, stirring frequently, until grains are translucent around edges, about 3 minutes. Add wine and cook, stirring frequently, until fully absorbed, 3 to 5 minutes.

4. Add 2 cups hot broth and one-half of reserved squash to rice. Simmer, stirring every 3 to 4 minutes, until liquid is absorbed and bottom of pan is almost dry, about 12 minutes.

5. Stir in ½ cup hot broth and cook, stirring constantly, until absorbed, about 3 minutes. Repeat with additional broth 2 or 3 more times until rice is al dente. Off heat, stir in remaining 1 tablespoon butter, Parmesan, and sage, then gently fold in remaining cooked squash. Season with salt and pepper to taste and add remaining broth as needed to adjust consistency of risotto. Serve immediately.

VARIATION

Butternut Squash Risotto with Spinach and Pine Nuts

Heat 1 teaspoon olive oil in 10-inch nonstick skillet over medium heat until shimmering. Add 2 ounces (2 cups) baby spinach, cover, and cook until leaves begin to wilt, about 2 minutes. Uncover and continue to cook, stirring constantly, until fully wilted, about 30 seconds longer. Transfer spinach to colander and set aside while making risotto. Stir drained spinach into risotto along with remaining squash in step 5. Sprinkle each serving of risotto with 2 tablespoons toasted pine nuts.

STUFFED ZUCCHINI

ENRICHED WITH CHEESE AND MADE MORE FILLING with the addition of grains or beans, stuffed vegetables are a hearty way to turn a humble collection of ingredients into a simple meatless meal. Though bell peppers seem to hog the limelight when it comes to stuffed vegetables, alternatives abound, from stuffed tomatoes to stuffed squash. We set our sights on the latter and had an entrée of brightly flavored stuffed zucchini in mind. After all, a pair of zucchini would be perfect for two diners, plus they cook relatively quickly, meaning dinner would be on the table in no time at all.

To start, we tried several different recipes, all claiming to be the best way to make stuffed zucchini. Sadly, each one turned out to be a disappointment. In the simpler recipes the raw zucchini were stuffed with rice and vegetables and thrown in the oven. Not only did the zucchini take a while to cook through, but also the top

SEEDING ZUCCHINI

To remove seeds from zucchini, halve zucchini lengthwise and run small spoon inside each zucchini half to scoop out seeds.

of the filling dried out while the bottom of the filling absorbed the zucchini's moisture and became mushy. In other recipes the squash were blanched in water or broth before they were stuffed, which drained the zucchini of flavor and left behind a dull, limp shell. In still others the squash were filled raw and baked in canned tomato sauce, which merely imparted a tinny tomato flavor. For the fillings, most recipes used precooked rice, which absorbed the moisture in the zucchini, thereby creating a gummy texture and monotonous flavor. It was clear we had two issues to contend with. First, we had to find the best way to prepare the zucchini for stuffing, then we had to figure out the right mix of ingredients that would create a flavorful filling with a toothsome texture.

We knew that the zucchini would require at least some parcooking to drive off excess moisture that would lead to soggy stuffed squash. Roasting, with its hot, dry heat, seemed a promising way to ditch this moisture while also jump-starting the squash's cooking. We experimented by roasting the zucchini whole, halved, and halved and seeded. The whole zucchini took too long to cook and steamed itself soggy. Although the halved squash cooked in less time, the seeds still held on to some moisture, leaving behind a waterlogged shell. The seeded squash, on the other hand, retained the yielding yet firm texture we were looking for and also developed a more concentrated flavor. Because the heat of the oven was able to hit the flesh of the zucchini directly, more moisture evaporated, leading to squash that had a more intense flavor.

Next we conducted a few tests to determine whether we should roast our zucchini cut side up or cut side down. When the zucchini were roasted cut side up, the moisture that did not evaporate pooled in the hollow space once occupied by the seeds and later seeped into the stuffing, making it watery. When roasted cut side down, however, the moisture from the squash dripped onto the hot roasting pan and turned into steam that got trapped under the squash and cooked it more quickly. Using a preheated pan further enhanced this effect, reducing the roasting time even more while also creating a flavorful, golden brown crust along the rim. Salt and pepper brought out the flavor of the squash, and a bit of olive oil prevented the halves from sticking to the pan. With its lightly browned edges and tender texture, the seeded squash, roasted cut side down on a preheated pan, was by far the best of its class. Now we could turn our attention to the filling.

Right off the bat, we set up a few guidelines. We didn't want to call for any special ingredients or hard-to-find items, and we wanted to be able to prepare the filling while the squash roasted. To start, we tried using a simple combination of sautéed vegetables and cheese, but our tasters were left wanting something more substantial. We then tested fillings made with rice, couscous, bread cubes, and last, canned cannellini beans, all of which added some bulk. The rice and couscous tasted fine but didn't contribute too much overall. The bread cubes became mushy and broke down in the oven. The cannellini beans ended up stealing the show, giving the dish a satisfying and creamy oomph that none of the other contenders could match.

For the other filling ingredients, tasters liked a simple mix of sautéed garlic and shallot. A single tomato, chopped, and a good amount of basil contributed freshness and brightness. Shredded cheese, which helped to bind the filling and added richness to an otherwise lean dish, was a given. After trying eight different types of cheese, tasters voted unanimously for Monterey Jack cheese. The flavor of the cheese was noticeable without being overpowering, and the cheese melted and became nicely browned when sprinkled on top of the stuffed zucchini.

Our zucchini were almost there now, but tasters felt they were lacking a little in the texture department. Panko bread crumbs, toasted in olive oil and sprinkled over the zucchini before baking, solved the problem and lent our vegetarian entrée some appealing crunch.

Stuffed Zucchini with Cannellini Beans, Tomato, and Monterey Jack Cheese
SERVES 2

See page 54 for a recipe to use up the leftover cannellini beans.

- **3 tablespoons olive oil**
- **2 zucchini (8 ounces each), halved lengthwise and seeded**
- **Salt and pepper**
- **⅓ cup panko bread crumbs**
- **1 shallot, minced**
- **3 garlic cloves, minced**
- **¾ cup canned cannellini beans, rinsed**
- **1 large tomato, cored, seeded, and cut into ½-inch pieces**
- **3 ounces Monterey Jack cheese, shredded (¾ cup)**
- **¼ cup chopped fresh basil**

1. Adjust oven rack to upper-middle position, place baking sheet on rack, and heat oven to 400 degrees.

2. Brush 1 tablespoon oil over cut sides of zucchini and season with ⅛ teaspoon salt and ⅛ teaspoon pepper. Carefully place zucchini halves, cut side down, on hot baking sheet. Roast until slightly softened and skins are wrinkled, about 10 minutes. Flip zucchini halves over and set aside on baking sheet.

3. Meanwhile, heat 1 tablespoon oil in 10-inch skillet over medium heat until shimmering. Add panko, ⅛ teaspoon salt, and ⅛ teaspoon pepper and cook, stirring frequently, until crumbs are golden brown, 3 to 5 minutes. Transfer panko to bowl and wipe out skillet.

4. Heat remaining 1 tablespoon oil in now-empty skillet over medium heat until shimmering. Add shallot and cook, stirring occasionally, until softened and beginning to brown, 3 to 5 minutes. Stir in garlic and cook until fragrant, about 30 seconds. Add beans and tomato and cook until heated through, about 3 minutes.

5. Off heat, stir in ½ cup cheese and basil and season with salt and pepper to taste. Divide filling evenly among squash halves and pack lightly. Sprinkle evenly with remaining ¼ cup cheese, then sprinkle with toasted bread crumbs. Bake stuffed zucchini until heated through, about 6 minutes. Serve.

STUFFED ZUCCHINI WITH CANNELLINI BEANS, TOMATO, AND MONTEREY JACK CHEESE

See page 116 for a recipe to use up the leftover canned black beans.

Substitute ¾ cup canned black beans for cannellini. Add 1 teaspoon minced canned chipotle chile in adobo sauce to skillet along with garlic. Add ½ cup fresh or frozen corn to skillet along with beans and tomato. Substitute ¼ cup minced fresh cilantro for basil.

CUBAN-STYLE BLACK BEANS AND RICE

RICE AND BEANS HAVE ALWAYS BEEN A VEGETARIAN cook's bread and butter—satisfying, surely, but a bit mundane. So we were intrigued when we read about a Cuban version in which black beans and rice are cooked together with aromatic vegetables and spices to create a hearty main course. Traditionally called *Moros y Cristianos*, this dish is unique in that the rice is cooked in the inky concentrated liquid left over from cooking the beans, which renders the grains just as flavorful. With its promise to ramp up the flavor of what's become a ho-hum meatless main, Cuban-style black beans and rice seemed the perfect addition to our collection of vegetarian suppers for two.

Most versions of this recipe follow the same method. Aromatics and spices are lightly browned in oil, then the uncooked rice is stirred in, followed by the cooked black beans and their reserved cooking liquid. Finally, the pot is covered and its contents are gently simmered until the liquid has been absorbed and the rice is tender. After we tested a few recipes, the issues became clear. Some recipes offered up bland rice studded with insipid beans—hardly worth the time or effort. Others offered less-than-stellar rice—either it cooked into a moist, gluey mass or the grains were scorched on the bottom but undercooked on the top (the liquid having boiled away). Our goal now was to make a vegetarian dish that was not just richly flavorful, but also foolproof.

To get the flavor right, we knew we needed to perfect the *sofrito*. This mixture of aromatic vegetables, spices, and herbs is a cornerstone of Latin cooking and the starting point for this dish. The specific elements in the mix differ from one Latin cuisine to another, but a Cuban sofrito usually consists of the trio of onion, green bell pepper, and garlic, typically flavored with cumin and oregano.

We started our sofrito by sautéing one shallot (scaled down from a whole onion) and a small green pepper in olive oil with cumin and oregano until the mixture was golden brown and flavorful. Then we added some garlic and a teaspoon of tomato paste to the mix to coax out as much flavor as possible from the vegetables and impart some rich, deep flavor.

Although the tomato paste added some depth, the sofrito still wasn't as flavorful as it needed to be. We wanted it to be the backbone to our pot of beans and rice, not just give our dish a mild flavor. Increasing the spices helped, but only to a point; overdoing it made the dish dusty and harsh. We thought that doubling the amount of sofrito would do the trick—and flavor-wise, it did—but the sheer volume of moist vegetables weighed down the rice and beans in a kind of sofrito sludge. We wondered if all of our vegetables had to go directly into the sofrito. Since we had been using plain water to precook the soaked beans (the test kitchen has found that soaking beans in salt water ensures that they are more tender and cook more evenly), we thought we could use the extra veggies to infuse the beans with flavor and thereby increase the overall flavor of the dish. With this in mind, we put half of our shallot and green pepper, a couple of cloves of unpeeled garlic, and a bay leaf in with the beans to simmer. When the beans were just cooked, we sampled them. It turned out to be a good idea—both the beans and their cooking liquid were full-flavored and would lend that quality to the rice as well.

With the flavor of the dish where we wanted it, we turned to the rice. It seemed that fixing the scorched yet undercooked rice would be a little trickier. Given that both the beans and the sofrito added moisture to the pot, every batch of beans and rice came out differently, with some tests resulting in gummy rice and others resulting in undercooked rice. We played around with the amount of liquid we were adding to the pot; after a few tests, we ultimately found that 1¼ cups was the correct amount of bean liquid to get ½ cup of rice cooked through in about 30 minutes. But even at the lowest heat setting, we found that the mixture at the bottom

THE BEST DRIED BLACK BEANS

In the cooking-for-two kitchen, canned beans offer the ultimate in convenience. But for dishes in which the beans truly take center stage, we prefer the flavor and texture provided by dried beans. To find the best dried black beans, we sampled three brands cooked plain and in our Cuban-Style Black Beans and Rice. Surprisingly, the single mail-order variety, a pricey heirloom bean, became mushy, while the beans from the two national supermarket brands were perfectly creamy. Our favorite was **Goya Dried Black Beans**, which offered "nutty," "buttery" bean flavor and a reliably uniform texture.

Salt

⅓ cup dried black beans, picked over and rinsed

2 cups water

1 small green bell pepper, stemmed, seeded, and halved, 1 half chopped into ¼-inch pieces

1 large shallot, peeled and halved, 1 half chopped into ¼-inch pieces

5 garlic cloves (2 unpeeled and whole, 3 minced)

1 bay leaf

1 tablespoon olive oil

1 teaspoon minced fresh oregano

1 teaspoon ground cumin

1 teaspoon tomato paste

½ cup long-grain white rice, rinsed

2 teaspoons red wine vinegar

1 scallion, sliced thin

Lime wedges

---

of the pot was still scorching while the rice grains at the top remained almost crunchy. The problem made sense: With the stove's flame hitting only the underside of the pot, the bottom layer of rice burned while the grains at the top barely cooked at all. That's when we considered moving our beans and rice to the oven, where the all-around, indirect heat would cook the pot's contents gently and evenly. We brought the rice, beans, and liquid (including a splash of red wine vinegar for brightness) to a simmer, gave the mixture a stir, covered the vessel, and slid it into a 350-degree oven.

After about the same amount of time as it took to cook on the stove, we removed the pot, fluffed the contents with a fork, and let the dish sit for five minutes. Finally, we had perfectly cooked rice from top to bottom. A sprinkle of thinly sliced scallion and a squeeze of lime added a final hit of fresh, bright flavor to our Cuban-inspired take on the classic beans and rice.

Cuban-Style Black Beans and Rice

SERVES 2

The success of the dish relies upon the texture and flavor of the black beans. Do not substitute canned beans for dried beans in this recipe. To quick-salt-soak the beans, combine 2 quarts water, beans, and 1½ tablespoons salt in a large saucepan and bring to a boil over high heat. Remove the pot from the heat, cover, and let stand for 1 hour. Drain and rinse well. Make sure you rinse the rice thoroughly until the water runs clear to prevent the rice from clumping together.

1. Dissolve 1½ tablespoons salt in 2 quarts cold water in large bowl or container. Add beans and soak at room temperature for at least 8 hours or up to 24 hours. Drain and rinse well.

2. In ovensafe medium saucepan with tight-fitting lid, stir together drained beans, water, 1 pepper half, 1 shallot half, whole garlic cloves, bay leaf, and ½ teaspoon salt. Bring to simmer over medium-high heat. Cover, reduce heat to low, and cook until beans are just soft, 35 to 45 minutes. Using tongs, remove pepper, shallot, garlic, and bay leaf. Drain beans in colander set over large bowl, reserving 1¼ cups bean cooking liquid. (If you don't have enough bean cooking liquid, add water to equal 1¼ cups.)

3. Adjust oven rack to middle position and heat oven to 350 degrees. In now-empty saucepan, heat oil over medium heat until shimmering. Stir in chopped pepper, chopped shallot, oregano, and cumin. Cook, stirring frequently, until vegetables are softened and beginning to brown, 10 to 15 minutes. Add minced garlic and tomato paste and cook, stirring constantly, until fragrant, about 30 seconds. Add rice and stir to coat, about 30 seconds.

4. Stir in beans, reserved bean cooking liquid, vinegar, and ½ teaspoon salt. Increase heat to medium-high and bring to simmer. Cover and transfer to oven. Bake until liquid is absorbed and rice is tender, about 30 minutes. Fluff with fork and let sit, uncovered, for 5 minutes. Serve, passing scallion and lime wedges separately.

GREEK SPINACH AND FETA PIE

A STAPLE OF GREEK DINERS EVERYWHERE, SPANA-kopita is a savory spinach pie featuring a flaky phyllo crust layered with a delectably moist filling of tender greens and salty feta, kicked up with lemon, garlic, herbs, and spices. With its contrasting textures and bright, addictive flavors, what's not to love? How about the fact that most recipes for spanakopita yield enough food to serve a small Greek army—way too much for two diners, and the leftovers don't exactly stay crisp and fresh tasting. We wanted a recipe for a scaled-down spanakopita that boasted the same lively flavor and crisp texture as the full-size version. It had to offer the perfect balance of zesty spinach filling and shatteringly crisp phyllo crust—and it had to make just enough for two.

Most recipes for spanakopita follow the same basic series of steps: Transparently thin sheets of phyllo—unleavened dough made from flour, water, and lemon juice or vinegar—are layered to form a bottom crust, usually in a 13 by 9-inch baking dish. Each layer receives a brush of melted butter to contribute rich flavor and boost browning. On top of that goes the cheesy spinach filling, followed by another layer of delicate phyllo sheets, which forms the top crust. Baked at a high temperature (to ensure a golden brown top), the piping-hot pie is cooled and sliced into serving portions. We decided to start with the spinach mixture.

Using a bare-bones filling of spinach, feta, and egg (for binding), we began testing whether frozen spinach, fresh baby spinach, or fresh curly-leaf spinach would work best. After just one test, we ruled out the frozen spinach. The weak flavor and woody, stringy texture were nonstarters. Baby spinach also proved to be too mild in flavor. In the end, tasters favored the bolder flavor of the fresh crinkly spinach. Happily, all the methods we tried for precooking it (sautéing, boiling, microwaving, steaming) worked well for these hearty leaves, so we went with the push-button convenience of the microwave. Follow-up tests revealed that coarsely chopping the spinach and thoroughly squeezing out the excess moisture yielded superior texture and maximum flavor.

With the spinach figured out, we moved on to the other major component of the filling: the dairy. Feta rides shotgun to spinach in spanakopita, and the right amount can make or break the dish; for our mini spinach pie, 4 ounces proved to be just right. We found that simply crumbling the rich, pungent cheese into fine pieces helped it spread evenly through the sea of green, ensuring a salty tang in every bite. To buffer the assertiveness of the feta and add textural contrast, many recipes include soft dairy in the mix as well. We tried cream cheese, but this gave our spinach pie the consistency of spinach dip; ricotta and cottage cheese cooked up into rubbery curds. Sour cream and yogurt fared better, but thicker Greek yogurt turned out the best batch to date.

Some of the recipes we tested even included a third dairy component in the filling: a hard sheep's milk cheese called *kefalograviera*, which builds complexity. We wanted depth of flavor, but not the hassle of scouring specialty markets for such an obscure item. In the end, another, far more readily available hard sheep's milk cheese, Pecorino Romano, made a stand-up substitute.

At this point, our filling needed a few final flavor tweaks. Grassy scallions trumped onions, leeks, and shallots; the more robust flavor of raw minced garlic beat out sautéed; a generous scattering of mint provided a burst of freshness. A little nutmeg, cayenne, and a dose of lemon (juice plus grated zest) added fragrant warmth and brightness, respectively.

With a filling worthy of Mount Olympus, we moved on to the crust. We were already using frozen phyllo sheets, which are easy to find and simply need to be thawed ahead of time so that they are pliable. Standard recipes for full-size spanakopita use the full 14 by 9-inch sheets of phyllo to form the phyllo layers, but for our scaled-down spinach pie, we need to cut these sheets into smaller pieces. We found that cutting them into quarters gave us the perfect amount of spanakopita for two. Once the quarters were stacked and the spinach filling layered in the middle, our petite pie fit nicely in a 7¼ by 5¼-inch baking dish.

We'd figured out how to assemble our spinach pie, but now we had to address an annoying problem that kept popping up during our testing. Though the top crust consistently came out flaky and golden brown, the bottom crust always ended up soggy. We tried adjusting the oven temperature, to no avail. Then it occurred to us that the thick, high walls of the baking dish we were using would still trap any moisture coming off the crust, in effect helping to "steam" it instead of crisping it. What if we swapped the traditional baking dish for a baking sheet, which would provide a flat surface that

GREEK SPINACH AND FETA PIE (SPANAKOPITA)

allowed excess liquid to evaporate more readily? Sure enough, this proved to be an excellent move.

As we were assembling the layers on the baking sheet, we felt it was taking more time to paint every layer with melted butter than we wanted. A fellow test cook suggested that we try painting and stacking the full-size phyllo sheets first, then quartering them. This worked great, and after covering our small stack of phyllo with the spinach mixture, we did the same for the top crust. At the last minute, we decided to sprinkle between the top layers some of the grated Pecorino Romano we were using in the filling, which helped glue them together and prevented the tissue-thin pastry from sliding off when we sliced it. We scored the top few layers of phyllo with the tip of a knife to make it easier to cut once cooked and transferred the baking sheet to a 425-degree oven.

Twenty-five minutes later, what emerged from the oven was a beautiful spinach and feta pie built for two. It offered bright, zesty flavor and an ultra-crispy crust, from top to bottom.

Greek Spinach and Feta Pie (Spanakopita)

SERVES 2

Full-fat sour cream can be substituted for the whole Greek yogurt. Don't thaw the phyllo in the microwave—let it sit in the refrigerator overnight or on the counter for four to five hours.

FILLING

- 5 ounces curly-leaf spinach
- ¼ cup water
- 4 ounces feta cheese, rinsed, patted dry, and crumbled into fine pieces (1 cup)
- ¼ cup whole Greek yogurt
- 2 scallions, sliced thin
- 1 large egg, lightly beaten
- 1 tablespoon minced fresh mint
- 1 garlic clove, minced
- ½ teaspoon grated lemon zest plus 1 teaspoon juice
- ¼ teaspoon ground nutmeg
- ⅛ teaspoon salt
- ⅛ teaspoon pepper
  Pinch cayenne pepper

PHYLLO LAYERS

- 4 tablespoons unsalted butter, melted
- 5 (14 by 9-inch) sheets phyllo, thawed
- ¼ cup grated Pecorino Romano cheese
- 1 teaspoon sesame seeds (optional)

1. **FOR THE FILLING:** Place spinach and water in medium bowl, cover, and microwave until spinach is wilted and decreased in volume by half, 3 to 5 minutes. Transfer spinach to colander set in sink. Using back of spatula or spoon, gently press spinach against colander to release excess liquid. Transfer spinach to cutting board and roughly chop. Transfer spinach to clean kitchen towel and squeeze to remove excess water. Place drained spinach in large bowl. Add remaining filling ingredients and mix until thoroughly combined.

2. **FOR THE PHYLLO LAYERS:** Adjust oven rack to lower-middle position and heat oven to 425 degrees. Line rimmed baking sheet with parchment paper. Using pastry brush, lightly brush 7 by 4½-inch rectangle in center of parchment with melted butter.

3. Lay 1 phyllo sheet on cutting board and brush thoroughly with melted butter. Repeat, stacking 2 more phyllo sheets on top and brushing each with butter. Cut phyllo into quarters. Layer quarters on top of one another to form bottom crust, then place on buttered parchment.

4. Spread spinach mixture evenly over bottom crust, leaving ¼-inch border on all sides. Lay 1 phyllo sheet on cutting board, brush with melted butter, and sprinkle evenly with Pecorino. Layer remaining phyllo sheet on top and brush with butter. Cut phyllo into quarters. Layer quarters on top of one another to form top crust, then place on top of spinach filling.

5. Working from center outward, using hands, compress layers and press out any air pockets. Using sharp knife, score pie in half through top layer of phyllo. Sprinkle with sesame seeds (if using).

6. Bake until phyllo is golden and crisp, 20 to 25 minutes. Cool on baking sheet for 10 minutes or up to 2 hours. Slide spanakopita, still on parchment, onto cutting board and cut in half. Serve.

MAKING GREEK SPINACH AND FETA PIE

1. For bottom crust, lay 1 phyllo sheet on cutting board and brush thoroughly with melted butter. Repeat, stacking 2 more phyllo sheets on top and brushing each with butter. Then, cut phyllo into quarters.

2. Layer quarters on top of one another to form bottom crust, then place on buttered parchment paper.

3. Spread spinach mixture evenly over bottom crust, leaving ¼-inch border on all sides.

4. For top crust, lay 1 phyllo sheet on cutting board, brush with melted butter, and sprinkle evenly with Pecorino. Lay remaining phyllo sheet on top; brush with butter. Cut phyllo into quarters and stack as in steps 1 and 2.

5. Place top crust on top of spinach filling. Then, working from center outward, using hands, compress layers and press out any air pockets.

6. Finally, using sharp knife, score pie in half through top layer of phyllo. Sprinkle with sesame seeds (if using).

TIPS FOR TAMING PHYLLO

Frozen packaged phyllo dough functions as light, flaky pastry in traditional Greek dishes such as spanakopita and baklava and as a ready-made tart crust or wrapper for both sweet and savory fillings. But the tendency of these paper-thin sheets to tear, dry out quickly, and stick together can be maddening. Here are some tips for mastering this delicate dough.

1. TRIM STUCK EDGES: When the sheets of phyllo emerge from the box fused at their edges, don't try to separate the sheets. Instead, trim the fused portion and discard.

2. COVER WITH PLASTIC AND A DAMP TOWEL: The usual approach to prevent phyllo from cracking is to cover the stack with a damp towel. But it's easy to turn the dough sticky. We cover the stack with plastic wrap and then a damp towel.

3. STAGGER THE CRACKS: Some sheets of phyllo may crack and even tear while still in the box. Don't worry about rips; just make sure to adjust the orientation of the sheets as you stack them so that cracks in different sheets don't line up.

THE BEST KITCHEN RULER

We often specify exact measurements in our recipes, and traditionally we've used an ordinary steel ruler to guide us. But do rulers specifically designed for the kitchen have anything special to offer? We picked up two regular 18-inch steel rulers and compared them with two specialty rulers. We sliced cookie dough and chopped vegetables, using the rulers to achieve uniform-size pieces to ensure even cooking. A good ruler must be accurate and have a straight edge; one of the specialty rulers failed on both counts. In the end, a basic office-supply-store ruler, the **Empire 18-Inch Stainless Steel Ruler**, $8.49, which has large, easy-to-read markings, was the best tool by any measure.

TEMPEH TACOS

TACOS ARE A SATISFYING WAY TO BRING A VARIETY of textures and flavors to the table for two. But while recipes for homemade meat-based tacos are easy to come by, vegetarian versions are not quite so common. Those that do exist usually rely on beans or grilled vegetables as the stand-in for the meat. These are fine, but sometimes they seem like tacos that are just missing the meat. With all the options for vegetarian meat substitutes available these days, we felt confident we could develop a taco recipe that had a filling with great savory flavor and texture comparable to meaty tacos—but was 100 percent vegetarian friendly.

First we set our sights on finding the best meat substitute. Soy products are a staple vegetarian protein source and were a logical starting point. We gathered tofu, tempeh, and textured vegetable protein (TVP, a soy product sold in dehydrated flake form) and cooked up three basic batches, sautéing onion and garlic, then stirring in the protein and simmering with basic seasonings until done. Tofu was an out-and-out failure. Silken and soft tofu disintegrated in the skillet as expected, and the extra-firm tofu crumbled into unappealing bits. TVP became swollen when cooked, with a spongy texture that won over no one. However, tasters were pleased by the tacos made with tempeh. A tender but firm soybean cake made from fermented whole soybeans, tempeh can taste slightly sour or yeasty on its own, but here it came across as mildly nutty when mixed with the bolder taco flavors. Also, the texture of these tacos was actually "meaty."

With our protein chosen, we moved on to seasoning our filling beyond the simple onion and garlic combination. We started with a basic mix of common taco spices: chili powder, cumin, coriander, oregano, and cayenne. Tasters agreed that cumin was too strong and smoky here, and coriander too mild. For the chili powder, we began with 1 tablespoon but quickly increased it by half for the right kick. A half-teaspoon of dried oregano provided herbal notes. This simple combination added the right depth without overpowering the tempeh. To make their flavor fuller and rounder, we bloomed the spices by heating them briefly in a skillet. This simple step gave the filling a rich, deep flavor that was markedly better than when they were stirred in raw.

Taco fillings are usually made cohesive by a light sauce, which also helps carry the flavors of the spices. Many taco recipes call only for water, but water produced a hollow-tasting mixture for these tacos. We tried making one batch with canned vegetable broth and another with canned tomato sauce. Made with all vegetable broth, the filling took on a sweet flavor and the sauce did not thicken enough. On the other hand, made with only tomato sauce, the sauce was too thick and overshadowed the flavor of the spices. A combination of the two was perfect, with a nice acidity from the tomato sauce but not so much as to mask the spices, and together they reduced into just the right consistency.

The last adjustments to the filling came in the form of sweet and sour. A bit of brown sugar complemented the spices, and some lime juice picked up where the tomato sauce left off, adding just enough acidity to brighten it up. We moved on to the shells.

After sampling our tasty tempeh filling in both soft corn tortillas and hard taco shells, tasters decided they liked the contrast between the potently flavored, saucy filling and the crunchy shells, so we stuck with the latter option.

Served with all the usual taco fixings—shredded cheese, lettuce, diced tomato, avocado, onion, sour cream, and hot sauce—our vegetarian tacos more than hold their own against the meat versions any day.

NOTES FROM THE TEST KITCHEN

ALL ABOUT TEMPEH
While tofu, which is made from drained and pressed soy-milk curds, has definitely hit the mainstream, its soy-based cousin, tempeh, might not be as familiar. Tempeh is made by fermenting cooked soybeans, which are then formed into a firm, dense cake. Because it's better than tofu at holding its shape when cooked, tempeh serves as a good meat substitute. Although it has a strong, almost nutty flavor, it tends to absorb the flavors of any food or sauce to which it is added, making it a versatile choice for many sorts of dishes, from chilis and stews to sandwiches and tacos. Tempeh is sold in most supermarkets and can be found with different grain combinations and flavorings. We prefer to use five-grain tempeh in our recipes, but any tempeh variety will work.

SERVES 2

Any type of tempeh will work well in these tacos. Serve with shredded cheddar cheese, shredded lettuce, diced tomatoes, diced avocado, finely chopped onion, sour cream, and hot sauce.

- 1 tablespoon vegetable oil
- 1 small onion, chopped fine
- 1½ tablespoons chili powder
- 2 garlic cloves, minced
- ½ teaspoon dried oregano
- 8 ounces 5-grain tempeh, crumbled into ¼-inch pieces
- ¾ cup vegetable broth
- ½ cup canned tomato sauce
- ½ teaspoon light brown sugar
- 1 tablespoon minced fresh cilantro
- 1½ teaspoons lime juice
  Salt and pepper
- 6 taco shells, warmed

1. Heat oil in 10-inch nonstick skillet over medium heat until shimmering. Add onion and cook until softened, about 5 minutes. Stir in chili powder, garlic, and oregano and cook until fragrant, about 30 seconds.

2. Stir in tempeh and cook until lightly browned, about 5 minutes. Stir in broth, tomato sauce, and sugar. Bring to simmer and cook until thickened, about 2 minutes.

3. Off heat, stir in cilantro and lime juice and season with salt and pepper to taste. Divide filling evenly among taco shells and serve.

BROWN RICE BOWLS WITH CRISPY TOFU

BRINGING THE BRIGHT, BOLD FLAVORS AND CRISP, fresh textures of sushi home is quite challenging. Not only does homemade sushi require an investment of time and manual dexterity, it also involves special equipment. And when you're making only enough for two, rolling your own sushi at home seems like an absurd way to satisfy your craving. Enter the sushi rice bowl: a deconstructed version of a sushi roll, with a collection of fresh vegetables tossed in a sweet yet tart dressing and draped over a bed of seasoned rice. Generally a protein accompanies this dish; options range from raw fish to cooked egg to cubed tofu. We thought the creamy texture and mild flavor of tofu would pair well with the assertive flavors of sushi and sought to create a recipe for two brightly flavored rice bowls garnished with tofu and a variety of vegetables.

We got straight to work on the base of our dish, the rice. When we think of eating sushi, the first thing that usually springs to mind is the fresh raw fish. But technically, the term *sushi* refers to the seasoned rice that accompanies that fish. This style of rice stands apart from the pilafs and plain long-grain rice dishes we're used to here in the States. Sushi rice's delicate seasoning balances sweet, salty, and tart, and its texture is both pleasantly sticky and firm. A little research into traditional recipes told us that sushi rice isn't actually all that hard to make, but as with a number of "simple" recipes, the devil is in the details. In order to achieve rice with the proper sticky yet firm texture—without turning it gummy—we would need to find the best grain of rice for the job.

It turns out that sushi rice isn't a single rice at all, but rather a blanket term to describe any of the short-grain rice varieties traditionally used in making sushi. Imported Japanese short-grain rice (typically labeled "japonica") and California-grown japonica are commonly used, so we included these in our testing. Numerous cookbooks suggested that several Italian varieties of short-grain rice are as suitable for sushi rice as they are for risotto, so we also considered carnaroli and Arborio rice. For one last option, we included everyday, easy-to-find short-grain brown rice.

Working with a standard-issue sticky rice recipe from a traditional Japanese cookbook, we started cooking several batches of rice. Not surprisingly, Japanese sushi rice had a great balance between firmness and stickiness without being mushy. The carnaroli and Arborio (both favorites for making risotto) didn't fare so well; tasters felt they had a gummy texture. The short-grain brown rice had a pleasantly sticky and firm texture, plus tasters appreciated its slightly nutty flavor. Given that it was more readily available and helped make our simple dish more satisfying, we decided to go with the short-grain brown rice.

Satisfied with our choice of rice, we broached the next question: Is it imperative to rinse the rice before cooking? We often rinse rice and grains before cooking to remove excess starch so that the grains stay separate—ideal when cooking long-grain rice for a pilaf. So we were surprised to find that nearly every sushi rice recipe we came across likewise included instructions to rinse

the rice. This step seemed counterintuitive to producing "sticky" rice, but sure enough, a side-by-side test of rinsed and unrinsed rice proved tradition has it right. Why? Short-grain rice naturally has more starch within each grain than long-grain, so it inherently develops a stickier texture. Rinsing removes surface starch (and additives) that, if left on the rice prior to cooking, lead to an unappealing gummy texture. Our tasting confirmed that unrinsed short-grain rice was in fact slightly gummier, while the rinsed rice was appropriately sticky without being starchy.

We had nutty, tender, and perfectly sticky rice on our hands, but we now needed to nail down the *sushi-su*, the seasoned vinegar dressing that gives the rice its appealingly bright flavor. Traditionally composed of rice vinegar, sugar, dashi (a type of stock made with dried tuna flakes and seaweed), and sometimes mirin, the sushi-su is gently folded into the cooling rice so that the flavors are absorbed and infuse each grain. We liked the savory richness that dashi brought to the mix, but we wanted to keep the ingredients simple and accessible. Rice vinegar lent a delicate acidity to the rice, and mirin, a low-alcohol rice wine, gave us enough sweetness that we didn't need to add any more sugar.

With our rice tender, sticky, and seasoned, we moved on to the tofu. After making a sushi bowl prototype using just the seasoned rice and tofu (we hadn't decided what vegetables we wanted to throw in yet), we realized that our tofu was in need of a little jazzing up. Pan-frying seemed like a good option; the crispy coating would make a good foil for the creamy, mild tofu interior. We coated and pan-fried extra-firm, firm, and soft tofus and tasted them side by side. Tasters preferred the soft tofu for its ultra-creamy texture. To prepare the tofu for the pan, we simply cut it into planks, and then into fingers, and placed them on paper towels to drain. For help with the coating, we turned to a number of stir-fry recipes. We'd had good luck in the past using pure cornstarch, which helps stir-fry sauce adhere to the pan-fried tofu. But we were disappointed when the resulting tofu lacked the crunchy texture we were craving. While skimming some Asian cookbooks, we stumbled across a couple of recipes in which cornmeal was added to the coating. We decided

NOTES FROM THE TEST KITCHEN

CUTTING TOFU INTO FINGERS

1. Slice block of tofu crosswise into ¾-inch-thick slabs.

2. Slice each slab in half to form 2 fingers.

3. Spread tofu on baking sheet lined with several layers of paper towels. Let sit for 20 minutes to drain. Gently press tofu dry with paper towels.

RINSING RICE

To remove excess starch from white or brown rice, rinse it under cold water until water runs clear.

to give it a try and combined ¼ cup of cornstarch with 2 tablespoons of cornmeal. This proved to be just the right combination, and after just a couple of minutes over medium-high heat, the coating was crispy and golden brown.

When it came to the vegetables, we decided to simply slice them and toss them with a simple dressing to give our dish some fresh texture and flavor. Cucumber was a given, as it makes frequent appearances in many sushi rolls and has a cool and crunchy texture. Creamy avocado contrasted nicely with the crispy tofu, and a thinly sliced scallion brought a subtle onion flavor to the table. Peppery radish, thinly sliced, contributed its slightly bitter notes and a pop of color. For the dressing, we used a bit more rice vinegar and mirin, which we'd used to season the rice, and added soy sauce for its savory, salty notes, ginger for zip, and orange zest and juice for their bright sweetness.

Though our two rice bowls were satisfying and boasted all of the best flavors and textures of our favorite sushi rolls, we noticed that one thing was missing: nori, the dried seaweed commonly used in rolled sushi. While a sprinkling of crumbled nori gave our dish an authentic sushi feel, our brown rice bowls with crispy tofu were delicious with or without it.

Brown Rice Bowls with Crispy Tofu and Vegetables
SERVES 2

To save time, prep the tofu and vegetables while the rice cooks. We prefer the creamier texture of soft tofu here; however, firm or extra-firm tofu will also work. Nori is seaweed that has been dried and pressed into sheets used for rolling sushi; you can find it in the international foods aisle of the supermarket.

RICE AND DRESSING
- 1½ cups water
- ¾ cup short-grain brown rice, rinsed
- 3 tablespoons rice vinegar
- 3 tablespoons mirin
- 1½ tablespoons soy sauce
- ½ teaspoon grated fresh ginger
- ¼ teaspoon orange zest plus 1 teaspoon juice

TOFU AND VEGETABLES
- 7 ounces soft tofu
- ¼ cup cornstarch
- 2 tablespoons cornmeal
- Salt and pepper
- 2 tablespoons vegetable oil
- ½ (8 by 7½-inch) sheet nori, crumbled (optional)
- 2 radishes, sliced thin
- ½ avocado, pitted and sliced thin
- ½ cucumber, peeled, halved lengthwise, seeded, and sliced thin
- 1 scallion, sliced thin

1. FOR THE RICE AND DRESSING: Bring water and rice to simmer in small saucepan over high heat. Reduce heat to low, cover, and continue to simmer until rice is tender and water is absorbed, 45 to 50 minutes. Off heat, lay clean folded kitchen towel underneath lid and let sit for 10 minutes.

2. Combine vinegar and mirin in small bowl. Measure 2 tablespoons vinegar mixture into second small bowl, whisk in soy sauce, ginger, and orange zest and juice, and reserve for serving.

3. Transfer rice to medium bowl, sprinkle with remaining ¼ cup vinegar mixture, and toss gently to combine. Let cool for about 20 minutes.

4. FOR THE TOFU AND VEGETABLES: Slice tofu crosswise into ¾-inch-thick slabs. Slice each slab in half to form two fingers. Spread tofu on paper towel–lined baking sheet and let drain for 20 minutes. Gently press tofu dry with paper towels.

5. Whisk cornstarch and cornmeal together in shallow dish. Season tofu with ⅛ teaspoon salt and ⅛ teaspoon pepper. Working with a few pieces at a time, coat tofu thoroughly with cornstarch mixture, pressing to help it adhere, then transfer to plate.

6. Heat oil in 10-inch nonstick skillet over medium-high heat until shimmering. Carefully lay tofu in skillet and cook until crisp and slightly golden on all sides, 10 to 12 minutes.

7. Divide rice between 2 serving bowls, sprinkle with one-half of nori (if using), and top with tofu, radishes, avocado, and cucumber. Sprinkle with scallion and drizzle with reserved dressing. Serve with remaining nori (if using).

GRILLED SEA SCALLOPS AND GRAPEFRUIT SALSA WITH FENNEL

GRILLED STEAK BURGERS WITH ROMAINE SALAD

MOST STEAKHOUSES FEATURE A BURGER ON THEIR menus. The meat is usually ground from intensely beefy steak trimmings, cooked on a ripping-hot grill (or under the broiler) to crusty perfection, and served with steak sauce. In essence, it's the steak experience on a bun. We wanted the same results from our backyard grill. To complement our burgers, we set out to develop a riff on another steakhouse classic: the wedge salad. But first we had to tackle the burgers.

In the test kitchen, we frequently opt to grind our own meat. For this dinner off the grill, however, we wanted an easier route to similarly big flavor. Therefore, we began our testing with three readily available varieties of ground beef: chuck, round, and sirloin. We patted portions of each cut into patties, seasoned them with salt and pepper, and grilled them over high heat to medium-rare. The ground round was perfectly fine and the chuck even better, but neither tasted as beefy as the sirloin. But sirloin is about 90 percent lean, so although these burgers offered ultra-meaty flavor, they were a bit on the dry side. Taking a cue from our Juicy Pub-Style Burgers (page 9), we decided to add melted butter to the meat; we found that this additional fat significantly improved the burgers' flavor and juiciness.

To give our burgers more complexity, we decided to add some aromatics. Onions and garlic are common burger additions, so that's where we started. We sautéed a small chopped onion and some minced garlic in our melted butter before mixing them into the meat. Unfortunately, the moisture from the chopped onion made for mushy burgers, so we nixed it; luckily, the garlic alone provided sufficient aromatic oomph. A hefty sprinkling of salt and pepper rounded out the flavor of our burgers. To shape the burgers, we used a proven test kitchen technique—making a small indentation in the patties to keep them from puffing up during cooking. Next up: the sauce.

Looking for inspiration, we sampled a number of commercial steak sauces—even A1—and tested a handful of recipes. Not surprisingly, they all tasted harsh, but they did provide a bit of direction. Following the lead of most recipes we tried, we sautéed garlic in butter, then added tomato paste, water, raisins, vinegar,

Worcestershire sauce, and mustard. This sauce got better when we traded white vinegar for balsamic and water for beef broth. We let it simmer for a few minutes, then buzzed the sauce in the blender until it was smooth.

At last, we were ready to cook our burgers. We heated the grill until it was hot, tossed the burgers on top, then pulled them off once they were perfectly medium-rare, which took a little over five minutes. We drizzled our steak sauce on top and served them up. While we loved the sweet and savory notes provided by the sauce, our burgers themselves hadn't picked up any real char. We couldn't leave them on the grill any longer without overcooking them, but perhaps we could boost caramelization on the surface of the patties by brushing them with something sweet. With tomato paste, raisins, and balsamic vinegar, our homemade sauce fit the bill, so we gave our patties a liberal coating before heading outside. After several minutes, our burgers were a perfect medium-rare—but now they also had a well-charred crust. For even more flavor, we brushed a little extra steak sauce mixed with butter onto our hamburger buns and toasted them on the grill.

Finally, it was time to address our salad. We aimed to complete our ultra-beefy steak burgers with a grilled wedge salad, but we suspected that the defining element, the iceberg lettuce, wouldn't take too well to the grill given its high water content. After just one test, it was clear we had to pick another lettuce—the grilled iceberg picked up no char or flavor whatsoever. For our next test, we traded the iceberg for romaine, which we simply halved, then grilled cut side down. Not only did the romaine become nicely charred and crisp in just a few minutes—and we had to let the burgers rest

NOTES FROM THE TEST KITCHEN

SHAPING BURGERS

To guarantee burgers with flat top and no bulge, press center of each patty down with your fingertips to form indentation that is about ¼ inch deep.

for five to 10 minutes anyway once they came off the grill—but one romaine heart was the perfect amount for two. Drizzled with a simple blue cheese dressing and rounded out with grilled tomato halves and red onion rings, our updated take on wedge salad was the perfect match to our ultra-satisfying steak burgers.

Grilled Steak Burgers with Romaine and Blue Cheese Salad

SERVES 2

You will need one 12-inch metal skewer for this recipe. We prefer these burgers cooked to medium-rare, but if you prefer them more or less done, see our guidelines on page 154. Don't remove the core from the lettuce; it will help keep the leaves together on the grill. You can substitute milk for the buttermilk, if desired, although the flavor of the dressing will not be as tangy. Don't brush the lettuce with oil or season with salt and pepper until just before placing it on the grill or the lettuce will wilt.

BURGERS

- 4 tablespoons unsalted butter
- 1 garlic clove, minced
  Salt and pepper
- 1 tablespoon tomato paste
- ⅓ cup beef broth
- 3 tablespoons raisins
- 1 tablespoon Dijon mustard
- 1 tablespoon balsamic vinegar
- 1½ teaspoons Worcestershire sauce
- 12 ounces 90 percent lean ground sirloin
- 2 hamburger buns

SALAD

- 1 ounce blue cheese, crumbled (¼ cup)
- 1 tablespoon plus 1 teaspoon buttermilk
- 1 small garlic clove, minced
- 2 tablespoons mayonnaise
- 1 teaspoon white wine vinegar
  Pinch sugar
  Salt and pepper
- 1 small red onion, sliced into ¾-inch-thick rings
- 1 tomato, cored and halved
- 2 tablespoons olive oil
- 1 romaine lettuce heart (6 ounces), halved lengthwise through core

1. FOR THE BURGERS: Melt butter in 8-inch skillet over medium-low heat. Add garlic, ½ teaspoon salt, and ½ teaspoon pepper and cook until fragrant, about 1 minute. Pour all but 1 tablespoon butter mixture into bowl and let cool, about 5 minutes.

2. Meanwhile, add tomato paste to skillet with remaining butter mixture and cook over medium heat until paste begins to darken, 1 to 2 minutes. Stir in broth, raisins, mustard, vinegar, and Worcestershire and simmer until raisins plump, about 5 minutes. Transfer sauce to blender and process until smooth, about 30 seconds; transfer to bowl.

3. Combine 2 tablespoons cooled butter mixture with ground sirloin and gently knead until well incorporated. Divide meat into 2 equal portions, then form gently into two ¾-inch-thick patties and press shallow divot in center of each patty. Measure out 1 tablespoon sauce and brush both sides of patties; cover and refrigerate until ready to cook. Combine remaining 1 tablespoon butter mixture with 2 tablespoons steak sauce and brush onto cut sides of buns.

4. FOR THE SALAD: In medium bowl, mash blue cheese, buttermilk, and garlic together with fork until no large clumps remain. Whisk in mayonnaise, vinegar, and sugar and season with salt and pepper to taste. Cover and refrigerate until ready to serve. Thread onion rounds, from side to side, onto 12-inch metal skewer. Brush skewered onion and tomato halves with 1 tablespoon oil and season with salt and pepper.

5A. FOR A CHARCOAL GRILL: Open bottom vent completely. Light large chimney starter filled with charcoal briquettes (6 quarts). When top coals are partially covered with ash, pour evenly over grill. Set cooking grate in place, cover, and open lid vent completely. Heat grill until hot, about 5 minutes.

5B. FOR A GAS GRILL: Turn all burners to high, cover, and heat grill until hot, about 15 minutes. Leave all burners on high.

6. Clean and oil cooking grate. Place burgers and onion skewer on grill. Cook burgers (covered if using gas) until they register 120 to 125 degrees (for medium-rare), 6 to 8 minutes, flipping them halfway through cooking. Cook onion until spottily charred on both sides, 8 to 12 minutes. Transfer burgers to plate, tent loosely with aluminum foil, and let rest for 5 to 10 minutes. Transfer onion to cutting board.

7. While burgers rest, brush romaine with remaining 1 tablespoon oil and season with salt and pepper.

Place tomato halves, romaine halves, and buns, cut side down, on grill. Cook buns until warm and lightly charred, about 30 seconds. Cook tomato and romaine until cut sides are spottily charred, 2 to 5 minutes. Transfer tomato and romaine to cutting board with onion and cut tomato halves into 2 wedges each.

8. Divide lettuce, onion, and tomato wedges between 2 plates, drizzle blue cheese dressing over top, and season with pepper to taste. Place burgers on buns and drizzle with remaining steak sauce. Serve with salad.

GRILLED BEEF AND VEGETABLE KEBABS

KEBABS MAKE FOR ONE EFFORTLESS GRILLED DINNER for two—simply thread meat and vegetables onto a few skewers, grill, and serve. Unfortunately, the pluses that kebabs offer—ease and speed—are often negated by their disappointing texture and flavor. Most of the time, the meat is either dry and tough with a burnt exterior, or at the other extreme, it's drab looking, with no visible char at all. The vegetables aren't much better—they usually turn out torched on the outside and still crunchy on the inside. We were determined to nail a foolproof approach to putting smoke, char, and flavor into our beef kebabs and achieving nicely browned, tender-firm vegetables at the same time.

Our testing started at the butcher case, where we rounded up five possible cuts of meat for skewering, ranging from bottom round to tenderloin. Though many recipes advise cutting the meat into 1-inch chunks, we opted to cube the beef into generous 2-inch pieces, which would cook through more slowly and increase our chances for perfectly cooked, tender meat. We then skewered the cubes and seasoned them with salt and pepper (we'd worry about the veggies and a marinade later) before throwing them onto the fire—for the moment, a full chimney of briquettes (6 quarts) spread into a single layer. Lean, pricey tenderloin turned out to be a waste of money, since tasters found it predictably bland, and bottom round was too chewy. The more marbled cuts—skirt steak, blade steak, and steak tips—all boasted respectable flavor, but the looser-grained steak tips outdid the others in both beefiness and tender texture. Best of all, it was easy to purchase just the right amount of meat (12 ounces) for a pair of diners.

When it comes to marinade, the test kitchen has developed a number of tricks to maximize its impact, so we had a head start on that front. First, we've found that salt is one of the few ingredients that penetrate to season the center of the meat, so we use a lot of it. Second, we always include oil. Though it won't seep beyond the meat's surface, oil is a key player when herbs and spices are part of the mix, since their flavor compounds are mostly fat-soluble. Third, we add a little sugar to lend a hint of sweetness and help the meat develop flavorful browning.

As for the other marinade ingredients, soy sauce is a common choice; it's packed with easily absorbable flavor enhancers, also known as glutamates, which make meat taste even more savory. But after just one test, we had to nix the soy sauce because it made our kebabs taste like teriyaki; we were after a more neutral flavor base. As we mentally ticked off other common pantry staples, we thought of tomato paste, also full of glutamates. Though tomato paste is an unorthodox addition to marinade, its fruity taste could be just the thing we were looking for when thinned with a little water. Trading the water for beef broth later on gave our marinade even more savory notes. For a little more flair, we added lemon zest, rosemary, and a few cloves of garlic. With all of these tricks and flavors in play, our beef needed only an hour to absorb all of the seasoning from the marinade. (We found we could leave the beef in for up to one additional hour with no harm done.)

For the vegetables, we singled out three grill favorites: bell pepper, red onion, and zucchini. One of each provided enough for two. After cutting our vegetables into fork-friendly pieces that were large enough to stay put on the skewer, we marinated them for 30 minutes, threaded them onto skewers with our beef, and cooked the kebabs over a hot fire. After about 15 minutes, our 2-inch beef chunks boasted a nicely charred exterior and perfectly tender, medium-rare interior, but our vegetables were blackened and tasted like charcoal. Clearly, they would do better cooked over more gentle heat. The obvious solution was to place the two components on separate skewers and build a fire with a hotter area and a slightly cooler area, where they could cook simultaneously but over their own optimal degree of heat.

GRILLED BEEF AND VEGETABLE KEBABS WITH NORTH AFRICAN MARINADE

For our next batch of kebabs, we spread our coals in the center of the grill (to enhance the char on the beef, we piled on even more coals), leaving a 2-inch gap between the grill wall and the charcoal. The heat flamed up the center, bonfire-style, and charred the beef pieces perfectly. Meanwhile, the veggies rested over the cooler perimeter of the coals, where they slowly bronzed and charred at the tips over the less intense heat. (For a gas grill, we mimicked the charcoal setup by turning the primary burner to high and the secondary burner(s) to medium-low.)

Our grill properly heated, both our vegetable and meat skewers came off the grill with just the right amount of char and smoky flavor. In fact, tasters were so pleased that we decided to come up with a couple of different marinade variations. First, we borrowed flavors from North African cuisine and replaced the lemon and rosemary with cilantro, paprika, cumin, and cayenne. For a spicier dish, we combined red curry paste with fresh basil, lime zest, and ginger. Not only were our grilled kebabs quick and easy, but now they boasted great flavor and tender meat and vegetables.

Grilled Beef and Vegetable Kebabs with Lemon and Rosemary

SERVES 2

To ensure evenly sized pieces, we prefer to purchase whole steak tips (also known as flap meat) and cut them ourselves. However, if you have long, thin pieces of meat, roll or fold them into approximately 2-inch cubes before skewering. You will need three 12-inch metal skewers for this recipe. We prefer these kebabs cooked to medium-rare, but if you prefer them more or less done, see our guidelines on page 154.

MARINADE

- 1 small onion, chopped coarse
- 3 tablespoons beef broth
- 3 tablespoons vegetable oil
- 1½ tablespoons tomato paste
- 3 garlic cloves, chopped
- 2 teaspoons minced fresh rosemary
- 1½ teaspoons grated lemon zest
- 1 teaspoon salt
- ¾ teaspoon sugar
- ½ teaspoon pepper

BEEF AND VEGETABLES

- 12 ounces sirloin steak tips, trimmed and cut into 2-inch chunks
- 1 zucchini or summer squash, halved lengthwise and sliced 1 inch thick
- 1 red or green bell pepper, stemmed, seeded, and cut into 1½-inch pieces
- 1 small red onion, halved through root end, each half cut into 4 wedges and each wedge cut crosswise in half

1. FOR THE MARINADE: Process all ingredients together in blender until smooth, about 45 seconds. Transfer ½ cup marinade to medium bowl and set aside.

2. FOR THE BEEF AND VEGETABLES: Combine remaining marinade and beef in zipper-lock bag and toss to coat; press out as much air as possible and seal bag. Refrigerate for at least 1 hour or up to 2 hours, flipping bag every 30 minutes.

3. Add zucchini, bell pepper, and onion to bowl with reserved marinade and gently toss to coat. Cover and let sit at room temperature for at least 30 minutes.

4. Remove beef from bag and pat dry with paper towels. Tightly thread beef onto one 12-inch metal skewer. Thread vegetables onto two 12-inch metal skewers, in alternating pattern of zucchini, pepper, and onion.

5A. FOR A CHARCOAL GRILL: Open bottom vent completely. Light large chimney starter mounded with charcoal briquettes (7 quarts). When top coals are partially covered with ash, pour evenly over center of grill, leaving 2-inch gap between entire grill wall and charcoal. Set cooking grate in place, cover, and open lid vent completely. Heat grill until hot, about 5 minutes.

NOTES FROM THE TEST KITCHEN

ENSURING EVENLY COOKED MEAT FOR KEBABS
When shopping for meat for kebabs, it can be hard to find evenly thick pieces of beef or chicken that will produce uniform chunks and cook through evenly.

To ensure that thinner pieces cook at same rate as larger chunks, slice tapered beef into 2-inch by 4-inch pieces or chicken into 1-inch by 2-inch pieces; roll or fold to create thicker 2- or 1-inch pieces for skewer.

5B. FOR A GAS GRILL: Turn all burners to high, cover, and heat grill until hot, about 15 minutes. Leave primary burner on high and turn other burner(s) to medium-low.

6. Clean and oil cooking grate. Place meat skewer on hotter part of grill and vegetable skewers on cooler part of grill (near edge of coals if using charcoal). Cook (covered if using gas), turning skewers every 3 to 4 minutes, until beef is well browned and registers 120 to 125 degrees (for medium-rare), 12 to 16 minutes, and vegetables are tender and lightly charred, 17 to 21 minutes. Transfer skewers to serving platter, tent loosely with aluminum foil, and let beef rest for 5 to 10 minutes. Serve.

VARIATIONS

Grilled Beef and Vegetable Kebabs with North African Marinade

Substitute 10 cilantro sprigs, 1 teaspoon sweet paprika, ¾ teaspoon ground cumin, and ¼ teaspoon cayenne pepper for lemon zest and rosemary.

Grilled Beef and Vegetable Kebabs with Red Curry Marinade

Substitute ¼ cup packed fresh basil leaves, 1½ tablespoons red curry paste, 1½ teaspoons grated lime zest, and 1 teaspoon grated ginger for lemon zest and rosemary.

GRILLED STEAK TIPS AND RED POTATOES

GRILLED STEAK TIPS ARE A STEAKHOUSE FAVORITE for a reason: The tender cut of beef takes well to potent marinades and easily picks up flavorful char. We wanted a recipe that delivered perfect grilled steak tips for two—our goal was to find the right cut of meat, then build a flavorful marinade, and, finally, nail down the grilling method. While we were at it, we would create an inspired side dish to accompany our steak tips, for the perfect homemade steakhouse dinner for two.

First, we set out to find the right beef for the job. Though you occasionally find the dish made with tender, richly flavored, expensive cuts like strip steak, rib-eye steak, and tenderloin, we didn't want to pay top dollar for a simple grilled meal for two. We turned instead to cheaper cuts: flank steak, round steak, and,

of course, the most common choice, sirloin steak tips (also known as flap meat), cut from the sirloin area between the cow's short loin and back legs. This beefy cut has a wealth of internal marbling that melts into the coarse muscle fibers of the steak, adding tenderness when the meat is cooked to medium-rare. Flank steak wasn't nearly as meaty tasting, and round steak lacked intramuscular fat, easily turning bland and dry. Steak tips, which can easily be purchased in small quantities (12 ounces proved just right for two people), were ideal for this dish.

It was time to move on to the marinade. Most recipes we came across stressed the importance of a "secret" ingredient—beer, ketchup, barbecue sauce, Italian dressing, or cola. Intrigued by this eclectic mix of flavorings, we decided to put these recipes to the test. The beer-based marinade produced bitter, soggy tips, and Italian dressing gave us sour, mushy tips. Both ketchup and barbecue sauce produced significant char because they contain sugar, but these distinctively seasoned condiments produced tips that tasted as though they belonged in a barbecue joint, not a steakhouse. The only "secret" ingredient that promoted the right sort of char and flavor was cola, but the cola marinade was a drippy mess, which meant we had to dry off the tips—a sloppy endeavor at best—before grilling.

While none of these marinades was very good, at least we'd learned that sugar would play an important role in our recipe. We whisked together a working marinade of typical flavor boosters, starting with garlic, paprika, cayenne pepper, black pepper, vegetable oil, and soy sauce, then added light brown sugar and tomato paste for a double dose of sweetness. We cut our tips into 2½-inch pieces; this size gave us steak tips that were large enough to grill with ease but weren't so big that they were overwhelming on the plate. We marinated the chunks for an hour, which was the minimum time called for in many recipes.

After preheating the grill, we set our steak tips on the ripping-hot grate. We generally like our steak cooked to medium-rare, so we pulled the tips off the grill when they reached 120 degrees. They were well seasoned and flavorful, but the char needed a boost. To further bump up the char, we simply added more brown sugar, which encouraged caramelization on the surface of the meat. In addition, we switched from light brown sugar to dark brown sugar, which lent a deeper, more molasses-like flavor.

Now our tips tasted great, but more than one taster joked about jaw fatigue—the meat was a little tough. We tried the common trick of poking the meat with a fork before cutting it into chunks. It worked: The poking breaks long, tough muscle fibers into shorter, more tender pieces. Fork-tenderizing had the added advantage of exposing more surface to soak up the marinade. We also found that marinating the beef for two hours gave us maximum flavor, but, if necessary, it could sit in the marinade for up to one day with no harm done.

To complete our at-home steakhouse dinner, we turned to steak tips' natural partner: potatoes. We halved a few small red potatoes (which held their shape over the high heat of the grill better than other varieties) and skewered and grilled them with our tips. However, by the time the grilled tips had finished resting, our potatoes were still raw on the inside. We often give hardier vegetables a jump start in the microwave before grilling, so we decided to give it a go with our potatoes. After microwaving them until they were almost tender, we skewered our potatoes and placed them over the hot fire. This time, when the steak tips were ready for the plate, our spuds were tender and creamy on the inside and nicely charred on the outside. To gild the lily, we drizzled a rich, creamy sauce (sour cream and mayonnaise spiked with chives and lemon juice) over our grilled potatoes—the perfect finishing touch to our grilled steak and potatoes dinner.

Grilled Steakhouse Steak Tips and Red Potatoes with Sour Cream–Chive Sauce

SERVES 2

To ensure evenly sized pieces, we prefer to purchase whole steak tips (also known as flap meat) and cut them ourselves. We prefer to use extra-small red potatoes, measuring about 1 inch in diameter, in this recipe. You will need two 12-inch metal skewers for this recipe. We prefer these steak tips cooked to medium, but if you prefer them more or less done, see our guidelines on page 154.

STEAK TIPS

- 3 tablespoons soy sauce
- 3 tablespoons vegetable oil
- 1½ tablespoons packed dark brown sugar
- 3 garlic cloves, minced

- 1½ teaspoons tomato paste
- 1½ teaspoons paprika
- ¼ teaspoon pepper
- ⅛ teaspoon cayenne pepper
- 12 ounces sirloin steak tips, trimmed and cut into 2½-inch pieces

POTATOES AND SAUCE

- 1 tablespoon sour cream
- 1 tablespoon mayonnaise
- 1 tablespoon minced fresh chives
- 1½ teaspoons lemon juice
- 1 teaspoon water
  Salt and pepper
- 12 ounces extra-small red potatoes, halved
- 1 tablespoon olive oil

1. FOR THE STEAK TIPS: Whisk soy sauce, oil, sugar, garlic, tomato paste, paprika, pepper, and cayenne together in bowl until sugar dissolves; transfer to zipper-lock bag. Pat steak tips dry with paper towels and prick on all sides with fork. Add to bag with soy sauce mixture and toss to coat; press out as much air as possible and seal bag. Refrigerate for at least 2 hours or up to 24 hours, flipping bag occasionally.

2. FOR THE POTATOES: Combine sour cream, mayonnaise, chives, lemon juice, and water in small bowl and season with salt and pepper to taste. Cover and refrigerate until ready to serve. Toss potatoes with oil and season with salt and pepper. Place, cut side down, on plate and microwave until potatoes soften but still hold their shape, 5 to 7 minutes, flipping them halfway through cooking. Let cool for 5 minutes and thread, cut side down, onto two 12-inch metal skewers.

3A. FOR A CHARCOAL GRILL: Open bottom vent completely. Light large chimney starter filled with charcoal briquettes (6 quarts). When top coals are partially covered with ash, pour evenly over grill. Set cooking grate in place, cover, and open lid vent completely. Heat grill until hot, about 5 minutes.

3B. FOR A GAS GRILL: Turn all burners to high, cover, and heat grill until hot, about 15 minutes. Leave all burners on high.

4. Clean and oil cooking grate. Place beef and potato skewers, cut side down, on grill. Cook potatoes (covered if using gas), turning as needed, until tender and browned on both sides, about 5 minutes. Cook beef until charred on both sides and it registers 130 to 135 degrees (for medium), 8 to 10 minutes.

5. Transfer potatoes and beef to serving platter, tent loosely with aluminum foil, and let rest for 5 to 10 minutes. Slide potatoes off skewers, drizzle sauce over potatoes, and serve.

NOTES FROM THE TEST KITCHEN

SKEWERING POTATOES FOR THE GRILL

Place potato half, cut side down, on cutting board and pierce through center with skewer. Repeat, holding already-skewered potatoes for better leverage.

COMMON INGREDIENTS, UNCOMMON RESULTS

We engineered our marinade to give the steak tips maximum meaty flavor and satisfying texture. These familiar ingredients make a strong team, each with its own part to play.

DARK BROWN SUGAR
Delivers depth, complexity, and caramelized, crusty char.

TOMATO PASTE
Adds background savor and enough body to help marinade cling.

VEGETABLE OIL
Distributes flavors and activates oil-soluble flavor compounds, such as those found in garlic.

SOY SAUCE
Its salt penetrates to deeply season meat. Its glutamates boost meaty flavor.

GRILLED GLAZED PORK CHOPS WITH ARUGULA

PORK CHOPS AND HONEY ARE A NATURAL PAIRING, as the honey brings out all of the subtle sweetness in the mild-tasting pork. In theory, grilling should only enhance the combination—it allows the honey to caramelize and become a smoky, charred glaze—but there's a fine line between charred and burnt. We sought a foolproof method for grilling honey-glazed chops that delivered both tender meat and a flavorful (but not burnt) exterior. While we were at it, we wanted a well-crafted side dish to match the sweet and savory notes of the pork.

Recipes for honey-glazed pork chops abound, so we started by testing a few varied approaches. In some, raw chops were dipped in a glaze of honey, sugar, and liquid (vinegar, apple juice, and brandy are common) and then grilled. Sadly, when we tried these recipes, the glazes melted right off. In other recipes the chops were grilled, uncoated, and subsequently painted with a honey glaze. Though these chops absorbed some flavor, they never developed a nicely lacquered exterior. A third method, painting the chops with glaze partway through cooking, showed the most promise, as these chops retained at least some of the coating.

Using the best glaze from our initial tests (honey, brown sugar, cider vinegar, and cornstarch), we built a two-level fire, which provided two distinct cooking zones: a hotter area that delivered intense, direct heat and a slightly cooler area that provided more gentle, indirect heat. Then we followed the test kitchen's standard method for grilling pork chops: Cook over direct heat to sear, brush on the glaze, and finish the chops over indirect heat on the cooler side. Despite the cornstarch, which we hoped would thicken the mixture, the glaze ran off. Although honey is sticky at room temperature, heat causes it to thin and melt away. We reversed our method, cooking the chops over indirect heat, then applying the glaze, and finally searing them quickly over direct heat. We hoped the honey would caramelize before it had a chance to melt. Instead, the indirect heat released the meat's moisture, which meant we had to leave the chops over the heat longer so the moisture could evaporate and then the chops could brown. Not surprisingly, this led to overcooked chops.

In the past, we've relied on a light sprinkling of sugar to expedite browning on everything from pork tenderloin to tuna. We decided to give it a try here and rubbed our chops with some sugar, plus salt and pepper for flavor, and then cooked them over indirect heat until deeply browned and almost cooked through. In addition to the rich brown color, our chops now had a crackly, sugared exterior: the perfect surface to which our glaze could cling. We could now glaze and sear our chops with ease.

At this point, the chops were looking great, but tasters demanded more honey flavor. We had been using a glaze made up of equal parts honey and brown sugar, but tasters felt the brown sugar competed with the flavor of the honey. We cut out the sugar completely and added more honey to make up the difference. Not surprisingly, the new glaze had better honey flavor, but subsequent testing revealed why recipes usually combine honey with sugar. As we found out, brown sugar has a much lower water content than honey (2 percent or less versus honey's 17 percent), so the honey-only glaze was too watery and didn't adhere to our chops. To remove the extra moisture, we reached for a pot and reduced the glaze on the stovetop. Now our nicely thickened glaze stayed put when brushed on the chops.

With our honey flavor optimized, we considered other ingredients to amp up the glaze. Dijon mustard and cayenne pepper contributed a subtle heat, and thyme added savory complexity. After grilling, glazing, and searing another batch of chops, we gave them a final brush with the glaze just before serving. This last step took them from good to great.

Not quite done yet, we looked to create a brightly flavored salad that would provide a nice complement to the pork. A single peach, halved and grilled until lightly charred, offered a delicate sweetness, which we countered with peppery baby arugula. For some sharpness to keep the salad in balance, we added a grilled red onion to the mix. Tossed with a Dijon vinaigrette, this fruity, peppery salad was the perfect match to our sweet and savory honey-glazed pork chops.

NOTES FROM THE TEST KITCHEN

GETTING THE GLAZE TO CLING

1. Simmer glaze until it turns thick and sticky, which will help it cling to pork chops.

2. Rub pork chops with sugar to create bumpy, caramelized crust to which glaze can adhere.

3. Cook pork chops over indirect heat until almost done. Then brush with glaze and sear over direct heat.

Grilled Honey-Glazed Pork Chops with Peach, Red Onion, and Arugula Salad

SERVES 2

You will need one 12-inch metal skewer for this recipe. To prevent the pork chops from curling on the grill, score the fat at 2-inch intervals (see page 56).

- 2 teaspoons plus 2 tablespoons cider vinegar
- 2 tablespoons Dijon mustard
- 2 tablespoons extra-virgin olive oil
- Salt and pepper
- ¼ cup honey
- ½ teaspoon cornstarch
- ½ teaspoon minced fresh thyme or ⅛ teaspoon dried
- ⅛ teaspoon cayenne pepper
- 2 tablespoons sugar
- 2 (10-ounce) bone-in pork rib or center-cut chops, 1 inch thick, trimmed
- 1 small red onion, sliced into ¾-inch-thick rings
- 1 peach, halved and pitted
- 2 ounces (2 cups) baby arugula

GRILLED HONEY-GLAZED PORK CHOPS WITH PEACH, RED ONION, AND ARUGULA SALAD

1. Whisk 2 teaspoons vinegar, 1 teaspoon mustard, and oil together in medium bowl. Season with salt and pepper to taste and set aside. Whisk remaining 2 tablespoons vinegar, remaining 5 teaspoons mustard, honey, cornstarch, thyme, and cayenne together in small saucepan until no lumps remain. Bring to boil, reduce heat to medium-low, and simmer until glaze is reduced to ¼ cup, 5 to 7 minutes. Reserve 2 tablespoons glaze for serving.

2. Combine sugar, ½ teaspoon salt, and ½ teaspoon pepper in bowl. Cut 2 slits about 2 inches apart through fat around outside of each pork chop. Pat chops dry with paper towels and rub evenly with sugar mixture. Thread onion rounds, from side to side, onto one 12-inch metal skewer. Brush skewered onion and peach halves with 1 tablespoon vinaigrette and season with salt and pepper.

3A. FOR A CHARCOAL GRILL: Open bottom vent completely. Light large chimney starter filled with charcoal briquettes (6 quarts). When top coals are partially covered with ash, pour two-thirds evenly over grill, then pour remaining coals over half of grill. Set cooking grate in place, cover, and open lid vent completely. Heat grill until hot, about 5 minutes.

3B. FOR A GAS GRILL: Turn all burners to high, cover, and heat grill until hot, about 15 minutes. Leave primary burner on high and turn other burner(s) to medium-low.

4. Clean and oil cooking grate. Place chops on cooler part of grill and cook (covered if using gas) until chops register 140 degrees, 6 to 10 minutes, flipping them halfway through cooking. Brush chops with 1 tablespoon glaze and grill, glazed side down, over hotter part of grill until caramelized, about 1 minute. Repeat with second side of chops and remaining 1 tablespoon glaze and grill until chops register 145 degrees, about 1 minute. Transfer chops to platter, tent loosely with aluminum foil, and let rest for 5 to 10 minutes.

5. Meanwhile, place onion skewer and peach halves on hotter part of grill. Cook until peach and onion are spottily charred on both sides, about 5 minutes for peach and 8 to 12 minutes for onion. Transfer peach halves and onion to cutting board and remove onion from skewer. Slice onion into 1-inch pieces and peach halves into ¼-inch wedges.

6. Add onion, peach, and arugula to bowl with reserved vinaigrette and toss to combine. Season with salt and pepper to taste. Brush chops with reserved 2 tablespoons glaze and serve with salad.

GRILLED STUFFED PORK TENDERLOIN WITH SWEET POTATOES

WHEN WE HAVE PLENTY OF TIME (AND PLENTY OF guests) on our hands, the test kitchen's go-to grilled pork roast is a bone-in, well-marbled cut that we can throw on the grill for as long as it takes for the meat to become tender and juicy while picking up plenty of smoke flavor from the fire. But when you're grilling for two, a smaller, fast-cooking alternative like pork tenderloin can come in handy. This readily available cut has the added advantages of being supremely tender and uniformly shaped for even cooking and slicing. But throw the unpredictable heat of the grill into the equation, and you're well on your way to producing a dry, bland roast. Most recipes tackle this problem with relishes or sauces, but those solutions are only skin-deep. For a flavor boost that would have more impact, we wanted to try stuffing our tenderloin with a rich-tasting filling. Once we'd figured out our main dish, we could complete our bistro-worthy grilled dinner with an equally flavorful side.

A small, 12-ounce tenderloin makes just the right amount for two, but since these small roasts are only about 2 inches in diameter, we'd have to think carefully about the stuffing technique. We had two options in mind. One was a simple hinge method, in which the meat is bisected lengthwise about half an inch shy of its back edge, opened up like a book and stuffed, then closed and secured with twine. The other approach took this method further: the butterflied meat was pounded until it was wide and thin, stuffed, and then rolled. The first technique was less fussy, but we found that it allowed too much stuffing to ooze from the seam. Though it took a little more effort, the second method had a couple of benefits. Pounding the meat created more surface area for the filling, and rolling the pork around the stuffing prevented leakage during cooking and carving.

But even with this wider plane to work with, we had to keep the filling's bulk to a minimum. That meant forgoing a traditional bread stuffing in favor of an intense-tasting pastelike filling, of which a little would go a long way. We perused the test kitchen's pantry for flavor-packed ingredients that wouldn't require extensive prep or precooking. It didn't take us long to come up with a couple of robustly flavored combinations that required nothing more than a whirl in the food processor. The first featured briny kalamata olives, sweet sun-dried tomatoes, and a flavor-enhancing anchovy. For an easy variation, we kept the sun-dried tomatoes (for their robust flavor and stickiness) but swapped out the olives and anchovy for equally potent Manchego cheese, toasted almonds, and chopped parsley. With both options, we layered raw baby spinach leaves over the fillings to freshen their rich flavors and add vibrant color.

Now we had to nail down the grilling method. Lean pork tenderloin needs a forgiving heat source that won't parch the meat's exterior before the interior has a chance to cook through. We opted for a half-fire grill setup, where all the coals are spread evenly over one side of the grill, leaving the other side cooler. But when we grilled our roast across from the coals for 25 minutes, we found that the indirect heat produced mixed results. While the meat was quite tender with perfectly warmed-through fillings, it looked utterly pale. To boost browning on the lean meat, we mixed 2 teaspoons of dark brown sugar with the salt and pepper we were rubbing on the tenderloin just before grilling. Now our roast came off the fire nicely browned and with deeper flavor.

Our pork was now the perfect marriage of rich filling and buttery, tender meat, but we wanted to make use of the available space left on the grill. We considered a number of candidates, but sweet potatoes won out—with their sweet, tender flesh, we thought they'd make a nice match to the piquant filling of our pork tenderloin. But because sweet potatoes have a high sugar content, they burn quickly. To avoid having to scrape the blackened, charred remains of our sweet potatoes off the grill grate, we would have to parcook the potatoes in the microwave, just until they began to soften. We sliced two small sweet potatoes into easy-to-grill 1-inch wedges, tossed them with olive oil, and gave them a five-minute stint in the microwave. The wedges now needed only about five minutes on the grill, after we'd set the pork aside to rest, to become perfectly charred on the outside and creamy on the inside. A dash of cayenne pepper added subtle heat that played off the potatoes' sweetness.

Grilled Stuffed Pork Tenderloin with Spiced Sweet Potato Wedges
SERVES 2

We prefer small sweet potatoes, weighing about 8 ounces each, in this recipe.

STUFFING

- 2 tablespoons oil-packed sun-dried tomatoes, rinsed and patted dry
- 2 tablespoons pitted kalamata olives
- 1 anchovy fillet
- 1 small garlic clove, minced
- ¼ teaspoon grated lemon zest
  Kosher salt and pepper

PORK AND POTATOES

- 2 teaspoons packed dark brown sugar
  Kosher salt and pepper
- 1 (12-ounce) pork tenderloin, trimmed
- ⅓ cup baby spinach
- ¼ cup olive oil
- 2 small sweet potatoes, cut into 1-inch wedges
- ⅛ teaspoon cayenne pepper

1. FOR THE STUFFING: Pulse all ingredients together in food processor until coarsely chopped, 5 to 10 pulses. Season with salt and pepper to taste.

2. FOR THE PORK AND POTATOES: Combine sugar, 1 teaspoon salt, and ½ teaspoon pepper in bowl. Cut tenderloin in half horizontally, stopping ½ inch away from edge so halves remain attached. Open tenderloin, cover with plastic wrap, and pound to ¼-inch thickness. Trim any ragged edges to create rough rectangle about 10 inches by 5 inches. Season interior of tenderloin with salt and pepper.

3. With long side of pork facing you, spread stuffing mixture over bottom half of tenderloin and top stuffing with spinach. Roll away from you into tight cylinder, taking care not to squeeze stuffing out ends. Position tenderloin seam side down, evenly space 5 pieces of twine underneath, and tie to secure. Coat pork with 1 tablespoon oil, then rub evenly with sugar mixture.

4. Meanwhile, toss sweet potatoes with remaining 3 tablespoons oil and cayenne in bowl and season with salt and pepper. Microwave, covered, until sweet potatoes begin to soften but still hold their shape, 3 to 6 minutes, tossing them halfway through cooking.

5A. FOR A CHARCOAL GRILL: Open bottom vent completely. Light large chimney starter filled with charcoal briquettes (6 quarts). When top coals are partially covered with ash, pour evenly over half of grill. Set cooking grate in place, cover, and open lid vent completely. Heat grill until hot, about 5 minutes.

5B. FOR A GAS GRILL: Turn all burners to high, cover, and heat grill until hot, about 15 minutes. Leave primary burner on high and turn off other burner(s).

6. Clean and oil cooking grate. Place pork on cooler side of grill, cover, and cook until center of stuffing registers 140 degrees, about 20 minutes, flipping pork halfway through cooking. Transfer pork to carving board, tent loosely with aluminum foil, and let rest for 5 to 10 minutes.

7. While pork rests, place sweet potatoes on hotter side of grill and cook until browned on all sides, 2 to 3 minutes. Slide potatoes to cooler part of grill and continue to cook until potatoes are tender, 2 to 4 minutes longer. Transfer to platter and tent loosely with foil. Remove twine from pork and slice ½ inch thick. Serve with potato wedges.

VARIATION

Grilled Manchego and Almond-Stuffed Pork Tenderloin with Spiced Sweet Potato Wedges
Omit olives and anchovy. Pulse ¼ cup grated Manchego cheese, 2 tablespoons fresh parsley, and 2 tablespoons toasted slivered almonds with tomatoes, garlic, and lemon zest.

NOTES FROM THE TEST KITCHEN

TESTING MEAT FOR DONENESS

An instant-read thermometer is the most reliable method for checking the doneness of poultry and meat. To use an instant-read thermometer, simply insert it through the side of a chicken breast, steak, or pork chop. The chart below lists temperatures at which the meat should be removed from the heat, as the temperature of the meat will continue to climb between 5 and 10 degrees as it rests. (Thin cutlets cook too quickly for an actual doneness test and you will have to rely more on visual cues and cooking times.)

WHEN IS IT DONE?

MEAT	COOK UNTIL IT REGISTERS	SERVING TEMPERATURE
Chicken Breasts	160 degrees	160 degrees
Chicken Thighs	175 degrees	175 degrees
Pork Chops and Tenderloin	145 degrees	150 degrees
Beef and Lamb		
Rare	115 to 120 degrees	125 degrees
Medium-rare	120 to 125 degrees	130 degrees
Medium	130 to 135 degrees	140 degrees
Medium-well	140 to 145 degrees	150 degrees
Well-done	150 to 155 degrees	160 degrees

GRILLED CHICKEN KEBABS WITH CHARRED COLESLAW

BARBECUED CHICKEN KEBABS FOR TWO ARE A no-brainer: Prep and assembly take just a few minutes when making such a small batch, so that in record time, you can have char-streaked pieces of juicy dark meat lacquered with sweet-sharp barbecue sauce. But rarely is this ideal achieved. Without an insulating layer of skin, even the richest thigh meat can dry out and toughen when exposed to the blazing heat of the grill. Simply slathering barbecue sauce onto skewered chicken chunks—the approach embraced by most recipes—does little to address this fundamental problem. In fact, it's often one of the ruining factors: If applied too early or in too great a volume, the sauce drips off the meat, burns, and fixes the chicken fast to the grill. We set out to remedy the problem and deliver juicy, tender chicken with plenty of sticky-sweet, smoke-tinged flavor. We wanted an everyday sort of recipe: chicken brushed with a homemade barbecue sauce and accompanied by a no-frills grilled side dish. But before we got to the sauce (we would use a simple ketchup-based placeholder for now), we had to ensure that the meat was as moist and tender as possible.

With 12 ounces of boneless, skinless chicken thighs at the ready, we considered our options when it came to keeping the meat tender. Brining is the natural first step when cooking poultry, as it adds moisture and locks in flavor. But when we made kebabs with brined thigh meat, the brine made the meat so slick that the barbecue sauce dribbled off. Maybe a dry method would work better. Sure enough, ¾ teaspoon of kosher salt rubbed on the meat 30 minutes before grilling worked just as well as brining. We then rubbed a sweet and savory mixture of sweet paprika and sugar into the salted chicken before grilling to add flavor and to create a craggy surface to which the sauce could cling.

After giving the kebabs a half-hour rest in the refrigerator, we grilled them over a half-fire setup that was moderately hot. (We had piled all of the coals on one side of the grill and left the other half empty to create a cooler "safety zone" on which to momentarily set the kebabs in the event of a flare-up.) We browned the kebabs on all sides, then slicked on our sauce. Another couple of minutes were enough to brown the sauce and cook the chicken through.

With its ruddy exterior, our chicken now looked the part, but the meat was still too dry for our tastes and lacked sufficient depth of flavor. We were scouring recipes, looking for a solution—something to keep our dark meat moist and tender and to flavor it throughout—when a colleague recalled a Turkish lamb kebab he'd tried that was skewered with extra lamb fat; during cooking, the fat melted and continually basted the lean meat. We knew we didn't want to add gamy lamb fat to our dish, but what about another fatty yet more complementary meat: smoky bacon? We tried a variety of methods for incorporating this addition.

First, we skewered bacon pieces between the chicken chunks, but by the time the chicken was done, the bacon had yet to render its fat and crisp. Next, we wrapped strips of bacon around the kebabs in a spiral-like helix. This time, the bacon turned crunchy, but its flavor overwhelmed the more delicate taste of the chicken. Brushing our kebabs with rendered bacon fat was a flop, too, leading to flare-ups and blackened chicken. The bites that weren't burnt, however, were moist and tasted addictively smoky.

Looking for an in-between solution, we tried dicing a strip of bacon and mixing the tiny bacon pieces with our chicken before skewering it. On the grill, the bacon bits clung tenaciously to the chicken, producing the best results yet. Unfortunately, the bacon didn't cook evenly: Some bits were overly crisp and others still a little limp. A colleague had an idea that would

take care of the problem: grinding the bacon into a spreadable paste.

For our next test, we placed one strip of raw bacon in a food processor and ground it down to a paste, which we then tossed with the chicken chunks and sugar-paprika mixture. This time, our grilled chicken kebabs were deeply browned, covered in a thick, shiny glaze, and, best of all, juicy and tender, with a smoky depth that totally outshone our simple sauce.

Taking another look at the sauce, we punched up its flavor by adding minced shallot and Worcestershire sauce. A spoonful of molasses added just enough bittersweet flavor to counter the ketchup's tanginess. Simmered for a few minutes, the mixture tasted bright and balanced and boasted a thick, smooth texture.

To complete our dish, tasters were enthusiastic about pairing our chicken kebabs with another barbecue classic: coleslaw. For a new take on this cookout staple, we decided to grill the cabbage. We needed only a quarter of a head for two servings and grilled the cabbage in one piece, with the core intact to hold the layers together. This way, we could turn the cabbage and it would pick up some char and flavor. Unfortunately, once shredded, the charred surface area—and the smoky flavor it had absorbed—virtually disappeared. To increase the surface area, we cut the cabbage into small wedges, still leaving the core intact. Now, when the cabbage was chopped and tossed with grated carrot, minced shallot, and a mayonnaise-based dressing, the smokiness had a stronger presence that permeated the whole dish.

Finally, we had perfected two cookout classics. Though our approach to the kebabs was a little more involved, the results were well worth it.

NOTES FROM THE TEST KITCHEN

MAKING BACON PASTE

To keep chicken moist when grilling, chop 1 slice of bacon, pulse in food processor until smooth, then toss resulting paste (along with sugar and paprika) with raw chicken pieces.

Grilled Chicken Kebabs with Charred Coleslaw

SERVES 2

You will need two 12-inch metal skewers for this recipe. If you have thin pieces of chicken, cut them larger than 1 inch and roll or fold them into 1-inch cubes before skewering (see page 146). Do not remove the core from the cabbage; it will keep the leaves intact on the grill.

KEBABS

- 12 ounces boneless, skinless chicken thighs, trimmed and cut into 1-inch pieces
- ¾ teaspoon kosher salt
- ¼ cup ketchup
- 2 tablespoons molasses
- 1 small shallot, minced
- 1 tablespoon Worcestershire sauce
- 1 tablespoon Dijon mustard
- 1 tablespoon cider vinegar
- 2 teaspoons sugar
- 2 teaspoons paprika
- 1 slice bacon, cut into ½-inch pieces

SLAW

- 2½ tablespoons mayonnaise
- 1 small shallot, minced
- 2 teaspoons cider vinegar
  Kosher salt and pepper
- ¼ small head green cabbage (4 ounces), cut into 2 wedges
- 1 tablespoon olive oil
- 1 small carrot, peeled and shredded
- 1 tablespoon minced fresh cilantro

1. FOR THE KEBABS: Toss chicken and salt together in bowl, cover, and refrigerate for at least 30 minutes or up to 1 hour.

2. Combine ketchup, molasses, shallot, Worcestershire, mustard, vinegar, and 1 teaspoon sugar in small saucepan. Bring to simmer over medium heat and cook, stirring occasionally, until sauce is reduced to ½ cup, 5 to 7 minutes. Reserve half of sauce for serving.

3. Combine remaining 1 teaspoon sugar and paprika in small bowl. Process bacon in food processor until smooth paste forms, 30 to 45 seconds, scraping down bowl as needed. Pat chicken dry with paper towels. Add bacon paste and paprika mixture to chicken and toss until chicken is completely coated. Thread meat onto two 12-inch metal skewers.

4. FOR THE SLAW: Whisk mayonnaise, shallot, and vinegar together in medium bowl and season with salt and pepper to taste. Cover and refrigerate until ready to serve. Brush cabbage wedges with oil and season with salt and pepper.

5A. FOR A CHARCOAL GRILL: Open bottom vent completely. Light large chimney starter three-quarters filled with charcoal briquettes (4½ quarts). When top coals are partially covered with ash, pour evenly over half of grill. Set cooking grate in place, cover, and open lid vent completely. Heat grill until hot, about 5 minutes.

5B. FOR A GAS GRILL: Turn all burners to high, cover, and heat grill until hot, about 15 minutes. Leave primary burner on high and turn off other burner(s).

6. Clean and oil cooking grate. Place kebabs on hotter side of grill and cook (covered if using gas), turning every 2 to 3 minutes until well browned and slightly charred on all sides, 8 to 12 minutes. Brush top surface of kebabs with 2 tablespoons barbecue sauce; flip and cook until sauce is caramelized, about 1 minute. Brush second side with remaining 2 tablespoons barbecue sauce; flip and continue to cook until sauce

---

USE IT UP: CABBAGE

Roasted Cabbage Wedges

SERVES 2

Do not remove the core from the cabbage; it will keep the leaves intact on the baking sheet.

- ½ teaspoon sugar
  Salt and pepper
- ½–¾ small head green cabbage, cut into 1-inch wedges
- 2 tablespoons vegetable oil
- 1 teaspoon balsamic vinegar

1. Adjust oven rack to upper-middle position. Place rimmed baking sheet on rack and heat oven to 450 degrees. Combine sugar, ½ teaspoon salt, and ⅛ teaspoon pepper in small bowl. Brush cabbage wedges with oil and sprinkle with sugar mixture.

2. Carefully place cabbage wedges on hot baking sheet and roast until cabbage is tender and lightly browned around edges, 15 to 20 minutes. Drizzle cabbage with vinegar and serve.

an hour, and we didn't want to wait that long. To speed up the process, we needed to increase the surface area of the wings. We cut them into sections and pierced the pieces all over with a fork. This step allowed the brine to soak down to the bone in just 30 minutes. Now, our 180-degree wings were both tender and juicy.

This approach had one downside, though: The moisture from the brine caused the wings to steam and stick to the grill again. A colleague suggested tossing the wings with a little cornstarch before grilling to discourage sticking. The thin layer of cornstarch worked like a charm—no more sticking. Tossed with just a little salt and pepper, these simple wings were bursting with chicken-y goodness. While we liked their simplicity, we wanted to come up with a few different, yet equally easy and pantry-friendly, spice variations. For a barbecue-style rub, we added chili powder, paprika, garlic powder, oregano, and sugar for sweet and savory balance; in a spicy Creole version, we bumped up the garlic powder and oregano and added onion powder, white pepper, and a sizable dose of cayenne; finally, we went exotic with a tandoori spice rub that included garam masala, cumin, garlic, ginger, and a touch of cayenne.

For the complete sports bar experience at home, we decided to pair our wings with an easy ranch-flavored dipping sauce that could do double duty as a salad dressing. Buttermilk and mayonnaise provided a cool, creamy foundation, and minced chives, garlic, and parsley added the traditional ranch flavors. For the salad, tasters preferred baby spinach over other salad greens; the spinach offered a nice, delicate flavor and fresh texture. Cherry tomatoes, which we skewered and grilled once the wings were done, contributed some brightness to our dish. Tossed with a bit of ranch dressing, this flavorful, fresh-tasting spinach salad completed our grilled wings dinner—the perfect menu for a sports-loving party of two.

NOTES FROM THE TEST KITCHEN

PREPPING GRILLED CHICKEN WINGS

1. Use fork to puncture each wing all over, letting brine easily penetrate wings and allowing rendered fat to be released.

2. Brine wings in saltwater solution for 30 minutes to keep them juicy.

3. Right before grilling, dust wings with mixture of cornstarch and pepper to prevent sticking and to season.

Grilled Chicken Wings with Tomato-Spinach Salad and Ranch Dressing

SERVES 2

You will need two 12-inch metal skewers for this recipe. Don't brine the wings for more than 30 minutes or they will be too salty.

DRESSING

- ¼ cup buttermilk
- ¼ cup mayonnaise
- 3 tablespoons sour cream
- 2 teaspoons minced fresh chives
- 2 teaspoons minced fresh parsley, dill, or cilantro
- 1 small garlic clove, minced
- ½ teaspoon lemon juice
  Salt and pepper

WINGS AND SALAD

- 2 pounds chicken wings, trimmed, separated at joints, and wingtips discarded
  Salt and pepper
- 1½ teaspoons cornstarch
- 12 ounces cherry tomatoes
- 1 tablespoon olive oil
- 2 ounces (2 cups) baby spinach

1. FOR THE DRESSING: Whisk all ingredients together in bowl until smooth. Season with salt and pepper to taste, cover, and refrigerate until ready to serve.

2. FOR THE WINGS AND SALAD: Prick chicken wings all over with fork. Dissolve ½ cup salt in 2 quarts cold water in large bowl. Submerge chicken in brine, cover, and refrigerate for 30 minutes.

3. Combine cornstarch, ¾ teaspoon salt, and 1 teaspoon pepper in bowl. Pat wings dry with paper towels and transfer to large bowl. Sprinkle wings with cornstarch mixture and toss to coat. Thread tomatoes through stem ends onto two 12-inch metal skewers, brush with oil, and season with salt and pepper.

4A. FOR A CHARCOAL GRILL: Open bottom vent completely. Light large chimney starter half filled with charcoal briquettes (3 quarts). When top coals are partially covered with ash, pour evenly over grill. Set cooking grate in place, cover, and open lid vent completely. Heat grill until hot, about 5 minutes.

4B. FOR A GAS GRILL: Turn all burners to high, cover, and heat grill until hot, about 15 minutes. Turn all burners to medium-low. (Adjust burners as needed to maintain grill temperature around 350 degrees.)

5. Clean and oil cooking grate. Grill wings (covered if using gas), thicker skin side up, until browned on bottom, 12 to 15 minutes. Flip wings and grill until skin is crisp and lightly charred and meat registers 180 degrees, about 10 minutes longer. Transfer wings to platter, tent loosely with aluminum foil, and let rest for 5 to 10 minutes.

6. While wings rest, place tomato skewers on grill and cook, turning as needed, until skins begin to blister and wrinkle on all sides, 3 to 6 minutes. Remove from grill, carefully remove tomatoes from skewers, and transfer to bowl. Add spinach and 2 tablespoons dressing to bowl, toss gently to coat, and season with salt and pepper to taste. Serve with chicken wings and remaining dressing for dipping.

VARIATIONS

Barbecue Grilled Chicken Wings with Tomato-Spinach Salad and Ranch Dressing

Reduce pepper in cornstarch mixture to ½ teaspoon and add 1 teaspoon chili powder, 1 teaspoon paprika, ½ teaspoon garlic powder, ½ teaspoon dried oregano, and ½ teaspoon sugar.

Creole Grilled Chicken Wings with Tomato-Spinach Salad and Ranch Dressing

Add ¾ teaspoon dried oregano, ½ teaspoon garlic powder, ½ teaspoon onion powder, ½ teaspoon white pepper, and ¼ teaspoon cayenne pepper to cornstarch mixture.

Tandoori Grilled Chicken Wings with Tomato-Spinach Salad and Ranch Dressing

We like the flavor of cilantro in the ranch dressing when serving these wings.

Reduce pepper in cornstarch mixture to ½ teaspoon and add 1 teaspoon garam masala, ½ teaspoon ground cumin, ¼ teaspoon garlic powder, ¼ teaspoon ground ginger, and ⅛ teaspoon cayenne pepper.

GRILLED CHICKEN WITH CORN ON THE COB

ALMOST EVERY MEXICAN TAQUERIA IN AMERICA serves grilled citrus-and-spice-marinated chicken. For such a standard dish, the quality differences can be dramatic. Sometimes you luck out with chicken that is juicy and full of flavor from the marinade of citrus juices, onions, garlic, oregano, and warm spices like cinnamon, cumin, and cloves. More often, though, the chicken is dry, leathery, and downright bland. We wanted to develop a recipe that delivered grilled chicken with bold, bright flavor from the marinade so that we could enjoy this dish at home—just for two.

We began by testing a number of recipes we uncovered in our research. Most called for marinating chicken pieces in a combination of orange juice and lime juice (a mixture that acted as a stand-in for the juice of hard-to-find but traditional sour oranges), along with aromatics, spices, and herbs. We needed just enough meat for a pair of diners, so we traded the chicken pieces for two bone-in breasts. After preparing several batches of citrus-and-spice chicken, we were dismayed to find that none of them delivered on the bold flavor we expected. We started tinkering with the seasonings, the ratio of juices, and the marinating times, but even then we were sorely disappointed—the chicken was bland, and the skin chewy and leathery.

Focusing on the flavor issue first, we decided to add citrus zest to the marinade. The zest is, after all, home to the oils that give citrus fruits much of their fragrance and flavor. Half a teaspoon of grated lime zest plus three times as much orange zest worked so well that we did away with the orange juice entirely. The flavor was much improved, but we still wanted our marinade to have more of a presence on the finished chicken. To turn our sauce into a paste with sticking power, we turned to the food processor. The ingredients needed less than a minute and just a drizzle of olive oil to turn into a thicker mixture that now clung to the chicken with ease. Grilled after an hour's rest in the pungent paste, this chicken had the best flavor yet.

But we still needed a grilling technique that would fix the chewy, leathery texture. With a gas grill, cooking the breasts over medium-low heat was just the ticket. But a medium-low charcoal fire was dicey: If the fire was a little too hot, flare-ups burned the chicken. If the fire was a little too cool, the fat didn't render properly by the time the meat was cooked. The solution for cooking over charcoal was to use indirect heat—that is, position the meat away from (and not directly over) the fire. For our grill setup, we placed a disposable aluminum pan in the center of the bottom of the grill, then poured half of the lit charcoal on either side. Now we could grill the chicken pieces over indirect heat with the skin side up; this allowed the paste to cook gently until the end, when we flipped the chicken and moved it over the fire for just a minute of direct heat to crisp the skin and give the paste a substantial char. (On a gas grill, we turned the primary burner to high and cooked the chicken over unlit secondary burners. To crisp the skin, we simply flipped the breasts and moved them to the hotter side.) Finally, no more flare-ups, and we got the succulent meat, crisp skin, and nicely caramelized seasonings we'd been aiming for.

With the available space left on the grill, we decided to grill two ears of corn. A quick stint on the hotter side of the grill cooked the corn and imparted a slight toastiness. The corn needed just a smear of butter, which we'd flavored with lime zest. At last, we had citrus-and-spice grilled chicken that was worthy of the name.

NOTES FROM THE TEST KITCHEN

CHECKING THE PROPANE LEVEL

Gas grills aren't as complicated as charcoal, but if you own one, there is a detail you should always make sure of: Do you have enough gas? If your grill doesn't have a gas gauge or propane level indicator, don't worry. We've come up with the following trick:

1. Bring 1 cup water to boil in kettle, then pour water over side of tank.

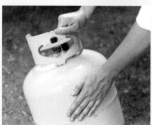

2. Where tank feels warm, tank is empty; where tank remains cool, there is propane inside.

Citrus-and-Spice Grilled Chicken with Corn on the Cob and Lime Butter

SERVES 2

Don't leave the chicken on the hotter part of the grill longer than 1 minute; otherwise, the skin will burn.

  1 **small onion, chopped coarse**
  1 **tablespoon olive oil**
  3 **garlic cloves, peeled**
1½ **teaspoons grated orange zest**
1½ **teaspoons grated lime zest plus 2½ tablespoons juice (2 limes)**
  1 **teaspoon dried oregano**
 ¼ **teaspoon ground cinnamon**
 ¼ **teaspoon ground cumin**
    Salt and pepper
  2 **(12-ounce) bone-in chicken breasts, trimmed and halved crosswise**
  2 **tablespoons unsalted butter, softened**
  2 **ears corn, all but inner layer of husk removed**
  1 **(13 by 9-inch) disposable aluminum roasting pan (if using charcoal)**

1. Process onion, oil, garlic, orange zest, ½ teaspoon lime zest, 2 tablespoons lime juice, oregano, cinnamon, cumin, ¾ teaspoon salt, and ¼ teaspoon pepper together in food processor until smooth, about 30 seconds; transfer to zipper-lock bag. Pat chicken dry with paper towels, add to bag, and toss to coat; press out as much air as possible and seal bag. Refrigerate for at least 1 hour or up to 24 hours, flipping bag occasionally.

2. Meanwhile, combine butter, remaining 1½ teaspoons lime juice, and remaining 1 teaspoon lime zest in small bowl and season with salt and pepper to taste.

3A. FOR A CHARCOAL GRILL: Open bottom vent completely and place roasting pan in center of grill. Light large chimney starter filled with charcoal briquettes (6 quarts). When top coals are partially covered with ash, pour into 2 even piles on either side of roasting pan. Set cooking grate in place, cover, and open lid vent completely. Heat grill until hot, about 5 minutes.

3B. FOR A GAS GRILL: Turn all burners to high, cover, and heat grill until hot, about 15 minutes. Leave primary burner on high and turn off other burner(s).

4. Clean and oil cooking grate. Place chicken, skin side up, on cooler part of grill (in center of grill if using charcoal). Cover and cook until bottom is browned and chicken registers 160 degrees, 25 to 30 minutes. Flip chicken skin side down, slide to hotter part of grill, and cook until well browned, 30 seconds to 1 minute. Transfer chicken to platter, tent loosely with aluminum foil, and let rest for 5 to 10 minutes.

5. While chicken rests, place corn on hotter part of grill and cook until lightly charred on all sides, about 10 minutes, turning as needed. Transfer corn to platter and remove husks and silk. Brush corn with lime butter and season with salt and pepper to taste. Serve with chicken.

GRILLED SALMON STEAKS WITH ZUCCHINI SALAD

CHOOSING SALMON STEAKS FOR THE GRILL WHEN cooking for two is an easy decision: Their bone and thickness make them a far sturdier cut than a fillet, but they still cook relatively quickly, making them a great choice for weeknight dining. But as with fillets, nailing the cooking time and method can be a challenge—by the time the interior is cooked through, what was a nicely grilled exterior can become blackened and dry. The two thin strips of flesh that come down on either side of the bone (which are the fish's belly flaps) can also easily become overcooked and dry. And no matter how much seasoning goes on the outside, it never seems to permeate the whole steak. We wanted to turn this supermarket staple into an easy fish dinner for two, boasting flavorful, moist fish rounded out with a bright-tasting side dish that would complement the richness of the salmon.

Our quest began by developing a way to ensure evenly cooked salmon steaks. We started by giving the salmon a much-needed tummy tuck: We gently removed the skin from one of the belly flaps and tucked it in toward the center of the steak, then wrapped the other flap around the side, securing the steak with kitchen twine. With that, we had neat medallions that cooked evenly and could be easily maneuvered around the grill.

As far as our grill was concerned, we'd need to be careful with our setup and take a gentle approach. First, as a precaution against sticking, we painted the grates with multiple coats of oil to create a super-slick nonstick cooking surface that wouldn't instantly burn off. For our coal setup, we knew that grilling over medium-low heat would produce a moist, tender interior—but at the steep cost of a good, flavorful sear. Instead, we needed a fire with two levels of heat: high heat to sear the steaks, and low heat to finish the job. Though using a half-fire setup (meaning the charcoal is arranged over half of the grill, leaving the other half empty) took up to 20 minutes total for a 1½-inch steak, our reward was that the steaks were now both moist and nicely browned.

But tasters were looking for a little more oomph in the salmon. We thought about another common high-heat cooking method for salmon—broiling—which often calls for slathering salmon steaks with a potent sauce that permeates the flesh as the fish cooks. Could we find a way to transfer this technique to the grill without risking flare-ups and burnt, stuck-on fish? One taster suggested bringing out one of our favorite grill tools: the disposable aluminum roasting pan. We could build a sauce while the steaks browned, then finish them gently in the sauce.

For a simple, yet traditional, flavor profile, we made a lemon-and-shallot butter sauce directly in the roasting pan while the steaks seared on the hot part of the grill. Then we transferred the browned fish steaks to the pan,

GRILLED SALMON STEAKS WITH ZUCCHINI AND FRISÉE SALAD

coating them with sauce. When they were done, the steaks were flavorful, juicy, and moist. But our modest two-person sauce was flecked with burnt butter and had reduced to almost nothing in the vast space of the roasting pan. It was clear we'd need a smaller vessel for our sauce. Normally used for corralling wood chips, a 9-inch disposable pie plate was just the solution. The steaks fit inside perfectly, and the sauce came together quickly. With the burnt butter now a nonissue, we noticed that the delicate sauce needed a boost to compete with the smoky flavor of the fish. We added a small amount of lemon zest and capers to the other ingredients in the pie plate, then stirred some minced parsley into the sauce when it came off the grill for a fresh finish. Now we had zesty, flavorful salmon steaks with a moist, succulent interior, garnished with a rich-tasting sauce.

NOTES FROM THE TEST KITCHEN

PREPPING SALMON STEAKS

1. To make salmon steaks sturdy enough to grill, first remove 1½ inches of skin from 1 tail of each steak.

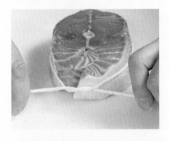

2. Next, tuck skinned portion into center of steak, wrap other tail around it, and tie with kitchen twine.

PREPARING ZUCCHINI FOR THE GRILL

Cut zucchini in half lengthwise. Peel two layers off skin side of zucchini using vegetable peeler; this will help stabilize zucchini on grill.

To round out our dinner off the grill, tasters wanted a light, fresh-tasting salad that would balance the richness of the fish and butter sauce. For the leafy component, we selected slightly bitter frisée; a single grilled zucchini gave the salad more presence. To make the zucchini easy to maneuver on the grill, we halved it. After we pulled the zucchini halves off the grill, we sliced them into fork-friendly half-moons. Thin slices of tomato added color and bright acidity, and a simple red wine vinaigrette gave the whole salad a subtle punch.

All the components of our grilled fish dinner had fallen into place: We had perfectly grilled salmon steaks with a tender center and just enough char, a bright and buttery sauce, and a salad with just the right amount of bite.

Grilled Salmon Steaks with Zucchini and Frisée Salad
SERVES 2

Before serving, lift out the small circular bone from the center of each steak.

    4   tablespoons olive oil
    1   tablespoon red wine vinegar
        Salt and pepper
    1   small tomato, cored and cut into thin wedges
    2   tablespoons minced fresh parsley
    1   zucchini, sliced in half lengthwise, skin side
        partially peeled
    2   (10-ounce) salmon steaks, 1 to 1½ inches thick
    1   small shallot, minced
    2   tablespoons unsalted butter, cut into 2 pieces
  1½   teaspoons capers, rinsed
    ½   teaspoon grated lemon zest plus 3 tablespoons juice
    1   (9-inch) disposable aluminum pie plate
    1   small head frisée (4 ounces), chopped coarse

1. Whisk 2 tablespoons oil, vinegar, ⅛ teaspoon salt, and ⅛ teaspoon pepper together in medium bowl. Add tomato and 1 tablespoon parsley and let sit while grilling. Brush both sides of zucchini with 1 tablespoon oil and season with salt and pepper.

2. Pat salmon steaks dry with paper towels. Working with 1 steak at a time, carefully trim 1½ inches of skin from 1 tail. Tightly wrap other tail around skinned portion and tie steaks with kitchen twine. Season salmon with salt and pepper and brush both sides with remaining 1 tablespoon oil. Combine shallot, butter, capers, lemon zest and juice, and ⅛ teaspoon salt in disposable pie plate.

3A. FOR A CHARCOAL GRILL: Open bottom vent completely. Light large chimney starter filled with charcoal briquettes (6 quarts). When top coals are partially covered with ash, pour evenly over half of grill. Set cooking grate in place, cover, and open lid vent completely. Heat grill until hot, about 5 minutes.

3B. FOR A GAS GRILL: Turn all burners to high, cover, and heat grill until hot, about 15 minutes. Leave primary burner on high and turn off other burner(s).

4. Clean cooking grate, then repeatedly brush grate with well-oiled paper towels until grate is black and glossy, 5 to 10 times. Place salmon and zucchini on hotter part of grill. Cook salmon (covered if using gas) until browned, 2 to 3 minutes per side. Meanwhile, set pie plate on cooler part of grill and cook until butter has melted, about 2 minutes. Transfer salmon to pie plate and gently turn to coat. Cook salmon, covered, until center is still translucent when checked with tip of paring knife and registers 125 degrees (for medium-rare), 6 to 14 minutes, flipping salmon and rotating pan halfway through grilling.

5. Meanwhile, cook zucchini, turning as needed, until softened and lightly charred on both sides, 8 to 10 minutes. Transfer to cutting board and slice ¼ inch thick.

6. Transfer salmon to platter and remove twine. Remove pie plate from heat, whisk remaining 1 tablespoon parsley into caper sauce, and drizzle sauce over salmon steaks. Add zucchini and frisée to bowl with tomatoes and vinaigrette and toss gently to coat. Season with salt and pepper to taste and serve with salmon.

GRILLED SEA SCALLOPS AND FENNEL

PAN-SEARING SCALLOPS IS ONE OF OUR FAVORITE ways to prepare them: The quick blast of heat deeply browns their exteriors while leaving their interiors moist and plump. Since achieving these results requires use of an incredibly hot skillet, we figured these bivalves would be tailor-made for the grill. In theory, the blazing-hot fire would produce even better results than a

stove, rendering the scallop crusts extra-crisp, with a hint of smoke. Unfortunately, the potential pitfalls are numerous. First and foremost, by the time the scallops develop a good sear, they're usually overcooked and rubbery. And then there's the more general problem of trying to flip them: No matter how well the scallops are coated with oil before cooking, it's inevitable that they'll end up sticking to the grate. Still, we were on a mission and set about to find a surefire way to grill scallops.

To combat the issue of overcooking, we knew that we wanted to use the largest sea scallops we could find—about 10 to 20 per pound. But we also needed to make sure that we were purchasing "dry," not "wet," scallops. Although they might be harder to find, dry scallops are worth seeking out because they have not been treated with the preservative solution that makes wet scallops taste metallic and causes them to leach water during cooking. Just 12 ounces of large scallops provided the right amount of seafood for two.

To ensure good browning, we blotted the scallops dry between layers of kitchen towels and threaded them onto doubled metal skewers so that all of the scallops could be flipped at the same time and wouldn't spin in the process. Then we brushed them with oil, seasoned them with salt and pepper, and considered our grill setup. To avoid overcooking the scallops but still develop a brown crust, we needed a quick blast of high heat. Our first thought was to double up on the briquettes for a taller and more intense fire that would be physically closer to the scallops, but this would require a ridiculous amount of charcoal for a grilled dinner for two. What if we simply piled as many coals as possible into a single chimney and concentrated the fire in the center of the grill?

The results were encouraging. Without anything to contain them, the coals didn't form an even layer, meaning that the skewers set over the center of the fire cooked faster than the others that were sitting farther away. It was clear we'd need to find a way to corral the coals and make the fire as level as possible. We turned to one of our favorite grilling tools, the disposable aluminum roasting pan, which we often use to separate piles of lit coals and to catch rendered fat dripping down from cooking meat. We placed the pan in the center of the grill, piled in the lit coals from the chimney, and proceeded with our recipe. At last, we had scallops with impressive char and juicy centers.

Only one problem remained: We still couldn't get the scallops off the grill in one piece. Painting the grate with multiple coats of oil created a super-slick cooking surface, but this wasn't enough. That's when we decided to try coating the scallops with something more protective than just oil. A trick developed in the test kitchen to protect lean chicken breasts from drying out during pan-searing sounded promising: lightly coating the meat with a slurry of melted butter, flour, and cornstarch. This seemed worth trying, although we wondered if such a coating would actually hold up in the much hotter fire of a grill. To our delight, it worked beautifully, with two tweaks. To save ourselves the trouble of melting butter, we went back to the vegetable oil we'd been using since the outset of our testing, and we added a little sugar to the mixture to expedite browning on our scallops. When we went to

pull this last batch of scallops off the grill, they were crisp-crusted but moist and tender within—and they released without hesitation.

Up to now, we'd been serving our scallops with just a spritz of lemon juice, but tasters encouraged us to take this one step further. We thought a simple citrus-based salsa, punched up with grapefruit, lime zest and juice, and minced jalapeño, would complement the mild, delicate flavor of our scallops. To keep things easy and streamlined, we made the salsa right before we fired up the grill and let the flavors meld in the refrigerator while we cooked our dinner. Just a few spoonfuls, dotted on top of the scallops, added bright color and a burst of flavor.

One thing was still missing: a grilled vegetable to turn our efforts into a satisfying meal. Fennel, with its bright, aniselike flavor and crisp texture, seemed like just the thing. Microwaving the fennel to jump-start its

---

NOTES FROM THE TEST KITCHEN

SKEWERING SCALLOPS FOR THE GRILL

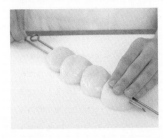

To double-skewer scallops, which makes flipping them much easier, thread 4 scallops onto one 12-inch metal skewer, then place second skewer through scallops parallel to and about ¼ inch from first skewer.

CUTTING CITRUS

1. Slice off top and bottom of grapefruit or orange, then cut away rind and pith using paring knife.

2. Cut grapefruit into 8 wedges or orange into 4 wedges. Working with 2 wedges at a time, slice citrus into ½-inch-thick pieces.

PREPARING FENNEL FOR GRILLING

1. Remove stems and feathery fronds.

2. Trim very thin slice from base and remove any tough or blemished outer layers.

3. Slice bulb vertically through base into ¼-inch-thick pieces resembling fans.

cooking was key; given the intensely hot fire needed for the scallops, the fennel would char quickly once it hit the grill. We quickly learned that slicing the fennel into thin strips wouldn't do—the strips fell through the grill grate and incinerated on contact. We had better luck when we sliced the bulb into wide, fan-shaped pieces (leaving the core attached ensured that the pieces stayed intact). Our fennel "fans" stayed put when placed on the grate and picked up a good amount of char in minutes.

With its perfectly cooked, tender scallops boasting a lightly browned, crisp crust, plus a boldly flavored salsa and lively side dish, this dinner off the grill was a resounding success.

Grilled Sea Scallops and Grapefruit Salsa with Fennel

SERVES 2

You will need four 12-inch metal skewers for this recipe. We recommend buying "dry" scallops, those without chemical additives. Dry scallops will look ivory or pinkish and feel tacky; wet scallops look bright white and feel slippery. If using wet scallops, soak them in a solution of 1 quart water, ¼ cup lemon juice, and 2 tablespoons salt for 30 minutes before step 2, and do not season with salt in step 3.

SALSA

- 1 grapefruit
- 1 small shallot, minced
- ½ jalapeño chile, stemmed, seeded, and minced
- 1 teaspoon grated lime zest plus 2 teaspoons juice
- 1 teaspoon sugar
   Salt and pepper

SCALLOPS AND FENNEL

- 2 small fennel bulbs, stalks discarded, cut vertically through base into ¼-inch-thick slices (see page 166)
- 3 tablespoons vegetable oil
   Salt and pepper
- 12 ounces large sea scallops, tendons removed
- 1½ teaspoons all-purpose flour
- ½ teaspoon cornstarch
- ½ teaspoon sugar
- 1 (13 by 9-inch) disposable aluminum roasting pan (if using charcoal)

1. FOR THE SALSA: Cut away peel and pith from grapefruit. Cut grapefruit into 8 wedges and slice each wedge crosswise into ½-inch-thick pieces. Combine grapefruit pieces, shallot, jalapeño, lime zest and juice, and sugar in bowl and season with salt and pepper to taste. Cover and refrigerate until ready to serve.

2. FOR THE SCALLOPS AND FENNEL: Toss fennel and 2 tablespoons oil in bowl and season with salt and pepper. Microwave, covered, until softened, about 6 minutes, tossing halfway through cooking. Place scallops on rimmed baking sheet lined with clean kitchen towel. Place second clean kitchen towel on top of scallops and press gently on towel to blot liquid. Let scallops sit at room temperature, covered with towel, for 10 minutes. With scallops on flat work surface, thread onto doubled skewers so that flat sides will directly touch grill grate, about 4 scallops per doubled skewer. Return skewered scallops to towel-lined baking sheet.

3. Whisk remaining 1 tablespoon oil, flour, cornstarch, and sugar together in small bowl. Remove towels from scallops. Brush both sides of scallops with oil mixture and season with salt and pepper.

4A. FOR A CHARCOAL GRILL: Open bottom vent completely and place roasting pan in center of grill. Light large chimney starter mounded with charcoal briquettes (7 quarts). Poke 12 holes in bottom of roasting pan with skewer. When top coals are partially covered with ash, pour into roasting pan. Set cooking grate in place, cover, and open lid vent completely. Heat grill until hot, about 5 minutes.

4B. FOR A GAS GRILL: Turn all burners to high, cover, and heat grill until hot, about 15 minutes. Leave all burners on high.

5. Clean cooking grate, then repeatedly brush grate with well-oiled paper towels until grate is black and glossy, 5 to 10 times. Place skewered scallops and fennel on hotter part of grill. Cook scallops (covered if using gas), without moving, until lightly browned, 2 to 4 minutes. Carefully flip skewers and continue to cook until second side is browned, sides of scallops are firm, and centers are opaque, 2 to 4 minutes longer.

6. Meanwhile, cook fennel until tender and lightly charred, 7 to 9 minutes. Transfer scallops and fennel to serving platter. Serve with salsa.

GRILLED PORTOBELLO BURGERS WITH GARLICKY EGGPLANT

WHEN YOU'RE GRILLING FOR TWO AND LOOKING to serve up a meatless main, you might be tempted to just throw a pair of frozen veggie patties on the grate. But these mealy, frostbitten disks never satisfy. For a hearty, flavorful vegetarian entrée off the grill, we turned to an increasingly popular option: the portobello mushroom burger. Infused with smoky flavor from the grill, portobello mushrooms develop a hearty, meaty taste and offer a thick, satisfying texture—plus it's easy to buy just what you need for two diners.

But making a portobello burger isn't as easy as tossing a few mushroom caps on the grill, waiting until they brown, then sandwiching them in a bun. Our initial tests brought up a variety of problems. Some mushrooms were the perfect size before cooking but shrank so much during cooking that they became overwhelmed by the bun. All of the mushrooms oozed moisture and made our buns soggy. And frankly, they were as bland as can be. With these challenges ahead, we fired up the grill and set out to create a hearty portobello burger that was properly cooked and packed with flavor.

First, we began with the size of the mushrooms. Because of their high moisture content, mushrooms shrink considerably when cooked, so we needed to start with caps that seemed a little oversized for them to end up just right. After testing various sizes, we found that although 6-ounce caps looked much too big in the raw state, they were the perfect size after grilling.

With the size squared away, we could turn to the next problem: soggy buns. The mushrooms were leaching so much water that they inevitably made our buns a mushy mess. If we grilled the mushrooms until their moisture was gone, the buns certainly remained dry, but the mushrooms were also leathery, overcooked, and inedible. Drawing on a test kitchen recipe for roasted mushrooms, we knew that scoring the flesh of the caps could help draw out excess moisture, and we had a hunch it would help out here as well. Using the tip of a sharp knife, we scored a shallow diamond pattern into each cap before placing the mushrooms on the grill.

This worked like a charm. In less than 10 minutes, the mushrooms were tender yet still moist, and they were no longer leaching liquid.

While they now had good smoky flavor and were properly cooked, our mushrooms still needed a boost. We settled on a two-pronged attack: infusing the mushrooms themselves with flavor, and picking the right toppings to take these burgers from ordinary to extraordinary. We tried brushing the mushrooms with a simple dressing before grilling, but the dressing's flavors mellowed too much during cooking, and the mushrooms didn't brown properly. Tossing the mushrooms with the dressing after they were cooked was more promising, but the mushrooms absorbed it like a sponge. In the end, we found that brushing the dressing on halfway through cooking gave us the best flavor boost and control. Tasters preferred a simple blend of oil, garlic, and woodsy thyme.

With the mushrooms complete, we began experimenting with toppings. Grilled onion added a charred sweetness that complemented the earthy mushroom flavor; slicing the onion into rounds and then skewering them ensured that they didn't fall through the grate when grilled. In addition to the grilled onion, tasters also wanted a fresh, crunchy element on the burger. Typical burger lettuces like iceberg couldn't stand up to the meatiness of the mushrooms, but arugula paired nicely with both the mushrooms and onion. For the cheese, we tested standard options like American and cheddar, but tasters found the pungent, tangy taste of goat cheese a better fit. Finally, a slice of tomato added a sweetness that paired well with the cheese and assertive arugula.

We had plenty of room left on the grill to cook an easy yet flavorful side dish and considered a few options, including sweet potato, zucchini, and eggplant. We thought eggplant, with its earthy, hearty nature, would pair well with the mushrooms. We sliced the eggplant into thick rounds, which browned in no time and turned pleasantly crisp in spots. For flavor and to prevent sticking, we brushed our rounds with some of the dressing we had used to flavor the mushrooms. Tasters liked the direction we were taking but wanted more flavor. Next time, when the eggplant came off the grill, we drizzled a little more dressing on top. But now we found the harsh notes of the raw garlic to be too much. Taking a step back, we decided to cook the mixture of garlic, thyme, and oil briefly at the outset to rid the garlic of its raw flavor. This took just a few minutes and led to a dish that had deeper flavor overall. The dressing was now so much richer in flavor that we even used a spoonful to dress our arugula before assembling the burgers.

Our vegetarian grilled meal was now far from ho-hum—in fact, it was so flavorful and satisfying, we didn't even miss the meat.

Grilled Portobello Burgers with Garlicky Eggplant

SERVES 2

We prefer to use portobello caps that measure 4 to 5 inches across. If your mushrooms are larger or smaller, you may need to adjust the cooking time accordingly. You will need one 12-inch metal skewer for this recipe.

    6   tablespoons olive oil
    3   garlic cloves, minced
    1   teaspoon minced fresh thyme or ¼ teaspoon dried
        Salt and pepper
   12   ounces eggplant, sliced into ¾-inch-thick rounds
    1   small red onion, sliced into ¾-inch-thick rings
    2   portobello mushroom caps
    2   ounces goat cheese, crumbled (½ cup)
    2   hamburger buns
   ½   cup baby arugula
    1   tomato, cored and sliced thin

1. Cook oil, garlic, thyme, ¼ teaspoon salt, and ¼ teaspoon pepper in 8-inch skillet over medium heat until fragrant, about 1 minute. Transfer to bowl.

2. Brush both sides of eggplant rounds with 2 tablespoons garlic oil and season with salt and pepper. Thread onion rounds, from side to side, onto 12-inch metal skewer, brush with 1 tablespoon garlic oil, and season with salt and pepper. Using paring knife, lightly score top of each mushroom cap on diagonal in crosshatch pattern.

3A. FOR A CHARCOAL GRILL: Open bottom grill vent completely. Light large chimney starter three-quarters filled with charcoal briquettes (4½ quarts). When top coals are partially covered with ash, pour evenly over grill. Set cooking grate in place, cover, and open lid vent completely. Heat grill until hot, about 5 minutes.

3B. FOR A GAS GRILL: Turn all burners to high, cover, and heat grill until hot, about 15 minutes. Turn all burners to medium-high.

4. Clean and oil cooking grate. Place mushrooms, gill side down, onion skewer, and eggplant rounds on grill. Cook mushrooms (covered if using gas) until lightly charred and beginning to soften, 4 to 6 minutes. Flip mushrooms, brush with 1 tablespoon garlic oil, and cook until tender and browned on second side, 4 to 6 minutes. Sprinkle goat cheese over mushrooms and cook until cheese softens, about 2 minutes.

5. Meanwhile, cook onion and eggplant, turning as needed, until spottily charred on both sides, 8 to 12 minutes. Transfer mushrooms, onion, and eggplant to platter and tent loosely with aluminum foil. Grill buns until warm and lightly charred, about 30 seconds; transfer to platter.

6. Toss arugula with 1 teaspoon garlic oil in bowl and season with salt and pepper to taste. Remove onion from skewer and separate rings. Assemble mushroom caps, onion rings, arugula, and tomato on buns. Drizzle remaining garlic oil over eggplant rounds and serve with burgers.

NOTES FROM THE TEST KITCHEN

SCORING PORTOBELLOS FOR GRILLING

To help mushrooms release excess moisture on grill, use tip of sharp knife to lightly score top of each mushroom cap on diagonal in crosshatch pattern.

PAN-SEARED SHRIMP WITH SPICY ORANGE GLAZE

ON THE LIGHTER SIDE

CURRIED LENTIL SOUP

MANY LENTIL SOUPS RELY ON LOTS OF OLIVE OIL or pork for a flavorful, rich backbone. But we wanted a lighter approach and instead turned to an Indian spin on this classic—flavor-packed curried lentil soup, which delivers on all the hearty, comforting qualities of this satisfying dish but ditches the hambone in favor of bold, potent spices.

After gathering a number of recipes, we headed into the test kitchen. Two discoveries quickly came to light. First, garlic, herbs, onions, and tomatoes are common denominators. Second, texture is a big issue. None of our tasters liked the soup that was thin and watery, or, at the other extreme, the one that was as thick as oatmeal. They also gave a thumbs-down to those that looked like brown split pea soup. Consequently, recipes that included carrots, tomatoes, and fresh herbs were praised for their bright flavor and color. With our preferences clearly identified, the next step was to determine which lentils to buy and how to cook them.

NOTES FROM THE TEST KITCHEN

ALL ABOUT LENTILS

Lentils come in various sizes and colors, and the differences in flavor and texture are surprisingly distinct. Because they are thin-skinned, they require no soaking, which makes them a most versatile legume. For our Curried Lentil Soup, we prefer to use *lentilles du Puy*, which are smaller than the more common brown and green varieties and take their name from the city of Puy in central France. They are dark olive green, almost black, in color and are praised for their "rich, earthy, complex flavor" and "firm yet tender texture." Brown and green lentils, which you'll see in most supermarkets, work well, too; both offer a mild yet earthy flavor. Red and yellow lentils are also quite common, but they will not work in this application; these small lentils, which are most frequently used in Indian and Middle Eastern cuisine, disintegrate completely when cooked.

THE BEST CURRY POWDER

Though blends can vary dramatically, curry powders come in two basic styles: mild or sweet and a hotter version called Madras. The former consists of as many as 20 different ground spices, herbs, and seeds. We tasted six of these curry powders, mixed into a simple rice pilaf and in a plain vegetable curry. Our favorite was **Penzeys Sweet Curry Powder**, though Durkee Curry Powder came in a close second.

Brown, green, and red lentils are the most common choices on supermarket shelves. At specialty markets and high-end supermarkets, you can also find yellow lentils and French green lentils (*lentilles du Puy*). We decided to test all of these. Red and yellow lentils, traditionally used in Indian cooking, were out—they disintegrated when simmered. All of the remaining choices produced an acceptable texture, but tasters preferred the earthy flavor and firm texture of the lentilles du Puy. However, the larger green and brown lentils fared reasonably well. We found that just half a cup of lentils provided the right amount of soup for two.

Now that we knew which lentil to use and how much we needed, we were ready to fine-tune our cooking method. A few recipes recommended soaking the lentils for a few hours, but we found that this was unnecessary since lentils cook rather quickly. Quite a few Indian cookbooks called for cooking, or sweating, the lentils with the aromatics in a covered pan before adding the liquid. After sautéing an onion, carrot, and tomato in canola oil (which has less saturated fat than olive oil or vegetable oil) until they began to soften, we added our lentils to the pan. We found that sweating them for about five minutes strengthened their outer skin and helped keep them intact while still ensuring a tender interior. These lentils were definitely firmer after simmering than lentils that had not been sweated.

Next, we settled on the cooking liquid. Water alone produced a soup that was not as rich in flavor as we desired, and a chicken broth–only soup tasted too chicken-y and salty. After several more tests, we concluded that a mix of 2 parts broth to 1 part water produced a hearty depth of flavor without being overpowering. For our small amount of lentils, 3 cups of liquid proved ample to create a brothy, but not watery, soup. To give our soup more heartiness, we simply pureed some of the lentils to thicken up the soup base, leaving plenty of whole, intact lentils for appealing texture.

At last, we turned to the flavor. For the curry powder, we decided to start with just a half-teaspoon. The resulting soup smelled great and had surprisingly deep flavor, but tasters wanted even more curry flavor; going up to ¾ teaspoon did the trick. Stirring in the curry with the aromatics helped intensify its warm spice notes. For more savory backbone, we added a few cloves of garlic and a bit of minced thyme with the aromatics and curry powder.

While we were pleased with our curried lentil soup thus far, we decided to amp up its flavor even further.

Rather than increasing the amount of curry powder, we stirred in a small amount of garam masala, an Indian spice blend made from up to 12 different spices, which gave the soup even more complexity. For a final burst of freshness, we sprinkled minced cilantro over the soup at the end of cooking.

Finally, our soup had gone from good to great—and great for you, too.

Curried Lentil Soup

SERVES 2

We prefer the flavor and texture of French green lentils (lentilles du Puy) in this soup; however, common brown lentils work fine, too.

    2 teaspoons canola oil
    1 onion, chopped fine
    1 carrot, peeled and cut into ¼-inch pieces
    1 tomato, cored, seeded, and chopped fine
    2 garlic cloves, minced
    1 teaspoon minced fresh thyme or ¼ teaspoon dried
    ¾ teaspoon curry powder
    ½ teaspoon garam masala
    ½ cup lentils, picked over and rinsed
    2 cups low-sodium chicken broth
    1 cup water
       Salt and pepper
    1 tablespoon minced fresh cilantro

1. Heat oil in small saucepan over medium heat until shimmering. Stir in onion, carrot, tomato, garlic, thyme, curry powder, and garam masala and cook until vegetables begin to soften, about 5 minutes. Stir in lentils, cover, reduce heat to medium-low, and cook until vegetables are softened and lentils have become darker, 5 to 8 minutes.

2. Stir in broth and water, scraping up any browned bits, and bring to simmer. Partially cover, reduce heat to medium-low, and cook until lentils are tender but still hold their shape, 35 to 45 minutes.

3. Process 1½ cups of soup in blender until smooth. Return processed soup to pot and stir to combine. Season with salt and pepper to taste and sprinkle with cilantro. Serve.

PER SERVING: Cal 260; Fat 7 g; Sat fat 0 g; Chol 0 mg; Carb 42 g; Protein 13 g; Fiber 11 g; Sodium 610 mg

ASIAN CHICKEN LETTUCE WRAPS

CONSIDERED COMMON STREET FOOD—FAST FOOD— in Thailand, the exotic-sounding *laab gai* consists of spicy, quickly cooked ground chicken that is eaten not with a fork but with the aid of a lettuce leaf. You spoon the filling onto a lettuce leaf, fold it shut, and eat it with your hands, much as you would a taco. Relying on a combination of fresh, bright aromatics for its flavor, laab gai is a naturally healthy dish. Though usually eaten as a starter, we thought it was the perfect inspiration for a light but not ho-hum weekday meal for two.

To start, we focused on the chicken. Most ground chicken is not finely ground, so it has an unappealing stringy texture when cooked. Wondering whether it would be better to mince boneless chicken breasts in the food processor or simply process store-bought ground chicken further, we gave each approach a try. The boneless chicken breasts that were processed in the food processor cooked into dry little morsels, and the ground chicken processed again in the food processor showed minimal improvement. We found that simply smashing store-bought ground chicken with the back of a spoon before cooking was the best option, and we made sure that we continued to break it into small pieces as it cooked.

Most laab gai recipes we found called for similar flavorings, including fish sauce, lime juice, scallions, and fresh chiles. Tasters preferred the flavor and heat of a Thai chile—just one proved sufficient—though a small jalapeño worked just as well. Lime zest gave our filling a good punch, which we tempered with brown sugar and fragrant basil. Though many laab recipes also include a unique ingredient, toasted rice powder, toasting and grinding rice just seemed too fussy for this casual weeknight meal for two, and tasters thought our filling was every bit as flavorful without it. However, the rice powder also serves as a thickener, so to keep our mixture from becoming too wet, we whisked in half a teaspoon of cornstarch with our liquid ingredients and let it simmer with the chicken for just a minute until thickened.

To turn our recipe into a meal, we decided to spoon some cooked rice into our wraps to serve as a bed for the chicken filling. We tried long-grain rice, but the loose grains started falling out of the wrap as soon as

THE BEST FISH SAUCE

Fish sauce, or *nam pla* or *nuoc cham*, is a salty, amber-colored liquid made from salted, fermented fish. Used in very small amounts, it adds a well-rounded, salty flavor to sauces, soups, and marinades. We tasted six brands of fish sauce—one from Vietnam, one from the Philippines, and the rest from Thailand. Tasters had preferences among the sauces, but those preferences varied from taster to taster. With such a limited ingredient list (most of the brands contained some combination of fish extract, water, salt, and sugar), the differences among sauces were minimal. But if you are a fan of fish sauce and plan to use it often, you may want to make a special trip to an Asian market to buy a rich, dark sauce, like **Tiparos**, that is suitably pungent. We used Tiparos when making our Asian Chicken Lettuce Wraps, so keep in mind that if you use another brand, the sodium content of the dish will change.

1   cup water
½   cup short-grain rice, such as sushi rice, rinsed
⅛   teaspoon salt
1½   tablespoons fish sauce
2¼   teaspoons packed brown sugar
1   teaspoon grated lime zest plus 1½ tablespoons juice
½   teaspoon cornstarch
8   ounces ground chicken
1   teaspoon canola oil
1   Thai chile, stemmed, seeds reserved, and minced
2   tablespoons chopped fresh basil
2   scallions, sliced thin
6   Bibb or Boston lettuce leaves (½ head)

1. Bring water, rice, and salt to boil in small saucepan over high heat. Cover, reduce heat to low, and cook for 10 minutes. Remove rice from heat and let sit, covered, until tender, about 15 minutes.

2. Meanwhile, whisk fish sauce, sugar, lime juice, and cornstarch together in small bowl and set aside. In medium bowl, mash ground chicken using back of spoon until smooth and no strandlike pieces of meat remain.

3. Heat oil in 8-inch nonstick skillet over medium heat until shimmering. Add chicken, lime zest, and chile and cook, breaking up meat into small pieces with wooden spoon, until chicken is no longer pink, about 5 minutes.

4. Whisk fish sauce mixture to recombine, then add to skillet and cook, stirring constantly, until sauce has thickened, about 45 seconds. Off heat, stir in basil and scallions. Transfer chicken to shallow serving bowl and serve with rice and lettuce leaves.

PER SERVING: **Cal** 400; **Fat** 12 g; **Sat fat** 3 g; **Chol** 75 mg; **Carb** 51 g; **Protein** 24 g; **Fiber** 2 g; **Sodium** 790 mg

we took a bite. Stickier short-grain sushi rice turned out to be the best choice. Spooned onto a lettuce leaf, it made a good bed for the chicken that absorbed the sauce and actually helped the wrap stay neatly together. Rinsing the rice was crucial, since rinsing rids rice of excess starch that coats the individual grains. We found that unrinsed rice had an unappealing, gluey consistency. We also found that if we used too much liquid when cooking our short-grain rice, it took on a creamy, risotto-like texture. Since we were cooking such a small amount of rice, we found that a 2-to-1 ratio of water to rice was ideal. Although any type of lettuce leaves could be used here, we liked the small leaf size and pronounced curvature of Boston and Bibb lettuces.

A few of these flavorful wraps left us feeling satisfied but not overstuffed, making them a great lighter option for two.

Asian Chicken Lettuce Wraps

SERVES 2

Do not use ground chicken breast here (also labeled 99 percent fat-free) or the filling will be very dry. To make this dish spicier, add the reserved chile seeds. If you can't find Thai chiles, substitute 1 small jalapeño. To make a lettuce cup, put a spoonful of rice in the middle of a lettuce leaf, top with the chicken, fold the leaf edges up to form a taco shape, and eat with your hands.

CHICKEN CHOPPED SALAD

CHOPPED SALADS HAD THEIR HEYDAY IN THE 1950s as a popular light menu item for ladies who lunched. If you encounter a good version, it's easy to see why they're making a comeback. The best are lively, thoughtfully chosen compositions of lettuce, vegetables, and sometimes fruit cut into bite-size pieces, offering a variety of tastes, textures, and visual appeal. Unfortunately, we've had more experience with the mediocre kind.

These are little better than random collections of cut-up produce from the crisper drawer exuding moisture that turns the salad watery and bland. To make matters worse, the whole thing is doused in a dressing overloaded with oil and topped with handfuls of fatty nuts and cheese. It would take some serious work to return the chopped salad to its fresher, lighter past. We headed to the test kitchen, set on creating a simple version that was light and flavorful, with a mixture of crisp, colorful vegetables tossed in a bright, well-balanced dressing. To give our chopped salad some heft and turn it into a substantial dinner salad, we decided we'd add some chicken to the mix as well.

Since one of the key problems we had encountered with poor versions of this salad was a random mishmash of ingredients, we made sure to choose cohesive major players right at the start. We settled on a mix of fresh flavors and crisp textures, selecting cucumber, fennel, apple, and some crisp romaine. We liked the savory flavor of shallot to cut the sweetness, and a modest amount of crumbled goat cheese offered a nice creamy textural contrast.

Salad ingredients selected, we were ready to address the issue of sogginess that had been prevalent in the recipes we had tasted. The cucumber had the potential to be the main offender in our lineup, so we focused our attention there. We started by salting it to remove excess moisture. Working with just half a cucumber, we scooped out its watery seeds before slicing it into half-moons, tossing it with salt, and allowing it to drain in a colander. After 15 minutes, the cucumber had shed a few teaspoons of unwanted water.

The apple, fennel, and romaine didn't release much liquid, so we quickly got chopping. Tasters liked them best in smaller pieces that were easily picked up by their forks. Slices worked great for the apples and fennel, and ½-inch pieces were preferred for the romaine.

With our vegetables and fruit ready to go, we moved on to the chicken. Since we needed just enough meat for two—a single boneless breast proved ample—we didn't want to make preparing it a production. We sought the flavor and color from browning, but browning both sides of the chicken breast required more oil than we wanted to use, and it gave our chicken a tougher texture than we wanted. We found our answer in a half-sautéing, half-poaching method that required very little fat. First we browned the chicken on one side in half a teaspoon of oil, then we flipped the chicken over, added water to

the skillet, reduced the heat, and covered the skillet until the chicken was cooked through. This method yielded a moist, flavorful chicken breast. Once the breast cooled, we cut it into chunks and combined the pieces with the other salad ingredients.

We were ready to tackle the dressing. After some early tests, it became clear that the dressings in most recipes weren't doing anything for the salads except weighing them down. Most called for a ratio of 3 parts oil to 1 part vinegar. This proportion is optimal for dressing tender, subtly flavored leafy greens, but it wasn't quite right here. Working with extra-virgin olive oil and cider vinegar, we found that a more assertive blend of equal parts oil and vinegar—2 tablespoons of each for now—was far better at delivering the bright, acidic kick needed in this hearty, chunky salad. But we had a big roadblock: While this ratio worked well at dressing our salad, it was loading it up with fat and calories. We needed a creative way to reduce the oil without taking away from the unctuous consistency of the dressing.

As we reviewed our ingredient list, our gaze settled on the quarter-cup of goat cheese that we planned

NOTES FROM THE TEST KITCHEN

THE BEST BONELESS, SKINLESS CHICKEN BREASTS
Given that boneless, skinless chicken breasts are easy to prepare and an excellent low-fat source of protein, it's not surprising that they are standard in many home kitchens. To find out which brand is best, we gathered six popular brands of boneless, skinless chicken breasts, broiled them without seasoning, and had 20 tasters sample the chickens side by side. Among the contenders were one kosher bird, two "natural," and one "free-range." The remaining two were just "chicken."

The koshering process involves coating the chicken with salt to draw out any impurities; this process, similar to brining, results in moist, salty meat. Natural—in the case of chicken—simply means there are no antibiotics or hormones, and the birds are fed a vegetarian diet. "Free-range" means exactly what it says: The birds are not confined to small cages but are allowed to roam freely. The tie for first place went to **Empire Kosher** (left) and the all-natural **Bell & Evans** (right). As the only kosher bird, Empire won points with tasters for its superior flavor, namely, salt.

FENNEL, APPLE, AND CHICKEN CHOPPED SALAD

to sprinkle over the salad before serving. What if we whisked some of it into the dressing in place of some of the oil? We tried multiple batches with varying amounts of the goat cheese, and the idea was getting there—we had a dressing that was creamy and rich but lower in fat—but even with the full amount of cheese and only 1½ teaspoons of oil, the dressing was missing some liveliness. We thought maybe a fresh herb would do the trick. In the end, a couple of tablespoons of minced tarragon solved the problem, infusing the whole salad with its aniselike notes.

Looking to enhance our salad further, we wondered if we could use the dressing to even greater advantage. We found that marinating the heartier ingredients in the dressing for just five minutes before adding the romaine infused every component with flavor while still keeping it fresh and light.

Fennel, Apple, and Chicken Chopped Salad
SERVES 2

Fuji and Gala apples are widely available year-round, but Jonagold, Pink Lady, Jonathan, and Macoun can be substituted. Avoid Granny Smith apples here; their tart flavor will upset the balance of the dressing.

½ cucumber, peeled, halved lengthwise, seeded, and sliced ½ inch thick
   Salt and pepper
1 (8-ounce) boneless, skinless chicken breast, trimmed of all visible fat
2 teaspoons extra-virgin olive oil
1 ounce goat cheese, crumbled (¼ cup)
2 tablespoons cider vinegar
2 tablespoons minced fresh tarragon
1 Fuji or Gala apple, cored, quartered, and sliced crosswise ¼ inch thick
1 small fennel bulb (8 ounces), stalks discarded, bulb halved, cored, and sliced ¼ inch thick (see page 50)
1 large shallot, minced
½ romaine lettuce heart (3 ounces), cut into ½-inch pieces

1. Toss cucumber and ¼ teaspoon salt together and let drain in colander for 15 to 30 minutes.

2. Meanwhile, pat chicken dry with paper towels and season with ⅛ teaspoon salt and ⅛ teaspoon pepper. Heat ½ teaspoon oil in 8-inch nonstick skillet over medium-high heat until just smoking. Brown chicken well on first side, 6 to 8 minutes. Flip chicken, add ½ cup water, and reduce heat to medium-low. Cover and continue to cook until chicken registers 160 degrees, 5 to 7 minutes longer.

3. Transfer chicken to cutting board, let rest for 5 minutes, then cut into ½-inch pieces.

4. Whisk goat cheese, vinegar, tarragon, and remaining 1½ teaspoons oil together in large bowl. Add drained cucumber, chicken, apple, fennel, and shallot and toss to combine. Let sit at room temperature until flavors meld, about 5 minutes. Add romaine and toss gently to coat. Season with salt and pepper to taste and serve.

PER SERVING: Cal 330; Fat 11 g; Sat fat 3.5 g; Chol 80 mg; Carb 28 g; Protein 30 g; Fiber 7 g; Sodium 690 mg

SAUTÉED CHICKEN BREASTS WITH ORANGES AND FETA

BONELESS, SKINLESS CHICKEN BREASTS ARE LIKELY a mainstay in the weekly rotation for anyone who wants to eat healthier. They are packed with protein and virtually fat-free—and they are also exceptionally easy to prepare. Though you could opt to broil or poach them, sautéing gives them a beautiful golden brown exterior that is both visually appealing and flavorful. But the major problem with sautéing is that it tends to dry out the meat. Ideally, a sautéed chicken breast should be juicy, with a golden, evenly browned crust. We felt sure we could find the best way to sauté boneless chicken breasts, and while we were at it, we also wanted to transform them into an appealing, flavorful meal without relying on sauces full of butter and heavy cream, as so many recipes do.

We began by investigating what pan was best for sautéing. In the end, we found that a large, heavy-bottomed skillet was best. Given that we were working with just two chicken breasts, we tried using an 8-inch pan first, but it crowded the chicken and caused it to steam, resulting in a pale, unappetizing-looking exterior. A 10-inch pan was clearly the way to go. We also found that a traditional skillet worked better than a nonstick pan. This may seem counterintuitive since nonstick pans allow you to cook with less fat, but we found that regardless of skillet type, a certain amount of fat is necessary for a good sauté. We also liked using a traditional skillet because we wanted the fond, the browned bits that get left behind after browning in a traditional skillet, to build flavor for our topping or sauce.

Just how much oil would we need? We wanted enough to brown the chicken evenly, while keeping the dish as light as possible. After cooking nearly 6 pounds of chicken, we found that 2 teaspoons was just enough. Sautéing the chicken with any less resulted in unattractive, spotty crusts (and slightly scorched pans).

In the test kitchen we know that a hot pan is necessary to get a good sear. We waited until our oil was just smoking before adding the chicken breasts to the skillet, but cooking the breasts at medium-high heat for the whole time resulted in a scorched pan and dry chicken. Turning the heat down when browning the second side of the breasts proved crucial to preventing the second side from turning to leather before the meat had cooked through.

Up to this point we had been using unfloured breasts, but we were curious whether flouring would make a difference. Indeed it did; the floured breasts were juicier, browned more evenly, and were less likely to stick to the skillet. A light coating was a definite plus.

Having nailed the cooking technique, we set out to determine how we would liven up our plain chicken breasts. We liked the idea of incorporating brightly flavored citrus and opted for a simple orange relish instead of a pan sauce. With a minimum of tests, our relish came together. While the chicken rested, we tossed some fennel seeds into the skillet, added the orange pieces, a little water, and minced garlic, and cooked the mixture just until the oranges began to soften. The fennel seeds, with their mild, aniselike notes, added a complexity that tasters wholeheartedly approved of, and the garlic contributed a subtle aromatic backbone. But what really gave our relish deep flavor was the fond left behind from browning the chicken; the juice from the orange pieces mingled with the fond, creating a topping for our chicken that boasted both fresh, bright flavor and savory depth.

A sprinkling of crumbled feta and sliced scallions completed our simple sautéed chicken breasts, giving this fresh-tasting dish a picture-perfect appearance.

Sautéed Chicken Breasts with Oranges and Feta

SERVES 2

Tangerines can be substituted for the oranges. For more information on cutting oranges, see page 166. Pounding the thicker ends of the chicken breasts ensures even cooking.

2 oranges
3 tablespoons all-purpose flour
2 (6-ounce) boneless, skinless chicken breasts, trimmed of all visible fat, pounded if necessary
   Salt and pepper
2 teaspoons canola oil
1 small garlic clove, minced
⅛ teaspoon fennel seeds
1 tablespoon water
2 tablespoons crumbled feta cheese
2 scallions, sliced thin

1. Slice off top and bottom of orange, then cut away rind and pith using paring knife. Quarter peeled orange, then slice each quarter crosswise into ½-inch-thick pieces. Spread flour in shallow dish or pie plate. Pat chicken dry with paper towels and season with ⅛ teaspoon salt and ⅛ teaspoon pepper. Dredge chicken in flour and shake off excess.

2. Heat oil in 10-inch skillet over medium-high heat until just smoking. Add chicken and cook until well browned on first side, 6 to 8 minutes. Flip chicken, reduce heat to medium, and continue to cook until chicken registers 160 degrees, 4 to 6 minutes longer. Transfer chicken to platter and tent loosely with aluminum foil.

3. Return now-empty skillet to medium heat, add garlic and fennel seeds, and cook until fragrant, about 30 seconds. Stir in oranges and water, scraping up any browned bits, and cook until oranges are just softened, 1 to 2 minutes. Stir in any accumulated chicken juices and season with salt and pepper to taste.

4. Pour relish over chicken breasts and sprinkle with feta and scallions. Serve.

PER SERVING: **Cal** 360; **Fat** 11 g; **Sat fat** 2.5 g; **Chol** 115 mg; **Carb** 25 g; **Protein** 40 g; **Fiber** 4 g; **Sodium** 420 mg

Sautéed Chicken Breasts with Cherry Tomatoes, Olives, and Feta

Omit fennel seeds. Substitute 6 ounces halved cherry tomatoes and 2 tablespoons coarsely chopped kalamata olives for oranges. Substitute 1 tablespoon shredded fresh mint for scallions.

PER SERVING: **Cal** 350; **Fat** 14 g; **Sat fat** 3 g; **Chol** 115 mg; **Carb** 13 g; **Protein** 39 g; **Fiber** 2 g; **Sodium** 660 mg

NOTES FROM THE TEST KITCHEN

POUNDING CHICKEN BREASTS

When buying packaged chicken breasts, it's important to note that packages often contain chicken breasts of varying sizes. Sometimes the thickness of a single breast can vary dramatically between the thick end and the thin tail.

To fix this, simply pound the thicker ends of the chicken breasts lightly until the breasts are all roughly the same thickness. Though some of the breasts will still be larger, they will at least all cook at a similar rate.

PARING KNIVES A CUT ABOVE

Nothing can compare with a chef's knife when it comes to sawing through large cuts of meat, chopping vegetables, or mincing fresh herbs. But for detail work—hulling strawberries, coring fruit, scraping out vanilla beans, or trimming silverskin from a roast—smaller, more maneuverable paring knives are far better tools. Since our last review a few years ago, two German makers have introduced changes to the geometry of their knives, and some of the cooks in the test kitchen raised concerns about the flimsiness of our previous favorite, from Victorinox. We decided to take another look. We armed ourselves with 10 of the latest models, most boasting our ideal blade length of 3 to 3½ inches, in a wide variety of prices—from our current favorite and bargain buy from Victorinox to a gleaming forged blade from Shun that cost 14 times as much. We then subjected the knives to a range of tasks to determine their maneuverability, comfort, and precision. The comfortable, well-proportioned, and solidly built **Wüsthof Classic 3½-Inch Paring Knife with PEtec** ("Precision Edge Technology"), $39.95 (left), won top marks as a near-perfect tool. Our old favorite, the **Victorinox Fibrox 3¼-Inch Paring Knife** (right), still won fans and remains our best buy with its mere $8.95 price tag.

TURKEY CUTLETS WITH CRANBERRIES

ONE QUICK LOOK AT THE SUPERMARKET MEAT CASE will confirm it: Turkey has spread its wings far beyond Thanksgiving. There's ground turkey, smoked turkey, turkey parts, turkey sausage, and turkey burgers—to name just a few. And for home cooks in need of a light, quick-cooking dinner for two, there are turkey cutlets. However, they do take some know-how to prepare. Because they are thin, usually no more than about ⅜ inch thick, and very lean, the margin of error between a perfectly cooked turkey cutlet and shoe leather is slim. Most recipes turn out flavorless meat with a tough, pale exterior. We knew we could do better, so we headed to the kitchen, determined to bring out the best in turkey cutlets by perfecting our cooking technique and coming up with a flavorful, easy pan sauce to dress them up.

Our first obstacle was settling on a cooking method. We knew for the best flavor and appearance, our cutlets needed to be nicely browned. Because the cutlets are so thin, a high-heat cooking method (broiling, sautéing) was essential; low or moderate heat (baking, poaching) would overcook the delicate meat before it could form that flavorful browned exterior. We tried broiling first, but it yielded mediocre results; one cutlet was cooked perfectly but the other was overdone. Sautéing on the stovetop was our best bet as it required a minimal amount of fat (cutlets are so thin they don't require very much) and offered us the most control. And as a bonus, once we sautéed the cutlets, we could build a sauce in the same pan.

We found recipes that called for butter, olive oil, canola oil, and a combination of butter and oil. To keep the saturated fat to a minimum, we opted for canola oil. In side-by-side tests, we wanted to see how much oil was really necessary to brown the cutlets without scorching them. Ultimately, we realized that we needed 1 tablespoon to evenly coat the pan; any less and our cutlets browned unevenly. A 12-inch skillet was key to giving our two cutlets enough room to brown, rather than steam in their own juices. We took a cue from our Sautéed Chicken Breasts with Oranges and Feta (page 178) and tried flouring our cutlets, which would not only encourage browning but would also protect the delicate meat and prevent the outside of the cutlets from overcooking before the inside cooked through. Two minutes on each side over medium-high heat did the trick.

CHOOSING RED WINE FOR COOKING

After testing more than 30 bottles of red wine, we divined a few guidelines about those that are best for cooking. First, save expensive wine for drinking. Although a few tasters perceived "greater complexity" in pan sauces made with $30 bottles, the differences were minimal at best; $10-and-under wines are usually fine. Second, stick with blends like Côtes du Rhône or generically labeled "table" wines that use a combination of grapes to yield a balanced, fruity finish. If you prefer single-grape varietals, choose medium-bodied wines, such as Pinot Noir and Merlot. Avoid oaky wines like Cabernet Sauvignon, which turn bitter when cooked. Finally, don't buy supermarket "cooking wines." These low-alcohol concoctions have little flavor, high-pitched acidity, and enormous amounts of salt.

The hard part was over; now we could focus on the sauce. We settled on a red wine sauce that was slightly rich but wouldn't overpower our delicate turkey. After gently sautéing a thinly sliced shallot, minced garlic, and fresh thyme in the skillet, we used red wine and chicken broth to loosen the flavorful browned bits left in the pan from browning the turkey. Dried cranberries added just the right tartness (and carried out our Thanksgiving-anytime theme), and a touch of honey lent just the perfect balancing sweetness.

Now there was no need to invite the whole family over just to enjoy the taste of turkey. Our recipe delivered two perfect portions of poultry, and they offered tender meat and a richly flavored sauce in record time.

Turkey Cutlets with Cranberries and Red Wine

SERVES 2

Pounding the turkey cutlets to a ¼-inch thickness ensures that they will cook through quickly and evenly without drying out.

CUTLETS

- 3 tablespoons all-purpose flour
- 2 (6-ounce) turkey cutlets, trimmed of all visible fat and pounded ¼ inch thick
  Salt and pepper
- 1 tablespoon canola oil

SAUCE

- 1 shallot, sliced thin
- 1 garlic clove, minced
- ½ teaspoon minced fresh thyme
- 1 teaspoon all-purpose flour
- ½ cup red wine
- ⅓ cup low-sodium chicken broth
- ¼ cup dried cranberries
- ½ teaspoon honey

1. FOR THE CUTLETS: Spread flour in shallow dish or pie plate. Pat cutlets dry with paper towels and season with ⅛ teaspoon salt and ⅛ teaspoon pepper. Dredge cutlets in flour and shake off excess.

2. Heat oil in 12-inch skillet over medium-high heat until just smoking. Add cutlets and cook until light golden brown on both sides, about 4 minutes. Transfer cutlets to plate and tent with aluminum foil.

3. FOR THE SAUCE: Add shallot to now-empty skillet and cook over medium heat until softened, 1 to 2 minutes. Stir in garlic and thyme and cook until fragrant, about 30 seconds. Stir in flour and cook for 30 seconds. Whisk in wine, broth, cranberries, and honey, scraping up any browned bits.

4. Bring to simmer and cook until sauce is slightly thickened, 1 to 2 minutes. Stir in any accumulated turkey juices and season with salt and pepper to taste. Spoon sauce over cutlets and serve.

PER SERVING: Cal 400; Fat 8 g; Sat fat 0.5 g; Chol 65 mg; Carb 28 g; Protein 44 g; Fiber 1 g; Sodium 400 mg

HEARTY STUFFED SHELLS

TRADITIONAL STUFFED SHELLS, WITH THEIR RICH, ultra-cheesy filling, are far from diet fare. Many recipes try to lighten the stuffing by using novelty ingredients like pureed beans or soft tofu as a primary filling, which results in a noticeably odd flavor; other versions resort to such unfortunate options as grainy low-fat ricotta cheese or plasticky fat-free mozzarella. After sampling a number of recipes that compromised either flavor or texture (or both), we set out to create our own recipe for low-fat stuffed shells that tasted every bit as good as the full-fat versions.

Our starting point was a full-fat test kitchen recipe for the filling, which uses ricotta, Parmesan, shredded mozzarella, and two eggs. We figured we would slice and whittle where we could. Fortunately, in the process of testing sample recipes, we had come across one "diet" ingredient that really worked: fat-free cottage cheese. We usually prefer reduced-fat products to fat-free in the test kitchen because they have better texture and no aftertaste from the stabilizers often added to nonfat ingredients. But in this case, we found that when the fat-free cottage cheese was processed to a creamy puree, its smooth texture was indistinguishable from that of the higher-fat versions, and its flavor was clean and mild. We substituted fat-free cottage cheese for the full-fat ricotta, and the dish remained fully satisfying.

Next, we cut the Parmesan down little by little until we were left with less than one-quarter of the starting amount—its flavor is so strong, it didn't take much to make an impact. Using part-skim mozzarella was an easy switch from the full-fat version, and tasters thought it also offered plenty of flavor even when we reduced the amount to just ½ cup—still enough to melt over the top as well as help bind the filling.

The filling was delicious at this point but too soupy—it ran right out of the shells. We drained the cottage cheese, but even this was runnier than the ricotta had been, and adjusting the amount and types of shredded cheeses in the filling had reduced their binding power as well. Removing the eggs made the raw filling firmer (and saved some calories), but it still wasn't firm enough to pipe into the shells. One at a time, we added a handful of various low-fat ingredients such as cooked rice, instant potato flakes, and bread crumbs. Each gave the filling body, but in every case either the taste or the

texture of these ingredients was notably wrong for stuffed shells. Finally, we reached for a box of saltines. We thought their relatively bland flavor might work in our favor. It did. When ground fine in the food processor with the cheeses, they disappeared into the filling, firming it up nicely and adding only a few calories and no fat per portion.

Now we moved on to the sauce. Initially, we set out to develop a hearty meat sauce to complement our lightened shells. But given that we were trying to cut fat and calories, and we were making a scaled-down sauce for two, we would need just a small amount of meat. Though we could have asked the butcher at the meat counter to portion out just an ounce or two of ground meat for us, it seemed silly, so we looked for another way to give our tomato sauce some heartiness. Thinking back to our Quick Mushroom Ragu (page 85), we suspected mushrooms might make a good stand-in and provide the hearty texture and rich, deep flavor we were after.

We chopped 2 ounces of mushrooms and sautéed them with a minced shallot, then stirred in a small can of diced tomatoes, which we'd processed for a somewhat smooth sauce with smaller chunks of tomato. Sure enough, the mushrooms provided great flavor, but the texture of the sauce wasn't quite right. Since we already had the food processor out to process the tomatoes, we thought we'd give the mushrooms a whirl first. Just a few pulses gave us the pebbly, ground-meat texture we were looking for, but now 2 ounces of mushrooms looked like a rather paltry amount. Doubling the amount solved the problem.

Though we'd figured out how to give our meat-free sauce some meaty texture, it was still lacking in flavor. We took a step back and considered other ingredients we could add to infuse our sauce with more meaty depth. In the test kitchen, we often rely on ingredients packed with glutamates—naturally occurring flavor compounds that enhance savory qualities—to add depth to sauces, stews, and braises. Tomato paste, which is one of these ingredients, seemed a natural inclusion. Indeed, a single teaspoon added substantial savory depth. But for even more savory character, we also considered soy sauce. Though it might seem unusual in a pasta dish, it actually did the trick. Just ¼ teaspoon gave our sauce a fuller, deeper flavor. After tasting the finished sauce, tasters agreed that no one would miss the beef in this hearty dish.

NOTES FROM THE TEST KITCHEN

FILLING STUFFED SHELLS

To fill shells, place cheese filling in zipper-lock bag, squeeze it into corner, and twist bag. Apply slight pressure to filling and snip corner of bag with scissors. Hold shell and squeeze 2 tablespoons of filling inside.

Since the rest of the sauce was so low in fat, and the stuffed shells finally had rich, hearty flavor combined with good texture, we called it a day. True, the amount of work involved in making the traditional version of this dish hadn't been reduced, but neither had the flavor of the creamy filling and hearty sauce.

Hearty Stuffed Shells

SERVES 2

You will need a shallow 2-cup gratin dish (measuring approximately 9 by 6 inches; see page 3), or you can substitute one 8-inch square baking dish. If the cottage cheese appears watery, drain it in a fine-mesh strainer for 15 minutes before you use it. Separate the shells after draining them to keep them from sticking together.

SAUCE

    4 ounces white mushrooms, trimmed and quartered
    ¼ teaspoon low-sodium soy sauce
    1 (14.5-ounce) can diced tomatoes
 1½ teaspoons olive oil
    1 large shallot, minced
    1 teaspoon tomato paste
    1 garlic clove, minced
    2 tablespoons chopped fresh basil
       Salt

STUFFED SHELLS

  10 jumbo pasta shells (4 ounces)
       Salt
    4 saltines, broken into pieces
    ¾ cup fat-free cottage cheese, drained if necessary
    2 ounces part-skim mozzarella cheese, shredded (½ cup)
    3 tablespoons grated Parmesan cheese
    2 teaspoons chopped fresh basil
    1 garlic clove, minced

1. FOR THE SAUCE: Adjust oven rack to upper-middle position and heat oven to 375 degrees. Pulse mushrooms and soy sauce together in food processor until well combined, about 4 pulses; transfer to bowl. Add tomatoes to processor and pulse until coarsely ground, about 4 pulses.

2. Heat oil in medium saucepan over medium heat until shimmering. Add mushrooms and shallot and cook until softened, 2 to 3 minutes. Add tomato paste and garlic and cook until fragrant, about 1 minute. Stir in processed tomatoes and simmer until sauce is slightly thickened, 2 to 3 minutes. Off heat, stir in basil. Season with salt to taste and set aside.

3. FOR THE STUFFED SHELLS: Meanwhile, bring 4 quarts water to boil in large pot. Add shells and 1 tablespoon salt and cook, stirring often, until al dente. Drain shells and transfer to kitchen towel–lined baking sheet. Reserve 8 shells, discarding any that have broken.

4. Using dry, clean food processor bowl, pulse crackers until finely ground, about 20 pulses. Add cottage cheese, ¼ cup mozzarella, Parmesan, basil, garlic, and pinch salt and process until smooth, about 1 minute, scraping down bowl as necessary; transfer to plastic zipper-lock bag. Using scissors, cut off one corner of bag and pipe 2 tablespoons of filling into each shell.

5. Spread one-half of sauce over bottom of 9 by 6-inch baking dish. Arrange filled shells, seam side up, over sauce in dish. Spread remaining sauce over shells. Cover with aluminum foil and bake until bubbling around edges, 25 to 35 minutes. Remove foil and sprinkle with remaining ¼ cup mozzarella. Bake until cheese is melted, about 5 minutes. Let cool for 5 minutes. Serve.

PER SERVING: Cal 460; Fat 11 g; Sat fat 4.5 g; Chol 25 mg; Carb 62 g; Protein 28 g; Fiber 5 g; Sodium 1460 mg

BEEF STROGANOFF

CLASSIC BEEF STROGANOFF IS ULTRA-RICH AND luxurious—and it's no wonder why. Typical recipes start with browning beef tenderloin in butter, then making a mushroom sauce, which is enriched with plenty of sour cream; the saucy dish is finally served with generously buttered egg noodles. We wanted to see if we could lighten this classic, while also scaling it down for two, but keep all of its satisfying, hearty appeal intact.

Unfortunately, the light recipes we tested cut back on fat and calories by way of skimpy portions, tough extra-lean beef, and curdled sauces made with fat-free dairy. One lower-fat recipe, however, did offer a glimmer of hope. It used more of the flavorful, hearty mushrooms already in the dish to replace some of the beef. We set out to create our own lighter take on stroganoff using this approach.

Working backward from the original recipe, we found that to significantly lighten the dish, we would have to

BEEF STROGANOFF

drastically reduce the meat—from about 8 ounces per person to 3 ounces. To compensate for the loss of beefy flavor, we went up on the mushrooms, eventually settling on 8 ounces. But with so many vegetables in the sauce, we could barely taste the mild beef tenderloin. We tried stronger-flavored eye round, sirloin, and flank steak. Only the flank steak was beefy enough to hold its own. Unfortunately, it was also tough and rubbery.

NOTES FROM THE TEST KITCHEN

SLICING BEEF FOR STROGANOFF

1. Using sharp chef's knife, slice steak with grain into 3-inch-wide strips.

2. Then cut each 3-inch-wide strip crosswise into ¼-inch-thick slices.

HOW MEAT TENDERIZERS WORK

The use of plants to tenderize meat dates back hundreds of years to the native peoples of what is now Mexico, who wrapped meat in papaya leaves. Both papaya and pineapple contain enzymes that break down collagen—the connective tissue that makes meat tough. These enzymes, papain (from papaya) and bromelain (from pineapple), are the active ingredients in bottles of meat tenderizer. We've dismissed these products in the past because they effectively tenderize only the outermost layer of a piece of meat—not much of an improvement for a thick, tough steak. But our thin, ultra-lean flank steak was just the right thickness for the bottled tenderizer to penetrate completely.

To see if brand mattered, we tested six tenderizers ("seasoned" and unseasoned varieties from Adolph's, Durkee, and McCormick) on tough veal cutlets. Adolph's and Durkee contain papain, while McCormick relies on bromelain to do the work. All of them worked equally well—neither the brand nor the type of enzyme mattered. Should you opt for seasoned or unseasoned? While the extra spices aren't enough to ruin dinner, we'd rather do the seasoning ourselves.

To ensure tender meat, we tried poking it with a fork to break up the fibers, cutting it very thin, and salting it, but nothing worked. Then a colleague suggested meat tenderizer. In the past, we've found that tenderizer doesn't penetrate deeply enough into large cuts of meat to be effective. But with our thinly sliced flank steak, the tenderizer showed dramatic results in just 15 minutes.

At this point, we took another look at the mushrooms. We had started our testing with white button mushrooms, but, like the tenderloin, they were too mild. Meaty portobello mushroom slices, however, could stand up to the flank steak in both flavor and texture. We were determined to use no more than a teaspoon of fat (and thus a nonstick skillet) to cook all the vegetables and beef. Yet the 8 ounces of mushrooms drank up the oil we had allotted for cooking them, plus we could barely contain them in the pan. We needed to find another easy way to cook them that would require less oil. Ultimately, we decided to spritz the mushrooms lightly with vegetable oil spray and roast them. The mushrooms browned in a single (mostly hands-off) batch, and their flavor became intense and concentrated.

Moving on to the creamy sauce, we started by sautéing some chopped onion, adding tomato paste and flour (the classic thickener used in stroganoff), and then adding the usual combination of beef broth, mustard, and white wine. Once the sauce reduced, it was time to add the sour cream. Obviously, full-fat sour cream wasn't going to cut it. We tried low-fat sour cream and nonfat yogurt, but the low-fat sour cream dulled the flavor of the sauce, and the nonfat yogurt curdled. We'd recently seen a recipe for braised lamb that called for stirring in an egg white with the yogurt to prevent the yogurt from curdling over the heat. It seemed odd, but it was worth a try. After stirring some egg white into a bit of yogurt, we slowly mixed the combination into the sauce. Miraculously, it stayed together. Our science editor explained that yogurt is acidic, and proteins, such as the casein in yogurt, are sensitive to both acid and heat. Also, the less fat there is, the more apt the yogurt is to curdle. The alkaline egg white was helping to neutralize the yogurt so it wouldn't curdle. Turning off the heat provided extra insurance against curdling.

With big, meaty bites of beef and mushrooms smothered in a rich, creamy sauce, our lightened stroganoff was so good that when we switched from regular egg noodles to yolk-free noodles—and skipped the butter altogether—tasters didn't even notice.

Beef Stroganoff

SERVES 2

Do not substitute Greek yogurt in this recipe, as its thicker texture will adversely affect the consistency of the sauce.

6	ounces flank steak, trimmed of all visible fat
½	teaspoon meat tenderizer
	Vegetable oil spray
8	ounces portobello mushroom caps, gills removed (see page 84), halved and sliced thin
	Salt and pepper
1	teaspoon canola oil
⅓	cup finely chopped onion
1	teaspoon all-purpose flour
¾	teaspoon tomato paste
¾	cup beef broth
2	tablespoons white wine
½	teaspoon Dijon mustard
3	ounces (2 cups) yolk-free egg noodles
3	tablespoons plain nonfat yogurt
1	tablespoon egg white
1	teaspoon minced fresh parsley

1. Adjust oven rack to middle position and heat oven to 425 degrees. Cut steak with grain into 3-inch-wide strips, then cut each strip crosswise into ¼-inch-thick slices. Toss meat and tenderizer together in medium bowl, cover, and refrigerate for 15 to 30 minutes.

2. Lightly spray rimmed baking sheet with vegetable oil spray. Place mushrooms on prepared baking sheet, lightly spray with vegetable oil spray, and sprinkle with pinch salt and pinch pepper. Roast mushrooms until golden brown, 7 to 10 minutes, stirring halfway through roasting; set aside.

3. Pat steak dry with paper towels. Heat ½ teaspoon oil in 10-inch nonstick skillet over medium-high heat until just smoking. Cook steak, without moving it, until browned around edges, 1 to 2 minutes. Toss steak and cook until no longer pink, about 30 seconds. Transfer to clean bowl.

4. Add remaining ½ teaspoon oil, onion, and pinch salt to now-empty skillet and cook over medium heat until softened and lightly browned, about 5 minutes. Stir in roasted mushrooms, flour, and tomato paste and cook until paste begins to darken, about 1 minute. Stir in broth, wine, and mustard and bring to boil. Reduce heat to medium-low and simmer until sauce is slightly thickened, 1 to 2 minutes.

5. Meanwhile, bring 4 quarts water to boil in large pot. Add noodles and 1 tablespoon salt and cook, stirring often, until al dente. Drain noodles and return to pot.

6. Stir steak into sauce, along with any accumulated juices, and cook until beef is heated through, about 30 seconds. Whisk yogurt and egg white together in small bowl until smooth. Off heat, stir yogurt mixture and parsley into sauce. Season with salt and pepper to taste. Serve over noodles.

PER SERVING: Cal 390; Fat 10 g; Sat fat 2.5 g; Chol 55 mg; Carb 42 g; Protein 31 g; Fiber 4 g; Sodium 800 mg

FISH CAKES

MARYLANDERS MAY RAVE ABOUT THEIR CRAB cakes, but here in New England we love a good cod cake. There is certainly no shortage of recipes, but most we've tried turn out to be more of a bread patty or potato cake than fish cake. They are laden with binders that not only mask the flavor of the fish but also pack on unnecessary fat and calories. We set out to develop a recipe for fish cakes that would make a New Englander proud: They would need to be moist, delicate, and tender yet still cohesive, and with seasoning and binding that complemented the clean, subtle flavor of the cod without drowning out the fish or weighing down the cakes.

Initial research turned up two basic approaches to making fish cakes: using cooked cod (usually bound by mashed potatoes) and using raw cod (bound by bread crumbs). After a few tests, tasters agreed that the cakes made with cooked cod and potatoes were heavy and the fish was overwhelmed by the potato flavor—not the clean-tasting, light cakes we were after. They were also much more time-consuming to prepare since we had to precook the cod and potatoes separately before forming and browning the cakes—way too much fuss and mess for a casual dinner for two. The few recipes we found that used raw cod showed more promise—they were light and cleaner-tasting, but still, they were not without faults, including the fact that they tended to fall apart in the pan (and those that didn't fall apart relied on far too much binder). But at least it was a starting point.

The next issue was how to prepare the raw cod before forming the cakes. Early tests told us a combination of textures was best. Finely chopped cod helped bind

FISH CAKES WITH REDUCED-FAT TARTAR SAUCE

the cakes (and kept the fish flavor at the forefront), and larger, bite-size chunks added heartiness and visual appeal. We started with 8 ounces of skinless cod fillets and cut half of them into 1-inch chunks, then tossed them into the food processor and pulsed them until finely minced. We chopped the other half by hand. This worked well, but then we realized we could eliminate a step by pulsing it all in the food processor for just two or three pulses and get similar results, since so few pulses produced an inconsistent texture anyway—annoying for some applications but exactly what we were looking for in this recipe.

As for a binder, we wanted to use as little as possible. We had already ruled out mashed potatoes, as they created a pasty, heavy cake and required precooking. Fresh bread crumbs absorbed too much moisture and created doughy, wet pockets in and around the cod—we wanted fish cakes, not dough balls. We eventually settled on finely ground dry bread crumbs. They didn't have an overwhelming flavor, they were easy to mix in, and they didn't mask the texture of the mild cod. The trickiest part was knowing when to stop. Fish cakes need just enough binder to hold together, but not so much that the filler takes over the flavor. We started with a half-cup of dry bread crumbs and eventually worked our way down to just 2 tablespoons. This gave us tender cakes with the cod flavor taking center stage. Any less and the cakes could not hold their shape.

Because cod is a lean, flaky fish, we knew we would need some moisture to supplement the bread crumbs and keep the cakes from falling apart. We tried a range of low-fat options. Low-fat yogurt and buttermilk were too wet and added too much moisture, and low-fat sour cream and cream cheese added unwanted tang. Finally, we tried light mayonnaise, which provided the right amount of moisture but came across as somewhat sweet. Some Dijon mustard provided just the right sharpness to balance it out. One tablespoon of mayonnaise combined with 2 teaspoons of mustard worked perfectly. To further help the binding, instead of the whole egg that most recipes call for, we tried adding a single egg white, but even that was too much liquid for our two cod cakes. We found that 1 tablespoon of egg white was all it took to keep our cod cakes together.

Careful mixing proved a must to avoid a pasty, mushy cake. We found that a rubber spatula worked best, and

we used it in a folding, rather than stirring, motion. Handling the mixture as little as possible was also key in keeping our cakes tender and light yet cohesive.

When it came time to cook our cakes, we still had some trouble making them hold together. We didn't want to add more binder, so we tried chilling the cakes before cooking, a technique we've used successfully for crab and shrimp cakes. Just half an hour in the refrigerator made a huge difference. We also tried different cooking methods. After baking, pan-frying, and broiling, we settled on sautéing our cod cakes in a nonstick skillet over medium heat. It was fast but still gave us complete control over how brown and crisp the cakes got. Dredging them lightly in flour before putting them in the pan helped create a crust and prevented sticking.

For seasonings, tasters preferred simplicity—some minced shallot and parsley, as well as lemon juice, accented the delicate cod and brought out its fresh flavor. Served with our lightened-up tartar sauce, these fish cakes made the perfect flavorful yet lean supper for a seafood-loving duo.

Fish Cakes with Reduced-Fat Tartar Sauce

SERVES 2

Be sure to use raw cod here; do not substitute cooked cod. Don't overprocess the cod in step 2 or the cakes will have a pasty texture. If sweet pickles are not available, substitute dill pickles in the tartar sauce.

    3 tablespoons light mayonnaise

    2 teaspoons minced sweet pickles plus ½ teaspoon juice

    1 teaspoon capers, rinsed and minced

    ¾ teaspoon lemon juice

    ½ teaspoon minced shallot

    ⅛ teaspoon Worcestershire sauce

       Salt and pepper

FISH CAKES

    8 ounces skinless cod fillets, cut into 1-inch pieces

    2 tablespoons plain dried bread crumbs

    1 small shallot, minced

1½ tablespoons minced fresh parsley

    1 tablespoon egg white

    1 tablespoon light mayonnaise

    2 teaspoons Dijon mustard

1½ teaspoons lemon juice

    ⅛ teaspoon salt

       Pinch pepper

    3 tablespoons all-purpose flour

    1 tablespoon canola oil

       Lemon wedges

1. FOR THE TARTAR SAUCE: Whisk all ingredients together in bowl and season with salt and pepper to taste. Refrigerate until needed.

2. FOR THE FISH CAKES: Pulse cod fillets in food processor until there is even mix of finely minced and coarsely chopped pieces, about 3 pulses. Transfer processed cod to bowl and sprinkle bread crumbs over cod.

3. Whisk shallot, parsley, egg white, mayonnaise, mustard, lemon juice, salt, and pepper together in bowl until combined. Using rubber spatula, gently fold mixture into cod and bread crumbs until cod mixture just holds together.

4. Divide cod mixture into 2 equal portions and shape each into round cake, about 3 inches across and 1 inch high. Transfer to plate, cover with plastic wrap, and refrigerate for at least 30 minutes or up to 24 hours.

5. Spread flour in shallow dish or pie plate. Dredge fish cakes in flour and shake off excess. Heat oil in 10-inch nonstick skillet over medium heat until shimmering. Carefully lay chilled fish cakes in skillet and cook until well browned on both sides, 7 to 9 minutes, flipping them halfway through cooking. Carefully transfer fish cakes to platter. Serve with lemon wedges and tartar sauce.

PER SERVING: **Cal** 310; **Fat** 15 g; **Sat fat** 2 g; **Chol** 55 mg; **Carb** 18 g; **Protein** 23 g; **Fiber** 1 g; **Sodium** 720 mg

PAN-SEARED SHRIMP

PAN-SEARING IS A WONDERFUL WAY TO PREPARE shrimp—it produces the ultimate combination of a well-caramelized exterior and a moist, tender interior. If executed properly, this cooking method also preserves the shrimp's plumpness and trademark briny sweetness. That said, a good recipe for pan-seared shrimp is hard to find. We've seen many that result in dry, pale, tough, or gummy shrimp—hardly appetizing. Given that shrimp are naturally low in fat and calories, we thought it was high time we figured out the best way to pan-sear this popular crustacean, so we could transform it into a simple light dinner for two.

We quickly uncovered a few basic principles for our recipe. First, tasters unanimously favored shrimp that were peeled before being cooked. Peeled shrimp are easier to eat, and unpeeled shrimp fail to pick up the delicious caramelized flavor that pan-searing provides. Second, oil was the ideal cooking medium, favored over both a dry pan (which made the shrimp leathery and metallic-tasting) and butter (which tended to burn). And third, the shrimp were best cooked in a 10-inch skillet, which proved just large enough that it kept our small amount of shrimp for two from being overcrowded in the pan and steaming—a surefire way to prevent caramelization. With these principles established, we moved on to refine our procedure.

Because in the test kitchen we like to brine shrimp before grilling them, we assumed that a successful recipe for pan-seared shrimp would include brining. Although brining did enhance their moistness and texture, the shrimp released just enough moisture to inhibit caramelization and prevent the nicely browned exterior we were after.

Although it seemed brining had its flaws, our tests yielded an unexpected benefit. We had been adding sugar to the brining solution with the hope of improving the shrimp's browning characteristics. While the sugar did not promote browning in the brined shrimp, it did accentuate their natural sweetness and nicely set off their inherent sea-saltiness. Capitalizing on this discovery, we added a pinch of sugar to some unbrined shrimp along with the requisite salt and pepper. This did indeed boost the flavor, as we had expected, and, absent the water from the brine, the sugar also encouraged browning. We could skip the brining step and move right to the skillet.

We'd already established that a 10-inch skillet was just the right size for our shrimp for two, but the trick now was to develop a technique that didn't overcook the shrimp while we achieved the perfect brown color. To prevent overcooking, we found that two minutes was the magic number to color and cook the shrimp through without turning them to rubber. A quick flip halfway though cooking ensured that both sides developed a flavorful and attractive sear. As for the oil, we found that 2 teaspoons were sufficient to sear 12 ounces of shrimp perfectly, while still keeping our dish squarely in the lighter category.

Now all we needed were a couple of quick, bright-tasting sauces. We came up with two Asian-inspired glazes made with assertive ingredients: one with orange juice, cilantro, and Asian chili-garlic sauce and another with fresh ginger, soy sauce, and hoisin sauce. While big on flavor, these sauces were naturally low in fat and kept the shrimp safely in the guilt-free zone. In order to give the sauces time to reduce (without overcooking the shrimp), we backed off the shrimp's cooking time by 30 seconds, then added the sauce and let the shrimp finish cooking while the sauce thickened. The big, bold flavors of both glazes perfectly complemented the sweet, briny shrimp and gave this easy weeknight entrée an exotic flair.

Pan-Seared Shrimp with Spicy Orange Glaze
SERVES 2

If using smaller or larger shrimp, be sure to adjust the cooking time accordingly. This dish is fairly spicy; to make it milder, use less Asian chili-garlic sauce. Serve with Simple White Rice (page 73).

½	teaspoon grated orange zest plus 2 tablespoons juice
1	tablespoon minced fresh cilantro
1⅛	teaspoons sugar
½	teaspoon Asian chili-garlic sauce
12	ounces extra-large shrimp (21 to 25 per pound), peeled and deveined
⅛	teaspoon salt
⅛	teaspoon pepper
2	teaspoons canola oil

1. Whisk orange zest and juice, cilantro, 1 teaspoon sugar, and chili-garlic sauce together in bowl.

2. Pat shrimp dry with paper towels and season with remaining ⅛ teaspoon sugar, salt, and pepper. Heat oil in 10-inch nonstick skillet over medium-high heat until just smoking. Add shrimp and cook until curled and lightly browned, about 1½ minutes. Add orange juice mixture and simmer, tossing to coat, until slightly thickened, about 30 seconds. Serve.

PER SERVING: Cal 180; Fat 6 g; Sat fat 0.5 g; Chol 215 mg; Carb 6 g; Protein 23 g; Fiber 0 g; Sodium 1150 mg

VARIATION
Pan-Seared Shrimp with Ginger-Hoisin Glaze
SERVES 2

If using smaller or larger shrimp, be sure to adjust the cooking time accordingly. Serve with Simple White Rice (page 73).

1	tablespoon hoisin sauce
1	tablespoon water
2	teaspoons grated fresh ginger
1½	teaspoons rice vinegar
¾	teaspoon low-sodium soy sauce
1	scallion, sliced thin
	Pinch red pepper flakes
12	ounces extra-large shrimp (21 to 25 per pound), peeled and deveined
⅛	teaspoon sugar
⅛	teaspoon salt
⅛	teaspoon pepper
2	teaspoons canola oil

1. Whisk hoisin sauce, water, ginger, vinegar, soy sauce, scallion, and pepper flakes together in bowl.

2. Pat shrimp dry with paper towels and season with sugar, salt, and pepper. Heat oil in 10-inch nonstick skillet over medium-high heat until just smoking. Add shrimp and cook until curled and lightly browned, about 1½ minutes. Add hoisin mixture and simmer, tossing to coat, until slightly thickened, about 30 seconds. Serve.

PER SERVING: Cal 180; Fat 6 g; Sat fat 0.5 g; Chol 215 mg; Carb 8 g; Protein 23 g; Fiber 0 g; Sodium 1450 mg

ARGENTINE-STYLE STEAK SALAD WITH CHIMICHURRI VINAIGRETTE

CHAPTER 7

ONE BIG ROAST, FOUR GREAT MEALS

EASY ROAST BEEF WITH GRAVY

MANY AMERICANS GREW UP WITH ROAST BEEF on the Sunday table. Maybe Sunday dinner with the family doesn't happen as often as we'd like today, but when the opportunity presents itself, why not indulge in some old-fashioned flavor, complete with rosy-pink meat, a browned, flavorful crust, and velvety gravy? We set out to resurrect the Sunday roast and, in doing so, to make it as easy and as foolproof as possible. And because we'd have a fair amount of leftovers, we'd come up with a few other creative suppers to enjoy later in the week.

We started out by purchasing a top round roast, which is not only affordable and easy to find but is also one of the most common cuts used for roast beef. For a nicely browned crust, we followed the path laid out by many recipes and started the roast in a hot 500-degree oven, then finished it at a moderate 350 degrees. Not surprisingly, this treatment produced a dry, tough roast with a gray ring of overcooked meat on the outside. A fast stovetop sear followed by a few hours in a low, slow oven (275 degrees) yielded a more tender roast that was a pretty pink from center to rich, dark crust. Curious how low we could go, we knocked down the temperature another 25 degrees, and then 25 more; the last roast was the most tender by far.

To develop its flavor, we salted the meat and let it rest, a step we often recommend for roasts in the test kitchen. Osmosis, our science editor explained, initially draws moisture out, dissolving the salt and allowing it to penetrate the meat. We tried resting the meat for various periods of time. Ultimately, an overnight rest was best, but even resting the meat for as little as one hour began to season it. Next, we moved on to the gravy.

We noticed that in many older recipes the roast is dredged in flour (and the roasting pan is even dusted) before roasting, to get both a good crust and a head start on the gravy. When we tried this, we got mixed results. Because our oven temperature was low, the flour just sat on the roast, remaining pasty and raw. But the flour in the roasting pan did brown, jump-starting a thick and toasty, if somewhat lumpy, base for gravy that we thinned slightly with water. To enhance its flavor, we added chopped celery, carrot, and onion to the fat left

in the skillet after browning the next roast. We stirred in the flour at this point (lumps solved), as well as tomato paste for more depth. Normally, we'd roast the beef on a V-rack, but it occurred to us to simply set the roast on top of the vegetables in a roasting pan—now we had one less piece of equipment to wash.

Over about three hours in the oven, the meat turned pink and tender, the vegetables softened and deepened in flavor, and the flour browned. As the meat rested, we poured the flavorful juices into a skillet. For even more flavor, we whisked canned beef broth instead of water into the drippings, let the gravy thicken, and then strained it, discarding the vegetables now that they'd done their work. Our roast beef dinner was good, but it wasn't quite hitting the mark yet. We scanned our pantry, looking for something to bump up the flavor. After a minute, we spotted a can of beef consommé, which we reconstituted with a little water. With this double-strength beef broth, our gravy turned dark, glossy, and deeply beefy.

Though our roast beef and gravy tasted perfect, the mechanics of the recipe were irksome. We had to brown the roast and vegetables in a skillet, move them to a roasting pan, and three hours later pour the drippings into a saucepan for gravy. We wondered if we could simply roast the beef in the very same skillet in which we browned it, and then make the gravy in that pan, too. The answer was a resounding yes. Our one-skillet roast beef was now not only delicious; it was dead simple, too.

Now that we had successfully streamlined this old-school classic for the modern-day dinner table, we focused on our spin-off meals, which would make use of the tender, beefy extras. First, inspired by Argentine cuisine, we created a simple steak salad dressed with a *chimichurri* vinaigrette. Traditionally, chimichurri is served alongside grilled meat to add a bright counterpoint and offset the richness of the meat. We started with the standard ingredients—parsley, cilantro, garlic, red pepper flakes, and red wine vinegar—but added a touch of honey for sweetness, a bit of Dijon mustard for more punch, and extra-virgin olive oil to bring the ingredients together and deliver a dressing that clung to the beef and salad greens. To reinforce the South American feel of our salad, we added jícama, cut into matchsticks. Halved cherry tomatoes rounded out our salad, and crumbled feta cheese (the perfect stand-in for hard-to-find but more authentic *queso fresco*) finished the dish with its salty, sharp bite.

Next, we set our sights on an upscale take on the roast beef sandwich. We started with a few slices of crusty bread, topping them with roast beef, bright, peppery arugula, and thin slices of red onion. Cheese was a given, but we had to figure out which kind. We tried a handful of contenders, but ultimately garlic-and-herb-rich Boursin cheese won the day, contributing both creaminess and aromatic punch. To elevate our sandwiches from lunch basic to bistro fare, we decided to press them. While a panini press works great for this, not everyone has one at home. We made do with a grill pan and a heavy Dutch oven; after preheating the pan, we placed our sandwiches in it and pressed them under the weight of the Dutch oven. Five minutes per side was just enough to turn the crusty bread golden brown, warm our tender slices of beef, and melt the creamy, rich Boursin cheese.

For our last recipe, we decided to use the extras to make a breakfast classic: hash. Though hash is usually made with corned beef, roast beef is often employed as a substitute in this dish of meat, potatoes, and seasonings combined in a skillet and cooked until the meat and spuds are crisped and well browned. Although many recipes call for boiling the potatoes in a separate pot, we found that we could simply simmer our diced potato (we needed just one) right in the same pan we'd use to cook the hash. Once the pieces were tender, we drained them and set them aside. Then we got to work building a good base of flavor for the rest of the dish. We started with finely chopped bacon, which lent smoky flavor, and an onion and garlic, which we sautéed in the rendered bacon fat. Then we added our beef, sliced thin and cut into small, bite-size pieces, followed by a small pour of heavy cream, which promised even more richness. A dash of hot sauce provided some heat. To ensure that the hash was crisped and browned on both top and bottom, we packed it down in the pan using a spatula and flipped it, piece by piece. Finally, we cracked two eggs on top and covered the pan until the egg whites were just set. Better than anything we could ever get at a diner, our roast beef hash was so rich and flavorful, it was hard to believe it started with leftovers.

Easy Roast Beef with Gravy

SERVES 2, WITH LEFTOVERS

You can use the leftovers to make all three of the following recipes: Argentine-Style Steak Salad with Chimichurri Vinaigrette (page 194), Roast Beef and Boursin Panini (page 195), and Roast Beef Hash (page 195). The leftover beef can be refrigerated in an airtight container for up to 3 days. You can substitute top sirloin for the top round. Look for an evenly shaped roast with a ¼-inch fat cap. We prefer this roast cooked to medium-rare, but if you prefer it more or less done, see our guidelines on page 154.

1 **(4- to 5-pound) boneless top round roast, fat trimmed to ¼ inch, tied at 1-inch intervals**
   Salt and pepper
1 **tablespoon vegetable oil**
2 **tablespoons unsalted butter**
2 **carrots, peeled and cut into 2-inch pieces**
1 **small onion, sliced into ½-inch-thick rings**
1 **celery rib, cut into 2-inch pieces**
2 **tablespoons all-purpose flour**
1 **teaspoon tomato paste**
1 **(10.5-ounce) can beef consommé**
¾ **cup water**

1. Pat roast dry with paper towels and rub with 2 teaspoons salt. Wrap in plastic wrap and refrigerate for at least 1 hour or up to 24 hours.

2. Adjust oven rack to middle position and heat oven to 225 degrees. Pat roast dry with paper towels and rub with 2 teaspoons pepper. Heat oil in 12-inch skillet over medium-high heat until just smoking. Brown roast on all sides, 8 to 12 minutes; transfer to plate.

3. Pour off all but 2 tablespoons fat from pan. Add butter to skillet and melt over medium heat. Stir in carrots, onion, and celery; cook until lightly browned, 6 to 8 minutes. Add flour and tomato paste and cook until flour is golden and paste begins to darken, about 2 minutes. Off heat, push vegetables to center of pan. Place roast, and any accumulated juices, on top of vegetables, and transfer skillet to oven. Cook until meat registers 125 degrees (for medium-rare), 2½ to 3½ hours. Using potholder (skillet handle will be hot), remove skillet from oven. Transfer roast to carving board, tent loosely with aluminum foil, and let rest for 20 minutes.

MAKING EASY ROAST BEEF WITH GRAVY

1. Pat roast dry with paper towels, season, and brown in hot skillet. Then brown vegetables.

2. Set roast on top of vegetables, which take place of V-rack.

3. Cook roast in low-temperature oven for 2½ to 3½ hours.

4. Use beef consommé and water to deglaze pan and make rich, beefy gravy.

THE BEST INEXPENSIVE INSTANT-READ THERMOMETER

An instant-read thermometer is the most foolproof way to determine the doneness of meat. It should have a broad range to cover high and low temperatures; a stem long enough to reach the interior of large cuts of meat; and, above all, speed, so you don't have to keep the oven door open too long. Our favorite remains the ThermoWorks Splash-Proof Super-Fast Thermapen, which meets all of these requirements (and it's water resistant), but the $96 price tag begs for an affordable alternative. We tested six models priced under $35. Although none of them bested the Thermapen, we did find the **ThermoWorks Super-Fast Pocket Thermometer**, $24 (shown), and CDN ProAccurate Quick-Read Thermometer, $18.99, to be reasonable stand-ins.

4. Meanwhile, being careful of hot skillet handle, set skillet with vegetables over medium-high heat and cook, stirring occasionally, until vegetables are deep golden brown, about 5 minutes. Slowly whisk in consommé and water, scraping up any browned bits, and bring to boil. Reduce heat to medium and simmer until thickened, 10 to 15 minutes. Strain gravy through fine-mesh strainer into serving bowl; discard vegetables. Season with salt and pepper to taste.

5. Remove kitchen twine from roast and thinly slice meat against grain. Serve with gravy.

Argentine-Style Steak Salad with Chimichurri Vinaigrette

SERVES 2

The cooked beef in this recipe is from Easy Roast Beef with Gravy on page 193.

VINAIGRETTE

- 3 garlic cloves, minced
- 2 tablespoons minced fresh parsley
- 2 tablespoons minced fresh cilantro
- 2 tablespoons red wine vinegar
- 1 teaspoon honey
- 1 teaspoon Dijon mustard
  Pinch red pepper flakes
- ¼ cup extra-virgin olive oil
  Salt and pepper

SALAD

- 8 ounces cooked beef, sliced thin, larger slices cut in half
- 3 ounces (3 cups) mesclun greens
- ½ small jícama (8 ounces), peeled and cut into 2-inch-long matchsticks
- 3 ounces cherry tomatoes, halved
- 1½ ounces feta cheese, crumbled (⅓ cup)

1. FOR THE VINAIGRETTE: Whisk garlic, parsley, cilantro, vinegar, honey, mustard, and pepper flakes together in medium bowl. Whisking constantly, drizzle in oil; season with salt and pepper to taste.

2. FOR THE SALAD: Divide beef between two plates and drizzle evenly with 3 tablespoons vinaigrette. Combine greens, jícama, tomatoes, and feta in large bowl. Drizzle remaining dressing over salad and toss gently to coat. Season with salt and pepper to taste and arrange over beef. Serve.

Roast Beef and Boursin Panini

SERVES 2

The cooked beef in this recipe is from Easy Roast Beef with Gravy on page 193. We like to use rustic artisanal bread for this recipe; don't use a baguette, but rather look for a wide loaf that will yield big slices. For easier slicing, place the beef in the freezer for 15 minutes before slicing. If you do not have a grill pan, you can use a 12-inch nonstick skillet instead.

¼ cup Boursin Garlic and Fine Herbs cheese, softened

4 (½-inch-thick) slices crusty bread

8 ounces cooked beef, shaved thin (1¾ cups)

1 cup baby arugula

⅓ cup thinly sliced red onion

1 tablespoon olive oil

1. Spread Boursin evenly over 1 side of each slice of bread. Assemble 2 sandwiches by layering beef, arugula, and onion between prepared bread slices (with Boursin inside sandwich). Press gently on sandwiches to set.

2. Heat 12-inch nonstick grill pan over medium heat for 1 minute. Brush outside of sandwiches lightly with oil. Place both sandwiches in pan and weight with Dutch oven. Cook sandwiches until bread is golden brown and crisp and cheese is melted, about 10 minutes, flipping sandwiches halfway through cooking. Slice sandwiches in half and serve.

NOTES FROM THE TEST KITCHEN

PRESSING PANINI

You don't need a sandwich press to make panini. Simply place the sandwiches in a 12-inch nonstick grill pan over medium heat and weight them with a Dutch oven.

Roast Beef Hash

SERVES 2

The cooked beef in this recipe is from Easy Roast Beef with Gravy on page 193. You will need a 10-inch nonstick skillet with a tight-fitting lid for this recipe.

1½ cups water

1 russet potato, peeled and cut into ½-inch pieces

2 slices bacon, chopped fine

1 small onion, chopped coarse
   Salt and pepper

3 garlic cloves, minced

¼ teaspoon minced fresh thyme

6 ounces cooked beef, sliced thin and cut into
   1-inch pieces (1¼ cups)

¼ cup heavy cream

¼ teaspoon hot sauce

2 large eggs

1. Bring water and potato to boil in 10-inch nonstick skillet over high heat. Reduce heat to low, cover, and simmer until just tender, 6 to 8 minutes. Drain potato and set aside.

2. Cook bacon in now-empty skillet over medium-high heat until fat has partially rendered, 3 to 5 minutes. Add onion, ¼ teaspoon salt, and ¼ teaspoon pepper and cook until browned at edges, 5 to 7 minutes. Add garlic and thyme and cook until fragrant, about 30 seconds. Stir in potato and beef and lightly press mixture into pan. Pour cream and hot sauce over top and cook, without stirring, for 4 minutes. Using spatula, invert hash, one section at a time, and lightly repack into pan. Repeat this process every few minutes until hash is partly crisp and potatoes are thoroughly cooked, about 8 minutes longer.

3. Make two 2-inch indentations in hash and crack egg into each indentation. Reduce heat to medium-low, cover pan, and cook until eggs are just set, about 5 minutes. Season with salt and pepper to taste. Cut hash into 2 pieces around eggs and serve.

HAWAIIAN-STYLE SMOKED PORK

IF YOU'VE EVER BEEN TO A HAWAIIAN LUAU, YOU'RE probably familiar with kalua pork—the succulent smoked suckling pig that's the centerpiece of this traditional feast. The word *kalua* refers to the traditional Hawaiian pit-cooking method using an *imu*, a deep hole in the ground with a native kiawe wood fire and a lining of hot rocks and banana leaves, which flavor the meat and help keep it moist. Seasoned with only local pink sea salt, the pork roasts at low heat in the pit for hours, emerging tender, juicy, and smoky and bearing the unique flavor stamp of the leaves. We wanted to find a way to translate this flavorful dish for the mainland—minus the whole pig, the banana leaves, and the imu—so that we could enjoy it whenever we wanted.

After a bit of research, we discovered that most modern Hawaiian cookbooks skip the imu, too. They use the oven, rely on bottled liquid smoke for the essential smoky flavor, and bypass the vegetation altogether. Imu aside, in terms of cooking method, true kalua pork resembles any barbecued pork in that it cooks "low and slow"—in other words, at a low temperature for a long time. The test kitchen has plenty of experience using a grill to barbecue pork, so we were confident that we could employ that technique here, too. Mimicking the elusive, herbaceous flavor of the banana leaves, however, would be another matter entirely.

To start, in place of the traditional but obviously impractical whole pig, we opted for boneless pork shoulder roast, often labeled "pork butt" or "Boston butt" in supermarkets. Comprising several well-exercised muscles with plenty of fat and connective tissue that melts during cooking to keep the meat moist, the rich, flavorful shoulder roast stands up well to long, slow cooking (it's the cut usually used for pulled pork).

Unlike most pulled pork and other types of barbecue, though, kalua pork is not sauced, so it wasn't a surprise that the first time we attempted to make it, some tasters found it a bit dry and bland. We decided to capture the flavorful juices that were dripping into the fire by placing the pork in a disposable aluminum pan on top of the grill grate. This allowed us to moisten the finished pork by adding back some of the collected—and defatted—juices, which are rich in meaty flavor. A few tests showed us that it was also necessary to loosely cover the pan with foil in order to replicate the steamy environment of the imu. Poking holes in the foil allowed the smoke to pass through.

Our pork was juicy now, but it was lacking in smoky flavor. To infuse grilled meats with smoky notes, the test kitchen usually relies on a packet of wood chips. After some research, we learned that mesquite is related to Hawaiian kiawe wood, so it was the natural choice for this recipe (both types of wood produce smoke that is more assertive than hickory or oak). Refueling the fire to keep it burning (and smoking) for an extended cooking time was inconvenient—it involved removing the roast, then the hot grill grate to add more charcoal, and replacing everything—so we decided to follow a hybrid cooking method: We started by smoking the meat over gentle indirect heat (on the cooler side of a banked fire), and then, when the coals and chips had burned out after two hours, we moved the meat to a 325-degree oven to finish, which took another two to three hours. With the cooking method figured out, it was time to address the flavor issue.

To get an idea of the flavor imparted by the banana leaves, we ordered some online, wrapped a pork butt with them, and slow-smoked it following our established cooking method. The herbal, mineral-y flavor played off the smoke perfectly and was quite unusual. Thinking about how to re-create that flavor, we went to the produce department at our local supermarket for inspiration, picking up various large, leafy greens to try wrapping around the pork.

We wrapped each of seven pork butts with a different type of leaf: collard greens, kale, Swiss chard, green cabbage, napa cabbage, savoy cabbage, and corn husks. It was an interesting experiment but not a successful one. The corn husks burned, and the rest of these vegetables infused the smoked pork with cabbagelike, sulfuric flavors. We rubbed more pork butts with pastes made from parsley, watercress, and spinach. Though these flavors weren't unpleasant, they weren't right for our kalua pork either.

We headed back to the supermarket produce aisle, this time staying tropical in theme and selecting bananas and pineapple. It took some doing, but we used kitchen twine to lash pork roasts with fancy patchworks of banana peels and pineapple rind. We got—not surprisingly—pork that tasted like bananas and pineapples.

We had one last banana leaf in the freezer, so we tried it again to further analyze the flavor: aromatic, earthy, and mildly grassy, with a distinctive tealike quality. Once again, we hit the market, this time selecting smoky Lapsang Souchong, a few herbal tea blends, and green tea, each of which we made into seasoning rubs. Several tests later, we were delighted to find that a rub made from 3 tablespoons of crumbled green tea and 4 teaspoons of kosher salt hit very close to the mark, and rubbing it on was far easier than tying leaves or peels around a large pork roast. A little brown sugar helped the rub caramelize and made the meat's crust a more attractive (and delicious) shade of deep brown.

Our smoked pork was finally luau-worthy, so now we needed to think of a few clever ways to use up the succulent extras. For our first recipe, we decided to create flatbreads for two. Using prebaked naan bread for the crust eliminated the need to flour the counter and roll out dough. After deciding on a Mediterranean theme, we chopped a few kalamatas and crumbled some feta for the toppings to go along with our pork. But we were still deliberating about the sauce. In the end, we whipped up an easy puree of roasted red peppers, which provided a piquant hit of flavor. We sprinkled the pork, feta, and olives over our red pepper sauce and popped our flatbreads in the oven for about 10 minutes, which turned them golden brown.

Next, we wanted something simple that wouldn't require a lot of time: quesadillas. Minced canned chipotles reinforced the smokiness in the pork and lent some heat, but this move still wasn't enough for tasters who wanted more punch. A squirt of lime juice, mixed in with the chipotles and shredded pork, gave our quesadillas a nice citrusy tang. We piled the pork onto two flour tortillas, scattered sliced avocado, cilantro, and shredded Monterey Jack over the top, and folded them in half before sliding our quesadillas into a skillet. In just minutes, the quesadillas were browned and crisp on the outside and nice and toasty on the inside.

For our last recipe, we were in the mood for a rustic, hearty Italian ragu. Having a good amount of shredded pork at the ready meant we could skip the hours-long simmering time—but we'd have to find another way to infuse our sauce with deep flavor quickly. Minced onion and garlic provided a strong aromatic foundation, and canned diced tomatoes offered bright acidity and just the right texture once we mashed them slightly in the pan and let them simmer briefly. But for really big flavor in record time, we turned to tomato paste, which the test kitchen has found gives sauces, stews, and braises deep flavor quickly, and a half-cup of red wine, which we simmered for a few minutes to concentrate its flavor. After just 15 minutes of simmering, the sauce was ready for the pork, which merely needed to be heated through before serving. A bed of soft, creamy polenta made the perfect partner to our richly flavored ragu, and it was ready in about the same amount of time.

With our Hawaiian pork, we had made three more flavorful dinners—and we even got to travel the globe, too.

Hawaiian-Style Smoked Pork

SERVES 2, WITH LEFTOVERS

You can use the leftovers to make all three of the following recipes: Baked Flatbreads with Pork, Roasted Red Peppers, and Olives (see below), Smoked Pork Quesadillas (page 200), and Quick Pork Ragu with Polenta (page 200). The leftover pork can be refrigerated in an airtight container for up to 3 days. If your pork butt comes with an elastic netting, remove it before you rub the pork with the tea. When using a charcoal grill, we prefer wood chunks to wood chips whenever possible; substitute 6 medium wood chunks, soaked in water for 1 hour, for the wood chip packets. Serve with Simple White Rice (page 73).

- 3 tablespoons green tea leaves (10 to 15 bags)
- 4 teaspoons kosher salt
- 1 tablespoon packed brown sugar
- 2 teaspoons pepper
- 1 (4- to 5-pound) boneless pork butt roast, trimmed
- 1 (13 by 9-inch) disposable aluminum roasting pan
- 6 cups mesquite wood chips, soaked in water for 15 minutes and drained

1. Combine tea, salt, sugar, and pepper in small bowl. Pat pork dry with paper towels and rub with tea mixture. Wrap meat tightly in plastic wrap and refrigerate for 6 to 24 hours. Place pork in roasting pan and cover pan loosely with aluminum foil. Poke about twenty ¼-inch holes in foil. Using large piece of heavy-duty foil, wrap 2 cups soaked chips in foil packet and cut several vent holes in top. Make 2 more packets with additional foil and remaining 4 cups chips.

2A. FOR A CHARCOAL GRILL: Open bottom vent halfway. Light large chimney starter three-quarters full with charcoal briquettes (4½ quarts). When top coals are partially covered with ash, pour into steeply banked pile against side of grill. Place wood chip packets on coals. Set cooking grate in place, cover, and open lid vent halfway. Heat grill until hot and wood chips are smoking, about 5 minutes.

2B. FOR A GAS GRILL: Place wood chip packets over primary burner. Turn all burners to high, cover, and heat grill until hot and wood chips are smoking, about 15 minutes. Turn primary burner to medium-high and turn off other burner(s). Adjust primary burner as needed to maintain grill temperature of 300 degrees.

3. Place pan on cool part of grill. Cover (positioning lid vent over meat if using charcoal) and cook for 2 hours. During last 20 minutes of grilling, adjust oven rack to lower-middle position and heat oven to 325 degrees.

4. Remove pan from grill. Cover pan tightly with new sheet of foil, transfer to oven, and bake until fork slips easily in and out of pork, 2 to 3 hours. Let pork rest, covered, for 30 minutes. When meat is cool enough to handle, shred into bite-size pieces, discarding fat. Transfer two portions to individual plates. Strain contents of pan through fine-mesh strainer into fat separator. Let liquid settle, then measure out 1 tablespoon defatted pan juices and drizzle over individual servings of pork. Serve.

Baked Flatbreads with Pork, Roasted Red Peppers, and Olives

SERVES 2

The pork in this recipe is from Hawaiian-Style Smoked Pork (see above). Be sure to rinse and dry the roasted red peppers, as the brine can impart a sour or acidic aftertaste.

- 3 tablespoons olive oil
- 2 naan breads
- ½ cup jarred roasted red peppers, rinsed and patted dry
  Salt and pepper
- 5 ounces cooked pork, shredded (1 cup)
- 2 ounces feta cheese, crumbled (½ cup)
- 2 tablespoons chopped pitted kalamata olives
- 2 tablespoons minced fresh parsley

1. Adjust oven rack to lowest position and heat oven to 500 degrees. Brush baking sheet with 1 tablespoon oil and lay naan on sheet. Process red peppers and remaining 2 tablespoons oil in food processor, scraping down sides of bowl as necessary, until smooth, about 30 seconds. Season with salt and pepper to taste.

2. Spread red pepper puree evenly over each naan, leaving ½-inch border around edge. Scatter pork, feta, and olives evenly over top. Bake until naan are golden brown around edges, 8 to 10 minutes, rotating sheet halfway through baking. Sprinkle with parsley and cut each naan into quarters. Serve.

BAKED FLATBREADS WITH PORK, ROASTED RED PEPPERS, AND OLIVES

Smoked Pork Quesadillas

SERVES 2

The pork in this recipe is from Hawaiian-Style Smoked Pork on page 198. You can serve these quesadillas with salsa, sour cream, or hot sauce if desired.

- 5 ounces cooked pork, shredded (1 cup)
- 1 tablespoon minced canned chipotle chile in adobo sauce
- 1 tablespoon lime juice
- 2 (10-inch) flour tortillas
- 3 ounces Monterey Jack cheese, shredded (¾ cup)
- ½ avocado, pitted (see page 121) and sliced thin
- 2 tablespoons fresh cilantro leaves
- 1 tablespoon vegetable oil
  Salt

1. Combine pork, chipotle, and lime juice in medium bowl. Heat 12-inch nonstick skillet over medium-low heat and toast tortillas, 1 at a time, until soft and slightly puffed on both sides, 2 to 3 minutes per tortilla, flipping them halfway through heating. Slide tortillas onto cutting board.

2. Spread pork mixture, cheese, avocado, and cilantro over half of each tortilla, leaving ½-inch border around edge. Fold tortillas in half and press to flatten. Brush tops generously with oil and sprinkle lightly with salt.

3. Place both quesadillas in skillet, oiled side down, and cook over medium-low heat until crisp and well browned, 1 to 2 minutes. Brush tops with oil and season lightly with salt. Flip tortillas and cook until second sides are crisp and well browned, 1 to 2 minutes. Transfer quesadillas to cutting board and let cool for 3 minutes. Cut each quesadilla in half and serve.

NOTES FROM THE TEST KITCHEN

COOKING QUESADILLAS

To cook 2 quesadillas at once, arrange folded edges of quesadillas in center of 12-inch nonstick skillet.

Quick Pork Ragu with Polenta

SERVES 2

The pork in this recipe is from Hawaiian-Style Smoked Pork on page 198. Be sure to use traditional dried polenta here, not instant polenta or precooked logs of polenta; dried polenta can be found alongside cornmeal or pasta in the supermarket (it looks like large-ground cornmeal). Do not omit the baking soda—it reduces the cooking time and makes for a creamier polenta.

PORK RAGU

- 1 tablespoon olive oil
- 1 small onion, chopped fine
  Salt and pepper
- 1 tablespoon tomato paste
- 2 garlic cloves, minced
- ⅛ teaspoon red pepper flakes
- ½ cup dry red wine
- 1 (14.5-ounce) can diced tomatoes
- ¼ cup water
- 5 ounces cooked pork, shredded (1 cup)
- 2 tablespoons chopped fresh basil

POLENTA

- 1⅔ cups water
  Salt and pepper
  Pinch baking soda
- ⅓ cup coarse-ground polenta
- 1 tablespoon unsalted butter
  Grated Parmesan cheese

1. FOR THE PORK RAGU: Heat oil in medium saucepan over medium heat until shimmering. Add onion, ¼ teaspoon salt, and ¼ teaspoon pepper and cook until softened and lightly browned, 5 to 7 minutes. Stir in tomato paste, garlic, and pepper flakes and cook until fragrant, about 30 seconds.

2. Stir in wine and cook until it has nearly evaporated, 3 to 5 minutes. Stir in tomatoes and water and mash with potato masher until tomatoes break into small pieces. Stir in pork, bring to simmer, and cook, stirring often, until thickened, about 15 minutes. Stir in basil and season with salt and pepper to taste.

3. FOR THE POLENTA: Meanwhile, bring water to boil in small saucepan over medium-high heat. Stir in ¼ teaspoon salt and baking soda. Slowly pour polenta into water in steady stream, stirring constantly with

THE SECRET TO SPEEDY POLENTA

Traditionally, polenta requires a long cooking time—no matter if you're making enough to serve 2 or 10. But we've found something that can speed up the cooking process: baking soda. For polenta to lose its hard, gritty texture and turn creamy, enough water must penetrate the corn's cell walls that the starch granules within swell and burst. Through much testing, we discovered that adding baking soda to the cooking liquid can reduce the time it takes for this to happen, thus shortening polenta's cooking time. A brief discussion with our science editor helped us understand why. It turns out that corn cell walls are held together by pectin. When alkaline sodium bicarbonate—also known as baking soda—is present, the pectin breaks down, weakening the corn's structure and allowing water to enter and the starch to swell and burst in less than half the time, delivering soft, creamy polenta in a speedy fashion.

wooden spoon or rubber spatula. Bring mixture to boil, stirring constantly, about 30 seconds. Reduce heat to lowest possible setting and cover.

4. After 5 minutes, whisk polenta to smooth out lumps, scraping down sides and bottom of pan. Cover and continue to cook, without stirring, until grains of cornmeal are tender but slightly al dente, 8 to 10 minutes longer. (Polenta should be loose and barely hold its shape; it will continue to thicken as it cools.)

5. Off heat, stir in butter and season with salt and pepper to taste. Let stand, covered, for 5 minutes. Spoon pork ragu over polenta and sprinkle with Parmesan. Serve.

GLAZED PICNIC HAM

SPIRAL-SLICED HAM—A LEAN CUT FROM THE REAR leg of a pig—gets its complex salty flavor from curing and smoking. But there's an even more flavorful cut that's given the same treatment: the picnic ham. Picnic hams, which come from the lower part of a hog's shoulder, are pleasantly smoky and salty like leg hams, but they taste richer and meatier because they have a lot more fat. Though many recipes for picnic ham call for simmering the meat, we were envisioning a bronzed, roasted picnic ham—one that could take center stage at one dinner and from which we could transform

the leftovers into a few other dishes to enjoy during the week.

To cook our picnic ham, we started with the test kitchen's basic method for spiral-sliced ham: After trimming off most of the tough rind (a step not needed for spiral-sliced hams), we slipped the ham into an oven bag, cinched the bag shut, cut slits in the top to vent the steam, and baked the bagged ham for a couple of hours in a 300-degree oven until the meat registered 100 degrees. We had high hopes as we carved samples for tasters, but our optimism was short-lived. The meat was unpleasantly chewy, and it was riddled with pockets of fat. Lesson learned: Although picnic hams are technically fully cooked, the extra fat means they need extra cooking (not just heating through, like leg ham) to become palatable.

For our next test, we upped the cooking time to three hours (still in the oven bag) to give the connective tissue enough time to render. The outside of the ham was leathery, and the meat was overcooked, dry, and still pocked with chunks of fat and gristle. Adding insult to injury, since the meat had dried out and concentrated, it was also too salty. Picnic ham was proving to be no picnic in the kitchen.

Was the oven bag actually impeding our goal of moist, tender meat? Through years of smoking similarly large, fatty cuts on the grill, we've learned that collagen (the tough, fatty connective tissue) renders most effectively in a moist, steamy environment (that's why we often use a drip pan when slow-smoking on the grill). But the vented oven bag, which traps enough moisture to keep a leg ham moist when reheating, wasn't trapping enough moisture to keep the picnic ham moist through the necessary extra cooking. We decided to bag the bag and instead place the ham directly on a rack in a large roasting pan. To create a contained moist environment (akin to covering the grill when smoking), we wrapped the whole roasting pan tightly with foil.

In a single test, the picnic ham improved dramatically. We sorted through the cooking details in subsequent tests and found that cooking the meat to 140 degrees in a 325-degree oven (which took anywhere from two to three hours, depending on the size of the ham) produced the best results—consistently moist, tender meat with much of the fat rendered out.

To balance the salty richness of the meat, we decided to make a sweet, spicy glaze. As soon as we put the ham in the oven, we got to work simmering a simple mixture of brown sugar, Dijon mustard, cloves, cayenne pepper, and apple cider vinegar. When the ham was almost done cooking, we carefully removed and discarded the foil, slathered the ham with the sticky glaze, and cranked the heat to 450 degrees so that the glaze could caramelize (it took about 20 minutes). The glaze nicely countered the ham's salinity, but tasters wanted more depth. Switching from cider vinegar to balsamic did the trick (and had the added benefit of giving the glaze a deep, rich color), and we thinned out a little extra glaze to a pourable consistency for spooning over slices at the table. This ultra-savory ham was better than any we'd ever tasted—and now we were ready to move on to our other recipes.

For our first dish, we set our sights on a frittata, perfect for a filling breakfast or casual supper. Armed with a nonstick skillet, we started by selecting a few other ingredients to round out our frittata. Mushrooms added hearty flavor and texture, and a shallot contributed some sweetness and aromatic depth. Once our vegetables were nicely browned, we added six eggs to the pan, plus a little cream and cubed cheddar cheese for richness and flavor. We followed standard test kitchen protocol for cooking frittatas: cooking the eggs until just set on the stovetop, then finishing them under the broiler. This method delivered a perfectly cooked frittata that was golden brown on top and firm yet tender on the inside.

Next, we decided to pay tribute to classic French comfort food and set out to make individual ham and potato gratins. Ham made the perfect salty-sweet counterpoint to the mild, creamy potatoes, but for even more flavor, we sautéed a thinly sliced leek, minced garlic, and fresh thyme in our small saucepan before adding a little flour (for thickening power) and heavy cream. We poured the creamy sauce over our thinly sliced ham and potatoes, then divided the mixture between two individual gratin dishes and baked them for about 35 minutes. Then we sprinkled a bit of shredded Gruyère cheese over the top and returned our mini gratins to the oven so that they could brown and the cheese could melt. After about 10 minutes, they were done, offering tender bites of potato and ham in a rich, creamy sauce.

Finally, we wanted to create a spin on classic spaghetti carbonara. We started by cooking the shaved ham in butter to crisp it (much as we would pancetta or bacon), then reserved it while we tackled the rest of the dish. Garlic and white wine added aromatic flavor and acidity. Instead of cooking the pasta in a separate pot, we simply added broth and water to our pan and stirred in the spaghetti. Not only did we have one less pot to clean, but also the starch from the pasta helped to thicken and flavor the cooking liquid. After about 10 minutes, the pasta was ready. Stirring in a mixture of heavy cream, egg, and grated Pecorino Romano cheese took the sauce from brothy to creamy in no time. When we added the ham back in, it provided the perfect salty complement to the rich-tasting sauce.

Each one of our spin-off suppers was so delicious, we could hardly believe that we had leftovers to thank for it.

Glazed Picnic Ham
SERVES 2, WITH LEFTOVERS

You can use the leftovers to make all three of the following recipes: Ham, Mushroom, and Cheddar Frittata (page 204), Ham and Potato Gratins (page 205), and Skillet Spaghetti Carbonara (page 205). The leftover ham can be refrigerated in an airtight container for up to 3 days. Crimp the foil tightly around the roasting pan to keep the ham moist and help the collagen render. Be sure to purchase the shankless version of the picnic ham.

1	(5- to 6-pound) bone-in smoked shoulder picnic ham
3	tablespoons dry mustard
1	teaspoon pepper
⅔	cup packed dark brown sugar
⅓	cup Dijon mustard
⅓	cup balsamic vinegar
⅛	teaspoon cayenne pepper
	Pinch ground cloves
1	tablespoon water

1. Adjust oven rack to lowest position and heat oven to 325 degrees. Line large roasting pan with aluminum foil. Remove skin from exterior of ham and trim fat to ¼-inch thickness. Score remaining fat at 1-inch intervals in crosshatch pattern. Combine 1 tablespoon dry mustard and pepper in small bowl. Rub ham all over with spice rub. Set ham on V-rack set inside prepared

GLAZED PICNIC HAM

roasting pan. Cover pan tightly with foil. Bake until ham registers 140 degrees, 2 to 3 hours.

2. Meanwhile, bring remaining 2 tablespoons dry mustard, sugar, Dijon mustard, vinegar, cayenne, and cloves to boil in small saucepan. Reduce heat to low and simmer until reduced to ¾ cup, about 10 minutes.

3. Remove ham from oven, remove foil, and let rest for 5 minutes. Increase oven temperature to 450 degrees. Brush ham evenly with ½ cup glaze. Return ham to oven, uncovered, and bake until dark brown and cara-melized, 15 to 20 minutes. Stir water into remaining ¼ cup glaze. Transfer ham to carving board, tent loosely with foil, and let rest for 30 minutes. Carve ham and serve with thinned glaze.

NOTES FROM THE TEST KITCHEN

A TALE OF TWO HAMS

A picnic ham is cut from the shoulder of the front leg of the pig, as opposed to a true ham, which is cut from the pig's back leg. They are both smoked and cured. The picnic ham is available either with the shank and hock attached (the full image) or as the smaller "shankless" cut (everything to the right of the dotted line). Since we didn't want our plates overflowing with too much ham for two (even with our recipes designed to take advantage of the extras), we opted for the shankless version of the picnic ham.

SMOKED PICNIC HAM
This is the whole smoked picnic ham. For our recipe, we use the shankless version, which consists of everything to the right of the line.

SCORING PICNIC HAM

To score ham, first trim fat layer as directed, then use sharp knife to score remaining fat at 1-inch intervals in crosshatch pattern.

Ham, Mushroom, and Cheddar Frittata

SERVES 2

The ham in this recipe is from Glazed Picnic Ham on page 202. You will need a 10-inch ovensafe nonstick skillet for this recipe. Because broilers can vary in inten-sity, watch the frittata carefully as it cooks.

    6   large eggs
    2   tablespoons half-and-half
        Salt and pepper
    1   tablespoon butter
    4   ounces white mushrooms, trimmed and sliced thin
    1   shallot, minced
    4   ounces cooked ham, sliced thin and cut into ½-inch
        pieces (¾ cup)
  1½   ounces cheddar cheese, cut into ¼-inch cubes
        (⅓ cup)

1. Adjust oven rack 6 inches from broiler element and heat broiler. Whisk eggs, half-and-half, pinch salt, and ⅛ teaspoon pepper together in bowl for 30 seconds; set aside.

2. Melt butter in 10-inch ovensafe nonstick skillet over medium heat. Add mushrooms and cook, stirring occasionally, until mushrooms begin to brown, 3 to 5 minutes. Add shallot and continue to cook until mushrooms are golden brown and tender and shallot is softened and lightly browned, 3 to 5 minutes longer.

3. Stir ham and cheese into eggs. Add egg mixture to skillet and cook, using rubber spatula to stir and scrape bottom of skillet, until large curds form and spatula begins to leave wake but eggs are still very wet, about 1 minute. Shake skillet to distribute eggs evenly and continue to cook without stirring to let bottom set, about 30 seconds.

4. Slide skillet under broiler and cook until surface is puffed and spotty brown, yet center remains slightly wet and runny when cut into with paring knife, 1 to 2 minutes.

5. Using potholder (skillet handle will be hot), remove skillet from oven. Let sit until eggs in middle are just set, about 3 minutes. Being careful of hot skillet handle, use rubber spatula to loosen frittata from skillet, then slide onto cutting board. Slice into wedges and serve.

Ham and Potato Gratins

SERVES 2

The ham in this recipe is from Glazed Picnic Ham on page 202. Prepare and assemble all of the ingredients before slicing the potatoes or the potatoes will begin to turn brown (do not store the sliced potatoes in water). Slicing the potatoes ⅛ inch thick is crucial for the success of this dish; use a mandoline, a V-slicer, or a food processor fitted with a ⅛-inch-thick slicing blade. You will need two shallow 2-cup gratin dishes (measuring approximately 9 by 6 inches; see page 3), or you can substitute one 8-inch square baking dish.

- 1 pound russet potatoes, peeled and sliced ⅛ inch thick
- 6 ounces cooked ham, sliced thin and cut into ½-inch pieces (1¼ cups)
- 1 tablespoon unsalted butter
- 1 leek, white and light green parts only, halved lengthwise, sliced thin, and washed thoroughly
  Salt and pepper
- 1 garlic clove, minced
- 1 teaspoon minced fresh thyme
  Pinch cayenne
- 1 teaspoon all-purpose flour
- ¾ cup heavy cream
- 1 ounce Gruyère cheese, shredded (¼ cup)

NOTES FROM THE TEST KITCHEN

THE BEST MANDOLINE

If you don't own a food processor, a mandoline can make quick work of turning out piles of identically sliced vegetables. We wanted to test the range of models being marketed to home cooks and were shocked by the assortment of sizes and prices (anywhere from $25 to $400). We gathered 13 mandolines and put them to the test. We preferred models with a V-shaped blade and rimmed, long-pronged hand guards. If we were going to own a mandoline, we figured it should be able to do the works—slice, julienne, and waffle-cut—while keeping our hands safe. We found our winner in the **OXO Good Grips V-Blade Mandoline Slicer**. Testers liked its wide, sturdy gripper guard, and its razor-sharp blade made short work of a variety of fruits and vegetables. Plus, it wasn't anywhere near $400— this savvy slicer sells for just $49.99.

1. Adjust oven rack to middle position and heat oven to 350 degrees. Grease two 2-cup gratin dishes. Place potatoes and ham in medium bowl and set aside.

2. Melt butter in small saucepan over medium heat. Add leek and ⅛ teaspoon salt and cook until softened, 3 to 5 minutes. Stir in garlic, thyme, ¼ teaspoon pepper, and cayenne and cook until fragrant, about 30 seconds. Stir in flour and cook until incorporated, about 1 minute. Whisk in cream and bring to simmer until thickened, about 1 minute.

3. Pour sauce over potatoes and ham and toss to coat thoroughly. Divide mixture evenly between prepared gratin dishes and gently pack potatoes into even layer, removing any air pockets. Cover dishes with aluminum foil and bake until potatoes are almost tender, 35 to 40 minutes. Remove foil and sprinkle with Gruyère. Continue to bake, uncovered, until cheese is lightly browned and potatoes are tender, about 10 minutes longer. Let gratins sit for 10 minutes before serving.

Skillet Spaghetti Carbonara

SERVES 2

The ham in this recipe is from Glazed Picnic Ham on page 202.

- 1 tablespoon unsalted butter
- 6 ounces ham, sliced thin and cut into ½-inch pieces (1¼ cups)
- 2 garlic cloves, minced
  Salt and pepper
- ⅓ cup dry white wine
- 2 cups water
- 1½ cups low-sodium chicken broth
- 6 ounces spaghetti, broken in half
- ¼ cup heavy cream
- 1 large egg
- ⅓ cup grated Pecorino Romano cheese
- 2 tablespoons minced fresh parsley or basil (optional)

1. Melt butter in 12-inch nonstick skillet over medium-high heat. Add ham and cook, stirring occasionally, until lightly browned and crisp, about 10 minutes. Using slotted spoon, transfer ham to paper towel–lined plate; set aside.

BREAKING LONG-STRAND PASTA IN HALF

To keep pasta from flying everywhere, roll it up in kitchen towel, center bundle over counter's edge, and push down to break pasta in middle of bundle.

2. Add garlic and ¼ teaspoon pepper to now-empty skillet and cook until fragrant, about 30 seconds. Stir in wine and simmer until nearly evaporated, 2 to 4 minutes.

3. Stir in water, broth, and pasta, increase heat to high, and cook at vigorous simmer, stirring often, until pasta is tender and liquid has thickened, 12 to 15 minutes.

4. Meanwhile, whisk cream, egg, and Pecorino together in small bowl. Off heat, pour egg mixture over pasta and toss to combine. Add ham, season with salt and pepper to taste, and gently toss to combine. Sprinkle with parsley (if using). Serve immediately.

ROAST TURKEY BREAST

A ROAST TURKEY BREAST MAKES A LOT OF SENSE for the for-two household. And even though leftover turkey sandwiches are welcome during the week, we had better ideas up our sleeves. But first, we wanted to tackle how to roast the perfect turkey breast—one that emerged from the oven with browned, crisp skin and tender, juicy meat.

Cooking experts have devised many clever and complex solutions to the problem of dry turkey breast, but we wanted to find a simple resolution. That's when we remembered an old-fashioned technique we've seen our grandmothers employ: cooking turkey in a bag. But while bag cookery promised a moist, juicy turkey breast minus any hassle, we soon found out that we had to solve a whole host of other problems.

Since experts now say that cooking in the brown paper grocery bag of the past is quite possibly toxic, we started with a box of ovensafe bags. The picture on the package of a plump, beautifully bronzed bird was certainly persuasive. Following the recipe card tucked inside, we sprinkled 1 tablespoon of flour inside the bag and shook it around, which supposedly prevents the bag from exploding in the oven. Next, as instructed, we brushed the turkey breast with oil and set it in the bag with chopped celery, carrot, and onion. We sealed the bag, cut slits in it, set it in a large roasting pan, and put the whole shebang in a 350-degree oven.

At the 2½-hour mark, we took the turkey breast out. The results were—no pun intended—a mixed bag. The meat was remarkably juicy, and the bag itself was full of juices that we could use for gravy—perhaps too full. As promising as this cook-in-a-bag approach was, it created problems: The skin was pale and flabby, and the meat at the bottom was waterlogged. Some adjustments were clearly in order.

To keep the turkey from braising in its own juices, we elevated it on a V-rack. The first time we tried this, the bag tore from the weight of the released juices. We decided to move the vegetables into the roasting pan, where they wouldn't contribute to the moisture in the bag. To keep them from burning, we added chicken broth and water to the pan. Our next turkey breast sat perched on the rack, snug yet remarkably moist at the end of cooking; meanwhile, the bag hung down through the rods of the V-rack, holding delicious turkey juices. Though one problem was solved, we still had to find a way to deliver a perfectly bronzed exterior.

We figured that crisping the skin would be as easy as opening the bag toward the end of cooking and cranking up the heat. Though this led to skin that was nicely crisped, the meat dried out, thus canceling out all of the work we had put into making it as moist as possible. To protect the breast meat, we found it necessary to cover it with several layers of cheesecloth before sealing the bag. This shield worked better when, for a subsequent test, we reinforced it with a layer of foil. We removed both cheesecloth and foil after we opened the bag to crisp the skin.

Getting nicely browned skin was not so easy. To take full advantage of the moist cooking method, we had been leaving the turkey inside the bag until the last possible moment—a method that ran counter to browning. So while our turkey finally tasted delicious, it sure didn't look it. We got the idea to give it a jump start on color, so we brushed the raw turkey with a few ingredients we thought would contribute to the bronzed exterior we were after. Though we tried everything from soy sauce and Gravy Master to a jar of carrot baby food, only soy sauce had any potential.

When we first tried brushing on a thin coat of soy sauce, it slid right off the turkey breast. For our next test, we reduced the soy sauce on the stovetop so that it would thicken and stay put. When it got nice and syrupy, we combined it with flour to make a paste (conveniently, this eliminated the need to toss flour into the oven bag at the start). To guarantee that the turkey breast would crisp once we opened the bag, and for good flavor, we mixed a dab of softened butter into the paste. We dried the turkey thoroughly so that the paste would adhere and massaged it over the bird before closing up the bag and moving it to the oven.

About two hours later, we took the turkey out, removed the bag (letting the drippings fall into the roasting pan), and raised the oven temperature to 475 degrees. In about 20 more minutes, the turkey had cooked through perfectly and was nicely bronzed. It showed all the advantages—and none of the disadvantages—of cooking in a bag. While the turkey rested, we made gravy from the flavorful pan drippings. Then we carved a few moist, succulent slices for dinner. Our turkey recipe was finally in the bag, and now it was time to think of a few ways to use up the rest of the meat.

Soup is one fallback way to use up extra turkey, but we had something a little more exciting than the humdrum egg-noodle-and-carrot version in mind. For a turkey soup boasting the bright, fresh flavors of Thai cuisine, we started by simmering store-bought chicken broth with ginger, lemon grass, garlic, and jalapeño. In just 10 minutes, our broth absorbed all the rich, potent flavor from these ingredients. After straining the broth to remove the aromatics, we stirred in a quarter-cup of jasmine rice, a Thai variety of long-grain rice. To avoid tough turkey, we waited until our rice was tender and fully cooked to stir it in, along with a handful of delicate, crunchy snow peas. The snow peas took just a few minutes to turn crisp-tender, at which point the turkey was heated through. For even more authentic flavor, we stirred in about half a can of coconut milk, which gave our broth body and a velvety texture and imparted a delicate sweetness that worked well with the bright notes of the lemon grass and ginger.

Next, we went in a totally different direction and set out to revamp a retro casserole: turkey tetrazzini. After sautéing a chopped onion and sliced mushrooms, we stirred in chicken broth, cream, and a touch of sherry for brightness, then we added our egg noodles right to the pan to simmer until tender. Peas, added toward the end of cooking, lent a hint of sweetness and some color. Along with our shredded turkey, we stirred in Gruyère for its rich, nutty tang. Super-crisp panko bread crumbs, toasted in butter, made the perfect golden, crunchy crown for our turkey tetrazzini, which needed just a 10-minute stint in the oven to become hot and bubbling.

Finally, we headed Southwest and set out to make turkey tamale pie for two. Tamale pie is popular Tex-Mex fare, and a good one boasts a juicy, spicy mixture of meat and vegetables topped with a cornmeal crust. We started by sautéing onion and garlic for the filling; chili powder gave it a subtle heat that we reinforced with a can of spicy Ro-Tel tomatoes (a blend of tomatoes, diced green chiles, and spices). Black beans added heartiness and bumped up the Tex-Mex feel of our dish. After letting the beans and tomatoes simmer briefly, we folded in our shredded turkey, a heaping pile of shredded cheddar, and a tablespoon of minced cilantro. Instead of a traditional tamale-style topping, which would be a bit dense for our saucy filling, we opted for a slightly sweet cornbread topping made from equal amounts of flour and cornmeal, a bit of sugar, baking powder and baking soda for leavening, and buttermilk, an egg, and melted butter for richness. A single 9-inch pie plate was much too large for our filling, so we opted to use two small pie plates for a pair of hearty individual tamale pies. We portioned both filling and topping into the pie plates, popped them into the oven, and waited. After about 20 minutes, our tamale pies were nicely golden and piping hot.

With a little creativity, we were able to enjoy our tender, flavorful roast turkey in a host of perfectly scaled-down dishes that were every bit as easy as they were delicious.

KEYS TO ROAST TURKEY BREAST

Roasting turkey in the moist environment of an oven bag ensures juicy meat—but flabby skin. We modified an old technique to take advantage of the moistness while achieving brown, crispy skin and an all-around perfectly cooked turkey breast.

1. Place turkey breast in bag and rub concentrated soy paste evenly and thoroughly over skin. Then lay cheesecloth, followed by aluminum foil, over turkey breast to insulate it.

2. Place vegetables, broth, and water in roasting pan. Set V-rack in pan and place bagged turkey breast (bag already tied, trimmed, and vented) on rack to keep from stewing.

3. When breast registers 150 degrees, cut bag open. Discard cheesecloth, foil, and bag, and let juices run into pan. Return turkey to 475-degree oven to brown and finish cooking.

THE BEST FAT SEPARATOR

Before gravy can be made from pan juices, the fat must be removed. If you have the time to wait, the fat will naturally rise to the top, where it can be spooned off. A faster method involves a specially designed fat separator. There are three distinct styles: pitcher-type measuring cups with sharply angled spouts; ladles with slots around the perimeter; and "fat mops," brushes with long, soft bristles made from plastic fibers.

Our favorite style of fat separator is the pitcher cup because of its efficiency and ability to handle fairly large volumes of stock. Our favorite brand is the **Trudeau Gravy Separator**, $10.99, which has a large, 4-cup capacity, a wide mouth that makes for easy filling, and an integrated strainer.

THE BEST CHICKEN BROTH

Store-bought chicken broth is a real time-saver, but which brand is best? Our winning broth, **Swanson Certified Organic Free Range Chicken Broth**, has two important characteristics: less than 700 milligrams of sodium per serving (others contain up to 1,350 milligrams per serving) and a short ingredient list that includes vegetables such as carrots, celery, and onions. Don't be intimidated by the large 32-ounce carton; extra chicken broth can be used in many applications, from cooking rice and grains to making soups and stews.

Roast Turkey Breast with Gravy

SERVES 2, WITH LEFTOVERS

You can use the leftovers to make all three of the following recipes: Thai-Style Turkey and Jasmine Rice Soup (page 209), Skillet Turkey Tetrazzini (page 209), and Turkey Tamale Pies (page 211). The leftover turkey can be refrigerated in an airtight container for up to 3 days. You will need a turkey-size oven bag and one 2-yard package of cheesecloth for this recipe. Don't let the oven bag touch the oven wall or it will melt. The soy sauce might seem out of place in this recipe, but it helps ensure the turkey breast turns a deep golden brown as it roasts. If you end up with less than 1½ cups of defatted pan juices, supplement them with additional low-sodium chicken broth.

¼ cup soy sauce

1 tablespoon unsalted butter, softened

2 teaspoons plus 2 tablespoons all-purpose flour
Salt and pepper

1 (6- to 7-pound) whole bone-in turkey breast, trimmed

3 cups low-sodium chicken broth

2 cups water

3 carrots, peeled and cut into 2-inch pieces

1 onion, peeled and quartered

1 celery rib, cut into 2-inch pieces

1. Adjust oven rack to lowest position and heat oven to 350 degrees. Bring soy sauce to boil in small saucepan over medium-high heat. Reduce heat to medium-low and simmer until reduced to 1 tablespoon, about 3 minutes. Transfer to small bowl and whisk in butter, 2 teaspoons flour, and ¼ teaspoon pepper. Set aside.

2. Lightly spray inside of oven bag with vegetable oil spray. Fold cheesecloth into 10 by 7-inch rectangle. Pat turkey dry with paper towels, transfer to prepared oven bag, and rub soy paste evenly all over skin. Place cheesecloth on top and cover with 10 by 7-inch rectangle of heavy-duty aluminum foil. Using kitchen twine, tie oven bag closed, trim bag end to 1 inch, and cut four ½-inch slits in top of bag. Add broth, water, carrots, onion, and celery to large roasting pan. Set V-rack inside pan and arrange bagged turkey in V-rack.

3. Roast turkey until meat registers 150 degrees, 2 to 2½ hours. Remove pan from oven and increase oven temperature to 475 degrees. Cut open oven bag. Discard cheesecloth, foil, and bag, letting juices fall into pan. Return turkey to oven and roast until meat registers 160 degrees, about 20 minutes. Transfer to carving board and let rest, uncovered, for 30 minutes.

4. Meanwhile, strain contents of roasting pan through fine-mesh strainer into fat separator; discard vegetables. Let liquid settle and reserve 1½ cups defatted pan juices.

5. Transfer 1 tablespoon fat from separator to small saucepan and heat over medium heat until shimmering. Stir in remaining 2 tablespoons flour and cook, stirring constantly, until golden, about 1 minute. Slowly whisk in reserved 1½ cups pan juices and bring to boil. Reduce heat to medium-low and simmer until gravy is slightly thickened, 3 to 5 minutes. Season with salt and pepper to taste. Carve turkey and serve with gravy.

Thai-Style Turkey and Jasmine Rice Soup
SERVES 2

The turkey in this recipe comes from Roast Turkey Breast with Gravy on page 208.

3½ cups low-sodium chicken broth
1 (¾-inch) piece ginger, peeled, cut into thirds, and bruised with back of knife
1 lemon grass stalk, trimmed to bottom 3 inches and bruised with back of knife
2 garlic cloves, unpeeled and smashed
1 jalapeño chile, stemmed, halved, and seeded
   Salt
¼ cup jasmine rice

6 ounces cooked turkey, shredded (1¼ cups)
¾ cup coconut milk
2 ounces snow peas, strings removed, cut into 1-inch pieces
2 tablespoons minced fresh cilantro
   Lime wedges

1. Bring broth to simmer in large saucepan over medium-high heat. Add ginger, lemon grass, garlic, jalapeño, and ¼ teaspoon salt, cover, and simmer until broth is fragrant and flavorful, about 10 minutes. With slotted spoon, remove ginger, lemon grass, garlic, and jalapeño.

2. Add rice and bring to boil, then reduce heat to medium and simmer, covered, until rice is tender, 12 to 15 minutes. Stir in turkey, coconut milk, and snow peas and simmer until turkey is heated through and snow peas are crisp-tender, 2 to 3 minutes. Ladle soup into individual bowls and sprinkle with cilantro. Serve with lime wedges.

Skillet Turkey Tetrazzini
SERVES 2

The turkey in this recipe comes from Roast Turkey Breast with Gravy on page 208. Do not substitute other types of noodles for the wide egg noodles here.

2 tablespoons butter
½ cup panko bread crumbs
   Salt and pepper
5 ounces white mushrooms, trimmed and sliced thin
1 small onion, chopped fine
1¾ cups low-sodium chicken broth
½ cup heavy cream
1 tablespoon dry sherry
3 ounces (2 cups) wide egg noodles
6 ounces cooked turkey, shredded (1¼ cups)
2 ounces Gruyère cheese, shredded (½ cup)
⅓ cup frozen peas
1 tablespoon minced fresh parsley

1. Adjust oven rack to middle position and heat oven to 475 degrees. Melt 1 tablespoon butter in 10-inch ovensafe nonstick skillet over medium-high heat. Add panko and ⅛ teaspoon salt; toast until just golden brown, 3 to 5 minutes. Transfer to small bowl and set aside.

TURKEY TAMALE PIES

2. Wipe out skillet with paper towels. Add remaining 1 tablespoon butter to now-empty skillet and melt over medium-high heat. Add mushrooms, onion, ¼ teaspoon salt, and ¼ teaspoon pepper and cook, stirring often, until mushrooms have released their moisture and are golden brown, 8 to 10 minutes.

3. Stir in broth, cream, and sherry, then add noodles and cook at vigorous simmer, stirring often, until noodles are nearly tender and sauce is slightly thickened, about 8 minutes.

4. Off heat, stir in turkey, cheese, peas, and parsley and season with salt and pepper to taste. Sprinkle panko over top, transfer skillet to oven, and bake until topping is crisp and casserole is bubbling lightly around edges, about 8 minutes. Serve.

Turkey Tamale Pies

SERVES 2

The turkey in this recipe comes from Roast Turkey Breast with Gravy on page 208. You will need two 6-inch pie plates for this recipe (see page 3). If you don't have buttermilk on hand, you can substitute ⅓ cup milk and 1½ teaspoons lemon juice; stir together and let mixture sit until it thickens, about 5 minutes. Serve with sour cream if desired. See page 116 for a recipe to use up the leftover black beans.

FILLING

- 1 tablespoon vegetable oil
- 1 small onion, chopped fine
- 2 teaspoons chili powder
  - Salt and pepper
- 1 garlic clove, minced
- 1 (10-ounce) can Ro-Tel tomatoes
- ¾ cup canned black beans, rinsed
- 6 ounces cooked turkey, shredded (1¼ cups)
- 4 ounces cheddar cheese, shredded (1 cup)
- 1 tablespoon minced fresh cilantro

CORNBREAD TOPPING

- ⅓ cup all-purpose flour
- ⅓ cup yellow cornmeal
- 1 tablespoon sugar
- ¼ teaspoon baking powder
- ¼ teaspoon salt
- ⅛ teaspoon baking soda
- ⅓ cup buttermilk
- 1 large egg
- 1 tablespoon unsalted butter, melted and cooled

1. FOR THE FILLING: Adjust oven rack to middle position and heat oven to 450 degrees. Line rimmed baking sheet with aluminum foil. Heat oil in 10-inch nonstick skillet over medium heat until shimmering. Add onion, chili powder, and ¼ teaspoon salt and cook until onion is softened, about 5 minutes. Stir in garlic and cook until fragrant, about 30 seconds.

2. Stir in tomatoes and beans and simmer until most of liquid has evaporated, about 5 minutes. Off heat, stir in turkey, cheddar, and cilantro and season with salt and pepper to taste. Divide mixture evenly between two 6-inch pie plates.

3. FOR THE CORNBREAD TOPPING: Whisk flour, cornmeal, sugar, baking powder, salt, and baking soda together in large bowl. In separate bowl, whisk buttermilk and egg together. Stir buttermilk mixture into flour mixture until uniform, then stir in butter until just combined.

4. Dollop cornbread topping evenly over filling, then spread into even layer, covering filling completely. Bake pies on prepared baking sheet until topping is golden and has baked through completely in center, about 20 minutes, rotating sheet halfway through baking. Let cool for 10 minutes before serving.

SLOW-COOKER TURKEY CHILI

CHAPTER 8

SLOW-COOKER FAVORITES

SLOW-COOKER BARBECUED STEAK TIPS

STEAK TIPS HAVE GREAT BEEFY FLAVOR AND JUST enough marbling to keep them moist and tender when quickly grilled. But grilling isn't a year-round option for many cooks, so we wanted to find a way to make steak tips in our slow cooker, for a (mostly) hands-off supper that would deliver the same tender meat, draped in a sweet and tangy barbecue sauce, even in the dead of winter.

We began by researching recipes for slow-cooker steak tips. In most of them, the raw steak tips were simply dropped into the cooker, bottled barbecue sauce was dumped on top, and the meat was cooked for upward of 12 hours. Though we were dubious, we decided to test this method anyway. As it turned out, our initial instincts were correct—after an all-day simmer, the meat was dry, stringy, and bland, and the sauce was so diluted by the released meat juices that it tasted like meat-flavored water. It was clear we had two issues to tackle. First, we'd have to figure out how to turn out tender, perfectly cooked steak tips using the slow cooker. Second, we'd need to create a sauce that stayed full-flavored and thick enough to cling to the meat even after an all-day simmer.

Our first correction was simple: We seared our sirloin steak tips in a skillet before they went into the slow cooker. Though most recipes skipped this step, we found it improved both the flavor and texture of the beef, and it gave us a flavorful fond (the browned bits left behind on the bottom of the pan) from which to build a concentrated sauce. Plus, it took just five minutes.

Once the beef was well browned, we moved it to the slow cooker and set about building a sauce with the richly flavored fond. We sautéed a shallot and a clove of garlic in the now-empty skillet, added a half-cup of tomato sauce and a couple of spoonfuls of ketchup (common ingredients in barbecue sauce recipes), and scraped up all the browned bits so they could dissolve in the sauce. Then we poured the sauce over the steak tips.

After about six hours on low, we removed the lid of the slow cooker and were severely disappointed. The meat had basically stewed in the sauce, which was now overly thick and scorched. It was clear we needed to find a way to preserve the flavorful, well-browned exterior of the meat, and having it sit in the sauce wasn't going to help us get there. We also needed to thin the sauce somewhat so it would coat our steak tips nicely at the end of the cooking time.

If our steak tips couldn't sit in the sauce, they'd need to sit above the sauce. We needed to find something to help elevate them. Looking around the test kitchen, we spied a steamer basket. Though it did elevate the meat enough to keep it out of the beefy hot tub, the chunks of meat cooked unevenly in the tight confines of the basket. Then we thought to apply a grilling technique: skewering the steak tips. We threaded the raw tips onto bamboo skewers, then browned the kebabs and laid them on top of a now-inverted (to give the skewers more breathing room) steamer basket in the cooker. Hours later, the texture of the cooked meat actually

---

NOTES FROM THE TEST KITCHEN

MAKING SLOW-COOKER BARBECUED STEAK TIPS
To simulate the flavor of grilled steak tips in the slow cooker, we needed to elevate the steak tips and build a rich sauce.

1. Brown skewered steak tips in 10-inch skillet to intensify flavor of meat and sauce.

2. Once meat is well browned, coat steak tips with potent wet rub made with soy sauce, tomato paste, and dark brown sugar.

3. Lay skewers on inverted steamer basket to keep them out of cooking liquid and preserve seared crust.

resembled that of grilled tips: tender and moist, with a nice seared crust.

To fix the sauce, we decided to try the simplest method first, so we stirred a half-cup of water into our tomato sauce mixture in the skillet. This new sauce was better than before, but now it was a little too thin. We tried reducing the amount of water, but this resulted in another scorched sauce. The culprit, we realized, was the meat itself; from batch to batch, our steak tips were releasing variable amounts of juices. We found that simmering the finished sauce on the stovetop for a couple of minutes was the best way to guarantee consistent results and a slightly thickened sauce. With a few final flavor tweaks—a splash of cider vinegar, a couple more spoonfuls of ketchup, and a dash of hot sauce—our sauce had real barbecue flavor.

Though the meat's texture was good and the sauce had plenty of flavor, the tips themselves needed more seasoning. What if we brushed them with something flavorful before moving them to the slow cooker? We combined a small amount of tomato paste, brown sugar, and soy sauce, which the test kitchen has found amplifies meaty flavors substantially, and then rubbed this mixture on our steak tips after browning them. The potent wet rub seasoned the meat as it cooked above the liquid in the slow cooker.

About six hours later, we couldn't believe how far our recipe had come: The beef, which we'd drizzled with our sweet and tangy barbecue sauce, was rich, meaty, and tender. Granted, it wasn't the genuine cooked-on-the-grill article, but it was so good, no one cared.

Slow-Cooker Barbecued Steak Tips

SERVES 2

This may seem like a lot of meat, but it will cook down substantially in the slow cooker. To ensure evenly sized pieces, we prefer to purchase whole steak tips (also known as flap meat) and cut them ourselves. However, if you have long, thin pieces of meat, roll or fold them into approximately 2-inch cubes before skewering (see page 146). You'll need a metal steamer basket and two 8-inch bamboo skewers for this recipe. *Cooking time: 5 to 7 hours on low or 4 to 5 hours on high*

1 **tablespoon soy sauce**
1 **tablespoon tomato paste**
1 **tablespoon packed dark brown sugar**
   Salt and pepper
1 **pound sirloin steak tips, trimmed and cut into**
   2-inch pieces
1 **tablespoon vegetable oil**
1 **shallot, minced**
1 **small garlic clove, minced**
½ **cup water**
½ **cup tomato sauce**
⅓ **cup ketchup**
¾ **teaspoon cider vinegar**
¼ **teaspoon hot sauce**

1. Lightly spray inside of slow cooker with vegetable oil spray. Combine soy sauce, tomato paste, sugar, and ⅛ teaspoon pepper in small bowl. Pat beef dry with paper towels and thread onto skewers.

2. Heat oil in 10-inch skillet over medium-high heat until just smoking. Brown beef on all sides, about 5 minutes. Transfer skewers to plate and brush soy sauce mixture evenly on all sides.

3. Add shallot and ⅛ teaspoon salt to now-empty skillet and cook over medium heat until softened and lightly browned, 2 to 3 minutes. Stir in garlic and cook until fragrant, about 30 seconds. Add water, tomato sauce, and half of ketchup and bring to boil. Transfer mixture to slow cooker.

4. Set inverted metal steamer basket in slow cooker. Place skewers on steamer basket, scraping excess soy sauce mixture over meat. Cover and cook until beef is tender and fork slips easily in and out of meat, 5 to 7 hours on low or 4 to 5 hours on high.

5. Transfer skewers to serving dish, slide beef off skewers, tent loosely with aluminum foil, and let rest for 5 to 10 minutes. Let cooking liquid settle for 5 minutes, then remove fat from surface using large spoon. Transfer liquid to small saucepan and stir in remaining ketchup. Bring to simmer over medium heat and cook until reduced to ¾ cup, about 5 minutes. Stir in vinegar and hot sauce and season with salt and pepper to taste. Pour ¼ cup sauce over steak tips. Serve with remaining sauce.

SLOW-COOKER PORK CHOPS WITH DRIED FRUIT COMPOTE

PORK CHOPS ARE PERFECT FOR THE FOR-TWO household—they're a mainstay at the supermarket, plus it's easy to purchase them in smaller quantities. But given their lean nature, they can overcook easily, resulting in a dry, flavorless dinner. We wanted to take advantage of this convenient cut, and the convenience of the slow cooker, but we'd have to figure out how to keep the pork moist and tender for the duration of cooking. Since pork chops and fruit are a natural combination, we set our sights on pairing our chops with a sweet and fruity sauce for a homey yet hands-off slow-cooker supper for two.

First we had to figure out which cut of chop would stay tender in the slow cooker. Rib chops are a common cut for braising, so that's where we started. We made sure they were about ¾ inch thick, thinking anything thinner would overcook quickly in the slow cooker. For a quick sauce (we'd finesse the flavors later on), we combined chicken broth, peeled, chopped apples, and a pinch of cinnamon. We moved this mixture to the slow cooker, added our pork chops, and set the cooker on low. When we pulled them from the slow cooker six hours later, they were dry and stringy. It appeared that thin was not in, and we'd need to consider thicker chops.

However, we didn't want to detract from the convenience of the slow cooker by specially ordering thick-cut chops. While considering other options for pork chop cuts, we landed on blade chops. Blade chops are cut from the shoulder end of the loin and contain a significant amount of fat and connective tissue, both of which make them ideal for long cooking times. When we tried cooking these chops, the fat melted into the meat, keeping it moist and tender, and the connective tissue all but disappeared over the long stay in the slow cooker. Though we often sear meat prior to braising, we found that in this case, searing sped up the cooking process, leading to the dry meat we were trying to avoid, so we could cross this extra step off the list.

NOTES FROM THE TEST KITCHEN

SLOW-COOKING FOR TWO
Using a slow cooker is a great way for the time-pressed cook to get supper on the table—no close monitoring of the stovetop or oven necessary. But most slow-cooker recipes make enough food to feed a crowd. In this chapter, you'll find an array of slow-cooker recipes scaled down to serve just two (although some recipes with multiple ingredients, such as our Slow-Cooker Brunswick Stew, page 220, didn't scale down perfectly, so these yield an extra serving, ideal for lunch or supper the next day). We developed these recipes with an oval 3- to 3½-quart slow cooker because we found it to be easier to maneuver and clean, more affordable, and less space-hogging than large slow cookers, but this collection of recipes works equally well in a standard 6-quart slow cooker. After developing lots of slow-cooker recipes over the years, we've learned a few tricks for ensuring success, no matter the size of your slow cooker.

SPRAY YOUR SLOW COOKER: Spraying the sides of the insert with vegetable oil spray, before adding food, eliminates any sticking (or burning) and makes cleanup easier. This is especially important when you are cooking a smaller amount of food, as with our scaled-down recipes for two.

USE THE MICROWAVE: When there is no need to get out a skillet to brown meat, we use the microwave to cook the aromatics and bloom the flavors of any spices. We also use the microwave to gently cook certain vegetables before stirring them into a finished dish, as in our Slow-Cooker Spicy Sausage Ragu with Red Pepper (page 224).

MAKE A FOIL PACKET: Depending on the cooking time and how the meat and vegetables are cut, it is sometimes necessary to wrap them in an aluminum foil packet to keep them from overcooking, as with our Slow-Cooker Brunswick Stew (page 220). The packet helps keep these delicate ingredients out of the cooking liquid and protects their flavors from fading.

INCLUDE FLAVOR-AMPLIFYING INGREDIENTS FOR DEPTH: We've found that a handful of key ingredients, such as tomato paste and soy sauce, can increase meaty richness and depth of flavor substantially.

BROWN YOUR MEAT—SOMETIMES: In recipes that use a lot of spicy or aromatic ingredients, we've found that we can get away with not browning. But when a deep flavor base is required, we need to get out the skillet and brown the meat. When it comes to ground meat, like the turkey in our Slow-Cooker Turkey Chili (page 227), we found that browning is important to ensure that it is tender and not grainy or mushy at the end of the long cooking time.

KEEP GROUND MEAT TENDER WITH A PANADE: Ground meat can become tough and sandy after hours in the slow cooker. To keep it tender, we use a panade, a mixture of bread and a liquid, which we mix with the meat before cooking.

But while our chops were now in great shape, our sauce was definitely not up to par. The apples had turned to flavorless mush and become waterlogged because of the liquid exuded from the pork. The chicken broth only served to dilute the sauce further. It was clear the apples wouldn't stand up to the heat of the slow cooker for such a long period of time, so we ditched them in favor of an ingredient that required no prep at all: applesauce. But simply braising our chops in applesauce gave us a one-note dish with a light coating of applesauce. For heartier, more complex flavor and a thicker sauce, we turned to dried fruit, which cooked down to a rich-tasting compote. Tasters preferred a combination of dried cherries and dried apricots; the dried cherries contributed a tartness that countered the sweet flavor of the applesauce, and the dried apricots turned jammy and absorbed the savory notes of the pork. With a few more refinements—a minced shallot for aromatic background, brown sugar for sweetness, and a dash of vinegar for acidity—our fruit compote offered bold, multidimensional flavor.

Our last challenge was to finesse the texture of the compote—the dried fruit had soaked up the moisture released by the chops, leading to a sauce that was over-reduced and sticky. We tried adding back some chicken broth, but its flavor now seemed out of place. If all we needed was a little extra liquid, and not necessarily extra flavor, why not use water instead? As it turned out, a few tablespoons were all we needed.

With a splash of vinegar and a sprinkle of fresh parsley, our dried fruit compote made the perfect partner to our pork chops, which were tender, sweet, and, best of all, a snap to prepare.

Slow-Cooker Pork Chops with Dried Fruit Compote

SERVES 2

To prevent the pork chops from curling during cooking, cut shallow slits in the fat on the side of the chop in 2-inch intervals (see page 56). *Cooking time: 6 to 7 hours on low or 3 to 4 hours on high*

½ cup applesauce

⅓ cup dried apricots, quartered

¼ cup water

3 tablespoons dried cherries

1 small shallot, minced

2 teaspoons packed brown sugar

1 teaspoon cider vinegar, plus extra for seasoning

1 small bay leaf

⅛ teaspoon ground cinnamon

2 (7-ounce) bone-in pork blade-cut chops, ¾ inch thick, trimmed

Salt and pepper

2 teaspoons minced fresh parsley

1. Lightly spray inside of slow cooker with vegetable oil spray. Stir applesauce, apricots, water, cherries, shallot, sugar, vinegar, bay leaf, and cinnamon into slow cooker. Cut 2 slits about 2 inches apart through fat around outside of each pork chop. Pat chops dry with paper towels and season with salt and pepper. Nestle chops into slow cooker, turning to coat with applesauce mixture. Cover and cook until pork is tender and fork slips easily in and out of meat, 6 to 7 hours on low or 3 to 4 hours on high.

2. Transfer pork chops to serving platter, tent loosely with aluminum foil, and let rest for 5 to 10 minutes. Let braising liquid settle for 5 minutes, then remove fat from surface using large spoon. Discard bay leaf, stir in parsley, and season with salt, pepper, and vinegar to taste. Spoon ¼ cup sauce over chops. Serve with remaining sauce.

SLOW-COOKER BRUNSWICK STEW

A SOUTHERN CLASSIC, BRUNSWICK STEW IS A hearty, rustic mix of meats (chicken, pork, and rabbit are most common) and vegetables (usually corn, lima beans, tomatoes, potatoes, and okra) cooked for many hours in a tomato-based broth. We thought this stew would translate well to the slow cooker, where it could simmer unattended for a good chunk of time, allowing the meat and vegetables to become ultra-tender and the broth to develop its bold character.

But when we began researching recipes for slow-cooker Brunswick stew, we found that most were simply a hodgepodge of ingredients dumped into the cooker and simmered all day, resulting in dry meats, mushy vegetables, and a bland broth. Our challenges were obvious. To keep this stew practical for the for-two household, we had to whittle down the list of ingredients. Then we had to figure out how to ensure perfectly cooked

SLOW-COOKER BRUNSWICK STEW

meat and vegetables and a broth that tasted bold and bright, even after the long cooking time.

Right off the bat, we narrowed the meat options to supermarket-friendly pork and chicken, nixing the hard-to-find rabbit. Then we dove in, testing various cuts of meat to see which could handle the lengthy cooking time. For the pork, we opted for a blade chop, which delivered consistently moist and tender meat (country-style ribs came in a close second). For the chicken, we preferred bone-in, skin-on thighs, which beat out split breasts. Though the fattier thighs fared better than the leaner breasts, they still came out a little overcooked by the time the chop was tender, about 6½ hours later. Since we didn't want to cut out the poultry completely, we'd need to figure out a different method to keep the thighs moist. Perhaps if we separated the chicken from the rest of the stew (and the slow cooker's heating element), we could slow down its cooking so it wouldn't dry out.

In the past, the test kitchen has used a foil packet to protect vegetables when preparing slow-cooker stews. The packet allows the vegetables to gently steam in the residual heat of the cooking stew, so they stay intact and tender. What if we used this method for our chicken thighs? We seasoned our thighs with salt and pepper, wrapped them in foil, and placed the packet on top of the pork chop and broth (a simple mixture of chicken broth and diced tomatoes for the time being). Several hours later, we were greeted with tender, moist chicken. We let the chicken cool briefly, then cut the meat into bite-size pieces (discarding the bone) and returned it to the stew along with the pork, which we also cut into fork-friendly bites.

At this point, we needed to revisit the broth. Though we'd been working with diced tomatoes up to now, some tasters found the large pieces of tomato distracting. We tried a variety of tomato products, looking for a smoother option, and ultimately swapped out the diced tomatoes in favor of tomato sauce. A spoonful of ketchup provided body and sweet-tart balance, and sautéed onion and garlic and a bit of cayenne provided an aromatic backbone and subtle heat. A quick simmer helped the flavors meld. With our broth and meat in order, we moved on to the vegetables.

We tested a number of options we'd encountered in our research, looking for a mix that kept the character

MAKING BRUNSWICK STEW

1. Brown pork chop in skillet before adding it to slow cooker to add savory depth to stew.

2. Create foil packet to protect chicken thighs and potatoes. Place them on one side of large piece of aluminum foil, fold foil over, shape into packet that will fit into slow cooker, and crimp edges to seal.

3. Place foil packet directly on top of stew, pressing gently as needed to make packet fit in slow cooker.

of the stew intact but also ensured that the shopping list was manageable for our scaled-down stew. Many traditional ingredients, like lima beans and okra, were met with mixed reactions from tasters, so we kept things simple and opted for just corn and potatoes. For convenience, we nixed fresh corn in favor of frozen corn, which we stirred in toward the end of cooking. But the potato (a single Yukon Gold, cut into small chunks) was a bit more troublesome. Added at the start of cooking, it overcooked and turned to sludge. Added at the end of cooking, it never became fully tender. Searching for a middle ground, we decided to try cooking the potato in the foil packet with the chicken, but it still wasn't completely softened by the time the chicken was done. For the next test, we simply stirred the potato back into the stew and let it cook a bit longer after we set the cooked chicken aside. Now our spud was both tender and richly flavored.

Though the meat and vegetables were now perfectly cooked, the stew still lacked the deep flavor of the authentic version. As we had discovered with our Slow-Cooker Barbecued Steak Tips (page 215), browning the meat before placing it in the slow cooker can go a long way toward boosting flavor. Since we were already getting out a skillet to sauté the aromatics and simmer the broth, we decided it wouldn't be that much of a hassle to brown the pork chop. After a brief stint in the pan, our chop had a nicely browned exterior and had released a small amount of fat that we could use to sauté our aromatics. Once the aromatics were softened, we added the tomato sauce, chicken broth, and ketchup to the pan, which mingled with the fond left behind from browning the pork chop. We moved the broth to the slow cooker with the pork chop, added the foil packet, and let it cook. At last, this stew offered the rich, meaty flavor we were after.

A final splash of cider vinegar reinforced the bright, tangy notes of our slow-cooked Brunswick stew, which now offered all the robust flavor and tender meat and vegetables of the original.

Slow-Cooker Brunswick Stew

SERVES 2, WITH LEFTOVERS

Wrapping the potatoes and chicken in a foil packet ensures that they do not dry out over the extended cooking time (see page 219). *Cooking time: 6 to 7 hours on low or 4 to 5 hours on high*

  1 (10-ounce) bone-in blade-cut pork chop, about 1 inch thick, trimmed
     Salt and pepper
  1 tablespoon vegetable oil
  1 small onion, chopped fine
  2 garlic cloves, minced
  ⅛ teaspoon cayenne pepper
  1 (8-ounce) can tomato sauce
  1 cup low-sodium chicken broth
  1 tablespoon ketchup
  2 (6-ounce) bone-in chicken thighs, trimmed
  8 ounces Yukon Gold potatoes, peeled and cut into ¾-inch pieces
  1 cup frozen corn, thawed
  1 teaspoon cider vinegar

1. Lightly spray inside of slow cooker with vegetable oil spray. Pat pork chop dry with paper towels and season with salt and pepper. Heat oil in 10-inch skillet over medium-high heat until just smoking. Brown chop on both sides, 6 to 8 minutes; transfer to slow cooker.

2. Add onion to now-empty skillet and cook over medium heat until softened and browned, 5 to 7 minutes. Stir in garlic and cayenne and cook until fragrant, about 30 seconds. Add tomato sauce, broth, ketchup, and ¼ teaspoon salt and bring to boil. Transfer sauce to slow cooker.

3. Season chicken thighs and potatoes with salt and pepper and place on one side of large piece of aluminum foil. Fold foil over, shaping it into packet that will fit into slow cooker, then crimp to seal edges. Lay foil packet in slow cooker on top of stew. Cover and cook until pork is tender and fork slips easily in and out of meat, 6 to 7 hours on low or 4 to 5 hours on high.

4. Transfer foil packet and pork chop to carving board and carefully open packet. Remove chicken and let cool slightly with pork chop, then chop into bite-size pieces, discarding skin, fat, and bones.

5. Stir potatoes, any accumulated juices, and corn into slow cooker. Cover and cook on high until potatoes are tender, about 30 minutes. Stir chicken, pork, and vinegar into slow cooker and let sit until heated through, about 5 minutes. Season with salt and pepper to taste. Serve.

SLOW-COOKER NORTH CAROLINA PULLED PORK

PULLED PORK IS A NATURAL FOR THE SLOW cooker—the low and slow cooking environment mimics the long stint in the smoker, which is required to turn the meat pull-apart tender. But most recipes for pulled pork start out with a 5-pound pork shoulder, which yields way too much food for two. We set out to develop our own scaled-down recipe, and looked to North Carolina–style pulled pork as our inspiration. With its thin and tangy vinegar-based sauce, we thought this bright-tasting barbecue classic would make the perfect addition to our roster of slow-cooked dishes for two. As we set out to bring this outdoors dish indoors, we would need to carefully consider not only the cut of pork, but also the cooking technique, and, of course, the sauce.

First things first, we started with the pork. In the test kitchen, we usually choose fatty pork shoulder when barbecuing. But it is nearly impossible to find a pork shoulder small enough for a two-person recipe (even if we did want a little left over). Instead, we picked up a few smaller, easy-to-find cuts of pork for testing: tenderloin; center-cut, rib-cut, and blade-cut chops; and boneless country-style pork ribs. The tenderloin, center-cut, and rib-cut chops were, not surprisingly, too lean for the slow cooker, turning bone dry after six hours on low. The blade chops were better but contained too much light meat to shred easily, so we opted for the fattier country-style ribs. This meat turned silky and fall-apart tender—that is, as long as we chose the right ribs.

Country-style pork ribs are cut from the fatty blade end of the loin, like blade chops, but contain more meat. They also can contain differing ratios of darker and lighter meat. The ribs with more dark meat performed much better than the lighter pieces. We found that 1½ pounds of meat gave us enough pulled pork for three sandwiches—two hearty portions for dinner that night, plus an extra serving for the next day. Ribs in hand, we turned to our technique.

Most slow-cooker recipes for pulled pork call for simply simmering the meat in bottled barbecue sauce. We knew from our Slow-Cooker Barbecued Steak Tips (page 215) that this wasn't going to cut it. Instead, we decided to try a riff on a traditional barbecue technique. First, we applied a dry spice rub (just paprika, chili powder, salt, and pepper) to our ribs and added the seasoned pork to the slow cooker with a simple ketchup- and vinegar-based barbecue sauce. This gave the meat some of the traditional sweet and tangy flavor, but it was too faint. To intensify the flavor in our next test, we let the rubbed meat rest overnight in the fridge. This helped, but the pork was even more flavorful when we poked the meat with a fork before rubbing it down.

But with our pork improving, the cooking liquid was becoming a glaring issue. Barbecue sauce wasn't working because the vinegar in it made the meat taste pickled. Given the lengthy cooking time, this problem shouldn't have been much of a surprise. In a slow cooker, some sort of cooking liquid is a must, but what should we use in place of the sauce? Chicken broth added a neutral, meaty flavor. Just a half-cup did the job, in part because the pork gave up so much moisture as it cooked. By the time the meat was tender, we had a cup of super-flavorful liquid left in the slow cooker. Unfortunately, once shredded, the meat itself was still not as juicy as we wanted. What the slow cooker had stolen from the pork in six hours, we had to put back.

We skimmed the fat from the liquid and reduced it by half while we shredded the pork. To transform the liquid into the characteristic vinegar-based barbecue sauce, we added cider vinegar, brown sugar, and some ketchup to the reduced elixir. We now had a cup of rich and tangy sauce with a touch of porky flavor. We poured ½ cup onto our shredded pork and watched as the meat drank it up. The elusive pork flavor was back where it belonged, but something was still missing: the smoke flavor that makes pulled pork so appealing.

We tried adding liquid smoke to the cooking liquid, but we cleared the kitchen with the awful campfire

NOTES FROM THE TEST KITCHEN

BUYING BONELESS COUNTRY-STYLE PORK RIBS
These meaty, tender ribs are cut from the upper side of the rib cage from the fatty end of the loin. They contain mostly fattier meat and are a favorite for braising, smoking, and slow cooking. Butchers usually cut them into individual ribs and package several together. When shopping, be sure to choose ribs with plenty of fat and dark meat to ensure tenderness.

ALL ABOUT LIQUID SMOKE
We were among the many people who had always assumed that there must be some kind of synthetic chemical chicanery going on in the making of "liquid smoke" flavoring, but that's not the case. Liquid smoke is made by channeling smoke from smoldering wood chips through a condenser, which quickly cools the vapors, causing them to liquefy (just like the drops that form when you breathe on a piece of cold glass). The water-soluble flavor compounds in the smoke are trapped within this liquid, while the nonsoluble, carcinogenic tars and resins are removed by a series of filters, resulting in a clean, smoke-flavored liquid. When buying liquid smoke, be sure to avoid brands with additives such as salt, vinegar, and molasses. Our top-rated brand, **Wright's Liquid Smoke**, contains nothing but smoke and water.

smell that resulted. We'd need to find another way to add smoky flavor to our barbecue sauce. Ham steak added barely-there smoke flavor, and smoked ham hocks added too much smoke flavor, overwhelming our pork. Then we tried an old standby: bacon. We tossed a couple of slices into the slow cooker as the pork cooked, and it was just the ticket, adding another layer of smoky complexity to our pork. And while the super-concentrated liquid smoke didn't work in the cooking liquid, we found it worked well in the finished sauce.

Piled high on a soft white bun, this pulled pork finally tasted like the real deal.

Slow-Cooker North Carolina Pulled Pork

SERVES 2, WITH LEFTOVERS

Try to buy country-style pork ribs with lots of fat and dark meat, and stay away from ribs that look overly lean with pale meat. Lean country-style pork ribs will taste very dry and will be hard to shred after the extended cooking time in the slow cooker. Do not omit the resting time in step 1; this step ensures flavorful meat. Serve on soft buns with pickle chips. *Cooking time: 6 to 7 hours on low or 3 to 4 hours on high*

- 1½ **tablespoons packed dark brown sugar**
- 1 **tablespoon paprika**
- 1½ **teaspoons chili powder**
- **Salt and pepper**
- 1½ **pounds boneless country-style pork ribs**
- 2 **slices bacon**
- ½ **cup low-sodium chicken broth**
- ¼ **cup cider vinegar**
- 3 **tablespoons ketchup**
- ¼ **teaspoon liquid smoke**

1. Lightly spray inside of slow cooker with vegetable oil spray. Combine 1 tablespoon sugar, paprika, chili powder, ½ teaspoon salt, and ¾ teaspoon pepper in bowl. Prick pork ribs all over using fork. Rub sugar mixture evenly over ribs, place ribs in zipper-lock bag, press out as much air as possible, and seal bag. Refrigerate for at least 8 hours or up to 24 hours.

2. Remove ribs from zipper-lock bag and place in slow cooker with bacon. Pour broth over ribs, cover, and cook until pork is tender and fork slips easily in and out of meat, 6 to 7 hours on low or 3 to 4 hours on high.

3. Transfer ribs to large bowl and discard bacon. Let cool slightly, then shred into bite-size pieces; cover to keep warm. Let braising liquid settle for 5 minutes, then remove fat from surface using large spoon.

4. Strain liquid through fine-mesh strainer into medium saucepan. Bring to simmer and cook until slightly thickened and measures ½ cup, 10 to 15 minutes. Whisk in remaining 1½ teaspoons sugar, vinegar, ketchup, and liquid smoke and bring to simmer.

5. Toss shredded pork with ½ cup sauce; add more sauce as needed to keep meat moist. Season pork with salt and pepper to taste and serve with remaining sauce.

SLOW-COOKER SPICY SAUSAGE RAGU

WE LOVE THE CLASSIC ITALIAN PAIRING OF SAUSAGE and peppers and set out to transform this duo into a hearty ragu using the slow cooker. Though most ragus require close monitoring of the stovetop and result in enough sauce to feed a big Italian family, we would use the slow cooker to deliver a richly flavored sauce that could simmer away during the day, so we could enjoy a satisfying spaghetti dinner for just two that night. We thought the big flavor of spicy Italian sausage would stand up to the long cooking time and moist environment of the slow cooker.

But before we addressed the meat, we had to determine the right mix of tomato products. Ideally, our ragu would be slightly chunky, with small bites of tomato throughout. The test kitchen usually relies on canned whole tomatoes, crushed by hand, to ensure the same texture in marinara sauce, so we decided to start there. After several hours in the slow cooker, our hand-crushed whole tomatoes gave us tender bites of tomato, but the sauce overall was too watery. We decided to give diced tomatoes a shot, but we got the same results. It was clear we'd need to use a combination of tomato products.

For the next test, we combined diced tomatoes with crushed tomatoes, which we thought would give us tender bites of tomato in a somewhat thickened sauce without dirtying our hands. The resulting sauce was fine, but tasters much preferred the batch where we swapped crushed tomatoes for canned tomato sauce, which offered

SLOW-COOKER SPICY SAUSAGE RAGU WITH RED PEPPER

a smoother consistency and deeper flavor. After six hours in the slow cooker, our sauce had body, discernible tomato chunks, and a robust, bold tomato flavor.

To round out the flavor of the sauce, we turned to our aromatics. A minced onion, a couple of cloves of garlic, and a sprinkling of fresh oregano added the characteristic Italian backbone. A dab of tomato paste added depth, and a pinch of red pepper flakes gave our sauce a hint of heat. After sautéing our aromatics for about five minutes to deepen their flavors and soften the vegetables, we added a splash of red wine for acidity. With our ragu in order, it was time to tackle the sausage and peppers.

After a number of tests, we determined that 8 ounces of sausage gave our scaled-down ragu plenty of spicy, meaty bites. We had hoped we could skip the step of browning the meat, but during our tests to figure out how much sausage we'd need, it became obvious that browning the meat was crucial. When we added raw sausage to the slow cooker, it released enough fat that the ragu was somewhat greasy. Fortunately, cooking the sausage to render its fat took mere minutes, plus we could use a portion of the fat to sauté our aromatics.

Finally, we turned to the peppers. We needed only one, and tasters preferred red over green for its vegetal sweetness. We cut our pepper into sizable ½-inch pieces so that it would retain its identity amid the sausage and tomatoes and sautéed it with the aromatics. Unfortunately, when we ladled out servings of our finished ragu, the pepper had become mushy and taken on a distractingly bitter flavor. We'd have to find a way to cook it more gently.

For our next test, we stirred in the raw pepper pieces toward the end of the cooking time, so that they would be in the slow cooker for just 20 minutes. This time, the pepper was far from overcooked—in fact, it was still crunchy. Not wanting to mind the slow cooker earlier than we had to—thus taking away from the walk-away convenience of our meal—we decided to change gears and turned to the microwave. After just five minutes, the pepper pieces were nicely softened but still retained some bite. We stirred the pepper, along with a couple of tablespoons of fresh parsley, into the sauce, then tossed it all with a pile of hot spaghetti.

With rich, meaty flavor and tender bites of sweet pepper, our sausage ragu was perfect—and the perfect comforting, hearty supper to come home to after a long day.

Slow-Cooker Spicy Sausage Ragu with Red Pepper

MAKES 3 CUPS, ENOUGH TO SAUCE 6 OUNCES PASTA

We like to serve this sauce with spaghetti. *Cooking time: 6 to 7 hours on low or 3 to 4 hours on high*

1½	tablespoons olive oil
8	ounces hot Italian sausage, casings removed
1	small onion, chopped fine
2	garlic cloves, minced
1½	teaspoons tomato paste
1½	teaspoons minced fresh oregano or ½ teaspoon dried
	Pinch red pepper flakes
¼	cup dry red wine
1	(14.5-ounce) can diced tomatoes
1	(8-ounce) can tomato sauce
1	red bell pepper, stemmed, seeded, and cut into ½-inch pieces
2	tablespoons minced fresh parsley
	Salt and pepper

1. Lightly spray inside of slow cooker with vegetable oil spray. Heat 1 tablespoon oil in 10-inch skillet over medium-high heat until just smoking. Add sausage and brown well, breaking up pieces with wooden spoon, about 5 minutes; transfer to slow cooker using slotted spoon.

2. Pour off all but 1 tablespoon fat left in skillet. Add onion, garlic, tomato paste, oregano, and pepper flakes and cook over medium heat until softened and lightly browned, 5 to 7 minutes. Stir in wine, scraping up any browned bits, and simmer until thickened, about 1 minute; transfer to slow cooker.

3. Stir tomatoes and tomato sauce into slow cooker. Cover and cook until sausage is tender and sauce is deeply flavored, 6 to 7 hours on low or 3 to 4 hours on high.

4. Let sauce settle for 5 minutes, then remove fat from surface using large spoon. Microwave bell pepper with remaining 1½ teaspoons oil in bowl, stirring occasionally, until tender, about 5 minutes. Stir softened bell pepper and parsley into sauce and season with salt and pepper to taste. Serve.

REMOVING SAUSAGE FROM ITS CASING

To remove sausage from its casing, hold sausage link firmly on one end and squeeze sausage out of opposite end.

SLOW-COOKER ITALIAN-STYLE STUFFED PEPPERS

STUFFED BELL PEPPERS ARE A POPULAR ITALIAN-American dish—and with their rich, savory filling and appealing mix of textures, it's easy to see why. But getting this hearty entrée to the table involves parcooking the peppers; cooking the rice; sautéing vegetables, meat, and other filling ingredients; and (finally) stuffing and baking the peppers—which adds up to a lot of work for a simple supper for two. We wanted to transfer our stuffed peppers from the oven to the slow cooker, and streamline the process as much as possible along the way, for a practically no-prep dinner.

Unfortunately, despite the bevy of slow-cooker stuffed pepper recipes available, not one could deliver a remotely edible result: Even the most successful recipe managed to turn what was a light and fluffy stuffing into a dense mass inside each pepper with blown-out rice and sodden globs of meatball. Not only that, but the slow cooker drained away any flavor contributed to the filling by the seasonings and cheese, a common ingredient in stuffed peppers that works to bind the filling ingredients. The one bright spot was that the long, low heat of the slow cooker eliminated the tiresome task of standing over a pot of boiling water and dropping in and fishing out the peppers to soften them before they are stuffed. The peppers just needed a little bit of water in the slow cooker insert so they could steam until tender and silken but still whole.

First things first, we tackled the rice. For our streamlined slow-cooker supper, we hoped to find a way to eliminate any extra steps, such as precooking the rice before stuffing it in the peppers. We tried additions of raw long-grain rice as well as instant rice, and neither came close to being acceptable—the raw rice never cooked through, and the instant rice turned completely to mush. Partially cooked rice fared better, but an extra 10 to 15 minutes of prep time was unacceptable for our goal of easy-prep stuffed peppers. Instead, we turned to leftover rice. When cooking for two, leftover rice is a common curse, so we thought this would be the perfect way to put those extras to good use (although packaged precooked rice works just as well). We added half a cup of rice to our mixture, making sure to keep the rest of the filling relatively dry (in the hope of preventing more rice blowouts). This time, the rice was close to perfect but was still just a little blown out at the edges. Hoping that better circulation inside the peppers would promote even cooking, we poked holes in the peppers. Now the rice emerged tender and evenly cooked.

Now that the rice was finally on target, we looked for ways to boost flavor in the other ingredients. To begin, we replaced the ground beef of traditional recipes with Italian sausage, which is seasoned with a number of herbs and spices. Fortunately, we found we could get away with not browning the sausage; any excess fat that would have been rendered was simply absorbed by the rice, which gave us an even more flavorful dinner and meant we didn't have to bother with lugging out a skillet.

Next, we tested a number of different cheeses. Mozzarella made the filling gummy without injecting much flavor. Cheddar added creaminess, but its strong flavor seemed out of place with the sausage. Monterey Jack, on the other hand, proved to be a creamy and neutral binding agent, and a small addition of Parmesan added another huge boost in flavor without adding much moisture.

As far as aromatics were concerned, we wanted to stick to a simple combination of onion, garlic, tomato paste, and red pepper flakes in order to enhance, but not overwhelm, the flavor of the sausage and peppers. But what would be the best method of incorporation? We tried adding the aromatics to the peppers raw and wound up with acrid, sweaty onion flavor permeating our peppers. To soften and temper the bite of the

SUPPORTING STUFFED PEPPERS

When using a large slow cooker, it is necessary to give the stuffed peppers extra support to keep them stable and prevent them from tipping over.

1. Create foil ring by loosely rolling 26 by 12-inch piece of foil into cylinder. Bend sides in to form oval ring that measures 8 inches long and 6 inches wide. Place in center of slow cooker.

2. Place peppers in slow cooker, leaning them against each other and foil ring, so that peppers remain upright during cooking.

onion and garlic, we'd need to cook them first. Since we weren't browning the sausage before stuffing, we turned to the microwave, which we've found works well to jump-start the cooking of aromatics in recipes where the stovetop isn't required (or desired). Five minutes was plenty of time to soften the aromatics and bloom the tomato paste. We stirred this potent mixture into our rice, sausage, cheese, and chopped pepper tops (for a burst of color); stuffed it all gently into our peppers; and popped them into the slow cooker.

A few hours later, our peppers were ready. With a sprinkling of grated Parmesan and chopped basil, our updated (and effortless) take on a typically labor-intensive Italian classic was complete.

Slow-Cooker Italian-Style Stuffed Bell Peppers
SERVES 2

Try to choose peppers with flat bottoms so that they stay upright in the slow cooker. This recipe works great with cold leftover rice, but packaged precooked rice (we prefer Uncle Ben's Ready Rice) works just as well. If using a 6-quart slow cooker, use a foil ring to keep the peppers upright during cooking. *Cooking time: 3 to 4 hours on low*

1 small onion, chopped fine
3 garlic cloves, minced
2 teaspoons extra-virgin olive oil
1½ teaspoons tomato paste
   Pinch red pepper flakes
2 red, yellow, or orange bell peppers
8 ounces hot or sweet Italian sausage, casings removed
½ cup cooked rice
1½ ounces Monterey Jack cheese, shredded (⅓ cup)
2 tablespoons grated Parmesan cheese, plus extra for serving
   Salt and pepper
1 tablespoon chopped fresh basil

1. Lightly spray inside of slow cooker with vegetable oil spray. Microwave onion, garlic, oil, tomato paste, and pepper flakes in bowl, stirring occasionally, until onion is softened, about 5 minutes.

2. Cut top ½ inch off of each pepper. Chop pepper tops into ¼-inch pieces, discarding stems. Set aside. Remove core and seeds from peppers. Using skewer, poke 4 holes in bottom of each pepper.

3. In large bowl, mix onion mixture, chopped pepper tops, sausage, cooked rice, Monterey Jack, Parmesan, ½ teaspoon salt, and ¼ teaspoon pepper together using hands. Pack filling evenly into cored peppers.

4. Pour ⅓ cup water into slow cooker and place foil ring in center of slow cooker, if using. Place stuffed peppers upright inside of foil ring. Cover and cook until peppers are tender, 3 to 4 hours on low.

5. Using tongs and slotted spoon, carefully transfer peppers to individual plates, discarding cooking liquid. Sprinkle with basil and extra Parmesan and serve.

SLOW-COOKER TURKEY CHILI

IN AN EFFORT TO LIGHTEN UP THE DINNER HOUR but keep all the rich, hearty flavor intact, many chili recipes swap the usual ground beef for ground turkey. Unfortunately, most of these recipes aren't pretty. While ground beef cooks up pleasantly tender with real meaty flavor, ground turkey often dries out or, worse, dissolves into flavorless, mealy pieces. The slow cooker exacerbates these problems, as the turkey has many hours in which to overcook. We didn't want to settle for lackluster chili and instead insisted that our turkey chili rival beef chili with hearty bites of moist, well-seasoned meat in a thick, mellow, gently spicy sauce. And our chili had to be scaled down for a smaller household.

To start our testing, we turned to the turkey. Many slow-cooker recipes call for adding raw ground turkey directly to the slow cooker. While it's certainly convenient, we had our doubts about whether this was really the best technique. To find out, we put together a basic working recipe with beans, tomatoes, and chili powder and pitted raw turkey against a browned competitor. After 4½ hours in the slow cooker, the raw turkey had disintegrated into mushy pellets, but the browned meat remained in more pleasant and discernible pieces. Unfortunately, even the browned turkey was flavorless and dry. To keep the meat moist, we borrowed a trick from test kitchen recipes for meatballs, in which a panade—a mixture of milk and bread—is employed to ensure that the meat stays tender. After mashing a slice of bread with a spoonful of milk, we added the turkey and browned the whole mixture before adding it to the slow cooker. Once we'd figured out the flavor profile of the rest of the chili, we'd return to the flavor of the turkey itself.

To build our chili base, we next turned to the aromatic components. Since we had already brought out the skillet to brown the turkey, we decided to go ahead and sauté our aromatics and spices in the pan. Onion, garlic, and chili powder were obvious inclusions, but our chili would need a little more oomph to stand up to the extended cooking time. We tested a variety of additions, but only a select few made the cut. Ground cumin added pleasant warmth, canned chipotle chiles contributed smoky complexity, and a little brown sugar balanced the heat of the chili powder. To add meaty depth, we browned a tablespoon of tomato paste in the skillet with the aromatics, then stirred 1½ tablespoons of soy sauce into the slow cooker with the aromatic mixture.

With our aromatics and spices in balance, we moved on to the other core components: tomatoes and beans. While both of these ingredients are often the subject of much debate concerning their rightful presence in chili, we found that we liked both in this recipe. Half a can of pinto beans was just the right amount to complement but not overwhelm the meat. The tomato issue was a little trickier. We liked the brightness added by canned

diced tomatoes, but one 14.5-ounce can wasn't enough to give our chili the volume it needed to cook without burning. We didn't want to have to use a portion of a larger can, and other tomato products, such as crushed tomatoes and tomato sauce, made our chili too sweet. Instead, we added a little extra liquid in the form of chicken broth, then bulked up the missing tomato flavor with another spoonful of tomato paste.

Our chili was humming along nicely, but the turkey was still glaringly bland. Wondering how we could ramp up its flavor, we evaluated the panade: Instead of milk, we tried using the soy sauce we'd been adding to the chili, then mashed in some of the chili spices and garlic for extra flavor insurance. This time, the turkey was beginning to turn a corner, but the spices in the meat weren't quite as prominent as we would have liked. One taster suggested toasting them in advance to bring out all of their flavor before incorporating them into the panade. This quick extra step did the trick, ensuring that our Slow-Cooker Turkey Chili was full of robust, hearty flavor.

Slow-Cooker Turkey Chili

SERVES 2, WITH LEFTOVERS

Be sure to use ground turkey, not ground turkey breast (also labeled 99 percent fat free), in this recipe. Serve with shredded cheese, sour cream, and lime wedges. See page 34 for a recipe to use up the leftover pinto beans. *Cooking time: 4 to 5 hours on low*

- 1½ tablespoons chili powder
- 1 teaspoon ground cumin
- 1 slice hearty white sandwich bread, crusts removed, torn into 1-inch pieces
- 1½ tablespoons soy sauce
- 2 garlic cloves, minced
  Salt and pepper
- 12 ounces ground turkey
- 1 tablespoon vegetable oil
- 1 small onion, chopped fine
- 2 tablespoons tomato paste
- 1 (14.5-ounce) can diced tomatoes
- ¾ cup canned pinto beans, rinsed
- ½ cup low-sodium chicken broth
- 1 teaspoon packed brown sugar
- ¾ teaspoon minced canned chipotle chile in adobo sauce

1. Lightly spray inside of slow cooker with vegetable oil spray. Heat chili powder and cumin in 10-inch nonstick skillet over medium heat, stirring frequently, until fragrant, about 1 minute. Transfer to small bowl.

2. Mash bread, soy sauce, 1½ teaspoons toasted spices, half of garlic, and ¼ teaspoon pepper into paste in large bowl using fork. Using hands, mix in ground turkey until well combined.

3. Heat oil in now-empty skillet over medium heat until shimmering. Add onion and cook until softened, 5 to 7 minutes. Stir in remaining toasted spices, remaining garlic, and tomato paste and cook until paste begins to darken, 1 to 2 minutes. Stir in turkey mixture and cook, breaking up meat with wooden spoon, until no longer pink, about 2 minutes. Transfer to slow cooker. Stir tomatoes, beans, broth, sugar, and chipotle into slow cooker. Cover and cook until turkey is tender, 4 to 5 hours on low.

4. Let chili settle for 5 minutes, then remove fat from surface using large spoon. Break up any remaining large pieces of turkey with spoon. Season with salt and pepper to taste. Serve.

SLOW-COOKER TUSCAN CHICKEN STEW

WHILE WE HAVE PLENTY OF EXPERIENCE COOKING chicken stew in a Dutch oven, we wondered if this type of hearty stew could be successfully replicated in a slow cooker and scaled down to serve two. Our goal was a chicken stew that would come together easily and could be left to simmer away on its own but, when it was dinnertime, still offered the same tender chicken, well-cooked vegetables, and velvety sauce. To keep our chicken stew from becoming ho-hum, we decided to add Italian sausage and creamy white beans to the mix, for a Tuscan take on this comforting dish.

Past tests have shown us that chicken thighs are the best choice for stew because they remain moist and tender over a long cooking time. In addition, the richer dark meat pairs especially well with the hearty flavors and thick sauce typical of stews. But we still had a few decisions to make: Should we use boneless or bone-in thighs, and did they need to be browned before going into the slow cooker? After a handful of tests, we had our answers. Though the bone-in thighs provided slightly more flavor, shredding them into fork-friendly, bite-size pieces (which we'd then stir back into the stew) was more cumbersome than shredding the boneless thighs, as we also had to remove the skin and bones. For convenience's sake, we opted to go with the boneless chicken. When it came to the browning question, we decided it was essential. Although it added a few minutes to our prep time, this step led to the development of a rich fond on the bottom of the pan that added deep flavor to our stew.

Moving on to the sausage, a single link gave our stew just enough meaty oomph without taking over. We sliced the sausage into rounds and browned them so that they would retain a noticeable presence in the finished dish. Now we could utilize the rendered sausage fat to sauté our aromatics.

For our aromatics, we found that an onion and a couple of garlic cloves provided the right backbone for our stew. To this mixture we added fresh thyme, a bay leaf, and a teaspoon of tomato paste for depth and complexity. A few spoonfuls of white wine worked to deglaze the pan and pull up all the rich, flavorful browned bits. After transferring this mixture to the slow cooker, we stirred in 1½ cups of chicken broth, half a can of cannellini beans, and our browned sausage and chicken. Four hours later, we reached for our forks. Sadly, the results were mixed. The good news was that the chicken was moist, tender, and flavorful; the bad news, however, was that the sauce was thin and watery, and the delicate white beans had blown out and turned to mush.

We decided to focus on the sauce before addressing the beans. To thicken stews and sauces, many slow-cooker recipes turn to flour or cornstarch, mixed with a small amount of liquid to create a slurry, which is stirred in at the end of the cooking time. While both of these options worked, the flour imparted a raw taste, and the cornstarch required at least a little extra cooking time to properly thicken the stew. Since we were already using our skillet to brown the chicken and sausage and sauté the aromatics, we decided to stick with the flour and cook it with the aromatics to rid it of its raw flavor. Once our garlic and onion were softened and nicely browned, we added a tablespoon of flour to the pan and let it cook for a minute. Then we added the broth and wine, transferred the sauce to the slow cooker, nestled in the meats, and hit the start button. A few hours later, our stew was nicely thickened, and not only was the sauce flavorful but it also had the ideal velvety texture.

Finally, we turned to the beans, which simply needed less cooking time. After we removed the chicken so it could cool and be shredded, we stirred in the beans and let them heat through. Just 10 minutes was enough for the beans to soften slightly and meld with the other elements of the stew.

At last, our rustic chicken stew boasted rich flavor and a thick, velvety sauce, but it needed a bit of green to perk it up. A few handfuls of baby spinach, stirred in at the end to wilt, did the trick.

With a sprinkling of nutty, salty Parmesan, our Tuscan-inspired chicken stew for two was just as flavorful as it was fuss free.

Slow-Cooker Tuscan Chicken Stew with Sausage, White Beans, and Spinach

SERVES 2

Serve with crusty bread. See page 54 for a recipe to use up the leftover cannellini beans. *Cooking time: 3 to 4 hours on low*

- 4 (3-ounce) boneless, skinless chicken thighs, trimmed
  Salt and pepper
- 2 tablespoons vegetable oil
- 4 ounces Italian sausage, sliced ½ inch thick
- 1 onion, chopped fine
- 2 garlic cloves, minced
- 1 teaspoon tomato paste
- ¾ teaspoon minced fresh thyme or ⅛ teaspoon dried
  Pinch red pepper flakes
- 1 tablespoon all-purpose flour
- 1½ cups low-sodium chicken broth
- 3 tablespoons dry white wine
- 1 bay leaf
- ¾ cup canned cannellini beans, rinsed
- 2 ounces (2 cups) baby spinach
  Grated Parmesan cheese

1. Lightly spray inside of slow cooker with vegetable oil spray. Pat chicken dry with paper towels and season with salt and pepper. Heat 1 tablespoon oil in 10-inch skillet over medium-high heat until just smoking. Brown chicken on both sides, 5 to 8 minutes; transfer to bowl.

2. Heat remaining 1 tablespoon oil in now-empty skillet over medium-high heat until just smoking. Brown sausage well, 3 to 5 minutes; transfer to bowl with chicken. Pour off all but 1 tablespoon fat left in pan and add onion, garlic, tomato paste, thyme, and pepper flakes. Cook over medium heat until vegetables are softened and lightly browned, 5 to 7 minutes.

3. Stir in flour and cook for 1 minute. Slowly whisk in ½ cup broth and wine, scraping up any browned bits and smoothing out any lumps; transfer sauce to slow cooker. Stir remaining 1 cup broth and bay leaf into slow cooker. Nestle browned chicken, sausage, and any accumulated juices into slow cooker and toss to coat with sauce. Cover and cook until chicken is tender and fork slips easily in and out of meat, 3 to 4 hours on low.

4. Transfer chicken to cutting board, let cool slightly, then shred into bite-size pieces. Let stew settle for 5 minutes, then remove fat from surface using large spoon. Discard bay leaf.

5. Stir beans and spinach into slow cooker, cover, and cook on high until spinach wilts and beans are heated through, about 10 minutes. Stir in shredded chicken and let sit until heated through, about 5 minutes. Season with salt and pepper to taste. Serve with Parmesan.

NOTES FROM THE TEST KITCHEN

TRIMMING CHICKEN THIGHS
Trimming and removing excess fat from chicken thighs before adding them to the slow cooker reduces the amount of fat that can be rendered and helps to prevent the dish from becoming greasy.

Holding one hand on top of chicken thigh, trim off any excess fat with sharp knife.

SLOW-COOKER BALSAMIC-BRAISED CHICKEN WITH SWISS CHARD

SLOW-COOKER BALSAMIC-BRAISED CHICKEN

RIDING HIGH ON THE SUCCESS OF OUR TUSCAN chicken stew (page 229), we now looked to create a simple braised chicken dish using the slow cooker. Inspired this time by the classic Italian pairing of chicken and balsamic vinegar, we wanted to develop a recipe that offered moist, tender meat accentuated by a brightly flavored sauce. The challenge would lie in keeping the assertive balsamic vinegar in check—we wanted the mild chicken to be coated in a sauce that was intensely flavored, yet not overpoweringly so.

The chicken was the natural starting point for our testing. Since we knew that we wanted rich, deeply flavored meat that would stand up to a hearty sauce, we opted for chicken thighs. Although boneless thighs proved the right cut for our stew, we thought bone-in thighs would provide the deeper flavor we wanted in our braise. After just one test with a working recipe, it turned out that our initial instincts were right—while the boneless thighs worked great in a stew, they couldn't compete with the bone-in option in this application. But we noticed that the skin made the finished dish far too greasy. Simply removing the skin prior to cooking solved this problem, and the intramuscular fat (along with the bone) kept even the skinless chicken moist throughout cooking. Finally, in the hope of keeping things simple, we decided to skip the browning step for now, figuring that the sauce would offer plenty of flavor.

To build our sauce, we tried the easiest approach first. We combined a handful of uncooked aromatics (a shallot, thyme, garlic, and red pepper flakes) with a few tablespoons of balsamic vinegar and a tablespoon of red wine in the slow cooker. For brightness and depth, we added half a can of diced tomatoes and a small amount of tomato paste, then nestled the chicken into the sauce. Four hours later, the chicken emerged moist and tender, but the sauce was bitter, acidic, and full of harsh-tasting shallot pieces. This wouldn't do. Wanting to avoid pulling out the skillet, we tried microwaving the aromatics with the tomato paste and a little oil to deepen their flavors and replicate the flavor that comes from browning. We added this mixture to the slow cooker and stirred in our liquid ingredients. After adding the raw chicken to the slow cooker, we hit the start button and busied ourselves elsewhere for a few hours.

The results were a mixed bag—the chicken was tender, but the sauce still needed help. The combination of vinegar and wine remained abrasive, and the sauce itself was thin and lacked depth. In the past, the test kitchen has found that reducing balsamic vinegar goes a long way toward improving its flavor. We knew that it would take quite a while to reduce vinegar in the microwave, so we settled on bringing our microwaved ingredients out to the skillet. In our next test, we sautéed our aromatics and tomato paste in olive oil, then added the balsamic vinegar and wine to the skillet. The small amount of liquid needed no time at all to reduce by half, and already the flavor had improved. Now we had to fix the consistency of the sauce.

As in our chicken stew, we decided this was a recipe where flour would work best as the thickening agent to create a full-bodied sauce. We added it to the skillet after we'd sautéed the aromatics, let its raw flavor cook off, then added the vinegar and reduced it. We transferred our new sauce base to the slow cooker and stirred in the tomatoes and a little chicken broth for balance.

Concentrating the flavor of the balsamic vinegar and thickening the sauce improved our final dish a great deal, lending silky and smooth texture with no hints of the harshness present in earlier tests. Yet our dish was still missing a bit of freshness. We thought that some greens, such as spinach, kale, or Swiss chard, might liven

NOTES FROM THE TEST KITCHEN

PREPARING SWISS CHARD

1. To prepare Swiss chard, first cut away leafy green portion from either side of stalk using chef's knife.

2. Next, stack several leaves on top of one another and slice crosswise into ½-inch strips. Wash and dry after leaves are cut, using salad spinner.

things up. Spinach didn't have enough presence to stand up to the robust sauce, and kale never fully integrated. Swiss chard worked better; it stood up to the hearty flavors of the braise, adding a touch of earthy bitterness.

Though our slow-cooker braise was updated for the modern-day cook, it still boasted all the great flavors and textures of old-world Italian cuisine.

Slow-Cooker Balsamic-Braised Chicken with Swiss Chard

SERVES 2

Serve with polenta. See page 54 for a recipe to use up the leftover diced tomatoes. *Cooking time: 3 to 4 hours on low*

1	tablespoon extra-virgin olive oil
1	shallot, minced
1½	teaspoons minced fresh thyme or ½ teaspoon dried
¾	teaspoon tomato paste
1	garlic clove, minced
	Pinch red pepper flakes
1	tablespoon all-purpose flour
2½	tablespoons balsamic vinegar
1	tablespoon dry red wine
½	cup canned diced tomatoes, drained
½	cup low-sodium chicken broth
1	bay leaf
4	(6-ounce) bone-in chicken thighs, skin removed, trimmed
	Salt and pepper
2	ounces Swiss chard, stemmed, leaves sliced ½ inch thick

1. Lightly spray inside of slow cooker with vegetable oil spray. Heat oil in 10-inch skillet over medium heat until shimmering. Add shallot, thyme, tomato paste, garlic, and pepper flakes and cook until shallot is softened and lightly browned, 2 to 3 minutes. Stir in flour and cook for 1 minute. Slowly whisk in vinegar and wine, scraping up any browned bits and smoothing out any lumps, and simmer until thickened, about 30 seconds. Transfer to slow cooker.

2. Stir tomatoes, broth, and bay leaf into slow cooker. Season chicken with salt and pepper and nestle into slow cooker, tossing to coat with sauce. Cover and cook until chicken is tender and fork slips easily in and out of meat, 3 to 4 hours on low.

3. Gently stir in chard, cover, and cook on high until tender, about 20 minutes. Transfer chicken to serving platter, tent loosely with aluminum foil, and let rest for 5 to 10 minutes. Let braising liquid settle for 5 minutes, then remove fat from surface using large spoon. Discard bay leaf. Season with salt and pepper to taste. Spoon ½ cup sauce over chicken and serve with remaining sauce.

SLOW-COOKER GINGERY CHICKEN BREASTS

NOW THAT WE HAD A COUPLE OF SUCCESSFUL SLOW-cooker recipes for chicken thighs under our belt, we moved on to another cut: the chicken breast. The mild flavor of white meat pairs well with many flavor profiles, but we were in the mood for an Asian-influenced dinner and looked to dress up our chicken with a boldly flavored ginger sauce. Given that the low, slow cooking environment of the slow cooker can dull big flavors, we'd have to find a way to ensure a potently flavored sauce, even after a few hours of cooking. But before we could even think about the sauce, we'd need to make sure we had the cooking method down pat.

We started by determining whether bone-in or boneless chicken breasts would work best in the slow cooker. We suspected that the bone-in pieces would be the optimum choice, as the bones would keep the chicken moist and tender. Just one test confirmed this theory. But even the bone-in breasts were dry if we cooked them any longer than four hours on low, which was our established upper limit for slow-cooked chicken thighs.

Although we could get away with not searing the chicken thighs in our richly flavored braise, we suspected our leaner chicken breasts would need to be browned to provide a deeper flavor base. We decided to run a few tests to confirm our hypothesis. We placed two unbrowned chicken breasts in one slow cooker. In a second slow cooker we placed two breasts that we'd seared in a skillet. Both were covered with a basic sauce of chicken broth, soy sauce, and ginger. Three hours later, we found that the browned chicken and accompanying sauce boasted richer, deeper flavor than the unbrowned chicken. Not only that, but we could also take advantage of the flavorful fond left behind to sauté the aromatics for our sauce, thereby giving it more depth. To ensure that the finished dish wasn't greasy, we removed the skin from the browned chicken before we placed it in the slow cooker. Next, we turned to building a flavorful sauce.

We sautéed a minced shallot, a tablespoon of grated ginger, and a couple of cloves of garlic in the fond left behind from searing the chicken. This mixture went into the slow cooker along with ½ cup of chicken broth and a tablespoon of soy sauce. A few hours later, the sauce was plenty fragrant, but its flavor was disappointing. The ginger had become muted over the long cooking time, giving us a one-note chicken dish that tasted of soy sauce alone. To add insult to injury, the sauce was thin and watery.

We decided to address the flavor of the sauce first and started by doubling the amount of grated ginger. Surprisingly, this made little difference in terms of flavor, but it did affect the texture of the sauce, which now had a distractingly stringy feel from the small pieces of ginger. We scaled back to our original amount and instead decided to reserve some of the ginger until the end of cooking. We sautéed 2 teaspoons of ginger with our aromatics, then stirred in the remaining teaspoon once the chicken was tender. Rich ginger flavor now permeated the entire dish. For one last flavor tweak, we stirred in a teaspoon of sugar, which worked to balance the savory notes of the sauce.

Finally, we needed to ensure that the sauce had body and would cling nicely to our chicken breasts. We'd had luck using flour to thicken slow-cooker sauces in the past, so we decided to give it a whirl here. Just a tablespoon did the trick, giving the sauce presence and body without making it too thick. Briefly cooking the flour with our sautéed aromatics helped to rid it of its raw flavor.

A sprinkle of thinly sliced scallions gave our gingery chicken breasts the perfect fresh finishing touch and a nice pop of color.

Slow-Cooker Gingery Chicken Breasts
SERVES 2

Serve with Simple White Rice (page 73). *Cooking time: 3 to 4 hours on low*

- 2 (12-ounce) bone-in split chicken breasts, trimmed
  Salt and pepper
- 1 tablespoon vegetable oil
- 1 shallot, minced
- 1 tablespoon grated fresh ginger
- 2 garlic cloves, minced
- 1 tablespoon all-purpose flour
- ½ cup low-sodium chicken broth
- 1 tablespoon soy sauce
- 1 teaspoon sugar
- 1 scallion, sliced thin

1. Lightly spray inside of slow cooker with vegetable oil spray. Pat chicken dry with paper towels and season with salt and pepper. Heat oil in 10-inch skillet over medium-high heat until just smoking. Add chicken, skin side down, and brown lightly, about 5 minutes; transfer to plate. Let chicken cool slightly and discard skin.

2. Add shallot, 2 teaspoons ginger, and garlic to now-empty skillet and cook over medium heat until softened and lightly browned, 2 to 3 minutes. Stir in flour and cook for 1 minute. Slowly whisk in broth, scraping up any browned bits and smoothing out any lumps; transfer to slow cooker.

3. Stir soy sauce and sugar into slow cooker. Nestle browned chicken and any accumulated juices into slow cooker and toss to coat with sauce. Cover and cook until chicken is tender, 3 to 4 hours on low.

4. Transfer chicken to serving platter, tent loosely with aluminum foil, and let rest for 5 to 10 minutes. Let braising liquid settle for 5 minutes, then remove fat from surface using large spoon. Stir in remaining 1 teaspoon ginger and season with salt and pepper to taste. Spoon ½ cup sauce over chicken and sprinkle with scallions. Serve with remaining sauce.

NOTES FROM THE TEST KITCHEN

GRATING GINGER

To grate ginger, first peel small section of large piece of ginger, then grate peeled portion with rasp-style grater, using remaining ginger as handle.

CLASSIC CAESAR SALAD

SIDE DISHES

CLASSIC CAESAR SALAD

THESE DAYS, CAESAR SALADS ARE HARD TO PICK OUT of a lineup, having been gussied up with chicken or shrimp, wrapped in pita breads, and stuffed into sandwiches. We wanted to strip away the superfluous ingredients that plague modern recipes and return to the basics that made this salad a star in the first place: crisp-tender romaine lettuce napped in a creamy, garlicky dressing, with crunchy, savory croutons sprinkled throughout. We also needed to keep the size of our salad scaled down for two—after all, even the best-dressed salads make soggy, unappealing leftovers.

After doing some research, we concocted a working recipe for our Caesar dressing. Most sources follow a similar formula, and we saw no reason to buck the trend. We built a preliminary dressing with extra-virgin olive oil, lemon juice, eggs, garlic, Worcestershire sauce, Parmesan cheese, and anchovies. We immediately knew we had our work cut out for us. For starters, tasters agreed that extra-virgin olive oil was too fruity and bitter. Plus, its robust flavor was at odds with the other assertive ingredients in the dressing. We decided to replace some of the olive oil with neutral-tasting vegetable oil. After a number of tests, we found that a greater ratio of vegetable oil to olive oil worked best, providing a nice balance of flavor.

Next, we considered the eggs, which in Caesar dressing have a dual purpose: They temper the strong ingredients without making the dressing greasy, and they effectively "glue" the dressing to the lettuce. We tried a whole egg, but the white washed out the flavor of the dressing, so we cut back to just a yolk.

Now we moved on to the garlic. In our experience, the dressing's flavor depends on how this key ingredient is prepared, so we worked our way through a series of tests—everything from finely chopping the garlic with salt to rubbing whole cloves around the interior of the serving bowl. Ultimately, tasters favored one clove transformed into pulp on a rasp-style grater. The fine paste virtually disappeared into the dressing, suffusing it with a robust flavor. Still, some tasters found the dressing a bit too harsh. In search of balance, we decided to test an old trick for taming garlic: steeping it in lemon juice. We compared three dressings, one made with unsteeped garlic, one with garlic steeped before grating,

and one with garlic steeped after grating. Not surprisingly, we found the grated and then steeped garlic to be much milder than the other two. Now our dressing had a significant, yet not overwhelming, garlic presence.

When it came to the anchovies, we started with a single fillet, but its flavor was far too subtle so we doubled the amount. When mashed to a paste, the anchovies' richly savory—not fishy—flavor was evenly dispersed throughout the dressing. Per tradition, a shot of Worcestershire sauce and a small pile of grated Parmesan added even more complexity.

But our work wasn't done. As the only other major component of Caesar salad, the croutons had to be perfect—nothing like the hard, desiccated specimens in most restaurant versions. We wanted croutons bursting with flavor, but also some contrast between a crunchy crust and chewy interior crumb. That goal eliminated the use of squishy supermarket sandwich loaves, as well as super-crusty French baguettes. In the end, a small ciabatta roll—with its bubbly, chewy center and crisp exterior—worked best.

To get our croutons golden brown, we toasted, broiled, and fried ¾-inch cubes, eventually discovering that crisping the bread in a hot pan with a little extra-virgin olive oil produced the most flavorful results—although the croutons were unevenly browned and a bit parched in the center. Brainstorming for ways to keep the middle moist (and just a bit chewy), one taster suggested adding a little water. On one hand, introducing water seemed silly, since part of our goal was a crisp crust. On the other hand, what if a small amount of water could preserve the croutons' interior moistness while allowing the exteriors to brown in the skillet?

We sprinkled the bite-size cubes with a little water and salt, transferred them to an oiled nonstick skillet, and proceeded. The results were better than we expected. Our croutons were perfectly tender on the inside and browned and crunchy as could be around the edges. For a flavor boost, we tossed the cubes with a paste of raw garlic and extra-virgin olive oil and dusted them with grated Parmesan.

Once a small heart of crisp romaine was sliced and dressed, there were just two last-minute tweaks: a tableside squeeze of fresh lemon juice for brightness and a shower of extra Parmesan. Finally, we'd brought the Caesar salad back to its original state of perfection.

Classic Caesar Salad

SERVES 2

You will need 1 small ciabatta roll for this recipe. The easiest way to turn garlic cloves into a paste is to grate them on a rasp-style grater.

CROUTONS

- 2 tablespoons extra-virgin olive oil
- 1 small garlic clove, peeled and grated to fine paste
- 2 ounces ciabatta bread, cut into ¾-inch pieces (1½ cups)
- 1 tablespoon water
  Pinch salt
- 2 teaspoons grated Parmesan cheese

SALAD

- 1½ teaspoons lemon juice, plus extra for seasoning
- 1 small garlic clove, peeled and grated to fine paste
- 1 large egg yolk
- 2 anchovy fillets, rinsed, patted dry, and mashed to fine paste
- ⅛ teaspoon Worcestershire sauce
- 2½ tablespoons vegetable oil
- 2½ teaspoons extra-virgin olive oil
- ⅓ cup grated Parmesan cheese
  Salt and pepper
- 1 small romaine lettuce heart (4½ ounces), cut into ¾-inch pieces

1. FOR THE CROUTONS: Combine 1 tablespoon oil and garlic in small bowl; set aside. Place bread cubes in medium bowl. Sprinkle with water and salt. Toss, squeezing gently until bread absorbs water. Heat remaining 1 tablespoon oil in 10-inch nonstick skillet over medium-high heat until shimmering. Add soaked bread cubes and cook, stirring frequently, until browned and crisp, 7 to 10 minutes.

2. Off heat, clear center of skillet, add garlic-oil mixture, and let heat until fragrant, about 10 seconds. Stir mixture into croutons, sprinkle with Parmesan, and toss to coat. Transfer croutons to bowl and let cool.

3. FOR THE SALAD: Whisk lemon juice and garlic together in large bowl and let sit for 10 minutes.

4. Whisk egg yolk, anchovies, and Worcestershire into lemon-garlic mixture. Whisking constantly, drizzle vegetable oil and olive oil into bowl in slow, steady stream until fully emulsified. Whisk in 3 tablespoons Parmesan and season with pepper to taste.

5. Add romaine to dressing and toss to coat. Add croutons and toss gently to distribute. Season with lemon juice, salt, and pepper to taste. Sprinkle with remaining Parmesan and serve immediately.

CUCUMBER SALADS

COOL AND CRISP, CUCUMBER SALADS MAKE THE perfect bright- and fresh-tasting accompaniment to many entrées. But we've sampled tons of recipes that were a letdown, with soggy disks awash in an insipid dressing. This should be such an easy dish, so what's the problem? The starring ingredient—the cucumbers—are full of water. While all that moisture gives the cucumber its fresh, clean bite, liquid begins to seep out as soon as the vegetable is cut, diluting the dressing once the two come together. We set out to perfect the cucumber salad, so that it offered all the crisp bites and big flavor we wanted, and it had to be scaled down for two diners.

To help draw out the excess moisture, the cucumbers are often salted and left to drain before being tossed with dressing. However, this process takes at least an hour and leaves the cucumbers slightly wilted. We found that we could get rid of some of the liquid with almost no added time by draining the slices on paper towels while we mixed the dressing, but this didn't entirely solve the problem. Could we do more?

We knew the variety of cucumber we chose would also affect the crispness of the salad. In past tests, the test kitchen has found that common American cucumbers have more crunch than their seedless English cousins. While all cucumbers contain a "softening" enzyme that's activated when the vegetable is cut, breaking down its cell walls, the cell structure of the English variety is naturally weaker and thus collapses more easily. We would stick with American cucumbers for our salad.

The cuke choice settled, we moved on to how we might compensate for the dressing's inevitable dilution. We tried doubling the amount of dressing to ensure a flavor-packed salad and lessen the impact of the cucumber water, but all the soupy liquid at the bottom of the bowl was unappealing. What if instead of trying to mask the excess water, we worked with it? For our next batch, we tossed the cucumbers with an ultra-potent dressing made with 2 tablespoons of vinegar and just 1 teaspoon of oil (reversing the usual salad dressing composition of more oil than vinegar). This latest batch was better, although its flavor was a bit harsh.

That's when we recalled a recipe we'd come across in which the flavor of the dressing was concentrated and smoothed out by reducing the vinegar. We did the same: We boiled ¼ cup of vinegar until it measured 2 tablespoons; let it cool; mixed it with oil, a little salt and sugar, and the cucumbers; and let the salad stand for a few minutes—just long enough for the cucumbers to shed some liquid into the dressing. But curiously, instead of tasting more concentrated, the flavor of the dressing had flattened out. It turns out that heating vinegar drives off some of the acetic acid that gives it its tartness, and boiling is the most detrimental way to heat it, driving off many of its other flavors. Perhaps a gentle simmer might preserve more of the vinegar's character while still mellowing its sharp bite. We gave it a whirl, this time reducing our vinegar over medium-low heat before proceeding. The results were remarkably improved. The dressing now had a concentrated depth that could hold up to an influx of water.

But all was still not perfect. We found we actually missed some of the brightness of the uncooked dressing. Adding back even a little raw vinegar reintroduced the harshness we were trying to avoid, so we swapped in another, more rounded source of acid: lemon juice. We cut the reduced vinegar to 1 tablespoon (2½ tablespoons before simmering) and added 1 teaspoon of fresh lemon juice. This dressing was much improved but still slightly harsh. We dropped the lemon juice to just ¾ teaspoon, which punched up the flavors nicely without contributing too much acidity.

The tasters' only outstanding complaint was that the cucumber slices, which we'd been cutting ¼ inch thick, were a bit chunky and didn't allow enough dressing to cling to them. We sliced the cucumbers very thin so that each piece would be coated with plenty of vinaigrette.

All our salad needed now was some jazzing up. Clean-tasting cucumbers take well to bolder elements, so we added minced fresh oregano, kalamata olives, and a handful of chopped almonds for a unique Mediterranean twist. For a spicy-salty spin, we swapped in lime juice and fish sauce for the lemon, then added a fresh Thai chile, mint, and toasted peanuts. Another version sprinkled with minced jalapeño, cilantro, and pepitas was a huge hit. For a final, milder (but certainly no less flavorful) take, we added sesame oil, grated ginger, scallions, and toasted sesame seeds.

Cucumber Salad with Olives, Oregano, and Almonds

SERVES 2

The texture of this salad depends upon thinly sliced cucumbers and shallots. Be sure to slice the vegetables ⅛ to 3⁄16 inch thick. This salad is best served within 1 hour of being dressed.

- 2 small cucumbers, peeled, halved lengthwise, seeded, and sliced thin
- 2½ tablespoons white wine vinegar
- 1 teaspoon extra-virgin olive oil
- 1 teaspoon sugar
- ¾ teaspoon lemon juice
- Salt and pepper
- 2 tablespoons chopped pitted kalamata olives
- 1 small shallot, sliced thin
- ½ teaspoon minced fresh oregano
- ½ teaspoon minced fresh parsley
- 1½ tablespoons sliced almonds, toasted and chopped coarse

1. Line baking sheet with paper towels and evenly spread cucumber slices on sheet. Refrigerate while preparing dressing.

2. Bring vinegar to simmer in small saucepan over medium-low heat; continue to simmer until reduced to 1 tablespoon, 3 to 5 minutes. Transfer to large bowl and let cool to room temperature, about 5 minutes. Whisk in oil, sugar, lemon juice, ½ teaspoon salt, and pinch pepper until well combined.

3. Add cucumbers, olives, shallot, oregano, and parsley to dressing and toss to combine. Let sit for 5 minutes, then toss to redistribute dressing. Season with salt and pepper to taste and sprinkle with almonds. Serve.

CUCUMBER SALAD WITH OLIVES, OREGANO, AND ALMONDS

SEEDING A CUCUMBER

Peel and halve cucumber lengthwise. Run small spoon inside each cucumber half to scoop out seeds and surrounding liquid.

VARIATIONS

Cucumber Salad with Chile, Mint, and Peanuts

To make this dish spicier, add the chile seeds.

Substitute vegetable oil for olive oil and increase sugar to 1¼ teaspoons. Substitute lime juice for lemon juice and omit pepper. Add 1½ teaspoons fish sauce and 1 seeded and minced Thai chile to dressing in step 2. Omit olives and shallot, and substitute 2 tablespoons minced fresh mint for oregano and parsley and 2 tablespoons coarsely chopped toasted peanuts for almonds.

Cucumber Salad with Jalapeño, Cilantro, and Pepitas

To make this dish spicier, add the chile seeds. Pepitas, or pumpkin seeds, are available in most supermarkets and natural foods stores.

Substitute lime juice for lemon juice. Omit pepper. Add 1 teaspoon grated lime zest and ½ seeded and minced jalapeño chile to dressing in step 2. Omit olives and shallot, and substitute ½ cup minced fresh cilantro for oregano and parsley and toasted pepitas for almonds.

Cucumber Salad with Ginger, Sesame, and Scallions

Substitute toasted sesame oil for olive oil and increase sugar to 1¼ teaspoons. Substitute lime juice for lemon juice and omit pepper. Add 1 teaspoon grated fresh ginger to dressing in step 2. Omit olives and shallot, and substitute 2 thinly sliced scallions for oregano and parsley and toasted sesame seeds for almonds.

ITALIAN BREAD SALAD (PANZANELLA)

RUSTIC ITALIAN CUISINE AT ITS BEST, *PANZANELLA* is a simple salad in which tomatoes are cut into chunks, tossed with bread pieces, and dressed with olive oil and vinegar. When the salad is done well, the tomatoes give up some of their sweet juice to mix with the tangy dressing and moisten the dry bread until it's soft and just a little chewy. We wanted to create a recipe for panzanella for two, as this would be the perfect way to turn the extras from a hearty, thick-crusted loaf into something more. To make the most of this rustic dish, we knew we'd want to use ripe, juicy tomatoes, and we'd need to get the bread just right so it was moderately soaked—not drenched—with a bright vinaigrette.

We started with the bread. Like many other peasant dishes, panzanella started out as a way to make use of day-old bread. But in the test kitchen, we prefer to skip the stale bread and start with a fresh loaf, which we cut into pieces that we "quick-stale" by drying them in a low oven. In the past, we've found that when bread stales naturally, it becomes hard and crumbly but not necessarily dry. This crumbly yet moist interior resists the absorption of liquid. Oven-dried bread, however, loses a fair bit of moisture, thereby enhancing its ability to soak up any added liquid.

Keeping these facts in mind, we began by slicing a small section of a crusty Italian loaf into bite-size (1-inch) pieces, tossing them with a little olive oil and salt, and spreading them in an even layer on a baking sheet to dry in a 225-degree oven. After about 15 minutes, we took the bread out of the oven, let it cool, and combined it with tomato pieces and a simple dressing of olive oil and red wine vinegar. Though this salad wasn't bad, it wasn't stellar either. We had the right amount of bread (1 cup of cubes per person), but it was a little dry and unevenly moistened. In addition, the dressing tasted flat, and the salad didn't meld into a whole: The bread and tomatoes seemed like two separate components occupying the same bowl.

Leaving the bread alone for the moment, we hoped we could fix the moisture issue by focusing on the tomatoes. We knew we wanted to use enough tomatoes to make our salad a substantial side and to generate enough juice to flavor our dressing. At the same time, we wanted to strike a balance between the fruit and the bread. Two medium tomatoes gave us the right amount of fruit, but the relatively small amount of juice they gave off didn't yield enough to coat our bread.

One taster hypothesized that instead of tossing the tomatoes directly with the bread, the process might work better if we removed some of the juice first and added it directly to the salad. We tossed the cut-up tomatoes with ¼ teaspoon of salt and set them in a colander to drain. Fifteen minutes later, they'd shed a good bit of juice from which we could build our dressing. We added the bread and tomatoes and called a tasting. Everyone agreed that the bread still hadn't absorbed much of the dressing's flavor. Even worse, the tomatoes themselves were far too salty. Cutting back on the salt was an easy fix (we dialed it back to just ⅛ teaspoon), but the flavorless bread took a little more work.

Reviewing our research, we remembered that the traditional approach to panzanella calls for giving the bread a lengthy soak in water before tossing it with the other ingredients—a frugal step that meant cooks didn't have to rely as much on tomatoes and olive oil to moisten the stale loaf. But since we wanted the bread to absorb tomato flavor, it seemed silly to saturate the pieces with water. Instead, we decided to give our bread cubes a few extra minutes in the dressing before adding the other components. We mixed up the dressing, added the bread, and let it soak for about 10 minutes before stirring in the tomatoes. Tasters said that the bread was now perfectly moistened, but they clamored for just a bit more flavor from the bread itself.

This problem had a simple solution. Our 225-degree oven was doing a great job of drying out the bread, but it wasn't adding any color. Since we know that more browning equals more flavor, we cranked up the oven to 400 degrees and baked the bread until it turned light golden brown before proceeding with the recipe. The browned bread pieces tasted nutty and were lightly saturated with the flavorful dressing.

Now we could turn to the finishing touches. Thinly sliced cucumber and shallot made the cut for their crunch and fresh bite, as did chopped basil. And because we knew that this salad would become a staple, we whipped up a few variations. First, we created a version with sweet red bell pepper and spicy arugula. A piquant version with garlic, a minced anchovy, and a couple of teaspoons of capers made for a robustly flavored dish. Finally, we put a Greek spin on this Italian classic with kalamata olives and crumbled feta cheese. Each salad was just as delicious as the last, and every bit as easy.

NOTES FROM THE TEST KITCHEN

CORING AND SEEDING TOMATOES

When we prep the tomatoes for our Italian Bread Salad, we like to remove the inedible stem, the tough core, and the texturally distracting seeds.

1. To remove core, use tip of paring knife to cut around stem, angling tip of knife slightly inward. Remove cone-shaped piece of stem and core from top of tomato.

2. To seed tomato, first cut tomato in half through equator, then use your finger to pull out seeds and surrounding gel.

THE BEST RED WINE VINEGAR

Red wine vinegar has a sharp but clean flavor, making it the most versatile choice in salad dressings. While acidity is the obvious key factor in vinegar, it is actually the inherent sweetness of the grapes used to make the vinegar that makes its flavor appealing to the palate. After tasters sampled 10 red wine vinegars plain, in vinaigrette, and in pickled onions, it was clear that they found highly acidic vinegars too harsh; brands with moderate amounts of acidity scored higher. Tasters also preferred those brands that were blends—either blends of different grapes or blends of different vinegars—as they offered more-complex flavor. In the end, tasters ranked French import **Laurent du Clos Red Wine Vinegar** first. Made from a mix of red and white grapes, this vinegar won the day with its "good red wine flavor."

Italian Bread Salad (Panzanella)

SERVES 2

Be sure to use ripe and juicy in-season tomatoes and a fruity, high-quality olive oil for this salad.

  3 ounces rustic Italian or French bread, cut into 1-inch pieces (2 cups)
  ¼ cup extra-virgin olive oil
     Salt and pepper
  2 tomatoes, cored, seeded, and cut into 1-inch pieces
  1 tablespoon red wine vinegar
  ½ cucumber, peeled, halved lengthwise, seeded, and sliced thin
  2 tablespoons chopped fresh basil
  1 small shallot, sliced thin

1. Adjust oven rack to middle position and heat oven to 400 degrees. Toss bread pieces with 1 tablespoon oil and ⅛ teaspoon salt and transfer to rimmed baking sheet. Toast bread pieces until light golden brown, 10 to 12 minutes, stirring them halfway through baking. Let cool to room temperature.

2. Gently toss tomatoes and ⅛ teaspoon salt in large bowl. Transfer to colander, set colander over bowl, and let drain for 15 minutes, tossing occasionally.

3. Whisk remaining 3 tablespoons oil, vinegar, and ⅛ teaspoon pepper into drained tomato juices. Add cooled bread pieces, toss to coat, and let sit for 10 minutes, tossing occasionally.

4. Add tomatoes, cucumber, basil, and shallot to bowl with bread pieces and toss gently to coat. Season with salt and pepper to taste and serve immediately.

VARIATIONS

Italian Bread Salad with Red Bell Pepper and Arugula

Substitute ½ red bell pepper, sliced ¼ inch thick, for cucumber and ½ cup chopped baby arugula for basil.

Italian Bread Salad with Garlic and Capers

Add 1 minced small garlic clove, 1 rinsed and minced anchovy fillet, and 2 teaspoons rinsed capers to drained tomato juices in step 3.

Italian Bread Salad with Olives and Feta

Add 2 tablespoons chopped pitted kalamata olives and 3 tablespoons crumbled feta cheese to salad in step 4.

SAUTÉED SNOW PEAS

THE TYPICAL DESTINATION FOR SNOW PEAS IS A stir-fry, where the pods almost always serve as filler—never as the focal point. And if the average stir-fry served up in Chinese restaurants is anything to go by, you wouldn't want the vegetable to be any more prominent. The pods are often greasy, limp, and drowning in a salty brown sauce, with all of their delicate flavor cooked out of them. But why should this have to be the standard? If executed properly, the high-heat method of stir-frying would seem like the ideal approach to preparing the quick-cooking pods, bringing out their sweet, grassy flavor while preserving their crisp bite. We wanted to perfect this dish so that we could have an easy and flavorful side for two on the table within minutes.

It took just one test to demonstrate that things weren't quite that simple. We heated a tablespoon of vegetable oil in a medium skillet over high heat and tossed in a few handfuls of snow peas. But after several minutes of constant stirring, we found that we had produced the oily pods we recognized from Chinese takeout. While some of the pods retained a bit of crisp texture, too many had gone limp, and their subtly sweet flavor had become far too subtle.

We never intended for the snow peas to stand entirely on their own—they'd need a few supporting ingredients to bolster their understated grassy sweetness. But still, we hoped we could enhance the pods' own natural flavor first. Browning seemed like the logical answer. When vegetables are cooked over high heat, they caramelize, which causes them to take on a nutty, concentrated flavor. But the food has to be relatively stationary to let browning happen—the constant motion of stir-frying only thwarts the process.

For our next test, we decided to treat the peas as if we were searing meat to create a well-browned crust: We didn't move them until the high heat had done its work. Sure enough, this approach put us on a better track. With 6 ounces of peas (just enough for two) in our skillet, most of the pods were in contact with the hot surface. After one minute of almost undisturbed cooking—we gave them a single stir—the peas emerged bright green, crisp, and freckled with a few spots indicative of good browning. We then reverted to constant stirring for another minute or two until the pods were fully cooked through.

This new sauté method helped considerably—and we were able to cut down the oil to just 2 teaspoons to stave off greasiness. But the peas still needed more depth. When we tried to increase browning by leaving them untouched in the pan for a few extra minutes, we were back to a skillet full of limp, overcooked pods. Then we had another idea, a trick that the test kitchen often uses to promote better browning: sugar. Just ⅛ teaspoon sprinkled over the peas as they went into the hot pan, along with salt and pepper, kicked up the color in the few minutes the vegetables needed to cook through.

Now it was time for those complementary additions to make their debut. Shallot seemed like a good place to start, but when we sautéed the minced aromatic before adding the snow peas to the skillet, it ended up burning and turning bitter by the time our peas had finished cooking. Instead, we treated the shallot like garlic, which also has a tendency to burn quickly. We made a clearing in the center of the skillet after the peas were well browned and cooked the shallot with half of the oil until just fragrant. This worked much better.

For a final flavor punch, we added some acidity in the form of lemon juice (lime juice or vinegar worked equally well in our variations), and a hit of fresh herbs drew out those shy grassy flavors. With just a few changes, we had turned these once-second-fiddle pods into a real standout side dish of their own.

NOTES FROM THE TEST KITCHEN

TRIMMING SNOW PEAS

Use paring knife and thumb to snip off tip of pea and pull along flat side of pod to remove string at same time.

Sautéed Snow Peas with Lemon and Parsley
SERVES 2

Chives or tarragon can be substituted for the parsley.

2 teaspoons vegetable oil
1 small shallot, minced
¾ teaspoon grated lemon zest plus
    ½ teaspoon juice
    Salt and pepper
⅛ teaspoon sugar
6 ounces snow peas, strings removed
1 tablespoon minced fresh parsley

1. Combine 1 teaspoon oil, shallot, and lemon zest in small bowl. Combine ¼ teaspoon salt, ⅛ teaspoon pepper, and sugar in separate small bowl.

2. Heat remaining 1 teaspoon oil in 10-inch nonstick skillet over high heat until just smoking. Add snow peas, sprinkle with salt mixture, and cook, without stirring, for 30 seconds. Stir, then continue to cook, without stirring, until snow peas are beginning to brown, 30 seconds. Continue to cook, stirring constantly, until peas are crisp-tender, 1 to 2 minutes longer.

3. Clear center of skillet, add shallot mixture, and cook, mashing mixture into pan, until fragrant, about 30 seconds. Stir shallot mixture into peas, transfer to bowl, and stir in lemon juice and parsley. Season with salt and pepper to taste. Serve.

VARIATIONS

Sautéed Snow Peas with Ginger and Scallion
Substitute 2 minced scallion whites, 1½ teaspoons grated fresh ginger, and 1 minced small garlic clove for shallot and lemon zest. Substitute pinch red pepper flakes for pepper. Substitute rice vinegar for lemon juice and 2 thinly sliced scallion greens for parsley.

Sautéed Snow Peas with Cumin and Cilantro
Substitute 1 minced small garlic clove and ¼ teaspoon toasted cumin seeds for shallot. Substitute ½ teaspoon lime zest for lemon zest. Substitute lime juice for lemon juice and minced fresh cilantro for parsley.

ROASTED CARROTS

WHEN WE WANT TO COAX MAXIMUM FLAVOR OUT of hardy vegetables like beets, broccoli, and cauliflower, we pull out a roasting pan and crank up the oven. The blast of heat concentrates the vegetables' sweet, earthy notes so effectively that we have a hard time transferring them from pan to plate without eating a few first. Humble carrots, however, never seem to attain the same heights—despite the fact that, as roasting candidates go, they would seem like one of the best: Carrots contain a good amount of water (about 87 percent by weight), which theoretically should help keep their interiors tender and moist while the oven's dry heat deepens their sweetness and browns their exteriors. But all too often, roasted carrots emerge

NOTES FROM THE TEST KITCHEN

CUTTING CARROTS FOR ROASTING
Cutting carrots to a uniform size is the key to evenly cooked results when roasting.

A. For large carrots (over 1 inch in diameter), cut carrot in half crosswise, then quarter each section lengthwise to create total of 8 pieces.

B. For medium carrots (½ to 1 inch in diameter), cut carrot in half crosswise, then halve wider section lengthwise to create total of 3 pieces.

C. For small carrots (less than ½ inch in diameter), cut carrot in half crosswise, then leave both sections whole.

from the oven dry, shriveled, and jerkylike. We knew there had to be a way to get carrots that were tender and buttery on the inside, with an irresistible caramelized outer layer. Given that even for-two kitchens have a bag of carrots on hand most of the time, this could become a go-to side that matched well with any number of main dishes.

As we started our testing, we had a basic method in mind: Cut up the carrots, toss them with some oil, put them on a baking sheet, and roast them at 425 degrees for about 30 minutes until browned and tender. Before we started cooking, we needed to pick the best way to cut our carrots. When we tried roasting carrots sliced into ½-inch rounds, they retained their moisture just fine. But unless we were willing to undertake the annoying task of flipping all the rounds midway through cooking, only the sides in direct contact with the pan achieved any kind of browning. Slicing the vegetables down the middle lengthwise created more surface area for browning but required that we buy loose carrots with the same diameter to ensure that the pieces cooked evenly. We then tried cutting the carrots into evenly sized batons that were about ½ inch thick. These gave us the most evenly cooked results with the best browning—but the pieces still shriveled and turned chewy.

We decided to back up and do a little research on the composition of carrots. It turns out that they contain more pectin than any other vegetable, and even many fruits. This reminded us of a technique we had developed a few years back that capitalizes on pectin to keep apples from turning mushy when baked in pie: gently precooking them on the stove before adding them to the crust. This step allows the apples to maintain an internal temperature of 130 to 140 degrees long enough for the pectin to convert to a heat-stable form that reinforces the fruit's cell walls. This in turn keeps the slices firm when their temperature rises further during the final cooking in the oven. We realized that precooking the carrots could trigger the same reaction as in the apples: Stronger cell walls could help keep moisture in, minimizing withering.

Given that this was a simple side for two, we wanted to keep things easy, so we brainstormed methods for precooking the carrots on the baking sheet we were already using—no need to dirty extra pans if we didn't have to. What if we covered the sheet with foil when the carrots first went into the oven? The foil would trap the moisture, creating an environment where the temperature could never rise above the boiling point of water (212 degrees), and the pectin in the carrots would become activated. After a short period, we would uncover the baking sheet to finish cooking and brown and caramelize the carrots.

When we uncovered the carrots after 15 minutes and poked a fork into one carrot, it wasn't mushy at all, and it resisted just a little. This was promising. Then we slid the uncovered baking sheet back into the oven until the moisture had burned off and the carrots took on deep notes of caramelization. At last, these carrots were tender-firm and distinctly sweet, with minimal withering. We got even better results when we swapped the oil for melted butter.

Tender, creamy, and deeply sweet, these carrots had more than earned their place on the for-two dinner table.

Roasted Carrots

SERVES 2

Be sure to cut carrots into uniform batons before roasting (see page 244); otherwise, they will not cook evenly or brown properly.

  4 carrots, peeled, halved crosswise, and cut lengthwise into ½-inch-wide batons
  1 tablespoon unsalted butter, melted
     Salt and pepper

1. Adjust oven rack to middle position and heat oven to 425 degrees. Line rimmed baking sheet with aluminum foil.

2. In large bowl, toss carrots with butter, ¼ teaspoon salt, and ⅛ teaspoon pepper. Transfer to prepared sheet and spread in single layer. Cover sheet tightly with foil and cook until carrots are almost tender, about 15 minutes.

3. Remove foil and continue to cook until carrots are well browned and tender, 20 to 25 minutes, stirring twice during cooking. Transfer to serving platter and season with salt and pepper to taste. Serve.

VARIATIONS

Roasted Carrots and Fennel with Toasted Almonds and Parsley

Reduce number of carrots to 3. Add ½ fennel bulb, cored and sliced ½ inch thick, to bowl with carrots. Toss roasted vegetables with 2 tablespoons toasted sliced almonds, 1 teaspoon minced fresh parsley, and ½ teaspoon lemon juice before serving.

Roasted Carrots and Shallots with Lemon and Thyme

Reduce number of carrots to 3. Add 3 shallots, peeled and halved lengthwise, and ½ teaspoon minced fresh thyme to bowl with carrots. Toss roasted vegetables with ¾ teaspoon lemon juice before serving.

Roasted Carrots with Chermoula

Chermoula, a fragrant mix of spices along with cilantro, lemon, and garlic, is often used in Moroccan cooking.

Substitute 1 tablespoon extra-virgin olive oil for butter. While carrots roast, heat 1 tablespoon additional oil, 1 minced small garlic clove, ¼ teaspoon paprika, ⅛ teaspoon ground cumin, and pinch cayenne pepper in 8-inch skillet over medium-low heat until fragrant, about 2 minutes. Transfer to bowl, let mixture cool, and stir in 1½ teaspoons minced fresh cilantro and 1 teaspoon lemon juice. Toss with roasted carrots before serving.

SAUTÉED MUSHROOMS

DEEPLY BROWNED AND ULTRA-SAVORY, SAUTÉED mushrooms make the perfect sidekick to a variety of dishes, from pan-seared steaks to a steaming bowl of creamy polenta. But take a wrong turn, and these luscious mushrooms can turn from silky and rich to rubbery and greasy. We wanted an easy, foolproof technique for preparing sautéed mushrooms.

We hoped success would be as easy as carefully browning our mushrooms and then stirring in a knob of butter and a scattering of aromatics. But when we prepared a handful of sample recipes unearthed in our research, we were disappointed by the results: shriveled mushrooms that were either bland and boring or slicked with excess butter. These were a far cry from the earthy, deeply flavorful specimens we craved. We knew we could do better.

Our first step was to select the right mushrooms. Though specialty and high-end markets offer a wide array of wild mushrooms, we wanted to limit ourselves to mushrooms that we could pick up at the local supermarket. In addition to white and cremini mushrooms, most markets stock shiitakes and portobellos, so we test-drove a handful of each of the four in our pan. Portobellos, which we knew were fantastic when grilled (see page 169), were springy and slimy when sautéed. White mushrooms worked well, and the robustly flavored cremini did even better. Tasters also liked rich and earthy shiitakes and were especially pleased when we combined the cremini and shiitakes. But in one test, in which we cooked equal amounts of the two, we found that the shiitakes overwhelmed the delicate flavor of the cremini. We tweaked the proportions gradually, eventually settling on a 2:1 ratio of cremini, which we halved, to shiitakes, cut into ½-inch slices, for the best flavor.

The problem with our choice in mushrooms, however, was that the characteristics of the cremini mushrooms directly impeded our goal of a silky texture and a browned exterior. Because of their absorbent, spongy texture, they soaked up any and all fat in the pan. Also, due to their high water content, they flooded the skillet, which hindered browning. The sliced shiitakes might be nicely browned after about eight minutes on their own in a hot skillet, but the cremini were swimming in a lake of exuded mushroom liquid.

Sound sautéing theory told us to crank up the heat, extend the cooking time, and leave some breathing room in the skillet. These changes kept the mushrooms from stewing, but the yield was now too meager. We didn't want to take the time to cook our mushrooms in batches (and risk our cooked mushrooms growing cold), but how could we cook all of our mushrooms in just one skillet and produce enough for a substantial side dish?

Unlike steaks or cutlets, which begin to sear immediately upon hitting a hot pan, mushrooms don't begin to brown until their water has been driven off. This gave us an idea. What if we overloaded the skillet to start, figuring that once the water evaporated and the mushrooms shrank, the pan would no longer be crowded? We melted butter in the skillet (we'd landed

at 1 tablespoon for richness without grease) and tossed all of our mushrooms (12 ounces) into the pan at once, then popped on the lid. After 10 minutes of covered cooking, all of the mushrooms had thrown off their liquid and shrunk.

It seemed a short dash from there to the finish line. We simply had to keep the heat high, stir the pan occasionally, and cook the contents until well browned. But now the skillet was too dry. Even over more moderate heat, the pan would begin to burn, which made the mushrooms taste bitter. The solution was simple enough. Once the mushrooms had given up their water, we added a little extra butter to prevent burning. With another 10 minutes of uncovered cooking, the liquid evaporated and the mushrooms—no longer crowded—browned beautifully.

It was time to refine the seasonings. Shallot and garlic added a backbone of flavor, and thyme provided an herbal note. A dash of white wine, stirred in at the end, not only contributed a welcome acidic punch but also helped dissolve the flavorful mushroom fond back into the buttery sauce, adding even more richness to our intensely flavored, ultra-tender mushrooms.

Sautéed Mushrooms

SERVES 2

Look for shiitakes that have caps between 2 and 2½ inches in diameter. You will need a 10-inch skillet with a tight-fitting lid for this recipe.

2 tablespoons unsalted butter

1 small shallot, sliced thin

8 ounces cremini or white mushrooms, trimmed
and halved

4 ounces shiitake mushrooms, stemmed and sliced
½ inch thick

Salt and pepper

¾ teaspoon minced fresh thyme or ⅛ teaspoon dried

1 small garlic clove, minced

2½ tablespoons dry white wine

1. Melt 1 tablespoon butter in 10-inch skillet over medium heat. Add shallot and cook until softened, 1 to 2 minutes. Add cremini, shiitakes, and ¼ teaspoon salt and increase heat to medium-high. Cover and cook, stirring occasionally, until mushrooms have released their moisture, 8 to 10 minutes.

2. Remove lid, add remaining 1 tablespoon butter, and cook, stirring occasionally, until mushrooms are deep golden brown and tender, 8 to 10 minutes. Stir in thyme and garlic and cook until fragrant, about 30 seconds. Add wine and cook, scraping up any browned bits, until liquid is nearly evaporated, about 30 seconds. Season with salt and pepper to taste. Serve.

FRIED GREEN TOMATOES

FRIED GREEN TOMATOES ARE JUST THAT—SLICES OF tart, unripe tomato coated in cornmeal or flour (or a mixture of the two) and fried until crisp. Though this dish is a favorite in many a Southern kitchen, it's still a relative unknown in the North. We wanted to develop our own recipe for this regional side dish so that we could enjoy its hallmark sweet-tart flavor and ultra-crunchy texture.

Unfortunately, the first sample recipes we tested—despite their bona fide Southern-cookbook roots—were disappointing. One called for dipping slices of tomato in a mixture of flour and cornmeal, but with no wet ingredients to cement the coating, it was soggy, thin, and patchy. Other recipes more sensibly required dipping the slices in milk or buttermilk combined with egg before dredging, a method that yielded more

substantial coatings, but they were soggy or slid off. In some recipes the green tomatoes were dredged in flour alone, but we found these to be lackluster, and tomatoes dredged in just cornmeal were delicious but gritty. It became clear that a combination of cornmeal and flour would work best.

But before turning to the coating, we considered the frying medium. Some Southern cooks swear by bacon fat, so we pitted this option against peanut oil, which is the test kitchen's usual choice for frying. After just one test, we nixed the bacon fat in favor of peanut oil. A number of tasters complained that its porky, smoky flavor overwhelmed the green tomatoes, plus cooking several batches of bacon to produce enough rendered fat for frying seemed impractical and time-consuming, especially since we were cooking for two. Given that we would be shallow-frying our tomatoes, the protocol followed by most recipes, we needed only 2 cups of oil. Now we could move on to the coating.

Based on our earlier tests, we started with a coating made up of equal amounts of cornmeal and flour. These tomato slices had a pleasantly crunchy coating, but they lacked any distinctive cornmeal flavor. Next time, we went up on cornmeal and down on flour slightly. This batch offered more corny oomph, but even when we were using finely ground cornmeal, the coating was too gritty. Wanting to strike a nice balance between crunch and grit, a colleague suggested processing a portion of the cornmeal so that it would be even finer. The only problem was that since we were processing such a small amount of cornmeal, it flew to the sides of the workbowl, escaping the blade entirely. Next time, we switched to a blender and added the flour as well for more volume. Finally, we were able to achieve a super-fine texture. When we combined this mixture with the rest of our (unblended) cornmeal, our dry coating achieved the right balance of full cornmeal flavor and subtle grit.

But our perfected coating continued to slip off the tomato slices somewhere between the pan and our mouths. To determine the function of each adhesion ingredient (egg, milk, and buttermilk), we tested each separately, dipping and then dredging. The egg dip gave us a coating that stayed in place but had a rubbery texture and tasted like overcooked eggs. The milk dip

FRIED GREEN TOMATOES

DRYING GREEN TOMATOES

To keep tomatoes from weeping when frying (which will loosen coating), let tomatoes sit between layers of paper towels for 20 minutes and then press dry.

yielded a soggy coating that slipped off. The buttermilk didn't improve adhesion, but its acid ensured a coating so crunchy that tasters gobbled up the bits that had fallen off. To get the coating to stick, we embarked on another series of tests, eventually learning that one egg beaten with ⅓ cup of buttermilk produced a crunchy, not eggy, coating that stayed put—almost.

The problem was that the green tomatoes released moisture while they fried. Despite our best efforts to make the coating stick, this moisture accumulated beneath the coating and loosened its grip. Fortunately, this problem had an easy solution: We just needed to dry off the excess moisture. We pressed the slices between paper towels, dipped them in the egg-buttermilk mixture, and then dredged and fried them.

Finally, our sweet-tart tomatoes were coated in an ultra-crunchy, *uber*-flavorful crust that stayed put—all the way from our plates to our mouths.

Fried Green Tomatoes

SERVES 2

We recommend finely ground Quaker cornmeal for this recipe.

- 2 green tomatoes, cored and sliced ¼ inch thick
- ⅓ cup cornmeal
- 2 tablespoons all-purpose flour
  Salt and pepper
  Pinch cayenne pepper
- ⅓ cup buttermilk
- 1 large egg
- 2 cups peanut or vegetable oil

1. Line large plate with paper towels. Place tomato slices on plate and cover with second layer of paper towels. Let sit for 20 minutes, then pat dry.

2. Meanwhile, process 2 tablespoons cornmeal and flour in blender until cornmeal is very finely ground, 1 to 2 minutes, scraping down blender jar as necessary. Combine processed cornmeal mixture, remaining cornmeal, ¾ teaspoon salt, ¼ teaspoon pepper, and cayenne in shallow dish. Whisk buttermilk and egg together in second shallow dish.

3. Working with 1 tomato slice at a time, dip tomato slices in buttermilk mixture, allowing excess to drip off, then coat with cornmeal mixture, pressing firmly to adhere; transfer to clean plate.

4. Set wire rack in rimmed baking sheet. Heat oil in 12-inch skillet over medium-high heat to 350 degrees. Carefully place 4 tomato slices in skillet and cook until golden brown, 4 to 6 minutes, flipping them halfway through cooking. Transfer to prepared wire rack and let drain. Bring oil back to 350 degrees and repeat with remaining tomato slices. Serve.

SWEET AND TANGY COLESLAW

SOMETIMES OUR GRILLED BURGERS AND CHOPS call out for a fresher, lighter partner than the usual mayo-based coleslaw. For these times, we turn to a slaw that has its roots in Amish cooking; this slaw relies on a dressing of oil, cider vinegar, and sugar. But like many slaws—no matter if they're creamy or tangy—it usually serves a small army. We wanted our own recipe for sweet and tangy slaw—and it had to make just enough to serve two, not 12.

Since cabbage is a relatively watery vegetable, our standard test kitchen protocol calls for salting the cabbage and letting it drain for several hours, eliminating moisture that would otherwise dilute the dish. We applied this technique to a basic slaw recipe (cabbage, onion, oil, vinegar, and sugar), allowing a quarter of a small head (our usual amount for two) of salted shredded cabbage to rest for three hours, which released a good quarter-cup of liquid. When we dressed the cabbage, the loss of moisture transformed the slaw, allowing its simple flavors to come to the forefront. But our quarter-head of cabbage shrank so much once it was salted and drained that our recipe hardly made enough for two. Doubling up on the cabbage worked much better; now we had two servings of slaw that were generous but not unreasonable. With a few more tweaks—we replaced the domineering onion with grated carrot and chopped parsley and added a pinch of celery seeds for zip—we had a refreshing slaw that would go with almost anything.

But it nagged at us that, for optimal results, this easy side dish for two required hours for salting (albeit unattended). In the past we found that combining the salting step with a quick stint in the microwave speeds moisture loss in other watery foods, including eggplant. Though heating a dish we planned to serve cold seemed counterintuitive, we decided to try it anyway. But after about a minute in the microwave—we didn't dare go longer for fear of wilting the cabbage—the salted leaves had released only a scant tablespoon of liquid.

NOTES FROM THE TEST KITCHEN

PREPARING CABBAGE FOR SLAW

1. Cut cabbage into quarters, then trim and discard hard core.

2. Separate cabbage into small stacks of leaves that flatten when pressed.

3. Cut each stack of cabbage leaves into thin strips, about ¼ inch thick.

At a loss for what to try next, we pulled out our science books and learned something new. It turns out that the speed with which water gets pulled to the surface of a salted food is determined by how many dissolved particles are in the solution. In other words, the more salt we used on the cabbage, the faster it should release water. We didn't want to increase the salt for fear of turning the slaw overly salty. But any dissolved particle will act similarly to the salt, and we hadn't yet considered the other water-soluble ingredient in our recipe: sugar. Though it doesn't break down as much as salt, and is therefore not quite as effective at drawing out moisture, it should still hasten water loss. We tossed a new batch of shredded slaw with ½ teaspoon of salt and 2 tablespoons of sugar and stuck it in the microwave. Remarkably, with both salt and sugar in the mix, it took just 90 seconds for the cabbage to shed the same ¼ cup of liquid it had released over three hours sitting at room temperature.

We had just one issue to contend with: We now had warm slaw that required chilling. We had worked so hard to cut back on the assembly time that we didn't want to add too much back. The easiest solution was to chill the dressing in the freezer for 15 minutes as we prepped the cabbage. For a final cool-down—and to let the flavors meld—we popped the finished slaw in the fridge for 15 minutes more. By the time we'd finished cleaning up, we had a bright, crisp slaw that was far from plain.

Sweet and Tangy Coleslaw

SERVES 2

If you don't have a salad spinner, use a colander to drain the cabbage and press out the residual liquid with a rubber spatula. See page 156 for a recipe to use up the leftover cabbage.

- 2 tablespoons cider vinegar, plus extra to taste
- 1 tablespoon vegetable oil
  Pinch celery seeds
  Salt and pepper
- ½ small head green cabbage, halved, cored, and shredded (4 cups)
- 2 tablespoons sugar, plus extra to taste
- 1 small carrot, peeled and shredded
- 1 tablespoon minced fresh parsley

1. Combine vinegar, oil, celery seeds, and pinch pepper in medium bowl. Place bowl in freezer until vinegar mixture is well chilled, at least 10 or up to 20 minutes.

2. While vinegar mixture chills, toss cabbage with sugar and ½ teaspoon salt in medium bowl. Cover and microwave until cabbage is partially wilted and has reduced in volume by one-third, 45 to 90 seconds, stirring cabbage halfway through.

3. Transfer cabbage to salad spinner and spin until excess water is removed, 10 to 20 seconds. Remove vinegar mixture from freezer, add cabbage, carrot, and parsley, and toss to combine. Season with vinegar, sugar, and salt to taste. Refrigerate until chilled, about 15 minutes. Toss again before serving.

VARIATIONS

Sweet and Tangy Coleslaw with Red Bell Pepper and Jalapeño

Substitute 2 teaspoons lime juice for celery seeds, ½ thinly sliced small red bell pepper and ½ seeded and minced jalapeño chile for carrot, and 1 thinly sliced small scallion for parsley.

Sweet and Tangy Coleslaw with Apple and Tarragon

Reduce cider vinegar to 1 tablespoon. Substitute ¼ teaspoon Dijon mustard for celery seeds, ½ Granny Smith apple, cut into matchsticks, for carrot, and 1 teaspoon minced fresh tarragon for parsley.

ROASTED SMASHED POTATOES

WHEN IT COMES TO POTATOES, THERE'S NOTHING like the silky creaminess of mashed potatoes—except for the satisfying crispness you get when they're fried. We recently discovered a quirky recipe for something called crispy smashed potatoes, which promised both textures in the same dish. The approach looked simple and straightforward: Whole skin-on potatoes are parcooked, then squashed with a potato masher until they're an even ½ inch thick. The potato disks are then coated with oil or butter and cooked at a high enough heat to render the roughened edges and torn skin browned and crispy and the interior flesh creamy and sweet. Determined to find out if creating these ultra-addictive spuds would really be that easy, we set out to develop our own recipe, and it had to yield just enough for two.

We began by consulting a number of recipes. In every one, the potatoes were parcooked by simmering them in water, but from there, the techniques divided. Some called for pan-frying, while others advocated roasting. Pan-frying produced nice crispness but required close supervision and lots of fat. We opted for the oven's more even heat and hands-off ease.

But when it came time to start smashing, some spuds cooperated better than others. Thick, oblong russets wouldn't budge under the press of a potato masher and needed the smack of a heavy skillet, at which point their starchy interiors crumbled into messy piles. Smaller Yukon Golds and Red Bliss potatoes (no more than 2 inches in diameter) worked far better, flattening evenly into disks that held their shape. We also liked the way their thinner skins crisped up nicely in the oven. In the end, we preferred Red Bliss for their slightly creamier, less starchy flesh.

For cooking fat, we first tried melted butter but found that its milk solids burned long before the potatoes fully crisped, leaving them marred by bitter black patches. We settled on olive oil; applying half before smashing and then drizzling on the rest afterward to ensure that it reached every nook and cranny.

So far, we'd managed to achieve creamy-crispy textures and pretty good flavor. But a certain rich earthiness still eluded us. Were we washing away some of the potato flavor during parcooking? Though simmering was standard among existing recipes, we knew it wasn't doing anything to improve the flavor of our spuds. We tried spiking the cooking water with bay leaves, smashed garlic, various herbs and spices, and even bacon slices, but no hint of these robust flavors came through in the finished dish.

Giving drier heat a try, we placed the potatoes in a large bowl and microwaved them until tender before roasting. These tasted better—but now the skins were tough and rubbery. Clearly, it would be necessary to use at least a little liquid to parcook the potatoes. What if we simply used less water than we had been using, effectively steaming our potatoes? The results were the best yet: Without the diluting effect of boiling, the creamy flesh tasted deeply sweet and earthy.

With this issue fixed, we turned to another problem that had arisen: The baking sheet we had been using to roast our potatoes was beginning to char a bit during the stint in the oven. We were about to swap in a smaller baking dish when we reconsidered. In the interest of keeping our recipe simple and streamlined, maybe we could find one vessel that we could use to both steam the potatoes on the stovetop and then roast them in the oven. Would our favorite multitasker, the 12-inch skillet, do the trick? In a word: yes. Its surface area allowed the potatoes to steam quickly, its sloped edges gave us room to smash the spuds with ease, and its insulated metal bottom helped crisp the bottoms nicely—plus, we'd cut back on dirty dishes.

NOTES FROM THE TEST KITCHEN

MAKING SMASHED POTATOES

Use bottom of greased 1-cup dry measuring cup to evenly smash potatoes to ½-inch thickness.

BUYING AND STORING POTATOES

When buying potatoes, look for firm specimens that are free of green spots, sprouts, cracks, and other blemishes. We generally prefer to buy loose potatoes, so that we can see what we are getting. Stay away from potatoes in plastic bags, which can act like greenhouses and cause potatoes to sprout, soften, and rot.

At home, keep potatoes in a cool, dark, dry place and away from onions, which give off gases that will hasten sprouting. Stored in a cool, dark place, most varieties should keep for several months. The exception is new potatoes—because of their thinner skins, they will keep no more than one month. To further extend their shelf life, we tried storing potatoes in a cool, dark place with an apple—a common old wives' tale that we wanted to put to the test. We found that because of the ethylene gas the apple released, it did indeed boost the storage time; these potatoes lasted almost two weeks longer.

After a 10-minute rest (very hot potatoes crumbled apart when smashed), we pressed the steamed spuds right in the pan, then returned them to the oven for an additional 30 minutes to finish: first on the top rack, where the ambient heat would thoroughly brown their exposed surfaces, then on the bottom rack to crisp their undersides.

These were the creamy spuds encased in rough, crispy skin we'd been after, but we had one last annoying problem to deal with: We were having trouble smashing the potatoes flat with our potato masher. Pieces of potato would stick up through the holes or get caught in the wires. We glanced around the kitchen for a more effective tool, landing on a flat-bottomed dry measuring cup. A little cooking spray prevented any sticking, and our nontraditional smasher worked like a dream.

Now we had perfectly smashed patties—and, once they were browned and crunchy, a great new potato dish to add to our weeknight rotation.

Roasted Smashed Potatoes
SERVES 2

We prefer to use small red potatoes, measuring 1 to 2 inches in diameter, in this recipe. You will need a 12-inch skillet with a tight-fitting lid. It is important to thoroughly cook the potatoes so that they will smash easily. Remove the potatoes from the skillet as soon as they are done browning—they will toughen if left on the hot surface for too long.

- 1 **pound small red potatoes**
- ¾ **cup water**
- 3 **tablespoons extra-virgin olive oil**
- ½ **teaspoon minced fresh thyme**
  Salt and pepper

1. Adjust oven racks to top and lowest positions and heat oven to 500 degrees. Place potatoes and water in 12-inch skillet and bring to simmer over medium-high heat. Reduce heat to medium-low, cover, and continue to simmer until paring knife can be slipped easily in and out of potatoes, 20 to 25 minutes. Uncover and let cool for 10 minutes. Drain potatoes and return to skillet.

2. Drizzle 1½ tablespoons oil over potatoes and toss to coat. Space potatoes evenly in skillet and use bottom of greased 1-cup dry measuring cup to flatten potatoes to ½-inch thickness. Sprinkle with thyme and season with salt and pepper; drizzle evenly with remaining 1½ tablespoons oil.

3. Roast potatoes on top rack for 20 minutes. Transfer potatoes to lowest rack and continue to roast until well browned, about 10 minutes. Carefully (skillet handle will be hot) transfer potatoes to serving platter and season with salt and pepper to taste. Serve.

JO JO POTATOES

CASTING ABOUT FOR ANOTHER POTATO RECIPE TO add to our roster of side dishes for two, we hit on Jo Jo potatoes, a popular roadside joint and tavern offering in the Western and Southern regions of the country. These appealing spuds boast a harmony of textures: They're shaggy and crunchy from seasoned bread crumbs, yet fluffy and tender in the middle. We set out to re-create this bar staple in the test kitchen, for another exciting spud dish for two.

We commenced testing by gathering a number of recipes and heading into the kitchen. However, we found that none of them delivered the real deal. In lieu of using the commercial pressure fryer traditionally employed to cook the spuds, recipes called for either deep-frying or baking. We tried deep-frying first, but the potatoes were burnt on the outside and raw on the inside. Plus, dealing with a pot of bubbling-hot oil, just to make two servings, was a pain. The baked versions were a mixed bag; though they were greasy, dense, and leaden, at least they were cooked through and required less mess and fuss. We picked the lesser of two evils and set out to develop a recipe for baked Jo Jo potatoes.

Every recipe agreed that russet potatoes were the way to go; the russet's high starch content is key to both fluffiness and crispness. Most recipes for baked Jo Jos call for baking the potatoes at 375 degrees or so, but we cranked the dial to 450 in hopes that a hotter oven would give us a better crust. We cut two small russets into fat wedges and, following the lead of most recipes, dipped them in melted butter and then in bread crumbs

(tasters preferred the big crunch of panko, Japanese-style bread crumbs, to homemade or standard store-bought crumbs) seasoned with paprika, dried thyme, garlic powder, dry mustard, cayenne, and salt. We placed the breaded wedges on a baking sheet and slid them into the oven. After we baked them for 15 minutes on each side, the potatoes were golden brown and crisp. Unfortunately, the interiors were dense and lacked fluffiness. Extending the baking time meant that the exteriors burned, so that wasn't an option. Lowering the temperature to 400 degrees helped a little, but any lower gave us soggy spuds.

Classic French fries get their crisp-on-the-outside, fluffy-on-the-inside texture from a double fry (first in moderately hot oil to cook them through, then in hot oil to crisp). Would a dual cooking method help us out here? Parboiling the potatoes gave us waterlogged fries that never came close to crisp in the oven. Steaming the spuds on the stovetop worked better, but it took at least 15 minutes for the potatoes to begin to soften, and we were left with an extra pot to wash. Perhaps the microwave would prove to be a faster solution.

For our next test, we microwaved the potatoes (covered) until they were barely softened before we breaded them. After 30 minutes in the oven, these Jo Jos had a fluffy interior. But though crisp, they lacked the crackly exterior that we were after. A couple of tests showed us that we could introduce serious crunch by preheating the baking sheet and then brushing it with melted butter before arranging the breaded wedges on it. But now the melted butter we used to help the panko adhere to the wedges scorched on the hot baking sheet. Substituting vegetable oil prevented the scorching, but the Jo Jos didn't taste as good. Fortunately, adding a good handful of grated Parmesan cheese to the panko allowed us to recoup the flavor. After a few tests, we settled on equal parts Parmesan and panko.

We had one last task ahead of us: upping the signature shaggy factor, which we'd never been entirely satisfied with. Instead of fiddling with additional ingredients to try to glue on extra crumbs, we wondered if we could employ the sticky potato starch to do the work for us. After the potatoes came out of the microwave, we tossed them with oil as usual. We continued to toss them, and toss them, and toss them some more, hoping to draw out the starch. In about a minute, the potatoes were coated in a starchy paste. We dredged the sticky wedges in the crumb mixture and let them sit for a few minutes to affix the coating before baking. It worked—with an extra benefit: Not only did the potato starch hold the ample breading in place, but it also promoted extra crispness on the exterior of the potatoes. Finally, our baked Jo Jo potatoes had reclaimed all their shaggy, crunchy, fluffy glory.

Jo Jo Potatoes

SERVES 2

Panko bread crumbs add a big crunch to these potatoes. Do not substitute standard store-bought bread crumbs.

2	small russet potatoes, cut lengthwise into ¾-inch-thick wedges
2½	tablespoons vegetable oil
⅓	cup panko bread crumbs
⅓	cup grated Parmesan cheese
1½	teaspoons paprika
1	teaspoon dry mustard
½	teaspoon garlic powder
½	teaspoon dried thyme
	Salt
	Pinch cayenne pepper

1. Adjust oven rack to middle position, place baking sheet on rack, and heat oven to 400 degrees. Microwave potatoes in medium bowl, covered, until edges of potatoes are translucent but centers remain slightly firm, about 5 minutes, tossing them halfway through cooking. Drain potatoes and return to bowl. Drizzle with 1½ tablespoons oil and stir continuously until potatoes are coated with starchy film, about 1 minute.

2. Combine panko, Parmesan, paprika, dry mustard, garlic powder, thyme, ½ teaspoon salt, and cayenne in shallow dish. Dredge potatoes in panko mixture, pressing gently to adhere. Transfer to platter and let sit for 15 minutes.

3. Remove hot sheet from oven and brush with remaining 1 tablespoon oil. Arrange potatoes, cut side down, in single layer. Bake until crisp and golden brown, about 25 minutes, flipping wedges halfway through cooking. Season with salt to taste. Serve.

SWEET POTATO SALAD

MAYO-BASED POTATO SALAD, COMPLETE WITH celery and hard-cooked eggs, is a cookout staple. But we recently discovered an alternative that makes a nice break from this barbecue basic: sweet potato salad. Unlike the typical American-style potato salad, sweet potato salad is tossed with a vinaigrette, which gives the dish an unexpected tangy and bright flavor. We wanted to liven up the dinner hour for two and set out to create our own scaled-down sweet potato salad.

All the recipes we found required boiling sweet potatoes, which had been peeled and cubed, before dressing them in vinaigrette. But this didn't work at all—the boiled sweet potatoes were mushy and waterlogged. We decided to test a couple of different methods. First, we tried roasting the cubed potatoes in a 400-degree oven. While the potato cubes came out creamy on the inside and caramelized on the outside, the distinct and crisp exterior formed a barrier to our vinaigrette; the resulting salad was greasy and underseasoned. Sautéing the potatoes didn't work much better. We still ended up with a crust on the potatoes, and the oil we used to cook the potatoes so that they wouldn't stick to the pan made the salad even greasier than before. Finally, we turned to steaming, which seemed to hold promise.

After a few minutes in a steamer basket, our potatoes had cooked through to fluffy perfection. It seemed we were on the right track, but then we stirred in our vinaigrette. Suddenly, the sweet potatoes turned from fluffy to oily. It turned out that steaming damages the cell walls of the sweet potatoes, so they absorb oil more easily. We made a few additional batches, adjusting our vinaigrette so that there was less oil and more vinegar.

This salad was already much improved, but the potatoes themselves tasted a little bland. When we make ordinary potato salad in the test kitchen, we often toss the warm potatoes with a little vinegar—they drink it up and become deeply seasoned. We did the same with the sweet potatoes, but their edges broke down. The fragile hot sweet potatoes just couldn't hold up to the agitation caused by stirring in the vinegar. Our science editor explained that there's less pectin to hold the cells together in sweet potatoes than in white potatoes; when the sweet potatoes are hot, the

SWEET POTATO SALAD

pectin begins to lose its grip, but cooling them would let the pectin rebond slightly. For our next test, we let the sweet potatoes cool before tossing them with the vinegar. This worked like a charm. The potatoes soaked up the vinegar with not one broken-down edge in sight. We then tossed these potatoes with our vinaigrette and dug in.

The texture of the salad was great, but the potatoes still lacked the bold flavor we were after. We needed to infuse our sweet potatoes with more than just vinegar. Thinking hot vinaigrette would be the solution, we microwaved the whole mixture and tossed it with the cooled potatoes. To our surprise, the salad was greasy once again, and the potatoes were even blander than before. Could the oil in the vinaigrette be blocking the absorption of the dressing?

The next time, we microwaved all of the remaining dressing components (cider vinegar, Dijon mustard, salt, and pepper) and waited to add the oil until the potatoes had had a chance to absorb the vinegar mixture. This salad was markedly more flavorful, but the oil failed to incorporate, giving our dressing a broken texture. We'd need a better way to incorporate the oil into the dressing while still fully flavoring our potatoes. Luckily, this would be an easy fix. We simply split the vinegar mixture in half, microwaving one portion before drizzling it over the potatoes, and then whisking the oil into the reserved vinegar mixture before tossing it with the vinegar-soaked spuds. Finally, our salad turned out perfectly dressed and seasoned.

Now that we had the technique down, we turned to additional flavorings. Our salad cried out for some heat and crunch, so we added a little cayenne pepper and chopped red bell pepper. To take it to the next level, we stirred in crisped bacon and thinly sliced scallions.

This salad now offered tender, deeply seasoned bites of sweet potato, plus crunch from the bacon and brightness from the scallions. At last, our potato salad was in a class all its own.

Sweet Potato Salad

SERVES 2

Be sure to cook the potatoes until they are just tender; otherwise the pieces will fall apart when the salad is assembled.

2 slices bacon, chopped
1 pound sweet potatoes, peeled and cut into ¾-inch pieces
½ red bell pepper, stemmed, seeded, and cut into ½-inch pieces
1 tablespoon cider vinegar
1½ teaspoons Dijon mustard
   Salt and pepper
   Pinch cayenne pepper
1½ tablespoons vegetable oil
2 scallions, sliced thin

1. Cook bacon in 10-inch skillet over medium heat until crisp, 6 to 8 minutes. Using slotted spoon, transfer bacon to paper towel–lined plate.

2. Meanwhile, fill large saucepan with 1 inch water. Bring water to boil. Place steamer basket in saucepan and add sweet potatoes. Reduce heat to medium-low and cook, covered, until potatoes are nearly tender, about 10 minutes. Add bell pepper and cook, covered, until vegetables are just tender, 2 to 4 minutes. Drain vegetables and rinse with cold water until cool, about 2 minutes. Transfer to large bowl.

3. Combine vinegar, mustard, ¼ teaspoon salt, ⅛ teaspoon pepper, and cayenne in bowl. Transfer half of vinegar mixture to small bowl and microwave until steaming, about 10 seconds. Drizzle hot vinegar mixture over vegetables and gently toss until evenly coated. Let sit at room temperature until flavors meld, about 15 minutes.

4. Whisking constantly, drizzle oil into remaining vinegar mixture in slow, steady stream until fully emulsified. Pour dressing over vegetables and gently toss until evenly coated. Stir in bacon and scallions, cover, and refrigerate until chilled, about 30 minutes. Season with salt and pepper to taste. Serve.

VARIATION

Asian-Style Sweet Potato Salad

Substitute 2 ounces snow peas, sliced ½ inch thick on bias, for bell pepper. Substitute 1½ teaspoons lime juice and 1½ teaspoons rice vinegar for cider vinegar, 1½ teaspoons grated fresh ginger for mustard, and 1½ teaspoons soy sauce for salt. Substitute 1½ teaspoons toasted sesame oil for 1½ teaspoons vegetable oil and 2 tablespoons chopped salted dry-roasted peanuts for bacon.

ISRAELI COUSCOUS WITH FENNEL AND SPINACH

PACKAGED COUSCOUS MIXES FROM THE SUPER-market are the ultimate in convenience, but they often yield a bland, unremarkable side dish. We wanted an effortless yet elegant couscous side dish that offered big flavor. To up the ante, we set out to use pearl-shaped Israeli couscous, which we planned to dress up with more than just dried herbs—in fact, we had a more refined couscous dish in mind, one in which the chewy, slightly nutty grains would be enhanced by a few thoughtfully chosen vegetables and/or greens.

First things first, we'd need to find the best method for preparing the couscous. Unlike fine-grained cous-cous, which is precooked and simply needs to be soaked in hot water or broth to turn tender, Israeli couscous requires more attention. In our research, we found two methods for preparing it: Either the couscous is cooked like rice in boiling water until the water is absorbed, or it's simmered like pasta in a large amount of water until tender. We first tried cooking the couscous like rice but found that the individual grains clumped together. Cooking the couscous in a large pot of water worked much better, giving us grains that were tender and distinct. Adding a tablespoon of salt to the cooking water, as we do with pasta, ensured that the couscous was well-seasoned from the outset.

Cooking method established, we moved on to the remaining elements of our dish. Looking to vegetables that would add an elegant touch, we first hit on fennel, which we sliced thinly and sautéed in a skillet. Covering it for the first 10 minutes of cooking worked to draw out its moisture (so our dish wasn't watery). Once it had softened, we removed the lid and turned up the heat so that the fennel would become nicely browned and richly flavored. For aromatic complexity, we added a sliced shallot and some minced garlic to the pan. Once everything was fragrant and all the vegetables had softened, we tossed in our cooked couscous, plus a bit more olive oil for richness, and reached for our forks. Tasters liked the flavor of the dish but thought it was missing something. We considered a few options but ultimately landed on baby spinach, which requires no prep other than a quick rinse. For our next test, we tossed a few handfuls into the skillet off the heat so that the spinach could wilt.

To finish off our dish, we needed to brighten up its seasoning. A bit of grated lemon zest and a little lemon juice contributed some much-needed acidity, but it was the final addition of minced fresh chives that really elevated this simple dish for two to another level.

Israeli Couscous with Caramelized Fennel and Spinach
SERVES 2

Do not substitute regular couscous in this dish.

- ¾ cup Israeli couscous
- Salt and pepper
- 1½ tablespoons extra-virgin olive oil
- 1 fennel bulb, stalks discarded, bulb halved, cored, and sliced thin (see page 50)
- 1 shallot, sliced ¼ inch thick
- 1 small garlic clove, minced
- ¼ teaspoon grated lemon zest plus 1½ teaspoons juice
- 2 ounces (2 cups) baby spinach
- 1 tablespoon minced fresh chives
- Lemon wedges

1. Bring 4 quarts water to boil in Dutch oven. Stir in couscous and 1 tablespoon salt and cook until tender, about 5 minutes. Drain couscous, transfer to bowl, and cover to keep warm.

2. Heat 1 tablespoon oil in 12-inch skillet over medium-low heat until shimmering. Add fennel, shal-lot, and ⅛ teaspoon salt, cover, and cook, stirring occa-sionally, until vegetables have softened and released their liquid, about 10 minutes. Uncover, increase heat to medium-high, and continue to cook, stirring often, until lightly browned and liquid has evaporated, about 10 minutes longer.

3. Stir in garlic and lemon zest and cook until fra-grant, about 30 seconds. Off heat, stir in spinach, cover, and let sit until spinach wilts, about 2 minutes. Add couscous to skillet with spinach and fennel. Stir in remaining 1½ teaspoons oil, chives, and lemon juice. Season with salt and pepper to taste. Serve warm or at room temperature with lemon wedges.

CHOCOLATE-RASPBERRY TORTE

BAKED GOODS & DESSERTS

MORNING GLORY MUFFINS

MORNING GLORY MUFFINS

MORNING GLORY MUFFINS ARE CINNAMON-scented breakfast treats, chock-full of carrots, nuts, coconut, and dried and fresh fruit. Created in the 1970s by a café owner in Nantucket, the morning glory muffin quickly started showing up in bakeries across the country. But since its heyday, this muffin has taken a detour. What used to be a moist, tender, flavorful baked good is now often overly sweet, dense, and heavy. It was clear we had our work cut out for us if we wanted to bring the glory back to these muffins and deliver a breakfast that was moist, tender, fruity, and balanced. Given that muffins tend to dry out after a few days, we set out to make just enough for breakfast and an afternoon snack for two.

We started with a version of the original 1970s recipe. In addition to some usual muffin-batter ingredients (flour, sugar, eggs, oil, salt, and leavener), the recipe contained grated carrots and apples, canned crushed pineapple, coconut, walnuts, raisins, and cinnamon. It was a long list of ingredients, and we'd need to tackle them one by one to create a foolproof recipe scaled down for two.

Our first step was to reconsider the amount of oil. Judging by the greasy fingerprints our tasters left behind after the first round of tests, we suspected that one of the main culprits in these less-than-glorious muffins was too much oil. Many muffin and quick-bread recipes include oil to keep the crumb moist, but we knew that the fruit in our muffins would contribute moisture, so we figured we could cut back on the oil with no ill effects. We started with ½ cup and worked our way down to a mere 3 tablespoons. The muffins were still moist, but tasters commented that the oil wasn't doing much for their flavor. Swapping the oil for melted butter was a step in the right direction.

Although we'd cut back on the oil, the muffins remained gummy and wet. We evaluated our moist stir-ins: carrot, apple, and pineapple. We had already scaled down to just a single carrot (any less, and the muffins didn't have any noticeable carrot flavor), so we decided to take a look at the pineapple and apple. To rid them of excess moisture, we placed them in a fine-mesh strainer, then pressed out and discarded their released juices before mixing the fruit into the batter.

As we had hoped, this method produced moist muffins, not soggy ones. Unfortunately, the missing fruit juice also resulted in missing fruit flavor.

When we make sauces in the test kitchen, we often reduce broth or wine to concentrate its flavor. We wondered if reserving the fruit juices and reducing them would have the same effect on our muffins. For our next test, after pressing the fruit, we boiled the juices down to 2 tablespoons, then added this syrup to the batter. This thickened liquid was exactly what the muffins needed. To compensate for the added syrup, we also cut back on sugar; although crystalline at room temperature, sugar adds moisture to baked goods. Using less sugar had the secondary benefit of letting the fruit flavors come to the forefront.

Although the moisture level was in check, tasters now complained about limp, stringy coconut and mealy nuts. We tried toasting them for heightened flavor and crunch, but once they hit the batter, they soaked up moisture and got soggy all over again. Texture aside, toasting worked wonders for the flavor. For our next test, we tried sprinkling the coconut and nuts on top of the muffins so that they would stay dry, instead of mixing them into the batter, but the muffins came out squat and flat-topped. It was clear that not only had the coconut and nuts added flavor, but they also had been giving our muffins structure. Perhaps we could find a better way to incorporate them into the flour mixture. For the next batch of muffins, we toasted the coconut and nuts as before, then ground them finely in the food processor and mixed the meal into the dry ingredients. Now our muffins had a deep, nutty flavor and nicely domed tops, with no mealy bits in sight.

Our muffins almost done, we quickly took stock of the flavors. Ground ginger and clove were included in some of the recipes we'd come across, but we found their flavors distracting and opted to nix them. That left just the cinnamon, which tasters found to be a bit overpowering. Reducing it to just ¼ teaspoon—some recipes included three times that much—worked much better and allowed the flavors of the fruit and nuts to take center stage.

At last, our Morning Glory Muffins were the perfect up-and-at-'em treat. They were moist, fruity, and nutty—and totally worthy of their name.

Morning Glory Muffins

MAKES 4 MUFFINS

Any size muffin tin will work here, and the batter can be placed in any of the muffin cups. Though we prefer golden raisins in these muffins, ordinary raisins will work, too.

- ¼ cup (¾ ounce) sweetened shredded coconut, toasted
- ¼ cup walnuts, toasted
- ¾ cup (3¾ ounces) all-purpose flour
- ¼ cup (1¾ ounces) sugar
- ½ teaspoon baking soda
- ¼ teaspoon baking powder
- ¼ teaspoon ground cinnamon
- ¼ teaspoon salt
- ⅓ cup canned crushed pineapple
- 1 small Granny Smith apple, peeled, cored, and shredded
- 3 tablespoons unsalted butter, melted and cooled slightly
- 1 large egg
- ¼ teaspoon vanilla extract
- 1 small carrot, peeled and shredded (⅓ cup)
- ⅓ cup golden raisins

1. Adjust oven rack to middle position and heat oven to 350 degrees. Grease 4 cups in muffin tin. Process coconut and walnuts together in food processor until finely ground, about 15 seconds. Add flour, sugar, baking soda, baking powder, cinnamon, and salt and pulse until combined. Transfer mixture to medium bowl.

2. Place pineapple and shredded apple in fine-mesh strainer set over liquid measuring cup. Press fruit dry (juice should measure about ⅓ cup). Bring juice to boil in 8-inch skillet over medium-high heat and cook until reduced to 2 tablespoons, 3 to 5 minutes. Let cool slightly. Whisk cooled juice, melted butter, egg, and vanilla together in small bowl until smooth. Stir wet mixture into dry mixture until just combined, then stir in pineapple-apple mixture, carrot, and raisins.

3. Divide batter evenly among prepared muffin cups. Bake until toothpick inserted in center comes out clean, 24 to 28 minutes. Let muffins cool in muffin tin on wire rack for 10 minutes. Remove muffins from tin and let cool for at least 10 minutes before serving.

USE IT UP: CRUSHED PINEAPPLE

Pineapple Sauce

MAKES ½ CUP

Serve over ice cream or cake.

- 2 tablespoons unsalted butter
- ¼ cup packed brown sugar
- ¼ cup water
- ⅔ cup canned crushed pineapple
- ¼ teaspoon vanilla extract
- Pinch ground cardamom
- Pinch salt

1. Melt butter in 8-inch skillet over medium-high heat. Add sugar and water and simmer until sugar has dissolved and liquid has thickened slightly, about 2 minutes.

2. Stir in pineapple and simmer until sauce is thickened and turns deep golden brown, 2 to 4 minutes. Off heat, stir in vanilla, cardamom, and salt. Serve warm.

ZUCCHINI BREAD

SERVED WITH A CUP OF COFFEE IN THE MORNING or tea in the afternoon, a moist, tender slice of zucchini bread makes a great pick-me-up. But most recipes we've tried result in dense, overly sweet loaves that hardly taste of zucchini, not to mention that they produce way too much for two. We set about creating a recipe for a mini zucchini bread that would deliver bright flavor, a moist crumb, and subtle zucchini flavor in every bite.

Zucchini bread recipes generally follow a simple technique: Stir the dry ingredients (flour, leavener, spices, and salt) together in one bowl, stir the wet ingredients and sweetener (oil, eggs, sugar, and often yogurt or sour cream) together in a second bowl, and then fold the dry ingredients into the wet and add the grated zucchini. We came up with a working recipe based on recipes for full-size zucchini breads, then scaled down the ingredients and commenced testing. As we've found with other baked goods, vegetable oil made our mini loaf greasy and dulled its flavor, so we swapped it for melted butter, which contributed a pleasant richness.

We had made some progress, but the flavor still tasted a bit flat. To brighten it up, we experimented with various acidic ingredients that the test kitchen has used in other quick-bread recipes: buttermilk, sour cream, and yogurt. While buttermilk worked well, we preferred the texture and flavor of the bread made with a tablespoon of plain yogurt. It had an appealing tanginess, and a small amount of lemon juice added a bit more acidity plus a bright citrus note. In addition to improving the flavor of our zucchini bread, the yogurt and lemon juice reacted with the baking soda to produce a lighter bread with more rise.

Next, we tackled the eggs and sugar. We found that one egg was all we could work into the batter without making it too runny or giving it an overly eggy flavor. To sweeten the loaf, we settled on ½ cup of sugar, which added the right amount of sweetness.

We had worked out a lot of issues, but we still had to face the biggest one of all: the zucchini, which can be quite watery and lead to a dense, soggy loaf. Standard recipes begin with a pound of zucchini; we tried cutting that amount in half and ended up with a heavy, wet batter that overflowed the pan. In the end, we couldn't fit more than 4 ounces of zucchini (about half a medium zucchini) into our pan, but even then, the loaf was too moist. Clearly we needed to find a way to drain the vegetable first. Placing the grated zucchini in a fine-mesh strainer and allowing the moisture to drip off had little effect; loaves made with zucchini prepared this way were still somewhat soggy. We needed to think

outside the box. If zucchini is basically a watery sponge, we figured, then why not treat it that way? We placed our grated zucchini in a kitchen towel and wrung out every drop of moisture we could. The resulting bread, dotted with green flecks of the squash, had a moist, but not gummy, texture.

Last, we tested other flavorings: ground cinnamon, ground allspice, grated nutmeg, ground ginger, vanilla, nuts, and raisins. We liked the effect of cinnamon and allspice in very small amounts (¼ teaspoon each). Except for the nuts, we found the rest of the flavoring agents out of place in our brightly flavored quick bread. After several tests, we found that ¼ cup of chopped toasted pecans or walnuts added a pleasant textural contrast to the moist bread without weighing it down. Finally, we had created a zucchini bread for two that was the perfect partner to morning coffee or afternoon tea.

Zucchini Bread

MAKES ONE 5½ BY 3-INCH LOAF

You will need a 5½ by 3-inch loaf pan or a pan of similar size for this recipe (see page 3). Make sure to squeeze the zucchini dry to prevent soggy zucchini bread.

½ zucchini (4 ounces)
½ cup (2½ ounces) all-purpose flour
½ teaspoon baking soda
½ teaspoon baking powder
¼ teaspoon ground cinnamon
¼ teaspoon ground allspice
⅛ teaspoon salt
½ cup (3½ ounces) sugar
1 large egg
1 tablespoon unsalted butter, melted and cooled
1 tablespoon plain whole-milk or low-fat yogurt
1 teaspoon lemon juice
¼ cup pecans or walnuts, toasted and chopped coarse

1. Adjust oven rack to middle position and heat oven to 350 degrees. Grease 5½ by 3-inch loaf pan.

2. Shred zucchini on large holes of box grater. Squeeze shredded zucchini between several layers of paper towels or clean dish towel until dry.

NOTES FROM THE TEST KITCHEN

REMOVING MOISTURE FROM ZUCCHINI

To prevent soggy zucchini bread, squeeze shredded zucchini between several layers of paper towels or clean dish towel until dry.

3. Whisk flour, baking soda, baking powder, cinnamon, allspice, and salt together in medium bowl. In separate bowl, whisk sugar, egg, melted butter, yogurt, and lemon juice together until smooth. Gently fold shredded zucchini and yogurt mixture into flour mixture with rubber spatula until just combined. (Do not overmix.) Gently fold in pecans.

4. Scrape batter into prepared pan and smooth top. Bake until golden brown and toothpick inserted into center comes out clean, 35 to 45 minutes, rotating pan halfway through baking.

5. Let bread cool in pan on wire rack for 5 minutes. Remove bread from pan and let cool completely for about 1 hour. Serve.

EASY CRÊPES

DESPITE THEIR APPARENT SIMPLICITY, CRÊPES HAVE a reputation for being fussy and finicky, calling for a specialized pan and requiring a just-so temperature and delicate handling. We sought to demystify this French classic and develop a recipe for the for-two household, so that we would have an easy and foolproof path to thin, lacy, rich-tasting crêpes.

We gathered a number of recipes and headed into the test kitchen. They were all pretty similar: Flour and milk (and sometimes water) were either blended or whisked with eggs, salt, and melted butter to form a creamy batter. Several recipes were spiked with brandy or lightly sweetened with sugar. The cooking instructions were universal: Spread the batter as thin as possible in the skillet (most recipes swapped out the specialty crêpe pan in favor of a 12-inch nonstick skillet), cook until the edges are golden and lacy, and then flip the crêpe to brown spottily on the other side. The biggest discrepancy we came across involved the resting time. About half of the recipes called for resting the batter for one to two hours after mixing, while others skipped straight to the cooking. The idea of having to rest the batter did not sit well with us, as we wanted this to be a relatively speedy dessert for two. We could test this later on, but first, we set out to perfect our crêpe batter.

A couple of quick tests confirmed that a 1½:1 ratio of milk to flour with a touch of sugar produced the best thin pancakes that were rich-tasting and lightly sweet. We tested several types of flour, from low-protein cake

flour to higher-protein all-purpose and bread flour, but tasters deemed the results indistinguishable, so we stuck with the more readily available all-purpose flour. Though brandy showed up as a flavoring in some ingredients, we felt it dominated in our crêpes, so we crossed it off our list and resolved to dress up our cooked crêpes with additional ingredients later on. When it came to the mixing method, we found that batters simply whisked together by hand turned out crêpes that were every bit as good as those made from batters whirled together by countertop or immersion blenders.

With our batter in good shape, we could tackle the issue of whether it needed to rest. The traditional justification is twofold: First, resting allows the starch granules in the flour to hydrate more fully, which purportedly produces a more tender crêpe. Second, a rest means that there is more time for any air incorporated into the batter during mixing to dissipate, so the crêpe will be as thin as possible. To find out if this step was really necessary, we made a batch of crêpe batter and placed it in the fridge. Two hours later, we made another batch and cooked both. Tasters tried crêpes from both batches, but there was no clear winner. We repeated the test to be certain, but again resting time made no difference; we could go straight from the mixing bowl to the pan.

Except for a few ingredient tweaks here and there, our recipe hadn't changed much since we began developing it. But these later batches of crêpes were noticeably better—more tender and uniformly brown—than earlier attempts. We realized that while the batter itself was relatively forgiving, there were some crucial crêpe-cooking tricks that we had picked up along the way.

First, we had to heat the pan properly. When we made it too hot, the batter set up before it evenly coated the surface, yielding a crêpe marred by thick, spongy patches and holes. When we didn't heat the pan enough, the crêpe was pale and flavorless and too flimsy to flip without tearing. To ensure steady, even cooking, we borrowed a technique that we use for French omelets: We slowly heated the oiled skillet over low heat for at least 10 minutes. To determine when the pan was ready, we placed a dollop of batter in the center of the preheated, oil-slicked pan; if it turned perfectly golden brown in 20 seconds, we were good to go.

Second, we needed to add just enough batter to coat the bottom of the pan. After much trial and error, we settled on ¼ cup of batter as the ideal amount. We tried the classic technique of tilting the pan to swirl the

CRÊPES WITH SUGAR AND LEMON

batter around it, but this wasn't distributing the batter as evenly as we had hoped. Making the minor adjustment of tilting the pan while simultaneously shaking it was a quick and effective fix.

Finally, we found that it was important to flip the crêpe at the right moment. If the batter was added to a properly heated pan, it took about 25 seconds for it to go from wet to ready to flip—appearing dry, matte, and lacy around the edges. But to truly loosen the crêpe, we nudged it from underneath with a rubber spatula before grasping its edge, then nimbly turned it to the flip side to cook until spotty brown, which took about 20 seconds.

Once we had these tactics down, we whipped up a few simple sweet fillings designed to satisfy every craving: sugar with lemon, banana-Nutella, honey-almond, and chocolate-orange. These crêpes were delicate, golden brown, and richly flavored—the perfect après-dinner treat for two.

NOTES FROM THE TEST KITCHEN

MAKING CRÊPES

1. Pour ¼ cup batter into far side of pan.

2. Tilt and shake skillet gently until batter evenly covers bottom of pan.

3. Gently slide spatula underneath edge of crêpe, grasp edge with fingertips, and flip crêpe.

Crêpes with Sugar and Lemon

SERVES 2

Crêpes will give off steam as they cook, but if at any point the skillet begins to smoke, remove it from the heat immediately and turn down the heat. Stacking the crêpes on a wire rack allows excess steam to escape so they won't stick together. To allow for practice, the recipe yields 5 crêpes; only 4 are needed for the filling.

½ teaspoon vegetable oil
½ cup (2½ ounces) all-purpose flour
½ teaspoon sugar, plus 4 teaspoons sugar
    for sprinkling
⅛ teaspoon salt
¾ cup whole milk
1 large egg
1 tablespoon unsalted butter, melted and cooled
   Lemon wedges

1. Heat oil in 12-inch nonstick skillet over low heat for at least 10 minutes.

2. While skillet is heating, whisk flour, ½ teaspoon sugar, and salt together in medium bowl. In separate bowl, whisk together milk and egg. Add half of milk mixture to dry ingredients and whisk until smooth. Add melted butter and whisk until incorporated. Whisk in remaining milk mixture until smooth.

3. Using paper towel, wipe out skillet, leaving thin film of oil on bottom and sides. Increase heat to medium and let skillet heat for 1 minute. After 1 minute, test heat of skillet by placing 1 teaspoon batter in center and cooking for 20 seconds. If mini crêpe is golden brown on bottom, skillet is properly heated; if it is too light or too dark, adjust heat accordingly and retest.

4. Pour ¼ cup batter into far side of pan and tilt and shake gently until batter evenly covers bottom of pan. Cook crêpe without moving it until top surface is dry and crêpe starts to brown at edges, loosening crêpe from side of pan with rubber spatula, about 25 seconds. Gently slide spatula underneath edge of crêpe, grasp edge with fingertips, and flip crêpe. Cook until second side is lightly spotted, about 20 seconds. Transfer cooked crêpe to wire rack, inverting so spotted side is facing up. Return pan to heat and heat for 10 seconds before repeating with remaining batter. As crêpes are done, stack on wire rack.

5. Transfer stack of crêpes to large microwave-safe plate and invert second plate over crêpes. Microwave until crêpes are warm, about 30 seconds (45 to 60 seconds if crêpes have cooled completely). Remove top plate and wipe dry with paper towel. Sprinkle upper half of top crêpe with 1 teaspoon sugar. Fold unsugared bottom half over sugared half, then fold into quarters. Transfer sugared crêpe to second plate. Continue with remaining crêpes. Serve immediately with lemon wedges.

VARIATIONS

Crêpes with Banana and Nutella

Omit 4 teaspoons sprinkling sugar and lemon wedges. Spread 2 teaspoons Nutella over top half of each crêpe followed by four to five ¼-inch-thick banana slices (from 2 bananas). Fold crêpes into quarters. Serve immediately.

Crêpes with Honey and Toasted Almonds

Omit 4 teaspoons sprinkling sugar and lemon wedges. Drizzle 1 teaspoon honey over top half of each crêpe and sprinkle with 2 teaspoons finely chopped toasted sliced almonds and small pinch salt. Fold crêpes into quarters. Serve immediately.

Crêpes with Chocolate and Orange

Omit 4 teaspoons sprinkling sugar and lemon wedges. Using fingertips, rub ½ teaspoon finely grated orange zest into 2 tablespoons sugar. Stir in 1 ounce finely grated bittersweet chocolate. Sprinkle 1½ tablespoons chocolate-orange mixture over top half of each crêpe. Fold crêpes into quarters. Serve immediately.

SKILLET APPLE CRISP

WHEN THE WEATHER TURNS COOL IN NEW ENGLAND, we start thinking about apple desserts. One of our favorites is apple crisp, which comes together quickly and easily—no fussy pie dough to mix and roll. But many recipes we've tried deliver a boring, flavorless filling with unevenly cooked apples and topping that can hardly be described as crisp. We wanted a great apple crisp that was as delicious as it was effortless—and it had to be scaled down for two.

We started by considering the best type of apple for our crisp, as experience with past recipes had taught us that not every variety is good for baking. For now, we cobbled together a working recipe to help us figure out which apple to use. We tossed 1½ pounds of peeled, sliced apples with sugar; transferred them to a baking dish; topped them with a blend of melted butter, sugar, and flour; and baked the whole thing in a 350-degree oven for 45 minutes.

We weren't surprised when McIntosh apples turned out mushy; they have a naturally pulpy texture when cooked. Granny Smiths, however, were another matter. Some batches made with this prized baking varietal virtually disintegrated into applesauce, while others held their shape. Baffled, we tested several other varieties until a more foolproof apple emerged: Golden Delicious (Braeburns and Honeycrisps measured up as well).

Confused as to why the normally reliable Granny Smith had performed so poorly, we did a little research. It turns out that some apples, like Granny Smiths, are more susceptible to the various gases, including ethylene, carbon dioxide, and oxygen, used in long-term storage, causing them to cook down more rapidly when heated, while other varieties, including Golden Delicious, are less susceptible to these gases. So that we could make our crisp year-round, not just when we had fresh-picked apples on hand, we decided to stick with the hardier Golden Delicious.

Though the Golden Delicious apples had held up well during baking and hadn't turned to mush, they still cooked unevenly within the baking dish, with some slices remaining too firm. But if we extended the oven time and baked the crisp until the apples in the center were fully tender, the fruit around the perimeter turned to pulp, and the topping burned. Stirring was the obvious solution to this problem—tossing the fruit as it transformed from crisp to softened would ensure uniformly tender slices, at which point we could add the topping. But frequently reaching into a hot oven to stir our apples was less than convenient.

We would need to find a way to jump-start the apples' cooking so that they'd cook through evenly in the oven. Parcooking our apples on the stovetop proved to be the answer. Now we could cook (and stir) the apples in a skillet until almost tender before transferring them to the oven. By adding a pat of butter to the pan, we were able to take advantage of the direct heat of the stovetop to amp up the Goldens' mild flavor. When cooked in the baking dish, the apples merely steamed in their own juices; on the stovetop, once the excess moisture was driven off, the fruit caramelized in the butter, leading to a sweet richness that would have been impossible to achieve in the oven.

Though our crisp was now richer in flavor, it still lacked a certain depth and roundness. To compensate for the Goldens' sweetness, we cut back on the sugar. For a tart edge, we added a touch of fresh lemon juice. And for full-fledged apple flavor, we turned to the concentrated form, cider, which we reduced in the pan before sautéing our apples. Added to the parcooked apples, this super-potent reduction contributed the intense fruity flavor we had been looking for.

We were about to transfer the fruit from the skillet to a baking dish when we realized the extra step wasn't necessary with our ovensafe skillet. We simply sprinkled on the topping and slid the whole thing into a 350-degree oven, where our parcooked apples would need only a short stint. Then it occurred to us: If we cranked up the heat even higher, the apples would need even less time to bake and we would be able to achieve some quick browning on the topping.

After only 15 minutes in a 450-degree oven, the "crisp" was just that: crunchy and golden, an ideal contrast to the luscious, flavorful fruit that lay beneath.

At this point, we simply needed to revisit the topping, which could use a bit more flavor. To play up the apples' caramel notes, we traded most of the white sugar for brown and added dashes of cinnamon and salt. But the biggest improvement came when we took a cue from some crisps we've made before, swapping part of the flour for chewy rolled oats and stirring in some crunchy chopped pecans.

Not only had we developed a scaled-down apple crisp that offered a richly flavored filling and a crunchy, browned topping, but we'd also found a way to make an easy dessert even easier.

Skillet Apple Crisp

SERVES 2

You will need an 8-inch ovensafe skillet for this recipe; if your skillet is not ovensafe, you can substitute an 8½ by 4½-inch loaf pan. We like Golden Delicious apples for this recipe, but any sweet, crisp apple such as Honeycrisp or Braeburn can be substituted; do not use Granny Smiths. While rolled oats are preferable in the topping, quick-cooking oats can be substituted. Serve the apple crisp warm or at room temperature with vanilla ice cream or Whipped Cream (page 276).

TOPPING

- ¼ cup (1¼ ounces) all-purpose flour
- ¼ cup pecans, chopped fine
- ¼ cup (¾ ounce) old-fashioned rolled oats
- 3 tablespoons packed light brown sugar
- 1 tablespoon granulated sugar
- ¼ teaspoon ground cinnamon
- ¼ teaspoon salt
- 3 tablespoons unsalted butter, melted

FILLING

- 1½ pounds Golden Delicious apples, peeled, cored, halved, and cut into ½-inch-thick wedges
- 2 tablespoons granulated sugar
- ¼ teaspoon ground cinnamon (optional)
- ½ cup apple cider
- 1 teaspoon lemon juice
- 1 tablespoon unsalted butter

1. FOR THE TOPPING: Adjust oven rack to middle position and heat oven to 450 degrees. Combine flour, pecans, oats, brown sugar, granulated sugar, cinnamon, and salt in medium bowl. Stir in melted butter until mixture is thoroughly moistened and crumbly; set aside.

2. FOR THE FILLING: Toss apples, sugar, and cinnamon (if using) together in medium bowl; set aside. Bring cider to simmer in 8-inch ovensafe skillet over medium heat; cook until reduced to ⅓ cup, 2 to 3 minutes. Transfer reduced cider to bowl or liquid measuring cup and stir in lemon juice.

3. Melt butter in now-empty skillet over medium heat. Add apple mixture and cook, stirring frequently, until apples begin to soften and become translucent, 12 to 14 minutes. (Do not fully cook apples.) Off heat, gently stir in cider mixture until apples are coated.

4. Sprinkle topping evenly over fruit, breaking up any large chunks. Place skillet on baking sheet and bake until fruit is tender and topping is deep golden brown, 15 to 20 minutes. Let crisp cool on wire rack for at least 15 minutes before serving.

VARIATIONS

Skillet Apple Crisp with Raspberries and Almonds
Substitute ¼ cup slivered almonds for pecans in step 1. Add ⅛ teaspoon almond extract to reduced cider with lemon juice in step 2. Stir ¼ cup fresh raspberries into apple mixture along with reduced cider in step 3.

Skillet Apple Crisp with Vanilla, Cardamom, and Pistachios
Substitute ¼ cup finely chopped pistachios for pecans in step 1. Substitute ¼ teaspoon ground cardamom for cinnamon in step 2. Add seeds from ¼ vanilla bean to apple and sugar mixture in step 2.

PEAR TARTE TATIN

CLASSIC TARTE TATIN IS A TIME-CONSUMING endeavor that involves making puff pastry from scratch, which demands not only several hours but also manual dexterity with a rolling pin. But when you're making dessert for two, the effort and time investment doesn't seem worth it. Nixing the homemade pastry, we set out to utilize convenient store-bought puff pastry to transform this labor-intensive French classic into a streamlined yet impressive dessert for two that delivered all the rich, sweet flavor of caramelized fruit and buttery, flaky pastry crust of the original. Since we were already taking some liberties with this dish, we decided to put one more spin on it and use pears in place of the apples, which we thought would up the elegance factor.

Traditionally, tarte Tatin is made by arranging fruit in a skillet, heating it until soft in a butter and sugar mixture that caramelizes into a rich syrup, and then covering it with pastry and baking the whole thing in the oven. Once baked, the tart is cooled and inverted, so the tender fruit that was initially on the bottom is now resting on top. Though the dish might sound simple, the sample recipes that we tried proved that the ideal flavors and textures might be harder to achieve than we expected. Most of the unsuccessful recipes we tested exhibited one of two flaws. One mistake was using sliced or chopped fruit, which made for a loose, wet tart that sprawled and fell apart when inverted. The second big mistake we saw was the decision to caramelize the fruit on top of the stove after the tart was completely baked. If the tart turned out juicy, it would not caramelize at all, and if it baked up dry, it burned. We resolved not to make these same mistakes and decided to forge ahead, starting with our caramel sauce, which we would make right in the skillet for convenience's sake.

After getting out a small pan, we began testing various amounts of butter and sugar, looking for the optimum ratio that would give us a richly flavorful but not overly sweet sauce. After a few tests, we found the sweet spot by combining 2 tablespoons of butter with ½ cup of sugar. We let the mixture cook for a couple of minutes until it began to turn lightly golden; if we cooked it any longer, the caramel burned in the time it took for the pears to cook through.

Next, we had to select our pears. We narrowed it down to the readily available varieties—Bosc, Anjou, Comice, and Bartlett—and cooked several of each to discern flavor differences. The Anjou and Comice pears developed a rather ordinary flavor once cooked. The Bartlett and Bosc pears fared better; tasters liked both the sweet, slightly spicy Bosc and the floral, sweet Bartlett. When it came to the level of ripeness, we found that moderately firm pears worked best and were able to withstand enough heat that they cooked up tender.

While tarte Tatin is typically made with fruit that's been cut into quarters, we encountered a few recipes that called for using halves. We decided to give the halved

PEAR TARTE TATIN

pears a go but quickly booted this idea as we had trouble getting the caramel to penetrate all the way through the large pieces. When we cooked the halves longer, we ended up with mushy pears that were overcooked.

Without a doubt, the pear quarters worked much better. We placed them cut side down in the pan, supporting each piece while we laid the next one so that none of them tipped over. In the end, we found we were able to cram an entire extra pear into the skillet by using quarters, for an even more flavorful dessert. To caramelize the other side of the pear quarters, we gently flipped them with a paring knife after a few minutes of cooking. Even though the caramelized sides of the pears

were soft, the sides facing up remained firm enough not to tear when we did this. A nonstick skillet helped prevent the quarters from sticking.

Now we could move on to the crust. We cut a circle out of a large sheet of thawed frozen puff pastry, making it an inch wider than the rim of our small 8-inch skillet so that we would have a nice outer crust on our finished tart. Then we chilled the puff pastry round on a large plate until we were ready to use it. Once our pears were cooked, we simply slid the round off the plate and onto the skillet, tucking the crust up so that it fit snugly in the pan. About 20 minutes in a 425-degree oven were enough to brown the pastry, which was now superbly flaky.

After allowing our tarte Tatin to cool briefly, we embarked upon the last major hurdle—flipping it over, which would give it its trademark upside-down presentation. Using a paring knife, we separated the tart from the inside edge of the skillet, then held a platter over the top of the skillet and flipped it over to ease the tart onto the platter. Though it looked flawless and tasted great, some of the puff pastry had become dense and soggy due to the lengthy cool-down time (it took about half an hour for the piping-hot caramel to come down in temperature). We took a cue from our pie crust recipes and tried cutting a few vents in the puff pastry dough before placing it on top of the pears. The pears now had an outlet for their steam, and our crust was considerably crisper.

Our tarte Tartin was every bit as impressive as the original French version, but now it was incredibly easy and perfectly scaled down for *deux*.

NOTES FROM THE TEST KITCHEN

PREPARING PEAR TARTE TATIN

1. Arrange pear quarters, cut side down, around edge of skillet, lifting each quarter to place next one. Then place remaining pears, cut side down, in middle of skillet.

2. After cooking pears in skillet until golden brown, and caramel is darkly colored, slide prepared dough round over pears.

3. Carefully tuck dough edges up against skillet wall. Bake and cool tart as directed.

4. Once tart has cooled, run paring knife around edge of pan. Place heatproof serving platter over skillet, hold tightly, and invert skillet and platter. Set platter on counter and lift skillet off, leaving tart behind.

Pear Tarte Tatin

SERVES 2

A 10-inch plate or pot lid can be used as a guide when cutting the pastry into a circle. When selecting the fruit, look for pears that are ripe but firm, which means the flesh at the base of the stem should give slightly when pressed. Use caution around the caramel—it is extremely hot.

1 (9½ by 9-inch) sheet frozen puff pastry, thawed

2 tablespoons unsalted butter

½ cup (3½ ounces) sugar

3 small Bosc or Bartlett pears (6 ounces each), peeled, cored, and quartered

1. Adjust oven rack to upper-middle position and heat oven to 425 degrees. Roll sheet of thawed puff pastry into 10 by 10-inch square. Cut pastry into 10-inch circle and, using sharp paring knife, cut four 1-inch slits in center of dough in circular pattern. Slide pastry onto lightly floured large plate and refrigerate until needed.

2. Melt butter in 8-inch nonstick skillet over medium-high heat. Stir in sugar and cook until foaming subsides and mixture is light golden, about 2 minutes.

3. Arrange pears around edge of skillet, lifting them on their cut sides so they stand up. Arrange remaining pears in middle of skillet. Cook pears over medium heat until pears begin to turn golden brown and caramel is darkly colored, 9 to 11 minutes, turning pears over, so cut sides are facing up, halfway through cooking time.

4. Off heat, slide chilled dough round over pears in skillet. Fold back edge of dough so it fits snugly into skillet. Transfer skillet to oven and bake tart until crust is golden brown and crisp, 20 to 25 minutes, rotating pan halfway through baking.

5. Using potholder (skillet handle will be hot), remove skillet from oven. Let tart cool in skillet for 30 minutes. Run small knife around edge, place inverted heatproof serving platter (or cutting board) over top, and gently flip tart onto platter, using oven mitts or kitchen towels if skillet is still hot. Scrape out any pears that stick to skillet and put back into place on tart. Slice tart into wedges and serve.

TEXAS-STYLE BLUEBERRY COBBLERS

WHEN WE THINK OF COBBLER, WE THINK OF LOTS of sweet, jammy fruit under a biscuit topping. But in some parts of Texas, the same word refers to a very different dessert, one with a moist, tender interior and a crisp, craggy top. As the cobbler bakes, the fruit (which starts out on top) sinks and forms juicy pockets throughout. But no matter the name, it tastes delicious. While this type of cobbler is usually prepared in a large baking dish, yielding enough dessert to feed at least 10 hungry cowboys, we wanted to scale it down using a pair of ramekins, to yield two individual desserts.

Working our way through a stack of Texas community cookbooks, we found a version of the homey recipe in almost every one. They went under several different names, but the techniques and ingredients were nearly identical: Butter is melted in a baking dish; a simple batter of milk, flour, baking powder, and sugar is poured over it; fruit is then scattered on top; and the whole thing is baked. Though peaches are standard cobbler fare in Texas, we decided to use blueberries, which would require no prep and fit nicely in our ramekins. We tested a number of recipes, swapping in blueberries, and although they were very easy, we did uncover a few problems: The cobblers were thin and a little bland, and the tops were underbaked. Clearly we had our work cut out for us, so we rolled up our sleeves and got to work.

Since all of our tasters had complained about a bland batter and weak berry flavor, we decided to address flavor first. We started by increasing the amount of butter that we melted in the ramekins, thinking this would add more richness. But now tasters complained that the bottoms of the cobblers were greasy. We found we could cut the grease, but keep the added richness and flavor, if we divided the butter between the ramekins and the batter. We settled on ½ tablespoon of melted butter in each ramekin and another 2 tablespoons stirred into the batter. This worked much better—now the cobbler's crisp brown edges were so good that our tasters fought over them.

To turn the berries into a more cohesive filling, we realized that we needed to get their juices flowing before the fruit went into the oven. We grabbed a potato masher and broke them up a bit. Adding a little sugar helped further break down the berries, and for a bright note, we stirred in grated lemon zest. But in the baked cobblers, the zest was barely discernible. In the past, we've found that processing citrus zest helps to release its flavorful oils. We were using such a small amount of zest, however, that using the food processor was out of the question. Instead, we reached for a spoon and used it to mash the zest with some of the sugar. This worked like a charm, and our baked cobblers now had a hint of bright lemon flavor.

Last, to get a crisp, nicely browned top, we knew what we had to do: We sprinkled the cobbler with sugar to help it caramelize. But before we did that, it occurred to us that now we had another chance to reinforce the lemon flavor. We mashed a portion of the lemon-sugar mixture with the berries, as before, but set some aside to sprinkle over the unbaked assembled cobblers.

After 35 minutes in a 350-degree oven, our pair of cobblers were golden brown with nicely crisped edges. And though they were scaled down in size, they delivered big, rich, Texas-size flavor.

Texas-Style Blueberry Cobblers
SERVES 2

You will need two 12-ounce ramekins with straight sides for this recipe (see page 3). Keep a close eye on the butter as it melts in the oven so that it doesn't scorch. If using frozen blueberries, thaw them first.

- 1 tablespoon unsalted butter, cut into 2 pieces, plus 2 tablespoons melted and cooled
- ⅓ cup (2⅓ ounces) sugar
- ½ teaspoon grated lemon zest
- 5 ounces (1 cup) blueberries
- ½ cup (2½ ounces) all-purpose flour
- ¾ teaspoon baking powder
- ¼ teaspoon salt
- ⅓ cup whole milk

1. Adjust oven rack to upper-middle position and heat oven to 350 degrees. Place two 12-ounce ramekins on aluminum foil–lined baking sheet and place 1 butter piece in each ramekin. Transfer to oven and heat until butter is melted, about 5 minutes.

2. Meanwhile, mash 1 tablespoon sugar and lemon zest with spoon in bowl until combined. In separate bowl, using potato masher, mash blueberries and 1 teaspoon lemon-sugar mixture together until berries are coarsely mashed.

3. Combine remaining sugar, flour, baking powder, and salt in large bowl. Whisk in milk and melted butter until smooth. Remove sheet pan with ramekins from oven and transfer to wire rack. Divide batter evenly between ramekins.

4. Dollop mashed blueberry mixture evenly over batter and sprinkle with remaining lemon sugar. Bake until cobblers are golden brown and edges are crisp, 35 to 40 minutes, rotating pan halfway through baking. Let cobblers cool on wire rack for 15 minutes. Serve warm.

MAKING TEXAS-STYLE BLUEBERRY COBBLERS

1. Melt butter in two 12-ounce ramekins in oven.

2. Divide batter evenly between ramekins over melted butter.

3. Scatter mashed berries evenly over batter, which will rise over berries in oven.

CRANBERRY UPSIDE-DOWN CAKE

THOUGH PINEAPPLE UPSIDE-DOWN CAKE SEEMS TO garner all the attention, we're just as enamored of its cranberry counterpart. This ruby-crowned cake is a visual stunner, and the delicate balance of sweet-tart cranberry topping and tender butter cake makes it every bit as appealing as the pineapple version. We set out to develop a recipe for a petite version of cranberry upside-down cake, which would make an elegant finale to a fancy holiday dinner for two.

As with all upside-down cakes, the inverted preparation (with the berries baked on the bottom, then turned out to the top) can easily spell disaster. We tested a number of recipes and encountered cakes in which the fruit topping was thin and runny or, worse, a super-sticky candied mess that we couldn't pry out of

CRANBERRY UPSIDE-DOWN CAKE

the pan. As for the cake itself, though a sturdy texture is a must to support the fruit, most recipes we tried went too far in this direction, resulting in cakes that were dry and dense. Our goals were obvious: We wanted a moist, tender cake topped with a nicely clingy cranberry topping. Clearly, we had our work cut out for us.

Putting the fruit aside for the moment, we started with the cake, scaling down the standard butter cake called for in the typical pineapple version of the recipe. After numerous tests, we cut the yield of the batter by about half, which fit nicely in a 6-inch round cake pan. For the main players in our cake, we settled on ½ cup of flour, ⅓ cup of sugar, 3 tablespoons of butter, and ¼ cup of milk. Though our testing progressed fairly smoothly, the eggs proved a bigger challenge to figure out.

We started out with two eggs, which gave us a cake with nice richness, but it was just too wet. On the other hand, a cake made with one egg felt lean and dry. Using one egg plus one yolk put us on the right path, but the texture was still too dense. Adjusting how we added the eggs proved key to producing the right structure. Rather than beating whole eggs into the batter, we added the yolks and whipped the egg white separately (with a pinch of cream of tartar to stabilize it). Folding the fluffy beaten white into the finished batter gave us the ideal texture—our cake was light and tender but still sturdy enough to support the heavy fruit topping.

It was time to move on to the fruit. Our sample recipes had taught us that simply lining the cake pan with cranberries tossed with sugar would lead to a watery, runny mess—far from our goal of a clingy berry topping. It was clear that precooking the cranberries and sugar to evaporate some of the fruit's moisture would be necessary. We simmered the berries with butter and sugar in a small skillet and quickly discovered that it was crucial to cook them briefly; otherwise they started to break down and turn to mush. Just a few minutes was enough to soften (but not burst) the berries and reduce the sugar and juices into a thick syrup that made the topping cohesive and clingy.

Though our topping now had the right consistency, tasters found it to be a little too tart. Increasing the sugar made the topping taste like candy, so we decided to add another sweetener. After trying honey, maple syrup, and corn syrup, our tasters settled on raspberry jam, which perfectly rounded out the tartness of the cranberries and enhanced the fruit flavor of the topping.

We baked our cake for 40 minutes, then let it rest briefly before flipping it out onto a platter. Our Cranberry Upside-Down Cake was the ultimate finish to any dressed-up dinner—and the best part was that it tasted just as good as it looked.

Cranberry Upside-Down Cake

SERVES 2

You will need a 6-inch round cake pan for this recipe (see page 3). It's important not to overcook the cranberries in step 2; stir gently and make sure to remove them from the heat before they burst. Make sure to scrape down the mixing bowl often when making the cake batter, to ensure that all ingredients are well incorporated. To prevent this cake from sticking, do not let it cool in the pan for more than 10 minutes. The finished cake can be held at room temperature for up to 8 hours before serving. Serve with Whipped Cream (recipe follows).

TOPPING

  2 tablespoons unsalted butter

  5 ounces (1¼ cups) fresh or frozen cranberries, thawed

  ⅓ cup (2⅓ ounces) sugar

  1 tablespoon seedless raspberry jam

  ⅛ teaspoon vanilla extract

CAKE

  ½ cup (2½ ounces) all-purpose flour

  ½ teaspoon baking powder

  ⅛ teaspoon salt

  ¼ cup whole milk

  ½ teaspoon vanilla extract

  3 tablespoons unsalted butter, softened

  ⅓ cup (2⅓ ounces) sugar

  1 large egg, separated, plus 1 large yolk

     Pinch cream of tartar

1. FOR THE TOPPING: Adjust oven rack to middle position and heat oven to 350 degrees. Grease one 6-inch round cake pan, line with parchment paper, grease parchment, then flour pan.

2. Melt butter in 8-inch nonstick skillet over medium-low heat. Add cranberries, sugar, and jam and cook, stirring gently, until cranberries are just softened, about 3 minutes. Off heat, stir in vanilla. Pour berries with juice into prepared pan, gently spread into even layer, and refrigerate for 30 minutes.

3. FOR THE CAKE: Whisk flour, baking powder, and salt together in medium bowl. Whisk milk and vanilla together in separate bowl.

4. Using stand mixer fitted with paddle, beat butter and sugar together on medium-high speed until pale and fluffy, about 3 minutes, scraping down bowl as needed. Add egg yolks, 1 at a time, and beat until combined, scraping down bowl after each addition. Reduce speed to low and add flour mixture in 3 additions, alternating with 2 additions of milk mixture, scraping down bowl as needed. Give batter final stir by hand, then transfer batter to large bowl.

5. Using dry, clean bowl and whisk attachment, whip egg white and cream of tartar together on medium-low speed until foamy, about 1 minute. Increase speed to medium-high and whip until soft peaks form, 2 to 3 minutes. Whisk one-third of whipped white into batter, then fold in remaining white.

6. Pour batter over chilled cranberry mixture and smooth top. Bake until toothpick inserted in center of cake comes out clean, 35 to 40 minutes, rotating pan halfway through baking. Let cake cool on wire rack for 10 minutes. Run paring knife around edge of cake and invert onto serving platter. Serve.

Whipped Cream

MAKES ABOUT ¾ CUP

The whipped cream can be refrigerated in a fine-mesh strainer set over a small bowl, wrapped tightly with plastic wrap, for up to 8 hours. For a boozy version of this whipped cream, add 1 to 2 teaspoons of bourbon.

⅓ **cup heavy cream, chilled**

1 **teaspoon sugar**

¼ **teaspoon vanilla extract**

Using stand mixer fitted with whisk, whip cream, sugar, and vanilla together on medium-low speed until foamy, about 1 minute. Increase speed to high and whip until soft peaks form, 1 to 3 minutes.

LEMON BUNDT CAKES

UNLIKE MOST CAKES, WHICH CALL FOR FUSSY mixing methods and intricately applied frosting, the Bundt cake is a straightforward cake that derives its elegance from its simplicity. We thought this unassuming cake would make the ideal addition to our lineup of scaled-down desserts, but instead of a single cake, we sought to create two mini Bundts. For some pizzazz, we decided to flavor them with lemon, which would infuse the tender, buttery crumb with a sweet, citrusy tang.

To start, we needed to find just the right bakeware. After a bit of digging around at our local kitchen supply shop, we found a pair of 1-cup Bundt cake pans. Our bakeware ready to go, we headed into the kitchen.

After looking at test kitchen recipes for Bundt cakes, we decided to adapt one that fell into the 1-2-3-4 cake category—it called for 1 cup of butter, 2 cups of sugar, 3 cups of flour, and 4 eggs, plus 1 cup of milk for a liquid component. But when we scaled the amounts down proportionally, our Bundt cakes were dry, with a coarse, crumbly texture. In addition to fixing the texture of our petite cakes, we'd need to figure out the best way to work in the light, bright citrus flavor we were after.

After a number of tests, we settled on ⅓ cup of sugar, ½ cup of flour, and a single egg for sweetness and structure. But we still had the dryness issue to resolve and set about adjusting the amount of butter (we had started with 2 tablespoons) to fix it. Four tablespoons greatly boosted the cakes' richness and tenderness but also left behind a greasy residue. Three tablespoons worked better. Swapping the milk for buttermilk (a trade we've successfully employed in other baked goods) also helped the texture, yielding a lighter, more tender crumb.

Most Bundt cake recipes follow the standard mixing technique of creaming the butter and sugar, adding the eggs, then alternating flour and liquid until combined. We wondered if we could streamline these steps, and tried a few versions of the ultra-easy dump-and-stir method. Sadly, they all produced rubbery, dense cakes, so we knew that creaming was indeed necessary to achieve a light and even crumb. The whipping action aerates the batter, contributing lightness to the final cakes.

But we still needed to find a way to maximize the lemon flavor; more than a teaspoon of lemon juice created cakes so tender that they practically fell apart when sliced, yet any less imparted merely a hint of flavor. For more potent lemon flavor, we decided to add some zest.

After some fiddling, we found that 2 teaspoons of zest, plus a teaspoon of lemon juice, gave the cakes perfumed lemon flavor without affecting the texture.

Though our two mini Bundts now offered bright lemon flavor and a moist, tender texture, tasters felt they were missing one thing: a sweet, citrusy glaze. A simple mixture of confectioners' sugar, lemon (or orange) juice, grated zest, and a pinch of salt was an easy and quick solution. After letting our baked cakes cool, we drizzled the glaze over the top. Not only did it reinforce the zippy lemon flavor of our cakes, but it also made a nice accent to their perfectly golden exteriors.

Glazed Lemon Bundt Cakes

SERVES 2

You will need two 1-cup Bundt pans for this recipe (see page 3). Don't be tempted to make the cake in another type of pan; the heavy batter was designed to work in a Bundt pan that has a center tube to facilitate baking. Make sure to scrape down the mixing bowl often when making the cake batter, to ensure that all ingredients are well incorporated.

CAKES

- 3 tablespoons unsalted butter, cut into chunks and softened, plus 1 tablespoon melted
- ½ cup (2½ ounces) plus 1 tablespoon all-purpose flour
- ¼ teaspoon salt
- ¼ teaspoon baking powder
- ⅛ teaspoon baking soda
- 2 tablespoons buttermilk, room temperature
- ½ teaspoon vanilla extract
- 2 teaspoons grated lemon zest plus 1 teaspoon juice
- ⅓ cup (2⅓ ounces) granulated sugar
- 1 large egg, room temperature

GLAZE

- ⅓ cup (1⅓ ounces) confectioners' sugar, plus extra as needed
- ¼ teaspoon grated lemon or orange zest plus 2¾ teaspoons juice
- Pinch salt

1. FOR THE CAKES: Adjust oven rack to lower-middle position and heat oven to 350 degrees. Stir together 1 tablespoon melted butter and 1 tablespoon flour to form paste. Using pastry brush, brush paste evenly over inside of two 1-cup Bundt pans. Whisk remaining ½ cup flour, salt, baking powder, and baking soda together in medium bowl. In small bowl, whisk buttermilk, vanilla, and lemon zest and juice together.

2. Using stand mixer fitted with paddle, beat remaining 3 tablespoons softened butter and sugar together on medium-high speed until pale and fluffy, about 3 minutes, scraping down bowl as needed. Beat in egg until fully incorporated, about 30 seconds, scraping down bowl halfway through. Reduce speed to low and add flour mixture in 3 additions, alternating with 2 additions of buttermilk mixture, scraping down bowl as needed. Increase speed to medium-high and beat until mixture is completely smooth, about 30 seconds. Give batter final stir by hand.

3. Divide batter evenly between prepared pans, smooth tops, and gently tap each pan on counter to release air bubbles. Wipe any drops of batter off sides of pans. Place pans on rimmed baking sheet and bake cakes until light golden brown and toothpick inserted into centers comes out clean, 20 to 22 minutes, rotating sheet halfway through baking.

4. Let cakes cool in pans on wire rack for 10 minutes. Remove cakes from pans and let cool completely on wire rack, about 30 minutes.

5. FOR THE GLAZE: Whisk sugar, lemon zest and juice, and salt together in bowl until smooth, adding extra sugar as needed to achieve thick consistency. Set wire rack with completely cooled cakes over baking sheet. Pour glaze over tops of cakes, letting glaze drip down sides. Let glaze set before serving, about 25 minutes.

NOTES FROM THE TEST KITCHEN

PREPARING BUNDT PANS

A Bundt cake is attractive only if you get it out of the pan in one piece. After unmolding lots of Bundt cakes unsuccessfully, we came up with a foolproof solution. This method works much better than the standard technique of greasing and flouring, which isn't as foolproof and often results in a cake with an unsightly pasty white film from the flour.

Make simple paste from 1 tablespoon melted butter and 1 tablespoon flour. Apply paste to inside of Bundt pans with pastry brush, taking care to reach all nooks and crannies.

NO-BAKE PUMPKIN PIE

SURE, PUMPKIN PIE IS A MUST-HAVE COME TURKEY day—and sometimes we crave this fall dessert other times of the year as well. But if you're baking for two, you may not want to go through all the paces (like making the dough and rolling it out) to put this classic pie on the table. Fortunately, there's an alternative: the no-bake pumpkin pie. Although often bypassed in favor of the baked kind, the no-bake pumpkin pie has a couple of benefits not offered by its traditional counterpart, one being a much easier press-in crust that requires just a quick stint in the oven, another being a creamier filling with a fresher, brighter pumpkin flavor. We thought this added up to the perfect pumpkin pie for two, so we set out to create our own scaled-down version.

We began by testing a number of recipes and were disappointed by the lackluster results. In some recipes the filling was thickened with so much gelatin that it became rubbery; in others, cream cheese was used as the binder, and the filling ended up dense and chalky. We wanted a creamy filling, but we also wanted it to be light. We came across several chiffon-style pies, which were certainly light, but the addition of whipped egg whites made them almost spongy. Despite these obstacles, the promise of producing a creamy pumpkin pie without the hassle of making pie pastry was appealing. Surely we could resolve these issues.

Luckily for us, we already had a press-in graham cracker crust in the test kitchen archives that we could work with. After scaling down the ingredients, we processed the graham crackers with melted butter and sugar, pressed the whole mixture into a small 6-inch pie dish, baked the crust, and set it aside to cool while we got started on the filling. For our preliminary test,

we combined ⅔ cup of pumpkin, ⅓ cup of sugar, and ¼ cup each of milk and heavy cream. We also needed a thickener. Though gelatin and cornstarch are the most common candidates, we also tested tapioca, arrowroot, and potato starch. In the end, we preferred the gelatin-thickened filling; just 1 teaspoon produced a pie that could be neatly sliced but wasn't excessively stiff.

Now that our pie filling was holding together, our tasters shifted their complaints to the fibrous texture of the pumpkin. Despite being labeled "pureed," canned pumpkin is not truly smooth. A quick whirl in the food processor yielded a silky mixture worthy of the label.

Although the consistency of our pie was better, it needed more richness. Switching from a blend of milk and heavy cream to all heavy cream helped. We also tried whipping the cream and folding it into the filling. Although the texture was lighter and fluffier, the pumpkin and the cream settled into an unattractive mottled mess. Ultimately, we found that pureeing some of the cream with the pumpkin worked better.

Our filling was getting pretty good, but our tasters still clamored for a richer and more velvety texture—like that of a baked pumpkin pie. Comparing the ingredient lists of our no-bake recipe and the test kitchen's favorite baked pumpkin pie, we saw one major difference: Our no-bake recipe didn't contain eggs. We had rejected chiffon-style pies because the whipped whites made them too mousselike. But what if we kept the yolks and cooked them with the sugar and cream to form a custard? We had to heat the cream anyway to dissolve the sugar. After a few tests, we found that two egg yolks gave our pie filling the luxurious texture we wanted.

Rich, creamy, and smooth, this pie filling now needed a refined flavor to match its texture. To add some complexity, we included a few spices. A mix of ground cinnamon, ginger, and nutmeg tasted best, but because the spices weren't cooked, their raw flavors quickly became overly harsh. We decreased the amount, but the harshness persisted. Next we tried heating them with the cream; this softened their hard edge while drawing out more of their heady, fragrant qualities.

To add some brightness and offset the warmth of the spices, we tried adding lemon juice, but it was too sour. Orange juice worked much better, adding a sweet, perfumed punch.

With these last adjustments, our no-bake pie was finally good enough to be a permanent fixture in our cooking-for-two repertoire—no matter the season.

NOTES FROM THE TEST KITCHEN

MAKING A GRAHAM CRACKER CRUST

To make graham cracker crust, press crumb mixture evenly and firmly across bottom and up sides of pie plate, using bottom of measuring cup.

No-Bake Pumpkin Pie

SERVES 2

You will need a 6-inch pie plate for this recipe (see page 3). Be sure to use pumpkin puree, not pumpkin pie filling. Serve with Whipped Cream (page 276).

CRUST

- 5 whole graham crackers, broken into 1-inch pieces
- 3 tablespoons unsalted butter, melted and cooled
- 2 tablespoons granulated sugar

FILLING

- ½ cup heavy cream, chilled
- ⅓ cup (2⅓ ounces) sugar
- 2 tablespoons orange juice, chilled
- 1 teaspoon vanilla extract
- ½ teaspoon ground cinnamon
- ¼ teaspoon salt
- ¼ teaspoon ground ginger
- Pinch ground nutmeg
- 1 teaspoon unflavored gelatin
- 2 large egg yolks
- ⅔ cup unsweetened canned pumpkin puree

1. FOR THE CRUST: Adjust oven rack to middle position and heat oven to 325 degrees. Process graham cracker pieces in food processor to fine, even crumbs, about 15 seconds. Sprinkle melted butter and sugar over crumbs and pulse to incorporate. Sprinkle mixture into 6-inch pie plate. Use bottom of measuring cup to press crumbs into even layer on bottom and sides of pie plate.

2. Bake until crust is fragrant and beginning to brown, 13 to 15 minutes. Transfer pie plate to wire rack.

3. FOR THE FILLING: Combine ¼ cup cream, sugar, orange juice, vanilla, cinnamon, salt, ginger, and nutmeg in small saucepan. Sprinkle gelatin over top and let sit until gelatin softens, about 5 minutes. Whisk egg yolks together in medium bowl.

4. Cook cream mixture over medium heat until gelatin dissolves and mixture is hot (but not boiling), about 2 minutes. Slowly whisk hot gelatin mixture into egg yolks to temper. Pour mixture back into saucepan and continue to cook over medium heat, stirring constantly, until slightly thickened, about 1 minute. Transfer mixture to medium bowl.

5. Puree pumpkin in food processor until smooth, about 15 seconds. With processor running, add remaining ¼ cup cream in steady stream. Scrape down bowl and continue to process, 10 to 15 seconds longer. Stir pumpkin mixture into warm cream mixture until completely smooth.

6. Pour pumpkin filling into baked and cooled pie crust. Refrigerate pie, uncovered, until chilled and set, about 6 hours. Serve chilled or at room temperature.

USE IT UP: CANNED PUMPKIN

Pumpkin Loaf

MAKES ONE 5½ BY 3-INCH LOAF

You will need one 5½ by 3-inch loaf pan for this recipe (see page 3).

- ¾ cup (3¾ ounces) all-purpose flour
- ¼ teaspoon baking soda
- ¼ teaspoon baking powder
- ¼ teaspoon ground cinnamon
- ¼ teaspoon salt
- ½ cup pumpkin puree
- ⅓ cup (2⅓ ounces) sugar
- 1 large egg
- 2 tablespoons unsalted butter, melted and cooled
- ½ teaspoon vanilla extract
- ¼ cup pecans or walnuts, toasted and chopped coarse (optional)

1. Adjust oven rack to lower-middle position and heat oven to 350 degrees. Grease 5½ by 3-inch loaf pan.

2. Whisk flour, baking soda, baking powder, cinnamon, and salt together in large bowl. In medium bowl, whisk pumpkin, sugar, egg, melted butter, and vanilla together until smooth. Gently fold pumpkin mixture into flour mixture until just combined. Gently fold in pecans (if using).

3. Scrape batter into prepared pan and smooth top. Bake until golden brown and toothpick inserted into center comes out clean, 35 to 40 minutes, rotating pan halfway through baking.

4. Let loaf cool in pan on wire rack for 10 minutes. Remove loaf from pan and let cool completely, about 1 hour. Serve.

RUSTIC WALNUT TARTS

WITH ITS RICH CARAMEL FLAVORS, CRUNCHY NUTS, and buttery crust, it's easy to see why pecan pie is so popular. But some occasions call for a dessert that's a bit more refined. We set our sights on developing a recipe for the dressed-up version of pecan pie: the nut tart. But instead of just one large tart, we would create two individual tarts. Ideally, they would deliver the same enticing textures and flavors of the homier pie version. Given that tart dough can be especially finicky, we were determined to develop a recipe that would be just as simple and foolproof as it was satisfying.

Starting with the foundation of our tarts, we considered the dough. Traditional tart dough recipes call for rolling and fitting a single tart shell into a pan, but since we were making two individual tarts, we wanted something simpler that wouldn't require a rolling pin, so we turned to testing pat-in-the-pan-style crusts. We tried several recipes, which included everything from shortening to eggs and even cream cheese, but they all produced crusts that were too cookielike and crumbly. More important, the intense buttery flavor we wanted was lost. We returned to a basic crust recipe that relied on butter for the dairy ingredient. Knowing that we wanted a prominent nut flavor throughout our tarts, and not just in the filling, we decided to incorporate nuts into the dough. We began our tests by cutting the butter into the flour but quickly turned to a food processor to speed things up. After we had combined the flour, sugar, toasted walnuts, a little baking powder, and salt in the food processor, we added the chilled butter, then pulsed everything to make a sandy-textured dough that was easy to press into our individual tart pans. We chilled the shells in the freezer, then baked them and set them aside to cool. Because the butter was evenly distributed throughout the dough (thanks to our food processor), we got big bites of crisp, buttery crust with each forkful.

Now we could move on to our filling. When it comes to pecan pie, many fillings tend to be overly sweet, thereby obscuring the flavor of the nuts, so we knew we'd have to look out for this potential pitfall. Starting with the basics, we combined ⅓ cup of sugar, 2 tablespoons of melted butter, and an egg. We also added a small amount of corn syrup, as we'd learned from past experience that it would prevent the filling from becoming gritty or separating. We poured our filling into the tart shells, then sprinkled toasted, chopped walnuts over the top and baked our tarts in a moderate 350-degree oven for about 30 minutes. When the tarts came out, we were disappointed with their cloyingly sweet, one-dimensional flavor.

For more complexity, we tried swapping out the granulated sugar for brown sugar. This worked wonders, and using this same tactic in our tart shells gave them a more nuanced flavor as well. Although the brown sugar had tamed the overt sweetness of the filling, tasters still commented that our tarts were a bit on the sweet side. A pinch of salt and a dash of vanilla kept the filling from being cloying and enhanced the rich, caramel-like flavors. But what really brought the nutty caramel notes to the forefront was a bit of bourbon—just 2 teaspoons gave the filling some oomph without making it taste overly boozy.

With the shells already baked, our walnut tarts needed just 25 minutes in the oven. After they'd cooled, we reached for our forks. Just one bite of the crisp, buttery crust and rich, caramel-y walnut filling told us we'd created a recipe we'd be making time and again.

Rustic Walnut Tarts

SERVES 2

You will need two 4-inch fluted tart pans with removable bottoms for this recipe (see page 3). Pecans can be substituted for the walnuts if desired. The baked and cooled tart shells can be held at room temperature for up to 1 day. Serve with plain or bourbon-spiked Whipped Cream (see page 276), if desired.

CRUST

- ½ cup (2½ ounces) all-purpose flour
- 2 tablespoons packed light brown sugar
- 2 tablespoons walnuts, toasted and chopped coarse
- ⅛ teaspoon baking powder
- ⅛ teaspoon salt
- 4 tablespoons unsalted butter, cut into ½-inch pieces and chilled

FILLING

- ⅓ cup packed (2⅓ ounces) light brown sugar
- 3 tablespoons light corn syrup
- 2 tablespoons unsalted butter, melted and cooled

RUSTIC WALNUT TARTS

2 teaspoons bourbon or dark rum

½ teaspoon vanilla extract

   Pinch salt

1 large egg

⅓ cup walnuts, chopped coarse

1. FOR THE CRUST: Grease two 4-inch tart pans with removable bottoms. Process flour, sugar, walnuts, baking powder, and salt in food processor until combined, about 5 seconds. Sprinkle butter over top and pulse until mixture is pale yellow and resembles coarse cornmeal, about 8 pulses.

2. Sprinkle mixture evenly into prepared pans. Press crumbs firmly into even layer over pan bottom and up sides using bottom of dry measuring cup. Set tart pans on plate, cover with plastic wrap, and freeze, for at least 30 minutes or up to 1 week.

3. Adjust oven rack to middle position and heat oven to 350 degrees. Set tart pans on rimmed baking sheet. Press double layer of aluminum foil into frozen tart shells, over edges of pans, and fill with pie weights. Bake until tart shells are golden brown and set, 20 to 25 minutes, rotating sheet halfway through baking. Remove weights and foil; let shells cool slightly while making filling.

4. FOR THE FILLING: Whisk sugar, corn syrup, melted butter, bourbon, vanilla, and salt together in medium bowl until sugar dissolves. Whisk in egg until combined. Pour filling evenly into tart shells and sprinkle with walnuts. Bake tarts on baking sheet until filling is set and walnuts begin to brown, 25 to 30 minutes, rotating sheet halfway through baking. Let tarts cool completely, about 1 hour.

5. To serve, remove outer metal ring from each tart pan, slide thin metal spatula between tart and tart pan bottom, and carefully slide tart onto plate.

NOTES FROM THE TEST KITCHEN

STORING BUTTER

When cooking for two, chances are that unless you're a frequent baker, it will take you a while to run through a pound of butter. And when stored in the refrigerator, butter (even when wrapped) can pick up odors and turn rancid within just a few weeks. To avoid bad butter, keep it in the freezer and transfer it, one stick at a time, to the fridge.

HOT FUDGE PUDDING CAKES

HOT FUDGE PUDDING CAKE IS THE ULTIMATE IN home alchemy: Cake batter, sprinkled with a mixture of sugar and cocoa and topped with boiling water, is transformed in the oven into a moist, brownie-like chocolate cake with a hidden reservoir of fudgy, gooey sauce built in underneath. But most recipes use a 13 by 9-inch baking dish, for a cake large enough to satisfy a big family (and ensure some leftovers). We thought scaling down this dessert to fit in individual ramekins would give this casual dish a touch of class, while ensuring that we still had enough for two bona fide chocoholics.

After pulling out a number of hot fudge pudding cake recipes from our cookbook library, we found they all followed the same basic method. The batter is made in the manner of a brownie batter—using cocoa powder or chocolate, flour, sugar, butter, and eggs, plus salt, vanilla, and a leavener—but with milk added. After the batter goes into the dish, things take an unusual turn. A mixture of sugar and cocoa is sprinkled over the batter, then liquid is poured on top, and the whole thing is popped into the oven. Though the step of pouring liquid over the batter might seem like a mistake, this is what transforms this dessert. The cake rises to the surface, and the liquid that started out on top sinks to the bottom, taking the sugar and cocoa with it, and morphs into hot fudge sauce. But as appealing as the recipes sounded on paper, they were all disappointing. Instead of tasting deeply chocolaty, they tasted dull and mild. And instead of providing enough spoon-coating sauce to accompany the cake portion, some were dry, with a disproportionate amount of cake, while the others were soupy, with a wet, sticky, underdone cake. We set out to right these wrongs.

We cobbled a working recipe together, modeled after the more successful versions but with reduced quantities of ingredients. Our first goal was to pump up the chocolate flavor, and we suspected that the problem was that most recipes call for cocoa rather than chocolate. In our experience, cocoa alone carries potent chocolate flavor, but it doesn't deliver the complexity or richness of chocolate. We tried adding different amounts of bittersweet chocolate to our cake base of ¼ cup of flour and ¼ cup of cocoa and eventually hit on the right amount (less than an ounce) to obtain deeper flavor.

Using Dutch-processed cocoa, instead of natural cocoa, ensured a fuller, rounder chocolate flavor.

For sweetness and to counter the bitterness of the cocoa, most recipes turn to granulated sugar. But cakes made with granulated sugar alone developed a sticky, tough crust with one-dimensional sweetness. We much preferred cakes that incorporated some brown sugar, too, as its rich molasses flavor added some complexity.

The next issue we needed to settle was how many eggs to use. We had encountered recipes that omitted the eggs completely, but the resulting cakes were mushy and crumbly. We conducted a number of tests but in the end opted to use just one yolk. This cake offered a dense and brownielike texture, with a nicely yielding crumb.

Moving on to the butter, which is always melted, we tried varying amounts, ultimately settling on 2 tablespoons, which provided ample richness without making our cakes greasy. In addition to butter, hot fudge pudding cakes contain some dairy, usually in the form of milk. We tried heavy cream and half-and-half to see if either had desirable effects, but both produced cakes that were at least a little bit on the greasy side. Milk was the way to go.

For lift, we relied on baking powder, finding that ¾ teaspoon gave the cakes the right stature. To heighten flavor, we added a pinch of salt and a teaspoon of vanilla (there was a lot of chocolate flavor to contend with).

Our last task was to figure out how much liquid we needed to pour over the cakes to create the sauce at the bottom of the ramekins. One-half cup total—proportionally more than what most recipes call for—was ideal, yielding an ample amount of sauce with the right consistency. Some hot fudge pudding cake recipes suggested using coffee instead of water, so we decided to give it a try. Indeed, we thought the coffee was a nice addition. It didn't interfere with the chocolate flavor but nicely complemented it, cutting through the sweetness of the cake and enriching its flavor.

After waiting patiently for our cakes to puff, which took about 15 minutes in a 400-degree oven, we were ready to dig in. Unfortunately, we were greeted with sodden cake and a thin sauce. For the next batch, we kept our patience in check and allowed the cakes to cool for 15 minutes. Now they had a brownielike texture with a rich, thick sauce underneath. At long last, we had achieved pudding cake perfection.

Hot Fudge Pudding Cakes

SERVES 2

You will need two 6-ounce ramekins for this recipe (see page 3). Serve with vanilla or coffee ice cream.

- ¼ cup (¾ ounce) Dutch-processed cocoa
- 2 tablespoons unsalted butter, cut into 2 pieces
- ⅔ ounce bittersweet or semisweet chocolate, chopped
- ¼ cup (1¼ ounces) all-purpose flour
- ¾ teaspoon baking powder
- 6 tablespoons (2⅔ ounces) granulated sugar
- 2 tablespoons whole milk
- 1 teaspoon vanilla extract
- 1 large egg yolk
  Pinch salt
- 2 tablespoons packed brown sugar
- ½ cup coffee

1. Adjust oven rack to lower-middle position and heat oven to 400 degrees. Grease two 6-ounce ramekins and arrange on rimmed baking sheet.

2. Microwave 2 tablespoons cocoa, butter, and chocolate together in medium bowl at 50 percent power, stirring occasionally, until smooth, 1 to 2 minutes; let cool slightly. In small bowl, whisk flour and baking powder together.

3. In large bowl, whisk ¼ cup granulated sugar, milk, vanilla, egg yolk, and salt together until combined. Whisk in cooled chocolate mixture, followed by flour mixture, until just combined. Divide batter evenly between prepared ramekins and smooth tops. (Ramekins can be covered and refrigerated for up to 1 day.)

4. Combine remaining 2 tablespoons cocoa, remaining 2 tablespoons granulated sugar, and brown sugar in bowl, breaking up clumps with fingers. Sprinkle 3 tablespoons of mixture into each ramekin, followed by ¼ cup coffee.

5. Bake until cakes are puffed and bubbling, 16 to 18 minutes. (Do not overbake.) Let cakes cool for 15 minutes before serving in ramekins (cakes will fall slightly).

CHOCOLATE ÉCLAIR CAKE

DESPITE ITS NAME, CHOCOLATE ÉCLAIR CAKE IS neither an oversized éclair nor a typical baked cake. It actually is closer to a classic easy icebox cake. Most recipes for this online phenomenon follow the same path; first a "mousse" filling is made from store-bought whipped topping and instant vanilla pudding, then this filling is alternated in a casserole dish with graham crackers and the whole thing topped with chocolate frosting. What results is almost ethereal: The creamy, light filling softens the graham crackers just enough to scoop up with a spoon, and the top layer adds just a hint of rich chocolate flavor. But though it sounds good on paper, the convenience products lead to an overly sweet dessert with an artificial flavor. We knew if we could revamp this dessert to ditch the processed ingredients, we could transform this lowbrow dish into a homey, satisfying dessert for two—the perfect finish to any comfort-food supper.

The first order of business was to select the right vessel for our scaled-down dessert. We knew that an 8-inch square baking dish, which is roughly half the size of the 13 by 9-inch dish usually called for in éclair cake recipes, would still be far too big for two people. Using two mini loaf pans was more reasonable, but assembling two cakes seemed like a hassle. After perusing our bakeware cabinet, we settled on a 3-cup baking dish. Now we could get to the real work.

To replace the instant pudding, we considered making a classic egg yolk–thickened pastry cream. But it was obvious that using a sensitive egg-thickened cream, necessitating a fine-mesh strainer and an ice bath to prevent any curdled egg, was too much hassle for a casual dessert for two. Instead, we turned to a classic cornstarch-thickened vanilla pudding. We combined 1½ tablespoons of cornstarch with ⅓ cup of sugar, poured in 1¼ cups of milk, and simmered everything in a saucepan until thick. Then, off the heat, we added butter and vanilla extract. The pudding was perfectly creamy, with subtle vanilla flavor. We assembled the cake, using real whipped cream in place of the artificial store-bought version. But rather than a perky mousse, we had a runny pool that nearly dissolved the grahams.

Doubling the cornstarch in the pudding made a stiffer filling and restored the soft (not soggy) crackers in the assembled cake. Unfortunately, the pudding was now stodgy and chalky rather than rich and creamy.

We had to back down on the cornstarch and find another way to set the filling. Maybe reinforcing the homemade whipped cream would help. Gelatin was an obvious choice. After about a dozen tests, during which we slowly decreased the cornstarch and increased the gelatin, we eventually found the sweet spot: 1½ tablespoons of cornstarch and ½ teaspoon of gelatin. This was just enough to set the filling without imparting any off-textures.

Having successfully booted the packaged ingredients in the filling, we refused to settle for canned frosting for the topping. Ganache, which is chocolate melted into hot cream, had too strong a flavor for such a mild and creamy cake. Instead, we tried a glaze made of cocoa powder, confectioners' sugar, and milk. It had a shine reminiscent of a true éclair glaze, but now tasters missed the rich melted chocolate. We circled back to the ganache, this time using chocolate chips (to save ourselves from having to chop the chocolate), taming the bitterness with extra cream (instead of milk) and adding corn syrup (for a smooth, shiny finish).

While this formerly lowbrow treat wasn't quite ready for high society, it was still utterly satisfying and totally irresistible.

Chocolate Éclair Cake

SERVES 2

You will need a 3-cup baking dish (measuring approximately 7¼ by 5¼ inches; see page 3) for this recipe, or you can substitute an 8½ by 4½-inch loaf pan. Depending on the exact dimensions of the dish you are using, you may not need to use all of the chocolate ganache in step 5. You can substitute 2 ounces of finely chopped semisweet chocolate for the chocolate chips.

⅓ cup (2⅓ ounces) sugar
1½ tablespoons cornstarch
¼ teaspoon salt
1¼ cups whole milk
1 tablespoon unsalted butter, cut into 2 pieces
1¼ teaspoons vanilla extract
½ teaspoon unflavored gelatin
1 tablespoon water
¾ cup heavy cream, chilled
4 ounces graham crackers
⅓ cup (2 ounces) semisweet chocolate chips
1½ tablespoons light corn syrup

1. Combine sugar, cornstarch, and salt in medium saucepan. Whisk milk into sugar mixture until smooth. Bring to boil over medium-high heat, scraping bottom of pan with heatproof rubber spatula. Immediately reduce heat to medium-low and cook, continuing to scrape bottom of pan, until thickened and large bubbles appear on surface, about 4 minutes. Off heat, whisk in butter and vanilla. Transfer pudding to large bowl and place plastic wrap directly on surface of pudding. Refrigerate until cool, about 1½ hours.

2. Sprinkle gelatin over water in small bowl and let sit until gelatin softens, about 5 minutes. Microwave until mixture is bubbling around edges and gelatin dissolves, 15 to 30 seconds. Using stand mixer fitted with whisk, whip ½ cup cream on medium-low speed until foamy, about 1 minute. Increase speed to high and whip until stiff peaks form, 1 to 3 minutes.

3. Rewhisk chilled pudding mixture briskly until smooth, then slowly whisk in melted gelatin until completely incorporated. Whisk one-third of whipped cream into pudding, then gently fold in remaining whipped cream, 1 scoop at a time, until combined.

NOTES FROM THE TEST KITCHEN

THE BEST GRAHAM CRACKERS
The original graham crackers, developed by Sylvester Graham some 200 years ago, were more like hardtack than like the sweet wafers we know today. Marketed as "Dr. Graham's Honey Biskets," the dense crackers were made largely from coarse whole-wheat flour. Graham might be faintly horrified by what's become of them: Yes, supermarket grahams still incorporate graham (or whole-wheat) flour, but white flour is now the primary ingredient, with sugar of some sort not far behind. They also contain oil, salt, and leaveners.

Looking for the best graham crackers, we recently tasted three brands, sampling them first plain, then in our Chocolate Éclair Cake, and finally in the crust of a Key lime pie. When it comes to baking, we prefer **Keebler Grahams Crackers Original**, which held up well in our éclair cake's creamy layers. However, if you're eating them straight from the box, we prefer **Nabisco Grahams Original** for their wheaty flavor, which is due to a high percentage of wheat flour, although this also contributed to their becoming mushy in our éclair cake.

4. Cover bottom of 3-cup baking dish with layer of graham crackers, breaking crackers as necessary to line bottom of dish. Top with half of pudding–whipped cream mixture and another layer of graham crackers. Repeat with remaining pudding–whipped cream mixture and remaining graham crackers.

5. Microwave remaining ¼ cup cream, chocolate chips, and corn syrup together in bowl on 50 percent power, stirring occasionally, until smooth, 1 to 2 minutes. Cool glaze to room temperature, about 10 minutes. Spread glaze evenly over graham crackers and refrigerate for at least 6 hours or up to 2 days before serving.

CHOCOLATE-RASPBERRY TORTE

CERTAIN FANCY DINNERS REQUIRE A PULL-OUT-all-the-stops finish. Enter Sachertorte, the ultimate indulgent dessert. In this classic Viennese cake, two layers of chocolate cake are separated by a thin coating of apricot jam and enrobed in an ultra-rich chocolate glaze. But though this dessert makes for an elegant centerpiece, rarely does it deliver the intense, fudgy flavor and texture expected. We wanted to create a rich, deeply chocolaty dessert, using the basic layered Sachertorte as inspiration, and giving it our own spin by pairing the chocolate with raspberries. Instead of the typical 9-inch cake, we planned to create a miniature version, just right for two.

Once we started looking at recipes, it was clear why most cakes lacked serious chocolate flavor—the typical sponge cake used in many recipes relied on a modest amount of chocolate. Rather than fiddle with this cake, we figured it would be better to ditch it altogether for a rich, fudgy cake. We started by scaling down a previously published test kitchen recipe for flourless chocolate cake (made from just eggs, chocolate, and butter) to fit into two small cake pans. This way, we could sandwich the two cakes together rather than struggle to horizontally halve a single delicate cake. After melting the chocolate and butter together to create a smooth mixture, we folded in the beaten eggs, transferred the batter to the cake pans, baked the cakes, and let them cool. After letting the layers cool, we spread raspberry jam on one. But when we picked up the second layer to stack it on top of the first, the dense cake tore and fell apart. Undeterred, we patched the layers together, poured a simple chocolate glaze over the top, and chilled the cake. Finally, we called tasters to the table. There was no denying the intense chocolate flavor, but the texture was too crumbly. Our cake needed more structure.

We tried to remedy this problem by adding a small amount of flour to the batter, but when we added enough to sufficiently strengthen our small cakes (about ¼ cup), we ended up with a heavy, pasty texture. For our next tests, we tried adding baking powder and baking soda, but these proved ineffective at lightening the heavy batter. Separating the eggs and folding in the beaten whites didn't work either. One thing that did help was adding an additional egg white, but it wasn't enough.

At a dead end, we went back to the books and came across a technique that we'd initially ignored. Many classic tortes contain either bread crumbs or ground nuts in place of some of the flour. We figured it was worth a shot. Though the bread crumbs merely created a spongy, mushy cake, substituting ground toasted almonds for half of the flour worked perfectly. The layers were still moist but had enough structure so that a filling could be added and the second layer placed on top of the first without any damage. What's more, the flavor of the cake benefited from the depth provided by toasted nuts.

The only problem now was that our cake—and the cleanup—was turning into too much of a project for a dessert for two (even an elegant dessert for two). Getting out the stand mixer to whip the eggs, and the food processor to grind the nuts, was a pain, so we looked for ways to make the method easier. For our next test, we processed the almonds and flour first, then transferred the mixture to a bowl. Next, we processed the eggs until they were almost doubled in volume, then added the sugar (just ⅓ cup proved ample). After combining the eggs with the melted chocolate and butter, we folded in the almond-flour mixture and baked the cakes. This worked beautifully, as the processor aerated the batter just as effectively as the stand mixer, and now we had a recipe that dirtied only one piece of equipment.

As for the filling, the raspberry jam we had been using wasn't providing enough bright, fruity flavor. Plain fresh raspberries added bright complexity but lacked sweetness and fell off during slicing. In the end, the winning approach was to combine jam with lightly mashed fresh berries for a tangy-sweet mixture that clung to the cake.

Finally, we turned to the glaze. Determined to keep things simple, we melted bittersweet chocolate with heavy cream to create a rich-tasting, glossy ganache that poured smoothly over the cake. For easy but impressive decorating, we dotted fresh raspberries around the top of the torte and pressed sliced, toasted almonds along its sides. At last, our modern-day yet scaled-down torte was a real beauty—inside and out.

Chocolate-Raspberry Torte
SERVES 2

You will need two 6-inch round cake pans for this recipe (see page 3). We recommend using either Callebaut Intense Dark L-60-40NV or Ghirardelli Bittersweet Chocolate Baking Bar, but any high-quality bittersweet or semisweet chocolate will work. If you're refrigerating the cake for more than 1 hour in step 7, let it stand at room temperature for about 30 minutes before serving. This recipe makes a generous amount for two; you may have some left over.

CAKE AND FILLING
- 4 ounces bittersweet chocolate, chopped fine
- 6 tablespoons unsalted butter, cut into ½-inch pieces
- 1 teaspoon vanilla extract
- ⅛ teaspoon instant espresso powder
- ¾ cup sliced almonds, lightly toasted
- 2 tablespoons all-purpose flour
- ¼ teaspoon salt
- 2 large eggs plus 1 large white
- ⅓ cup (2⅓ ounces) sugar
- ¼ cup fresh raspberries, plus 8 to 12 individual berries for garnishing cake
- 2 tablespoons seedless raspberry jam

GLAZE
- 2½ ounces bittersweet chocolate, chopped fine
- 4½ tablespoons heavy cream

1. FOR THE CAKE AND FILLING: Adjust oven rack to middle position and heat oven to 325 degrees. Line bottoms of two 6-inch round cake pans with parchment paper; set aside. Melt chocolate and butter together in large heatproof bowl set over saucepan filled with 1 inch simmering water, stirring occasionally until smooth. Remove from heat and cool to room temperature, about 30 minutes. Stir in vanilla and espresso powder.

2. Pulse ¼ cup almonds in food processor until coarsely chopped, about 6 pulses; set aside to garnish cake. Process remaining ½ cup almonds until very finely ground, about 30 seconds. Add flour and salt and continue to process until combined, about 15 seconds. Transfer almond-flour mixture to medium bowl.

3. Process eggs and egg white in now-empty food processor until lightened in color and almost doubled in volume, about 3 minutes. With processor running, slowly add sugar until thoroughly combined, about 15 seconds. Using whisk, gently fold egg mixture into chocolate mixture until some streaks of egg remain. Sprinkle half of almond-flour mixture over chocolate-egg mixture and gently whisk until just combined. Sprinkle in remaining almond-flour mixture and gently whisk until just combined.

4. Divide batter between prepared pans and smooth tops. Bake until center is firm and toothpick inserted into center comes out with few moist crumbs attached, 14 to 16 minutes. Transfer cakes to wire rack; let cool completely in pans, about 30 minutes. Run paring knife around sides of cakes to loosen. Invert cakes onto cardboard rounds cut same size as diameter of cake; remove parchment paper. Using wire rack, reinvert 1 cake so top side faces up; slide back onto cardboard round.

5. To assemble, place ¼ cup raspberries in medium bowl and coarsely mash with fork. Stir in raspberry jam until just combined. Spread raspberry mixture onto cake layer that is top side up. Top with second cake layer, leaving it bottom side up. Transfer assembled cake, still on cardboard round, to wire rack set on rimmed baking sheet.

6. FOR THE GLAZE: Melt chocolate and cream together in medium heatproof bowl set over saucepan filled with 1 inch simmering water, stirring occasionally until smooth. Remove from heat and gently whisk until very smooth. Pour glaze onto center of assembled cake. Use offset spatula to spread glaze evenly over top of cake, letting it flow down sides. Spread glaze along sides of cake to coat evenly.

7. Using fine-mesh strainer, sift reserved almonds to remove any fine bits. Holding bottom of cake on cardboard round with 1 hand, gently press sifted almonds onto cake sides with other hand. Arrange remaining raspberries around circumference. Refrigerate cake, still on rack, until glaze is set, for at least 1 hour or up to 24 hours. Transfer cake to serving platter and serve.

NOTES FROM THE TEST KITCHEN

ASSEMBLING CHOCOLATE-RASPBERRY TORTE

1. Run paring knife around sides of cakes and invert layers onto cardboard rounds. Then, using plate or wire rack, reinvert 1 cake so top faces up; slide back onto cardboard round.

2. Spread raspberry filling over cake layer with its top side facing up.

3. Top with second cake, leaving bottom facing up.

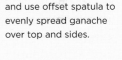

4. Pour glaze onto cake and use offset spatula to evenly spread ganache over top and sides.

5. Using cardboard round, lift and hold cake with one hand and gently press chopped nuts onto its sides with other hand.

6. Place 1 raspberry at top of cake at 12 o'clock, then another at 6 o'clock. Place third berry at 9 o'clock and fourth at 3 o'clock. Place remaining berries opposite each other until all are evenly spaced.

Conversions & Equivalencies

SOME SAY COOKING IS A SCIENCE AND AN ART. We would say that geography has a hand in it, too. Flour milled in the United Kingdom and elsewhere will feel and taste different from flour milled in the United States. So, while we cannot promise that the loaf of bread you bake in Canada or England will taste the same as a loaf baked in the States, we can offer guidelines for converting weights and measures. We also recommend that you rely on your instincts when making our recipes. Refer to the visual cues provided. If the bread dough hasn't "come together in a ball," as described, you may need to add more flour—even if the recipe doesn't tell you so. You be the judge.

The recipes in this book were developed using standard U.S. measures following U.S. government guidelines. The charts below offer equivalents for U.S., metric, and imperial (U.K.) measures. All conversions are approximate and have been rounded up or down to the nearest whole number. For example:

1 teaspoon	=	4.929 milliliters, rounded up to 5 milliliters
1 ounce	=	28.349 grams, rounded down to 28 grams

VOLUME CONVERSIONS

U.S.	METRIC
1 teaspoon	5 milliliters
2 teaspoons	10 milliliters
1 tablespoon	15 milliliters
2 tablespoons	30 milliliters
¼ cup	59 milliliters
⅓ cup	79 milliliters
½ cup	118 milliliters
¾ cup	177 milliliters
1 cup	237 milliliters
1¼ cups	296 milliliters
1½ cups	355 milliliters
2 cups	473 milliliters
2½ cups	591 milliliters
3 cups	710 milliliters
4 cups (1 quart)	0.946 liter
1.06 quarts	1 liter
4 quarts (1 gallon)	3.8 liters

WEIGHT CONVERSIONS

OUNCES	GRAMS
½	14
¾	21
1	28
1½	43
2	57
2½	71
3	85
3½	99
4	113
4½	128
5	142
6	170
7	198
8	227
9	255
10	283
12	340
16 (1 pound)	454

CONVERSIONS FOR INGREDIENTS COMMONLY USED IN BAKING

Baking is an exacting science. Because measuring by weight is far more accurate than measuring by volume, and thus more likely to achieve reliable results, in our recipes we provide ounce measures in addition to cup measures for many ingredients. Refer to the chart below to convert these measures into grams.

INGREDIENT	OUNCES	GRAMS
Flour		
1 cup all-purpose flour*	5	142
1 cup cake flour	4	113
1 cup whole wheat flour	5½	156
Sugar		
1 cup granulated (white) sugar	7	198
1 cup packed brown sugar (light or dark)	7	198
1 cup confectioners' sugar	4	113
Cocoa Powder		
1 cup cocoa powder	3	85
Butter†		
4 tablespoons (½ stick, or ¼ cup)	2	57
8 tablespoons (1 stick, or ½ cup)	4	113
16 tablespoons (2 sticks, or 1 cup)	8	227

* U.S. all-purpose flour, the most frequently used flour in this book, does not contain leaveners, as some European flours do. These leavened flours are called self-rising or self-raising. If you are using self-rising flour, take this into consideration before adding leavening to a recipe.

† In the United States, butter is sold both salted and unsalted. We generally recommend unsalted butter. If you are using salted butter, take this into consideration before adding salt to a recipe.

OVEN TEMPERATURES

FAHRENHEIT	CELSIUS	GAS MARK (IMPERIAL)
225	105	¼
250	120	½
275	135	1
300	150	2
325	165	3
350	180	4
375	190	5
400	200	6
425	220	7
450	230	8
475	245	9

CONVERTING TEMPERATURES FROM AN INSTANT-READ THERMOMETER

We include doneness temperatures in many of our recipes, such as those for poultry, meat, and bread. We recommend an instant-read thermometer for the job. Refer to the table above to convert Fahrenheit degrees to Celsius. Or, for temperatures not represented in the chart, use this simple formula:

Subtract 32 degrees from the Fahrenheit reading, then divide the result by 1.8 to find the Celsius reading.

EXAMPLE:

"Roast until chicken thighs register 175 degrees."
To convert:

$$175°\ F\ -\ 32\ =\ 143°$$
$$143°\ \div\ 1.8\ =\ 79.44°C,\ \text{rounded down to } 79°C$$

Index

NOTE: *ITALICIZED* PAGE REFERENCES INDICATE COLOR PHOTOGRAPHS.

Grains
cooking polenta, tip for, 201
Fried Green Tomatoes, 247–49, *248*
Mushroom and Farro Ragout, 123–25
Quick Pork Ragu with Polenta, 200–201
Quinoa and Vegetable Stew, 120–23, *122*
Turkey Tamale Pies, *210, 211*
wheat berries, about, 114
Wheat Berry and Arugula Salad, 114–16, *115*
see also Oats; Rice
Grapefruit
cutting up, 166
Salsa with Fennel, Grilled Sea Scallops with, *140,* 165–67
Graters
rasp, ratings of, 69
rotary, ratings of, 89
Gratin dishes, 3
Greek Spinach and Feta Pie (Spanakopita), 132–34, *133*
Greek-Style Shrimp with Tomatoes and Feta, 71–72
Greens
Argentine-Style Steak Salad with Chimichurri Vinaigrette, *190,* 194
Asian Chicken Lettuce Wraps, 173–74
Baked Tortellini with Radicchio, Peas, and Bacon, 106–8, *107*
Classic Caesar Salad, *234,* 236–37
Grilled Salmon Steaks with Zucchini and Frisée Salad, 162–65, *163*
Grilled Steak Burgers with Romaine and Blue Cheese Salad, 142–44
Radicchio-Apple Slaw, 108
Slow-Cooker Balsamic-Braised Chicken with Swiss Chard, *230,* 231–32
Swiss chard, preparing, 231
see also Arugula; Cabbage; Spinach
Green tea, taste tests on, 197
Grilled
Beef and Vegetable Kebabs with Lemon and Rosemary, 144–47
Beef and Vegetable Kebabs with North African Marinade, *145,* 147
Beef and Vegetable Kebabs with Red Curry Marinade, 147
Chicken, Citrus-and-Spice, with Corn on the Cob and Lime Butter, 160–62
Chicken Kebabs with Charred Coleslaw, 154–57
Chicken Wings, Barbecue, with Tomato-Spinach Salad and Ranch Dressing, 160
Chicken Wings, Creole, with Tomato-Spinach Salad and Ranch Dressing, 160
Chicken Wings, Tandoori, with Tomato-Spinach Salad and Ranch Dressing, 160
Chicken Wings, with Tomato-Spinach Salad and Ranch Dressing, 157–60, *158*
Hawaiian-Style Smoked Pork, 196–98
Honey-Glazed Pork Chops with Peach, Red Onion, and Arugula Salad, 149–52, *151*
Pork Tenderloin, Manchego and Almond-Stuffed, with Spiced Sweet Potato Wedges, 154
Pork Tenderloin, Stuffed, with Spiced Sweet Potato Wedges, 152–54

Grilled *(cont.)*
Portobello Burgers with Garlicky Eggplant, 168–69
Salmon Steaks with Zucchini and Frisée Salad, 162–65, *163*
Sea Scallops and Grapefruit Salsa with Fennel, *140,* 165–67
Steak Burgers with Romaine and Blue Cheese Salad, 142–44
Steakhouse Steak Tips and Red Potatoes with Sour Cream–Chive Sauce, 147–49
Grills, checking propane levels for, 161
Gruyère cheese
Ham and Potato Gratins, 205
Skillet Turkey Tetrazzini, 209–11

H

Ham
Mushroom, and Cheddar Frittata, 204
Picnic, Glazed, 201–4, *203*
picnic, scoring, 204
picnic, smoked, about, 204
and Potato Gratins, 205
Skillet Spaghetti Carbonara, 205–6
Hash, Roast Beef, 195
Hawaiian-Style Smoked Pork, 196–98
Hearty Chicken Chowder, 57–58
Hearty Stuffed Shells, 180–82
Herbs
fresh, storing, 88
see also specific herbs
Hoisin-Ginger Glaze, Pan-Seared Shrimp with, 189
Honey-Glazed Pork Chops, Grilled, with Peach, Red Onion, and Arugula Salad, 149–52, *151*
Hot Fudge Pudding Cakes, 282–83

I

Ice cream, vanilla, taste tests on, 268
Indonesian-Style Fried Rice, 73–74, *75*
Indoor Wisconsin Brats and Beer, 20–21
Ingredients, tastings of
black beans, 131
canned whole tomatoes, 80
cheese tortellini, 106
chicken breasts, boneless, skinless, 175
chicken broth, 208
curry powder, 172
elbow macaroni, 111
feta cheese, 72
fish sauce, 174
graham crackers, 285
green tea, 197
ketchup, 10
liquid smoke, 221
maple syrup, 15
mozzarella, 117
mustard, coarse-grained, 20
panko bread crumbs, 106
premium pork chops, 19
red wine vinegar, 241